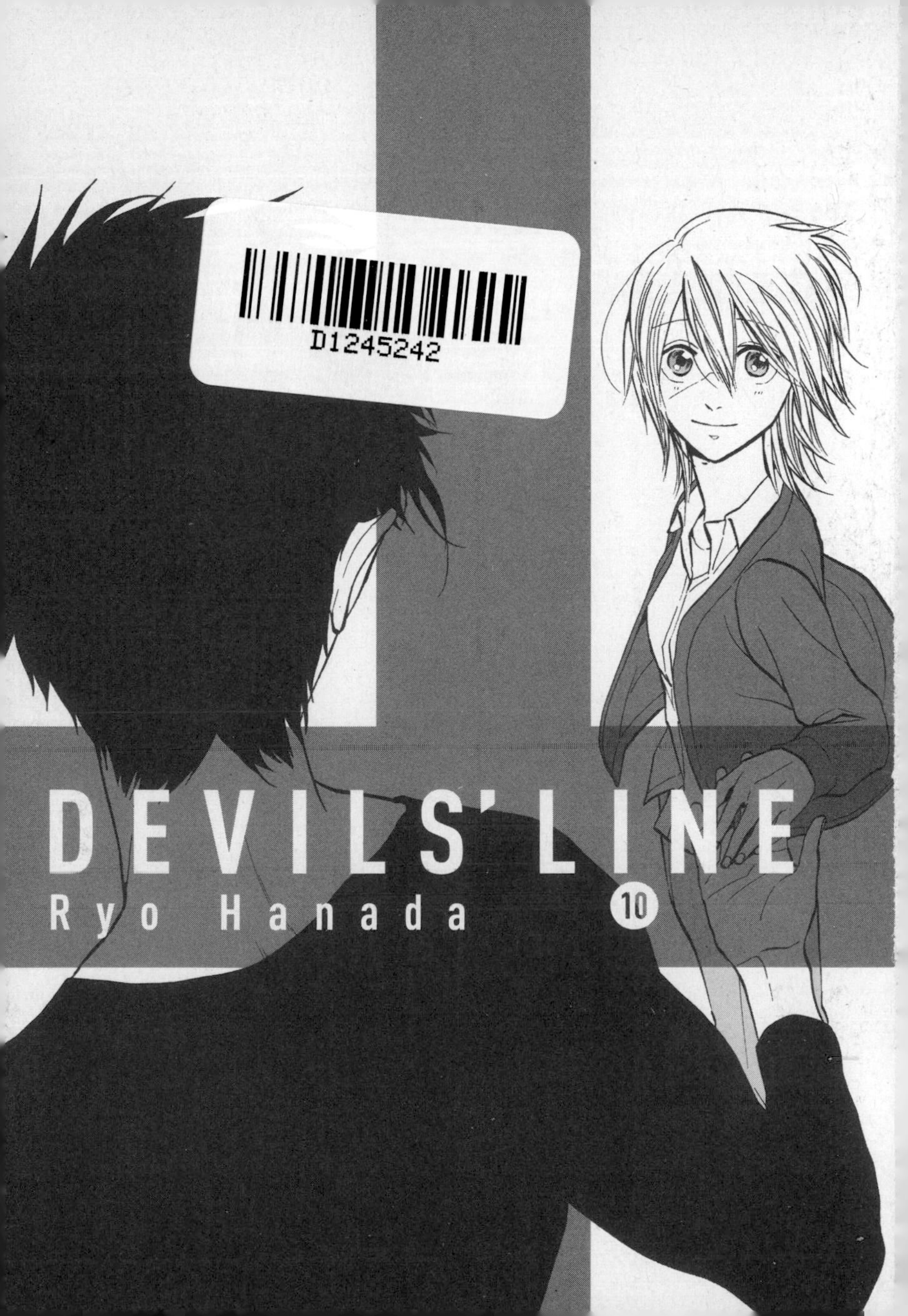

DEVILS' LINE

10

Ryo Hanada

Character and Relationship Diagram (based on relationships up to the last volume)

TAKESHI MAKIMURA
(Zero Six)

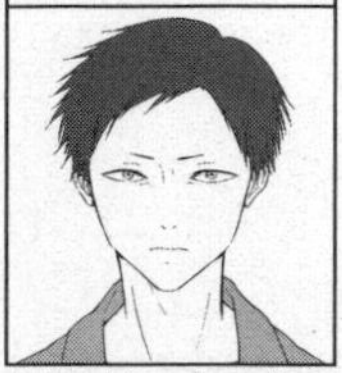

Came into contact with the CCC for an undercover investigation. He is currently in hiding somewhere in Tokyo with Mayu Sumimori.

NAOYA USHIO
(Zero Five)

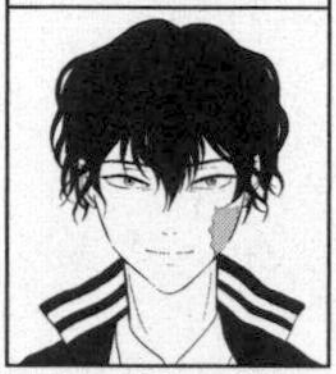

Former CCC member. He is currently under protection and surveillance by the police.

KIRIO KIKUHARA
(Zero Two)

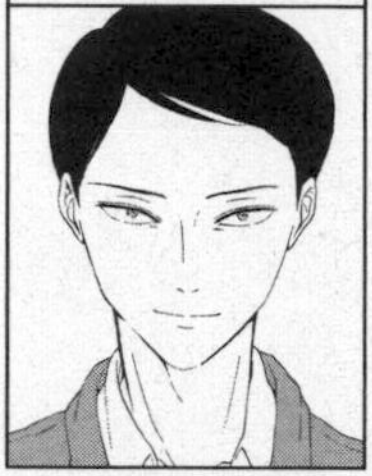

He was the leader of Public Safety Division 5's A Squad, but he was also secretly the commander of the CCC. Someone put a bomb in his car.

YUUKI ANZAI

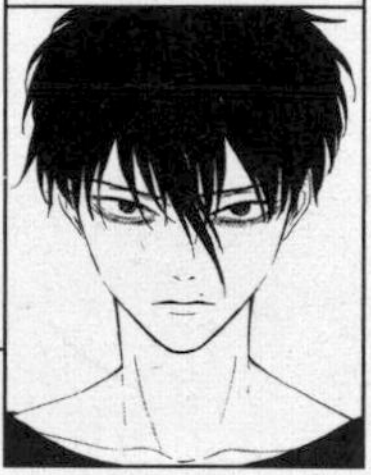

He was with the police's Public Safety Division 5, but has since resigned. Half-devil, half-human. He was dating Tsukasa, but they're on a break.

MEGUMI ISHIMARU

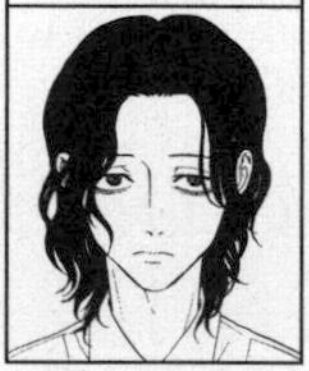

Made contact with the CCC while working with Division 5. Transferred back to Public Safety General Affairs.

TAKASHI SAWAZAKI

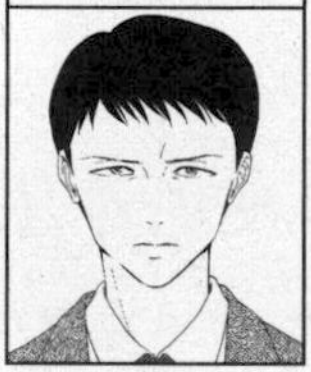

Senior police officer with Public Safety Division 5. Transferred to the General Admin department.

YOUSUKE ASAMI

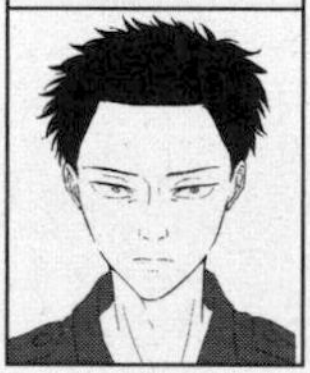

A member of Investigation Division 1, he was assigned to Public Safety Division 5 temporarily.

TOMOAKI OGATA

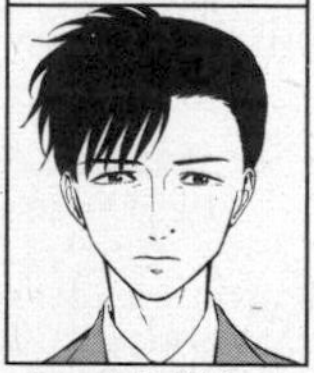

Sergeant with Riot Squad No. 9. Currently assigned to Division 5 as a bodyguard for Anzai.

JULIANA LLOYD

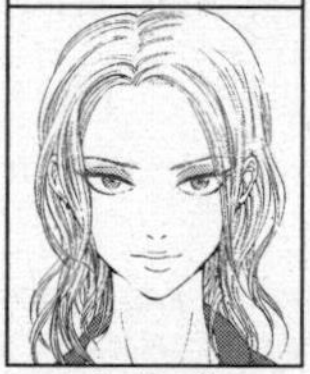

Devil police officer. Born and raised in Japan. She skillfully uses make-up to hide the bags under her eyes.

RYUUSEI YANAGI

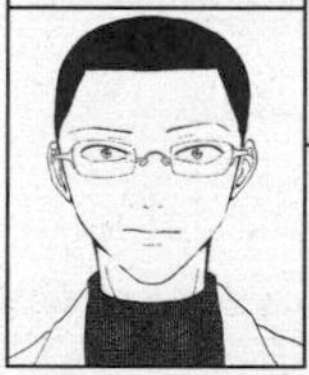

Doctor attached to F Squad specializing in the hematology of the redeye race (devils). He was apparently a punk in his youth.

Acquaintance

AKIO KANO

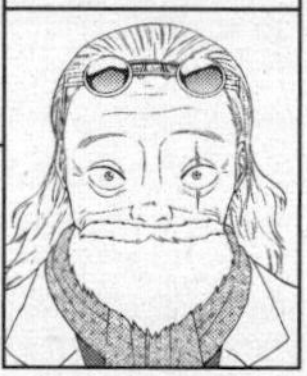

Psychosomatic doctor specializing in devil care, he is also a member of R2PC, a committee that works to protect devil rights.

FORMER CCC MEMBERS

KEN'ICHI YOSHII
(Zero Nine)

He fled the CCC with Zero Seven, but is currently under protection and surveillance by the police.

NANAKO TENJO
(Zero Seven)

She was a CCC sniper, but has deserted the group. Currently on the run alone.

MAYU SUMIMORI
(Eleven)

She was responsible for accounting and intel gathering. Makimura's quick thinking saved her life.

JOHANNES KLEEMAN
(HANS LEE)

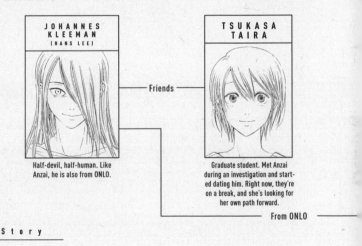

Half-devil, half-human. Like Anzai, he is also from ONLO.

Friends

TSUKASA TAIRA

Graduate student. Met Anzai during an investigation and started dating him. Right now, they're on a break, and she's looking for her own path forward.

From ONLO

DEVIL'S LINE

Story

Due to the secret maneuverings of the CCC, an organization intent on the annihilation of all devils, the existence of devils becomes known to the world at large, dramatically changing society. In the midst of this upheaval, Anzai was fatally wounded in a fierce battle with the CCC, and Tsukasa's blood saved his life. The weight of his actions heavy on his mind, Anzai decides to takes leave of the police force as well as break up with Tsukasa for the time being, in order to confront his devil self. Tsukasa accepts his decision and resolves to also move forward. With their own objectives, Tsukasa and Anzai head separately to Obihiro. Still unable to meet at present, will the time of their reunion come at last...?

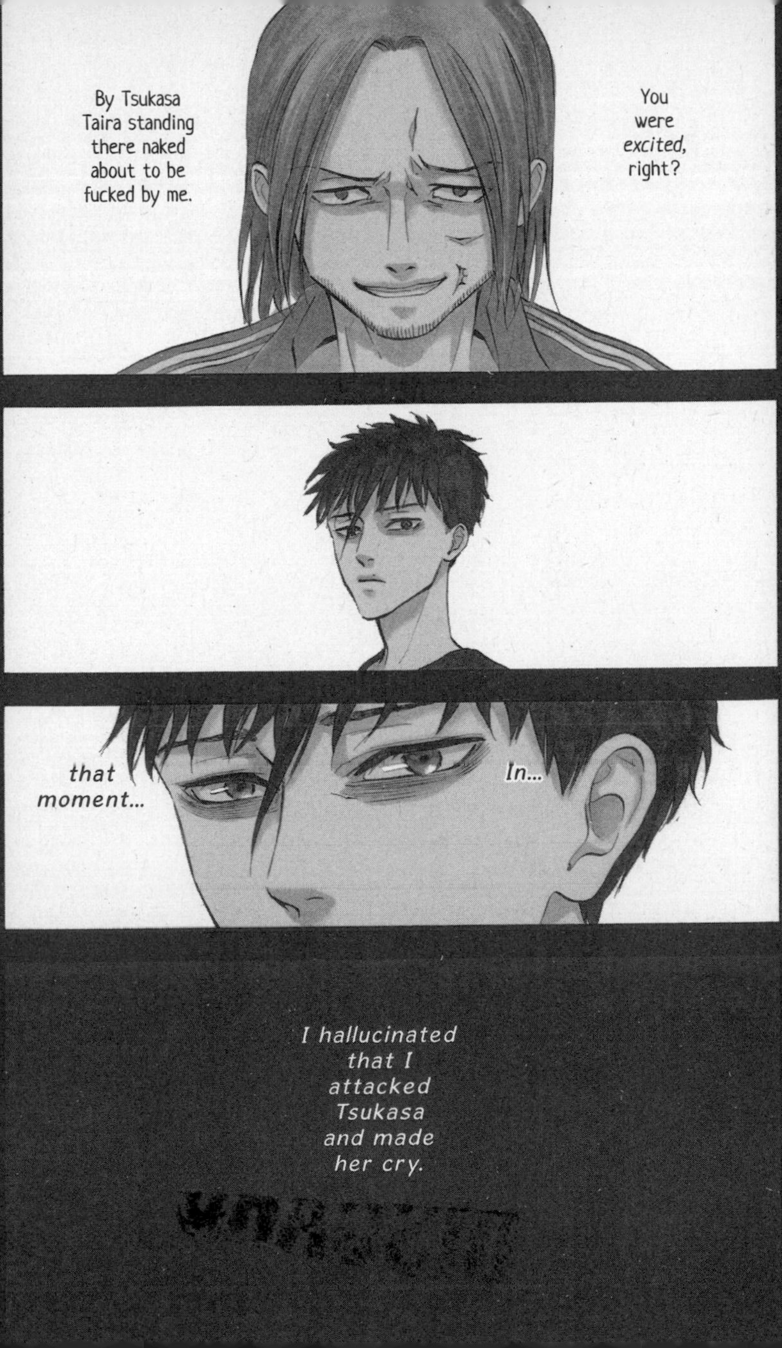
You were excited, right?
By Tsukasa Taira standing there naked about to be fucked by me.
In...
that moment...
I hallucinated that I attacked Tsukasa and made her cry.

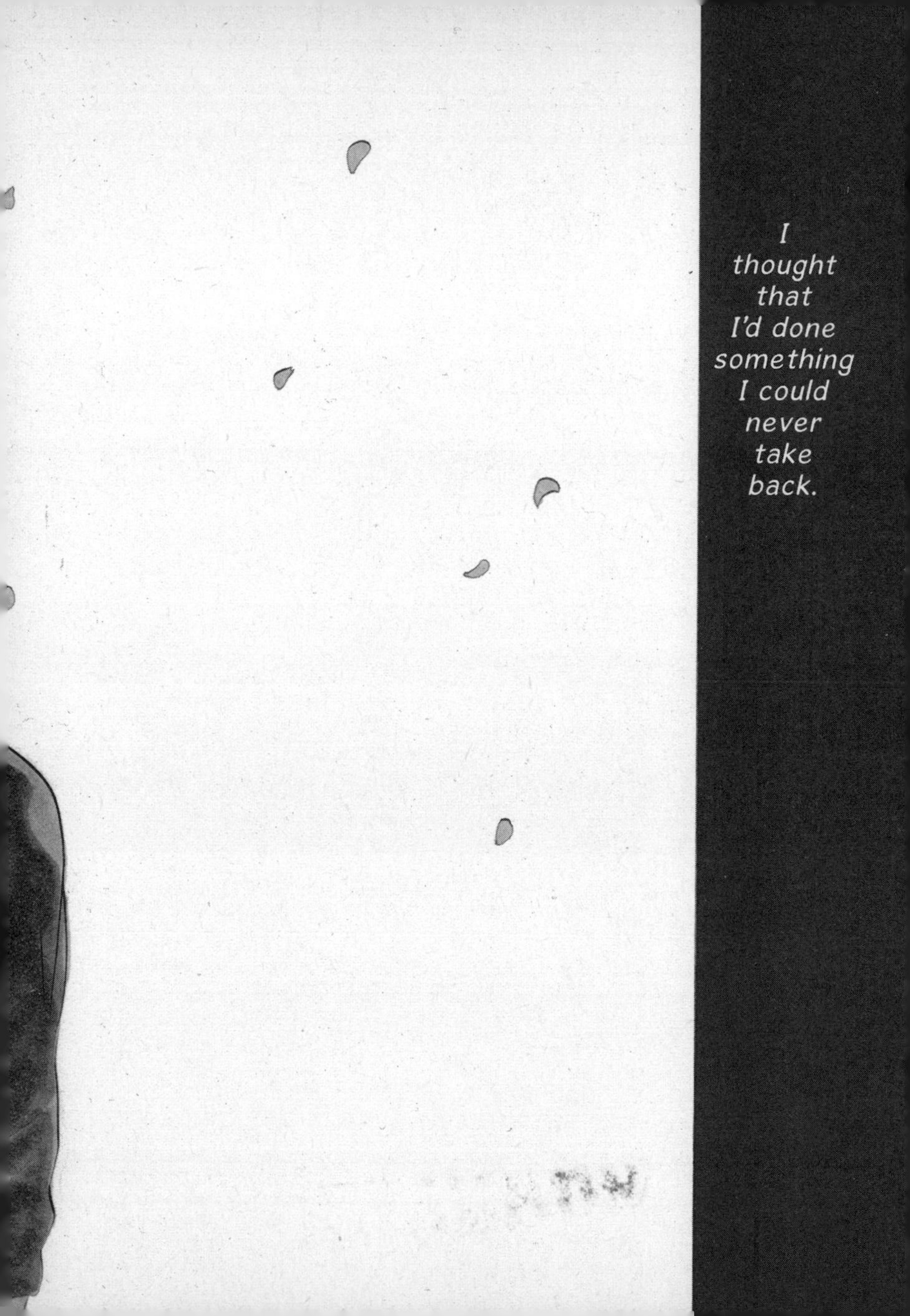
I thought that I'd done something I could never take back.

Line 48
Gate

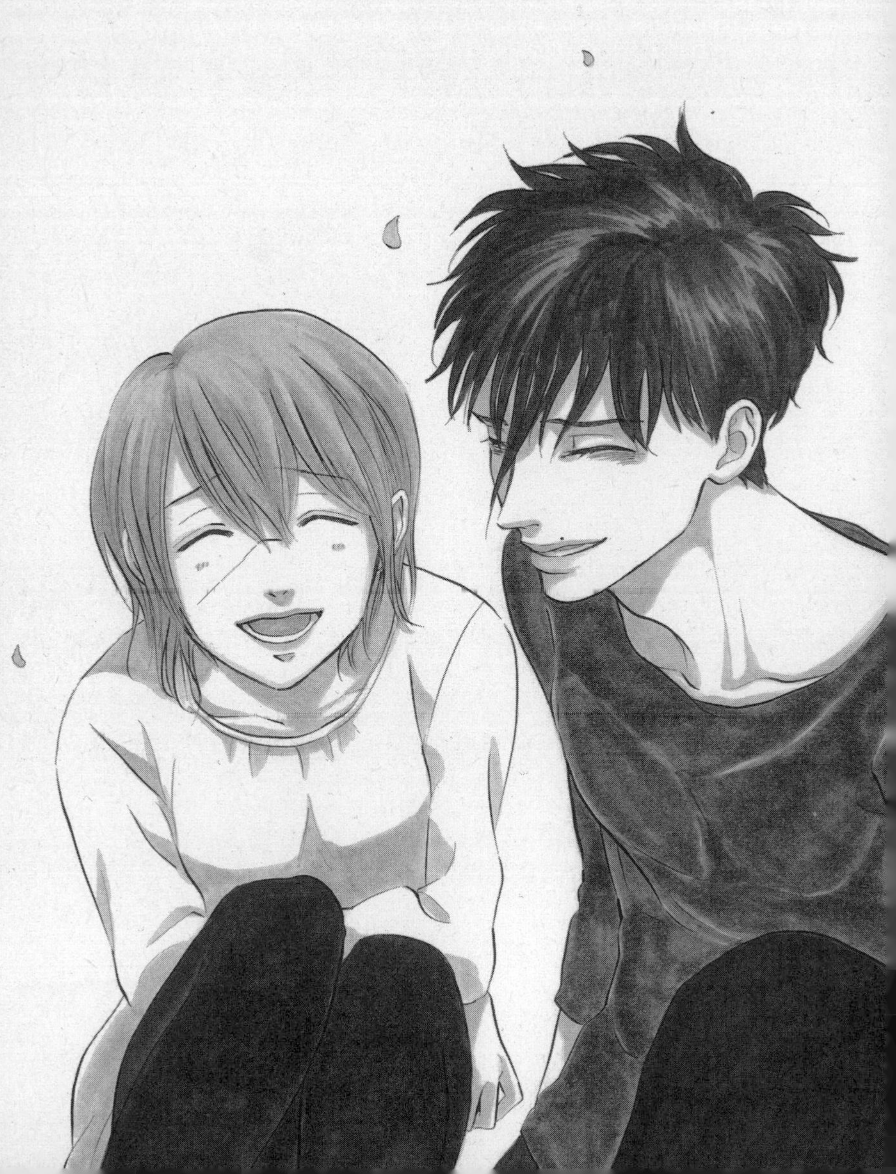

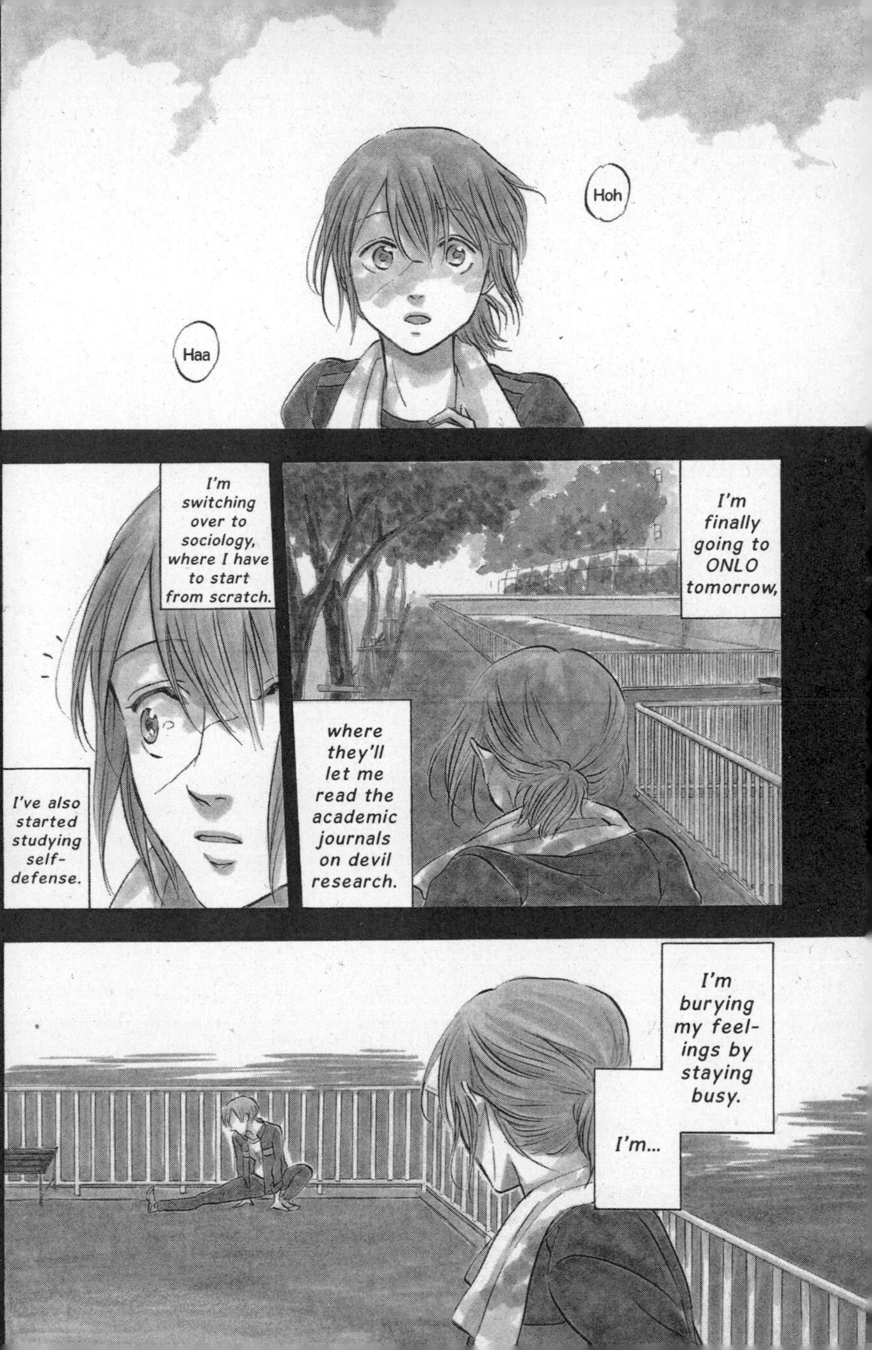
Hoh
Haa
I'm finally going to ONLO tomorrow,
where they'll let me read the academic journals on devil research.
I'm switching over to sociology, where I have to start from scratch.
I've also started studying self-defense.
I'm burying my feel-ings by staying busy.
I'm...

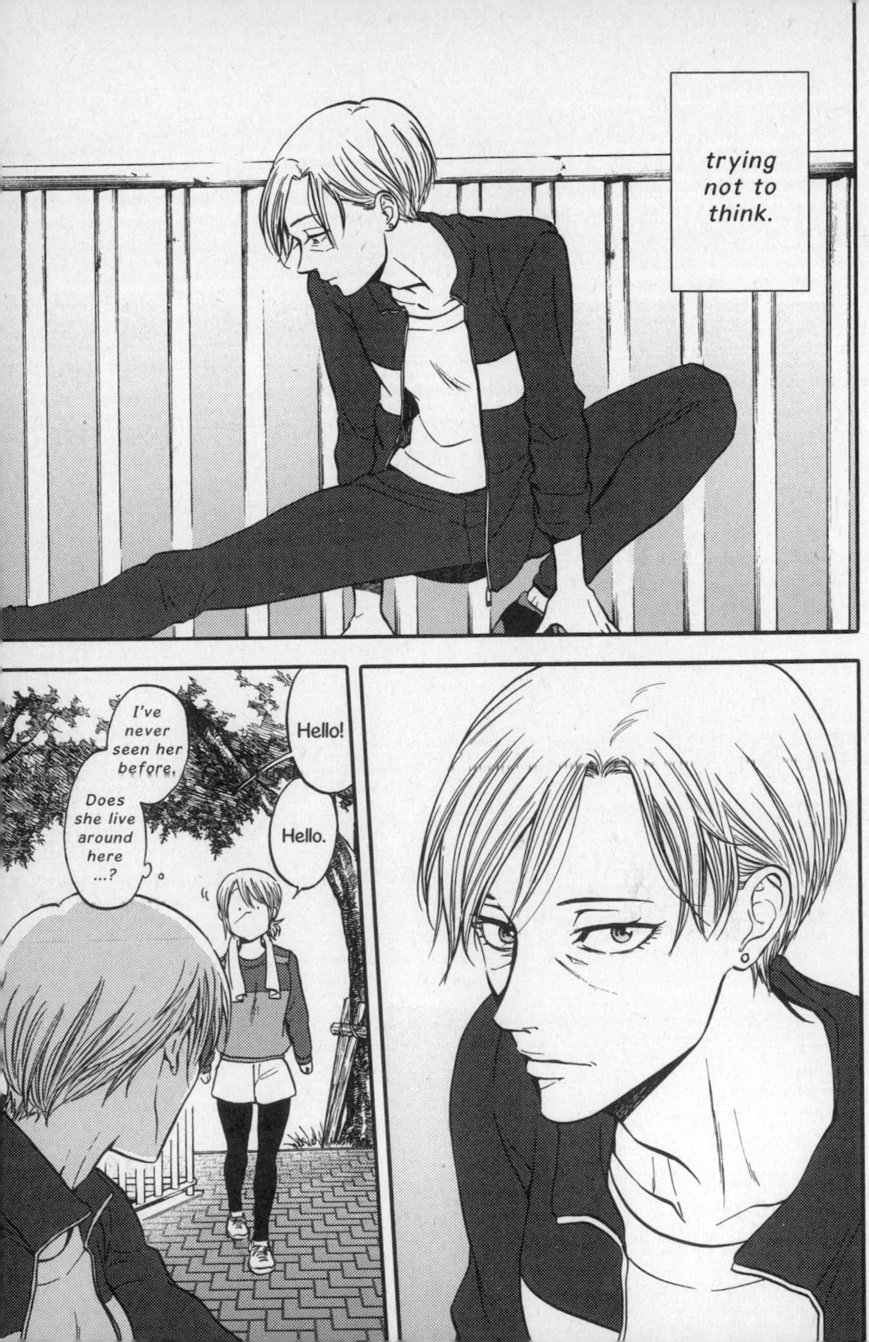
trying not to think.
Hello!
Hello.
I've never seen her before. Does she live around here ...?

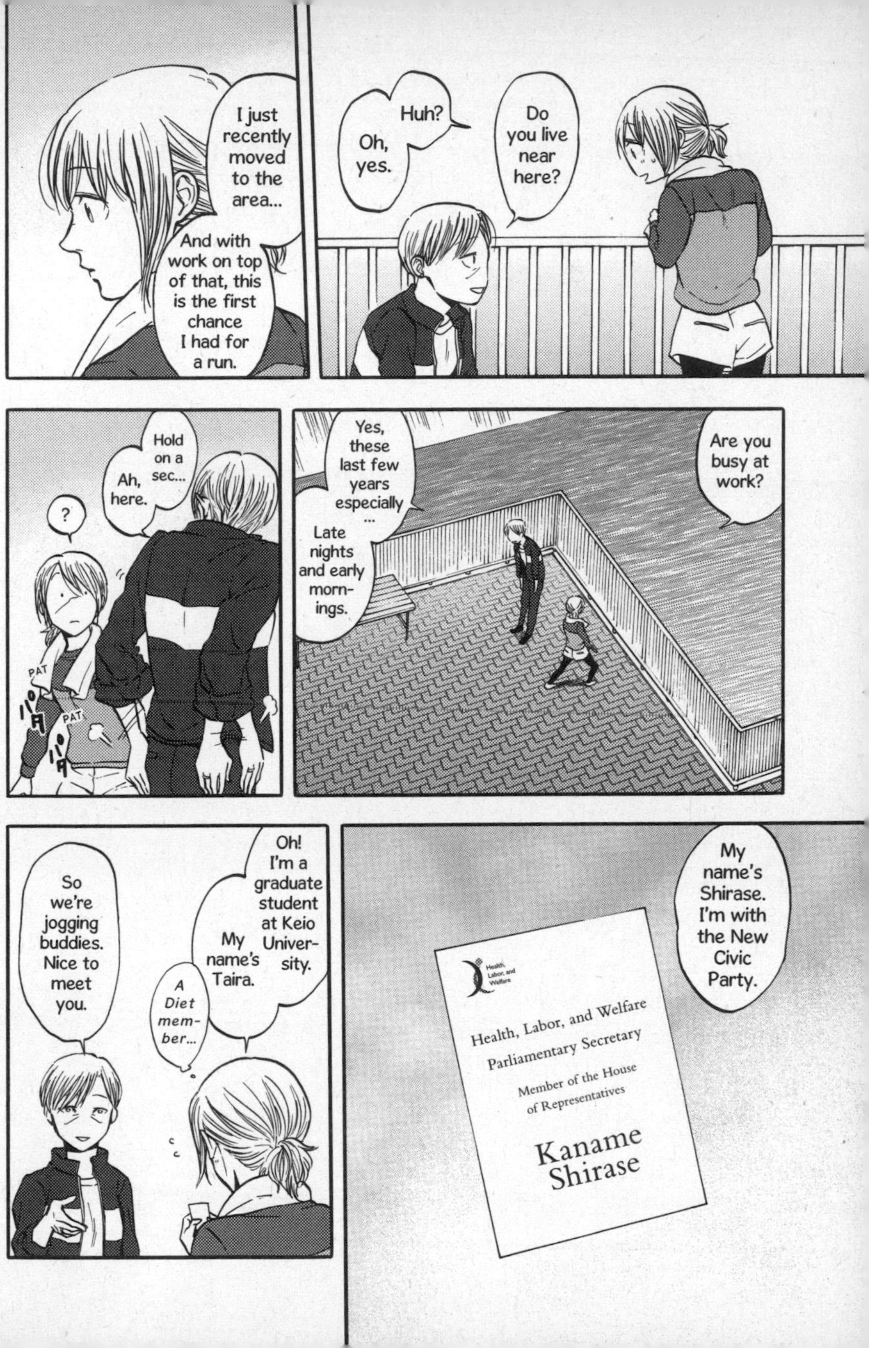
Do you live near here?
Huh?
Oh, yes.
I just recently moved to the area...
And with work on top of that, this is the first chance I had for a run.
Are you busy at work?
Yes, these last few years especially...
Late nights and early mornings.
Hold on a sec...
Ah, here.
?
PAT
PAT
My name's Shirase. I'm with the New Civic Party.
Health, Labor, and Welfare
Health, Labor, and Welfare Parliamentary Secretary
Member of the House of Representatives
Kaname Shirase
Oh! I'm a graduate student at Keio University.
My name's Taira.
A Diet member...
So we're jogging buddies. Nice to meet you.

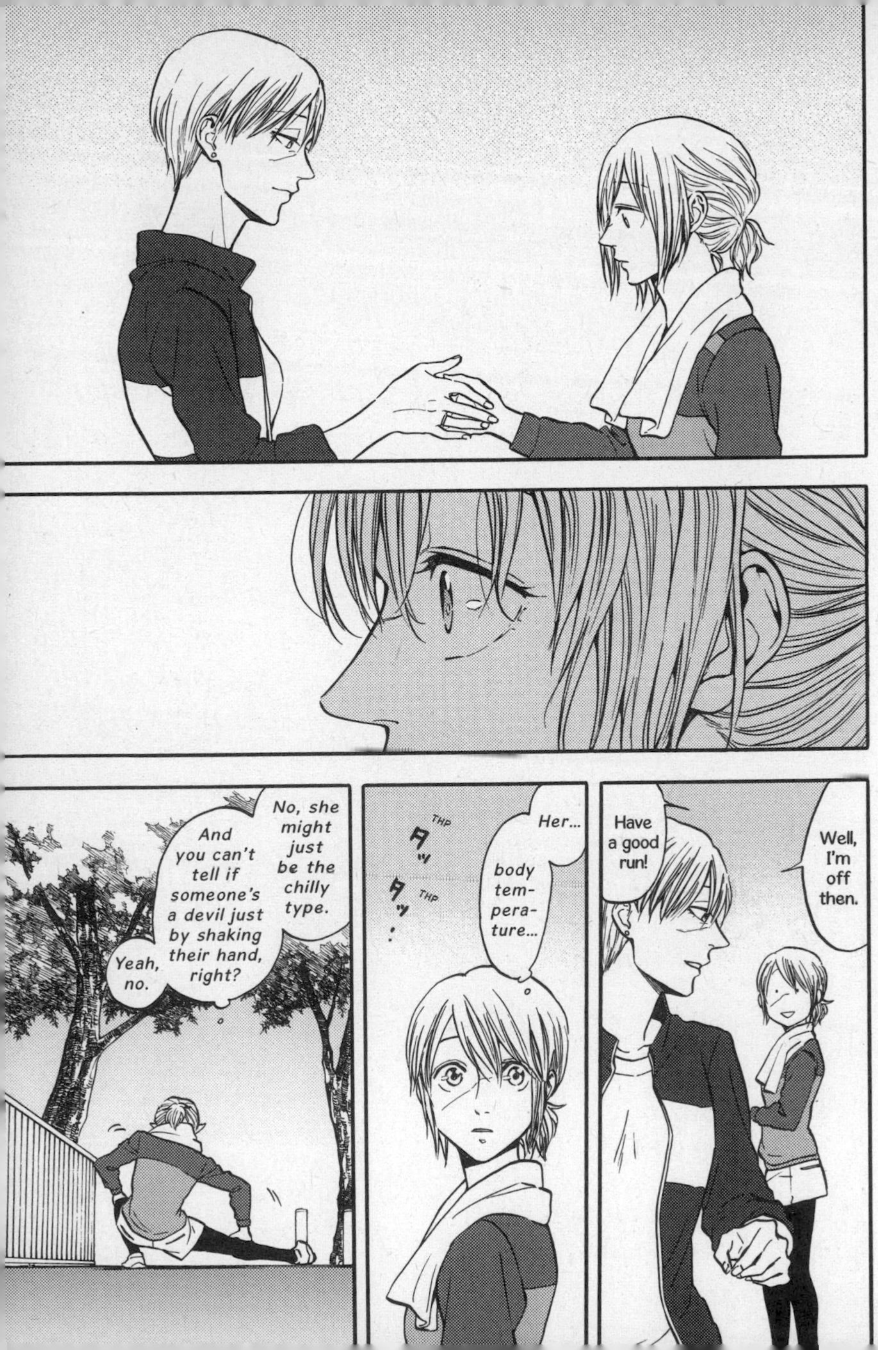
Well, I'm off then.
Have a good run!
タッ THP
タッ THP
Her...
body temperature...
No, she might just be the chilly type.
And you can't tell if someone's a devil just by shaking their hand, right?
Yeah, no.

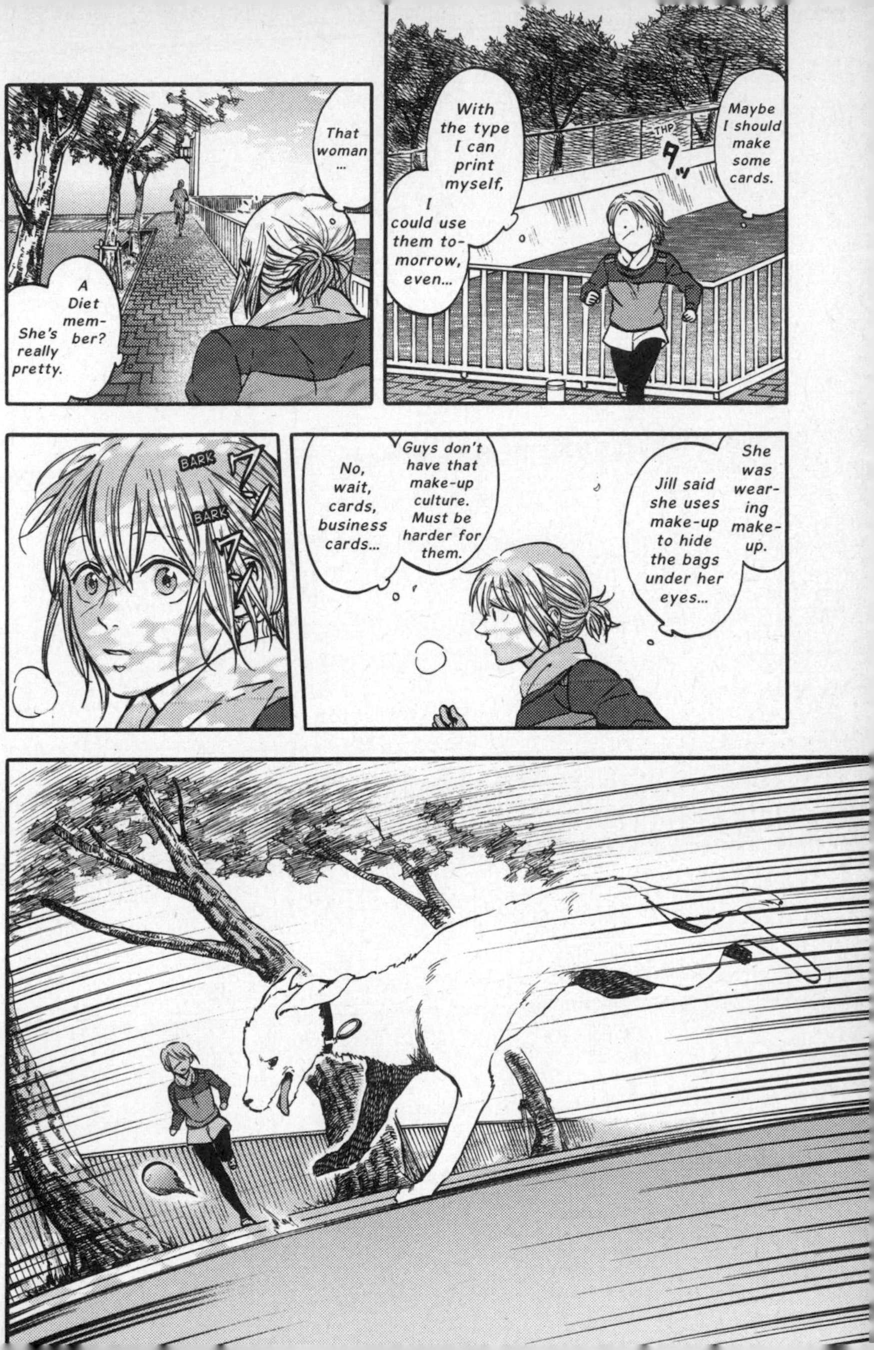
Maybe I should make some cards.
THP
With the type I can print myself,
I could use them to-morrow, even...
That woman ...
A Diet mem-ber?
She's really pretty.
She was wear-ing make-up.
Jill said she uses make-up to hide the bags under her eyes...
Guys don't have that make-up culture. Must be harder for them.
No, wait, cards, business cards...
BARK
BARK

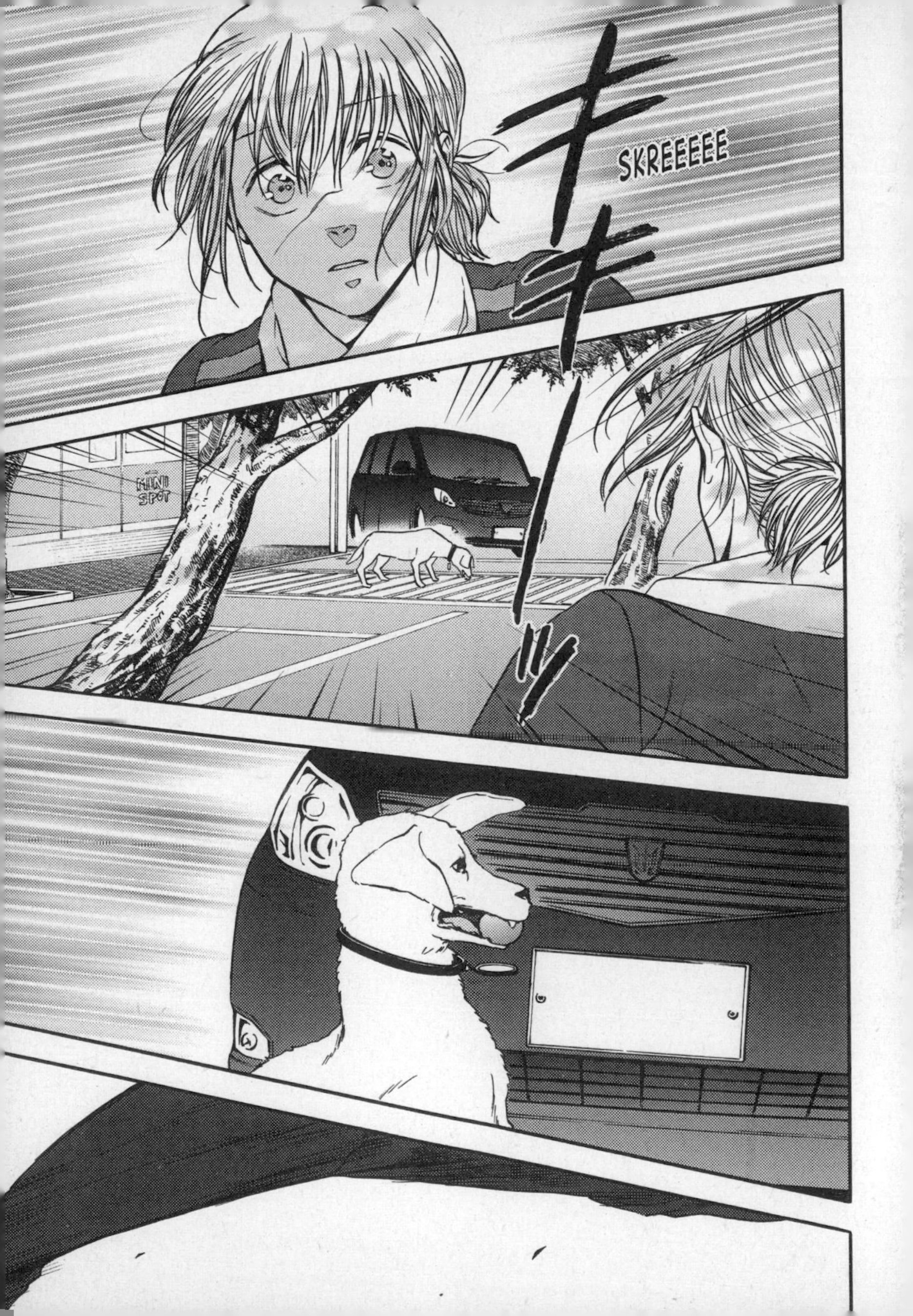
キキーッ
SKREEEEE
MINI SPOT

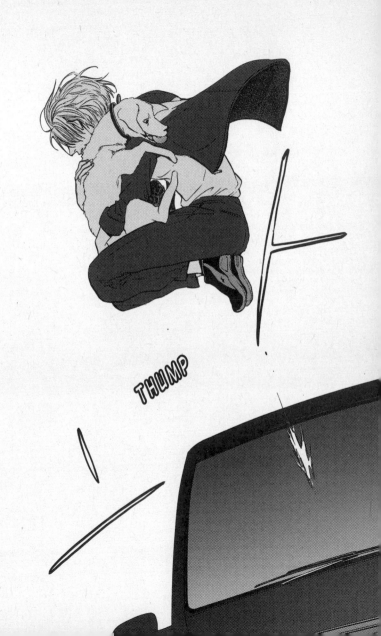

THUMP

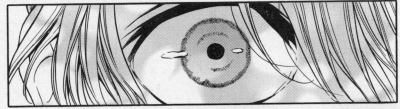

BARK

BARK

CHFF

SKRTCH

SKRTCH

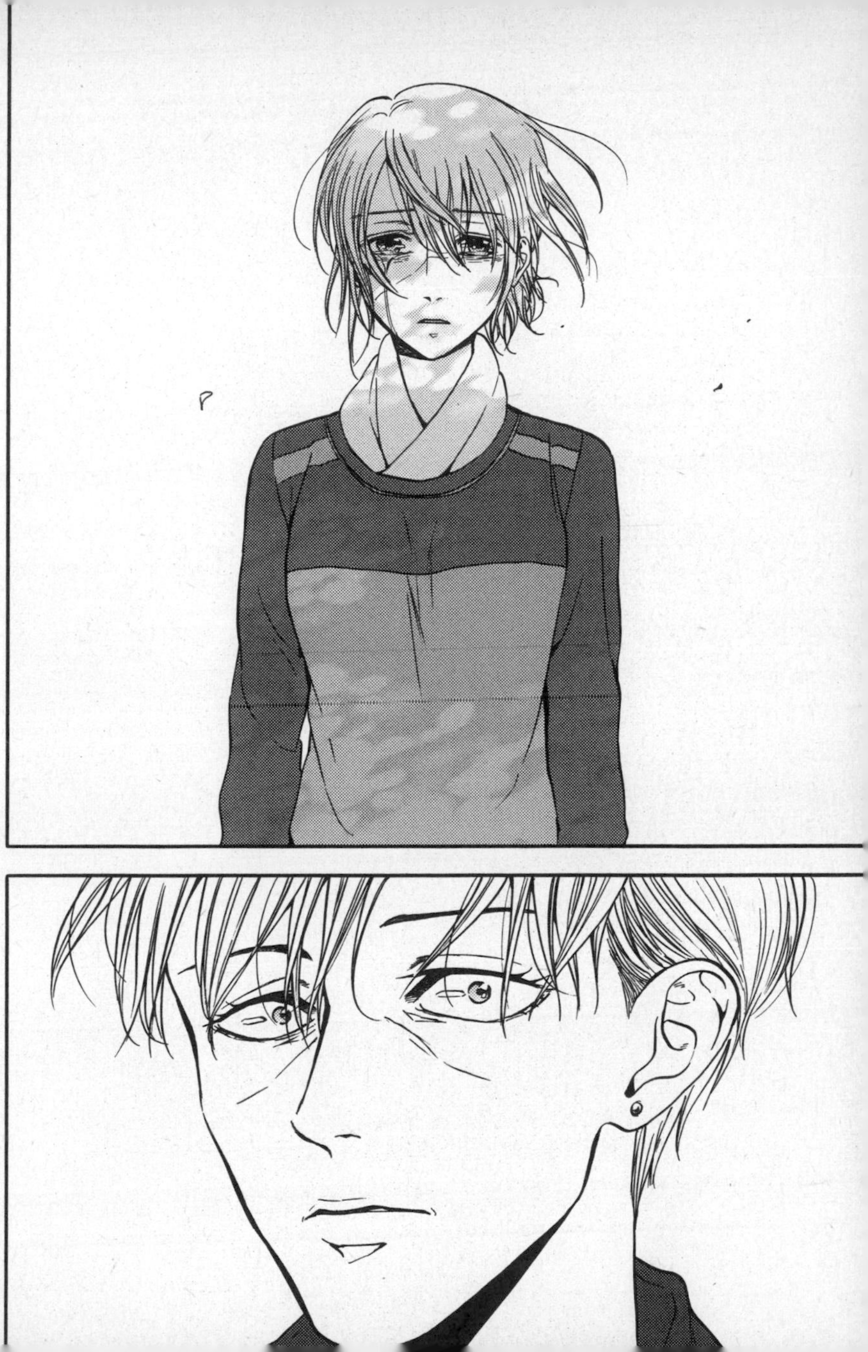

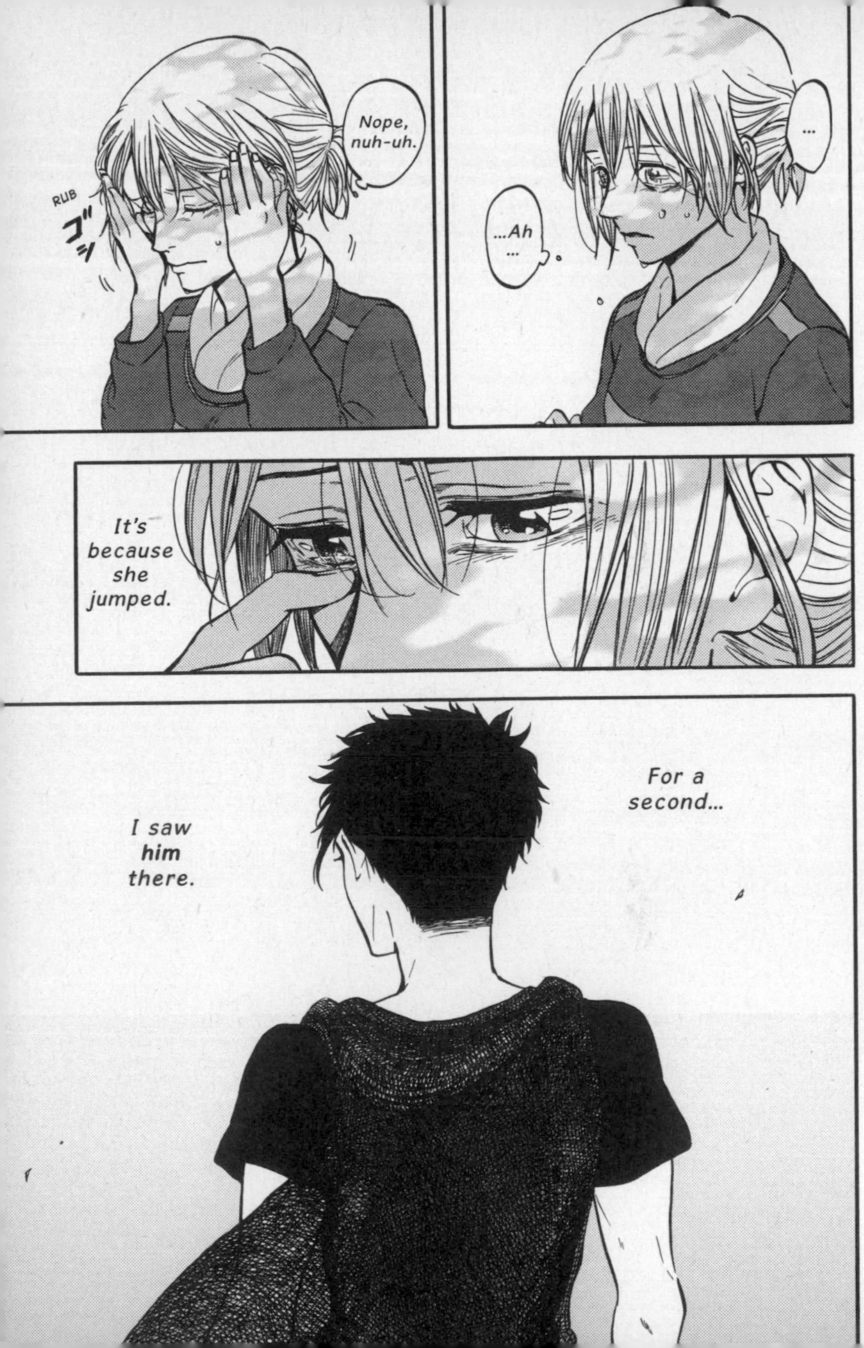
...
...Ah ...
Nope, nuh-uh.
RUB
ゴシ
It's because she jumped.
For a second...
I saw **him** there.

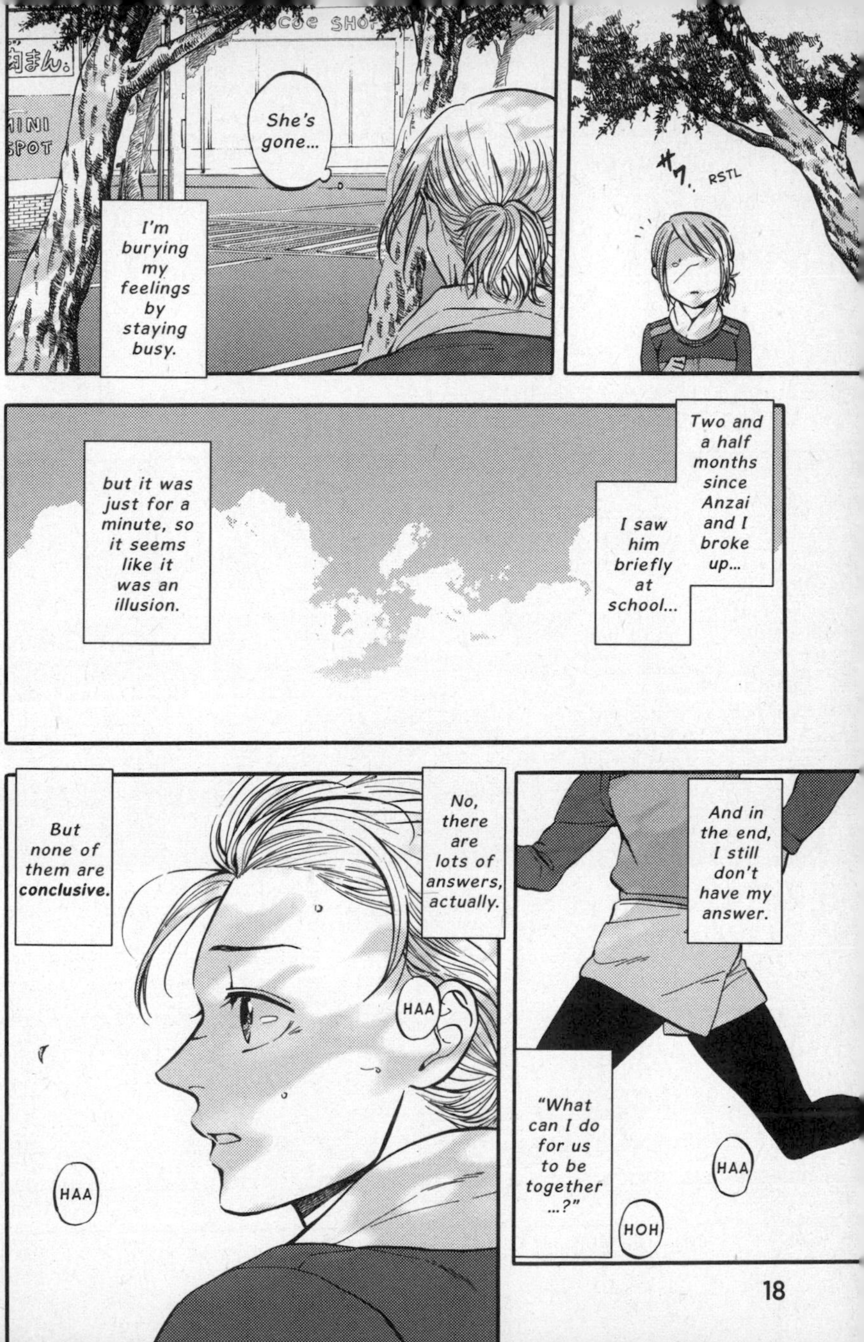
RSTL
She's gone...
I'm burying my feelings by staying busy.
Two and a half months since Anzai and I broke up...
I saw him briefly at school...
but it was just for a minute, so it seems like it was an illusion.
And in the end, I still don't have my answer.
"What can I do for us to be together ...?"
HAA
HOH
No, there are lots of answers, actually.
But none of them are **conclusive.**
HAA
HAA

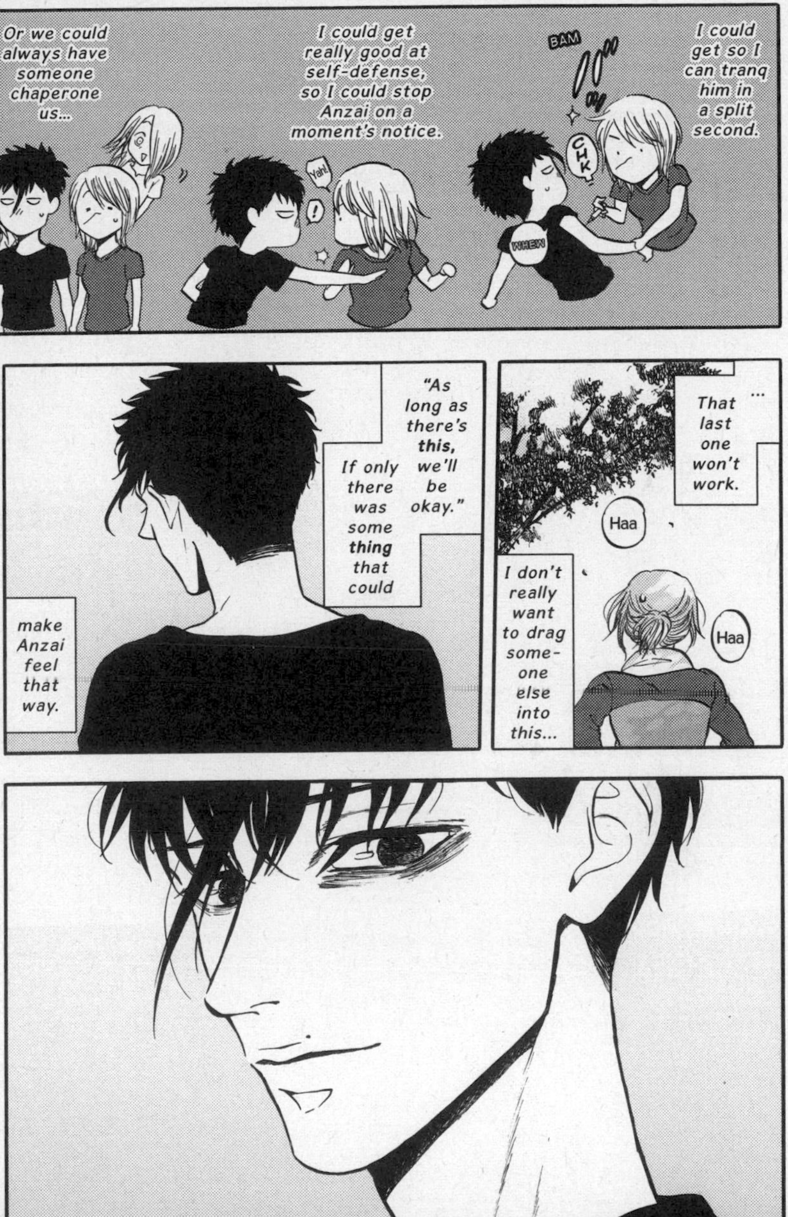
I could get so I can tranq him in a split second.
BAM
CHK
WHEW
I could get really good at self-defense, so I could stop Anzai on a moment's notice.
Yah!
!
Or we could always have someone chaperone us...
...
That last one won't work.
Haa
I don't really want to drag some-one else into this...
Haa
"As long as there's this, we'll be okay."
If only there was some thing that could
make Anzai feel that way.

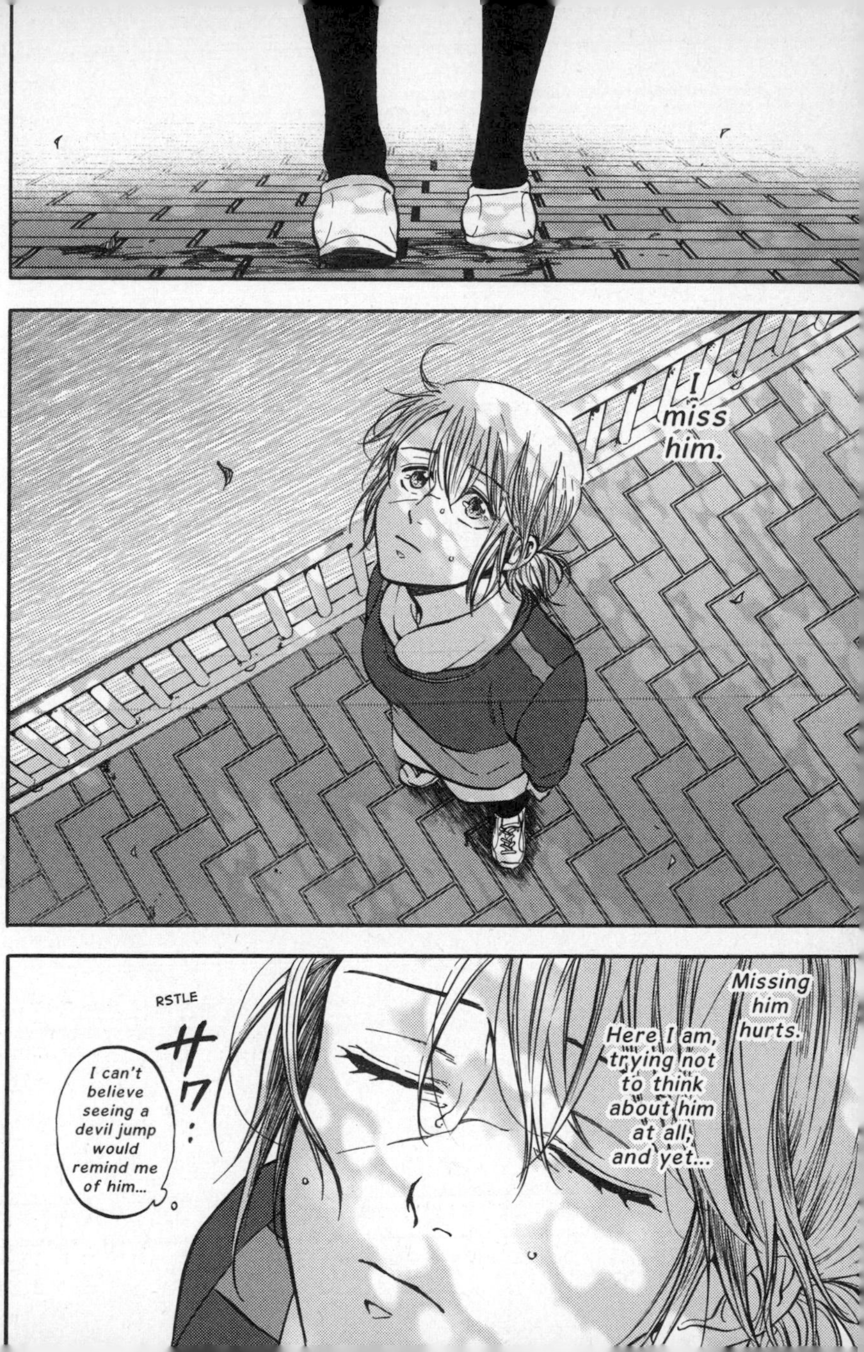
I miss him.
Missing him hurts.
Here I am, trying not to think about him at all, and yet...
RSTLE
サワ…
I can't believe seeing a devil jump would remind me of him...

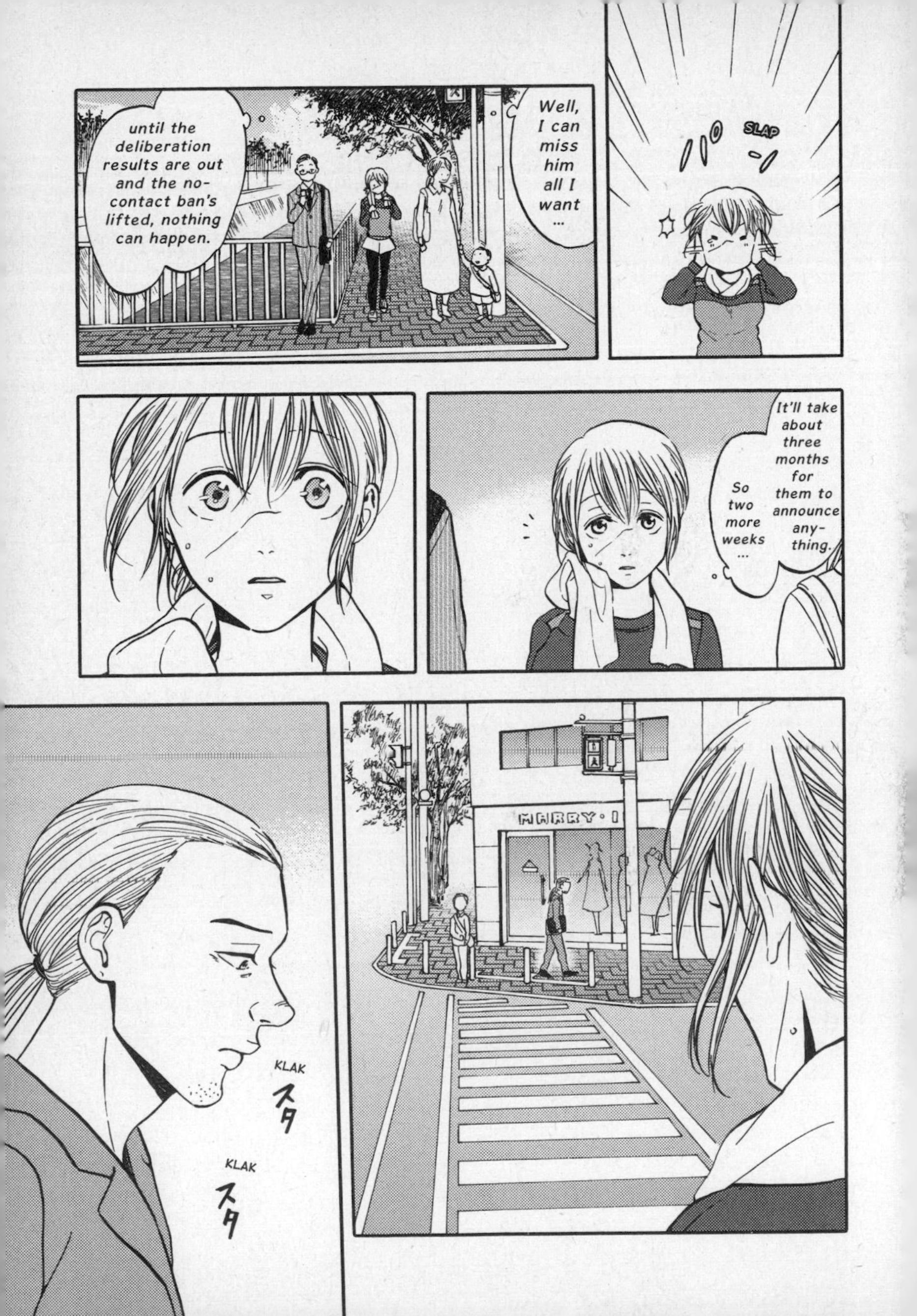
SLAP
Well, I can miss him all I want ...
until the deliberation results are out and the no-contact ban's lifted, nothing can happen.
It'll take about three months for them to announce anything.
So two more weeks ...
KLAK
スタ
KLAK
スタ

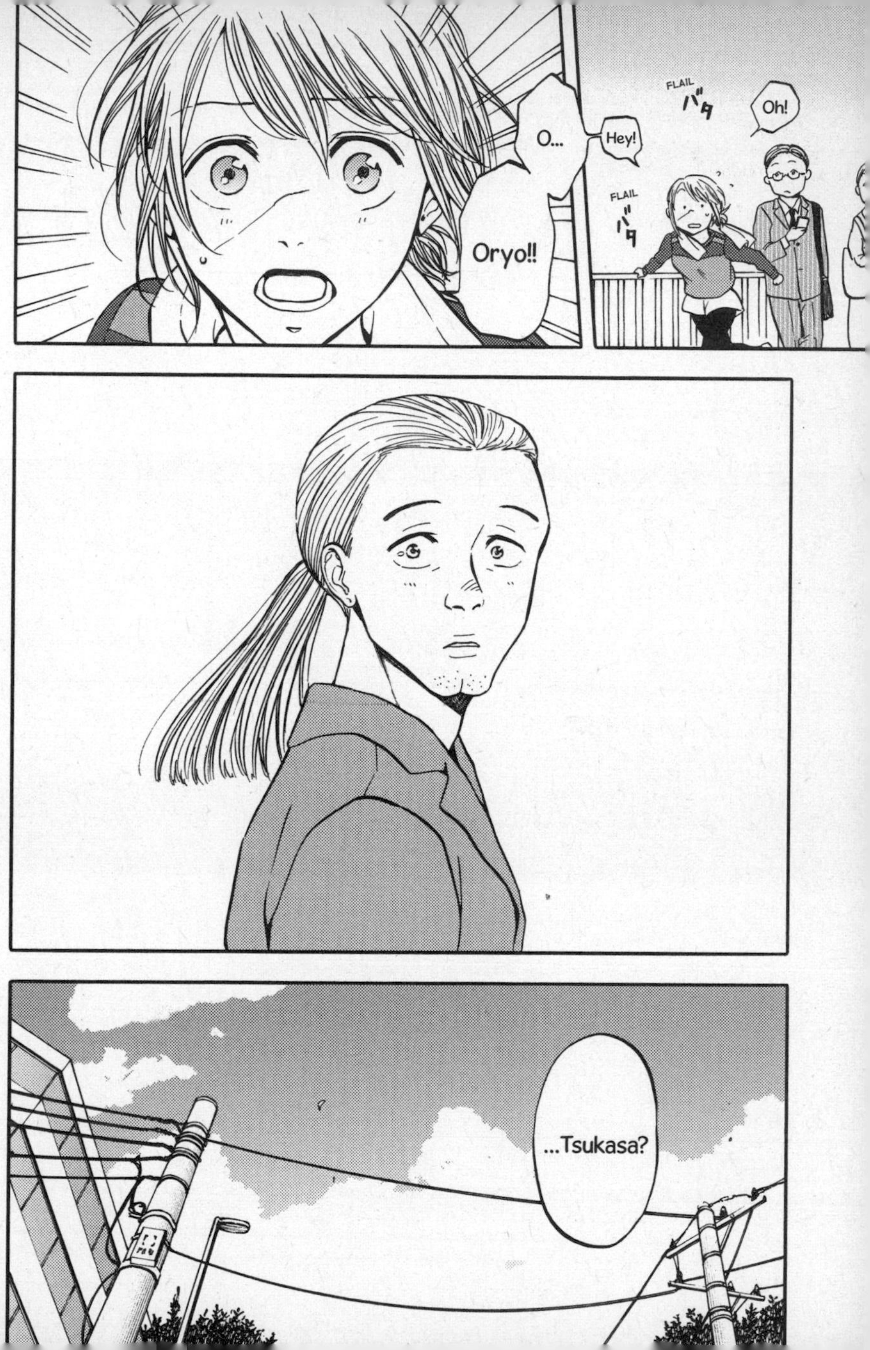
Oh!
FLAIL
バタ
Hey!
FLAIL
バタ
O...
Oryo!!
...Tsukasa?

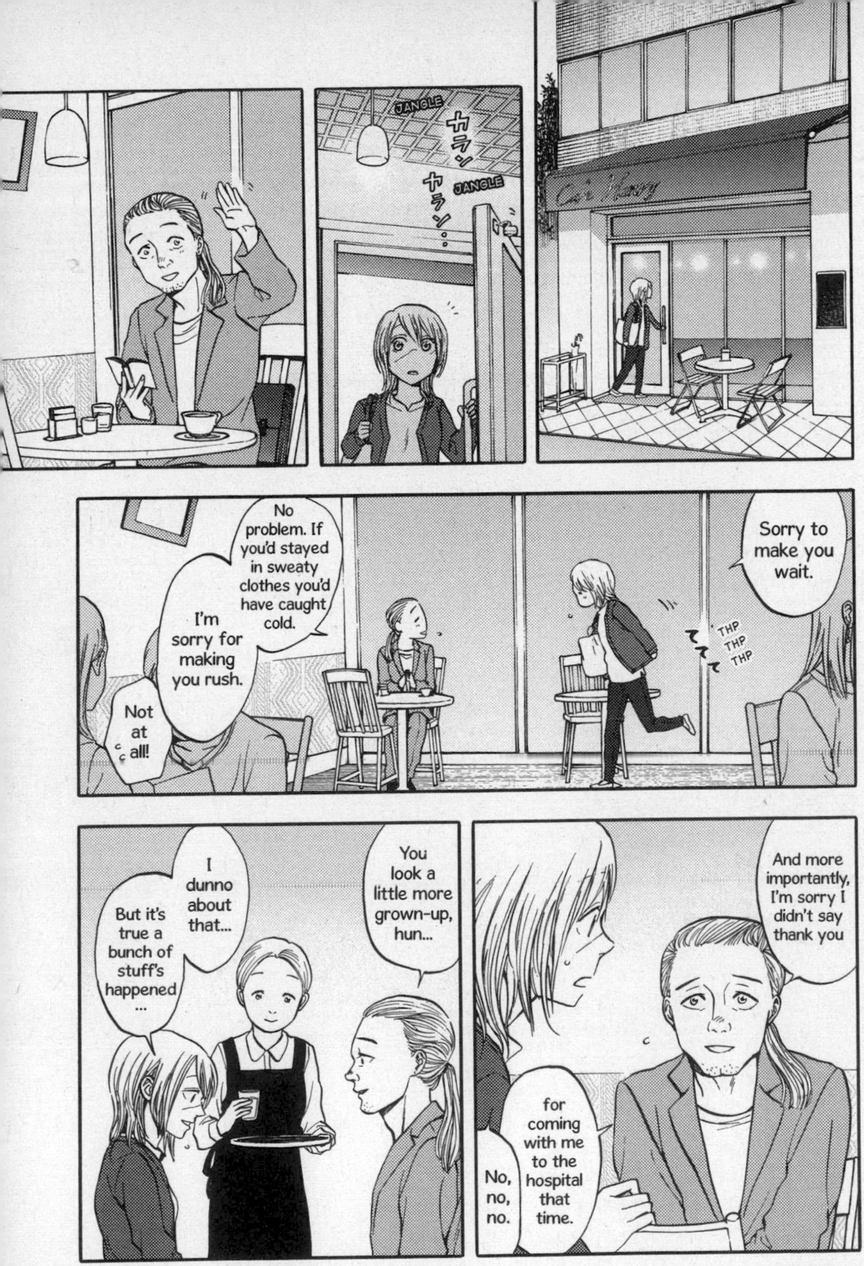
JANGLE
カラン
カラン
JANGLE
Sorry to make you wait.
てててて
THP THP THP
No problem. If you'd stayed in sweaty clothes you'd have caught cold.
I'm sorry for making you rush.
Not at all!
And more importantly, I'm sorry I didn't say thank you
for coming with me to the hospital that time.
No, no, no.
You look a little more grown-up, hun...
I dunno about that...
But it's true a bunch of stuff's happened ...

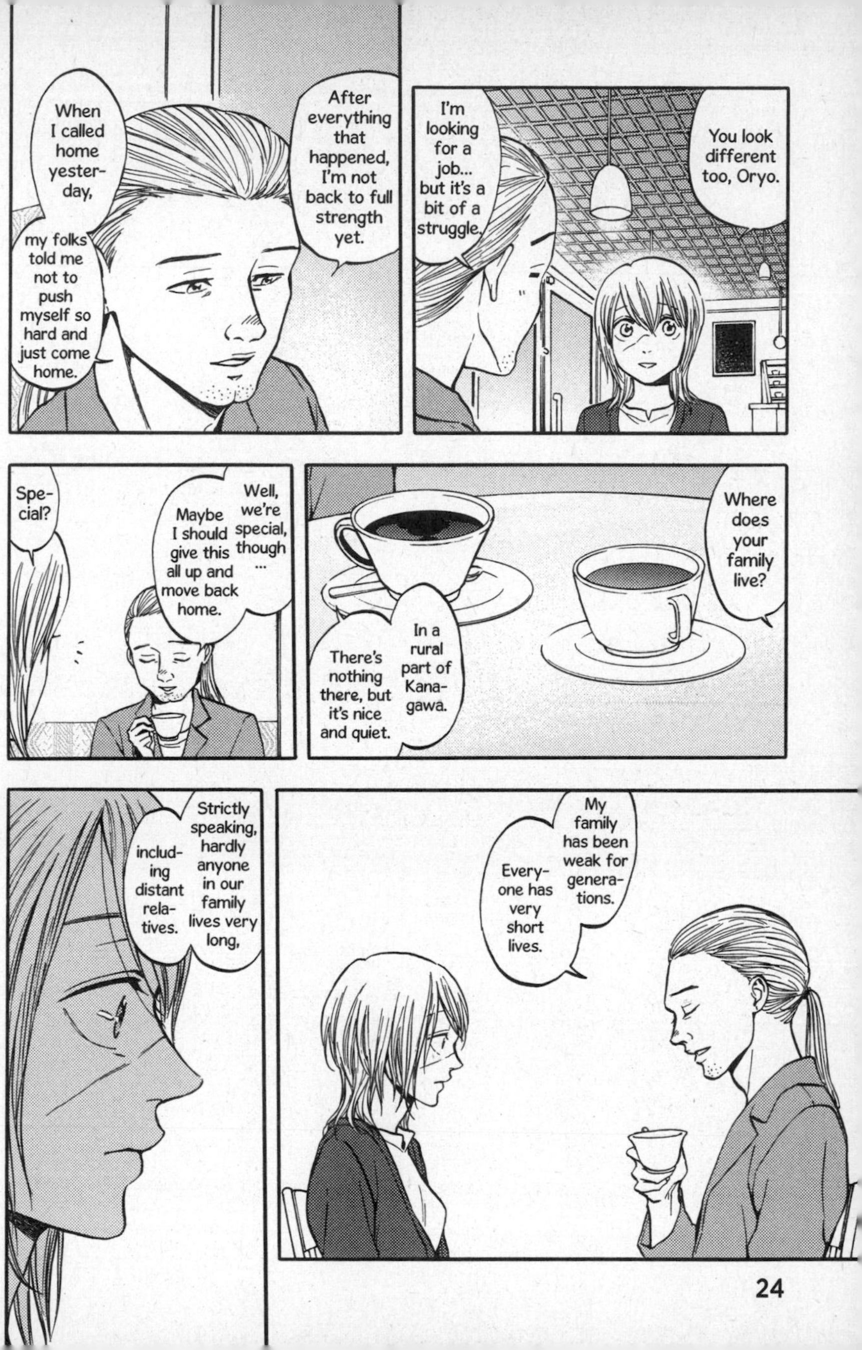
You look different too, Oryo.
I'm looking for a job... but it's a bit of a struggle.
After everything that happened, I'm not back to full strength yet.
When I called home yesterday,
my folks told me not to push myself so hard and just come home.
Where does your family live?
In a rural part of Kanagawa.
There's nothing there, but it's nice and quiet.
Well, we're special, though ...
Maybe I should give this all up and move back home.
Special?
My family has been weak for generations.
Everyone has very short lives.
Strictly speaking, hardly anyone in our family lives very long,
including distant relatives.

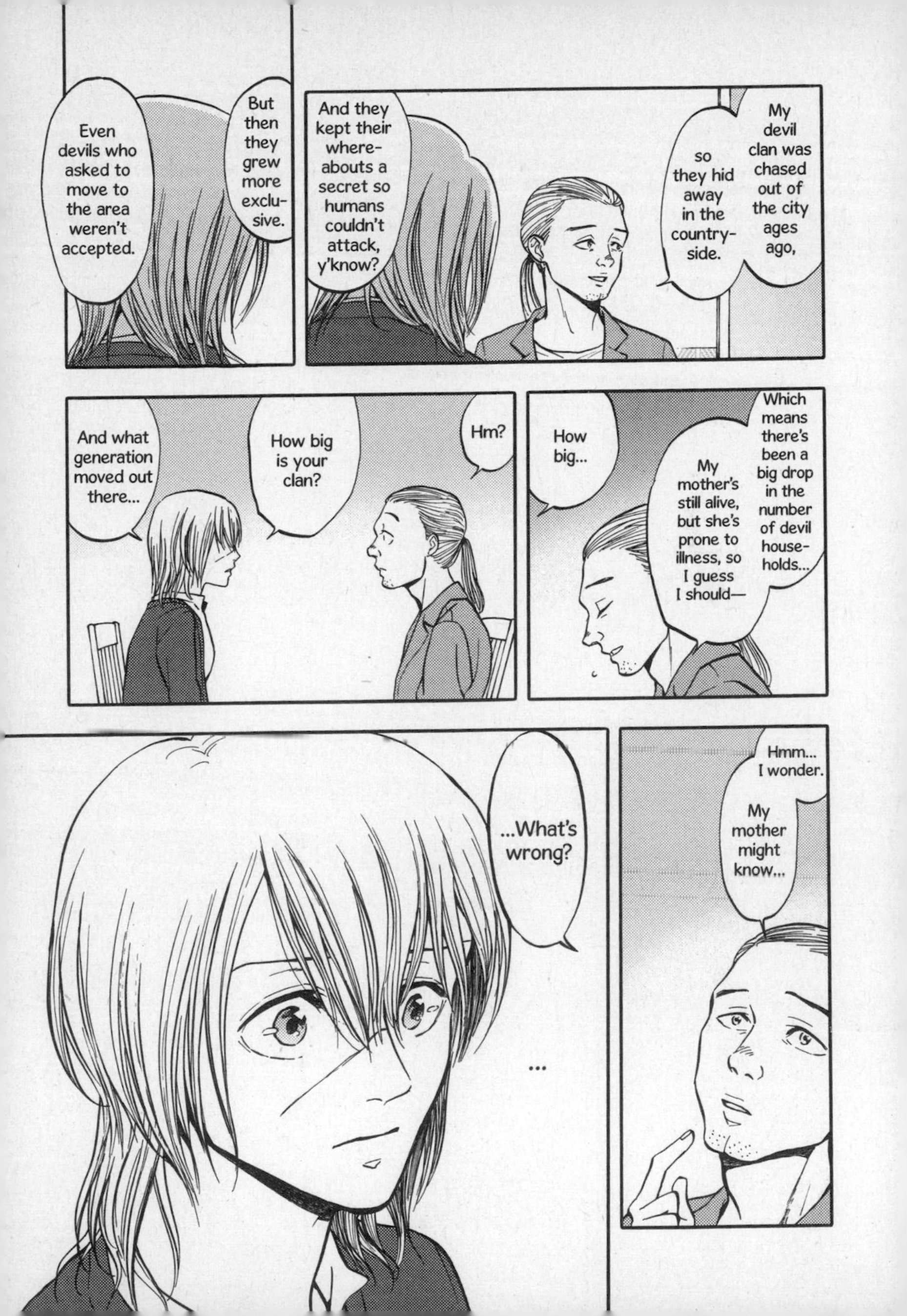
My devil clan was chased out of the city ages ago,
so they hid away in the countryside.
And they kept their whereabouts a secret so humans couldn't attack, y'know?
But then they grew more exclusive.
Even devils who asked to move to the area weren't accepted.
Which means there's been a big drop in the number of devil households...
My mother's still alive, but she's prone to illness, so I guess I should—
How big...
Hm?
How big is your clan?
And what generation moved out there...
Hmm... I wonder.
My mother might know...
...What's wrong?
...

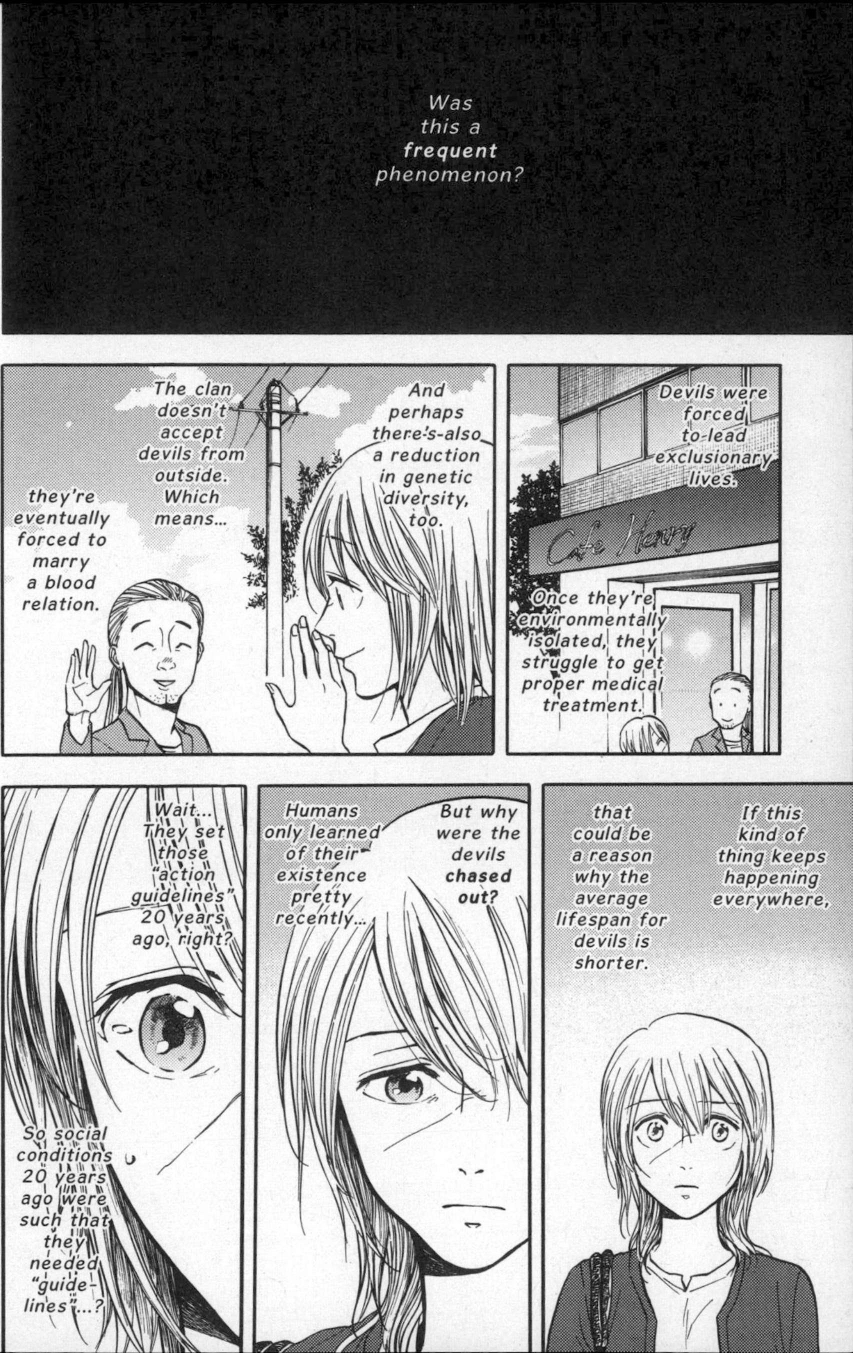
Was this a **frequent** phenomenon?
Devils were forced to lead exclusionary lives.
Once they're environmentally isolated, they struggle to get proper medical treatment.
And perhaps there's also a reduction in genetic diversity, too.
The clan doesn't accept devils from outside. Which means...
they're eventually forced to marry a blood relation.
If this kind of thing keeps happening everywhere,
that could be a reason why the average lifespan for devils is shorter.
But why were the devils **chased out?**
Humans only learned of their existence pretty recently...
Wait... They set those "action guidelines" 20 years ago, right?
So social conditions 20 years ago were such that they needed "guide-lines"...?

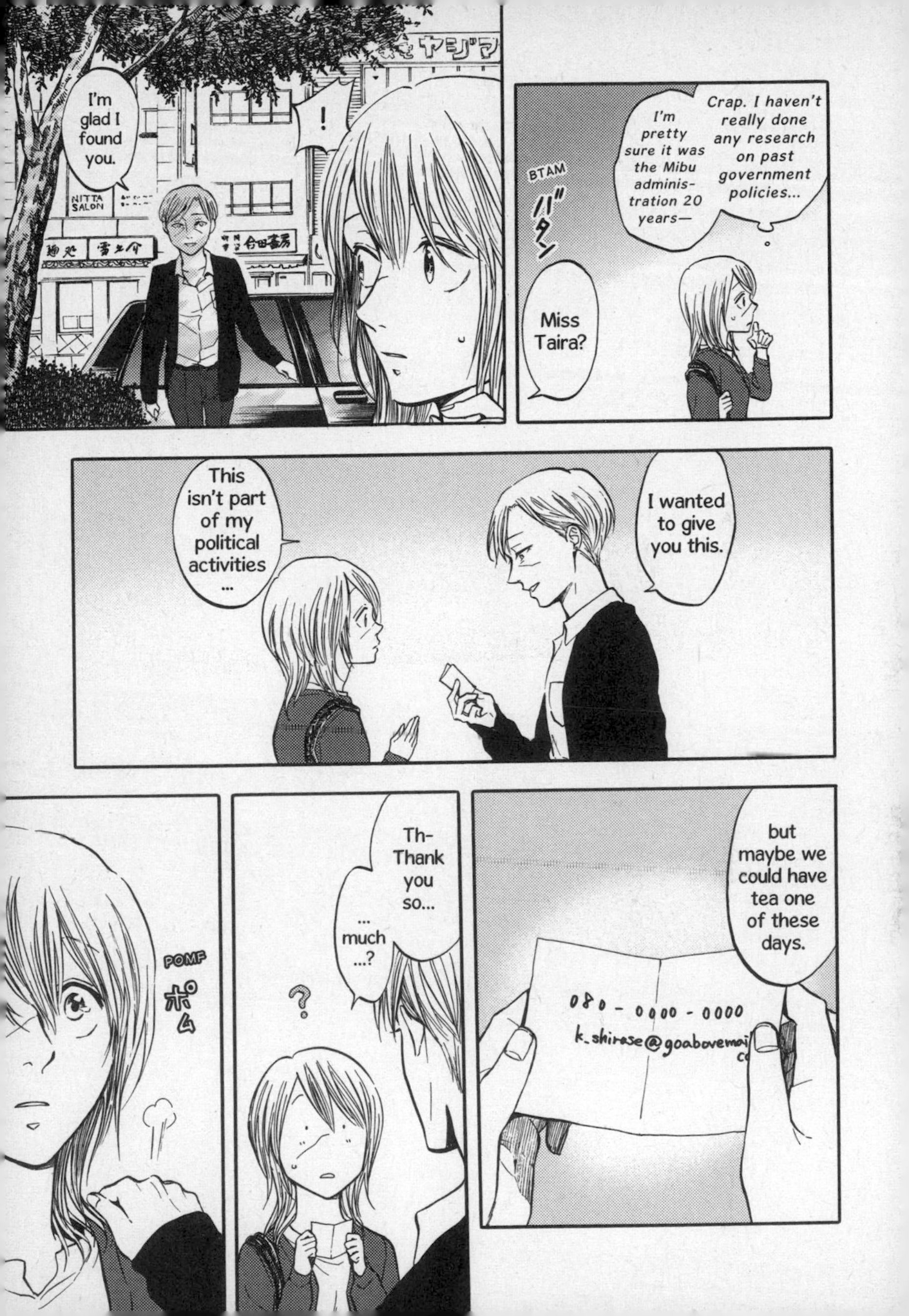
Crap. I haven't really done any research on past government policies...
I'm pretty sure it was the Mibu administration 20 years—
BTAM
バタン
Miss Taira?
!
I'm glad I found you.
ヤジマ
NITTA SALON
麺処 雪之介
合田書房
I wanted to give you this.
This isn't part of my political activities ...
but maybe we could have tea one of these days.
080 - 0000 - 0000
k_shirase@goabovemai
Th-Thank you so...
... much ...?
?
POMF
ポム

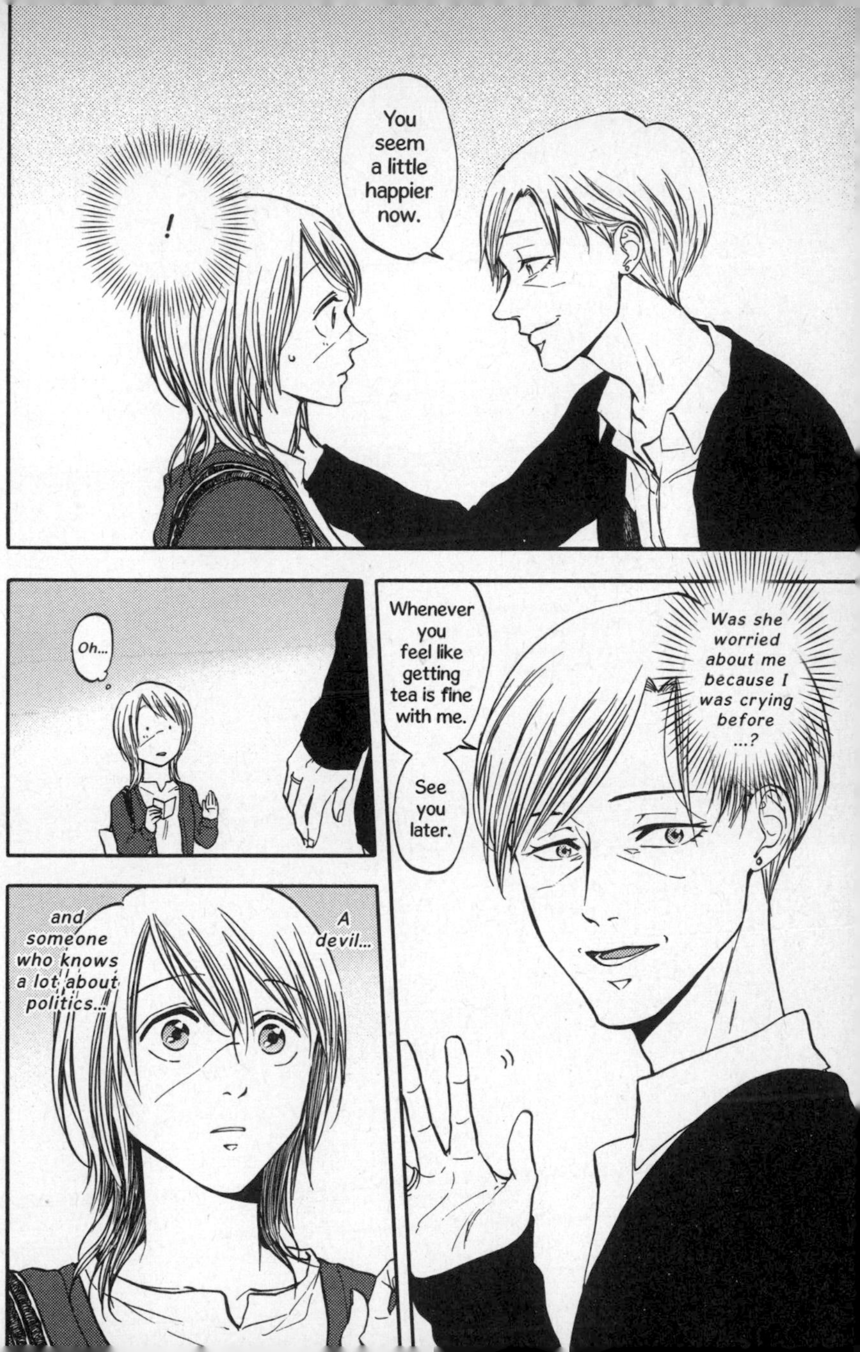
You seem a little happier now.
!
Was she worried about me because I was crying before ...?
Whenever you feel like getting tea is fine with me.
See you later.
Oh...
A devil...
and someone who knows a lot about politics...

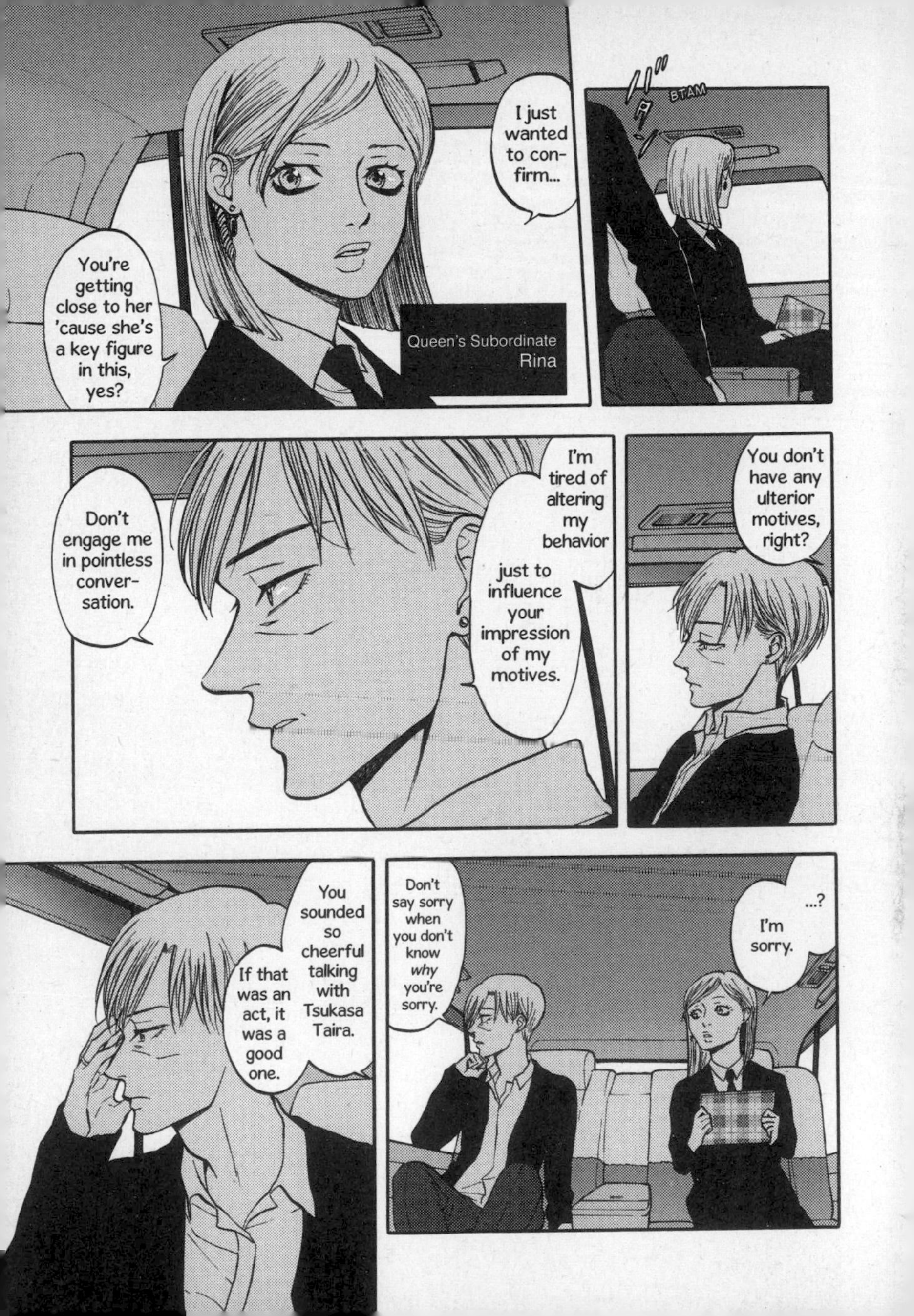
BTAM
I just wanted to confirm...
You're getting close to her 'cause she's a key figure in this, yes?
Queen's Subordinate Rina
You don't have any ulterior motives, right?
I'm tired of altering my behavior
just to influence your impression of my motives.
Don't engage me in pointless conversation.
...?
I'm sorry.
Don't say sorry when you don't know *why* you're sorry.
You sounded so cheerful talking with Tsukasa Taira.
If that was an act, it was a good one.

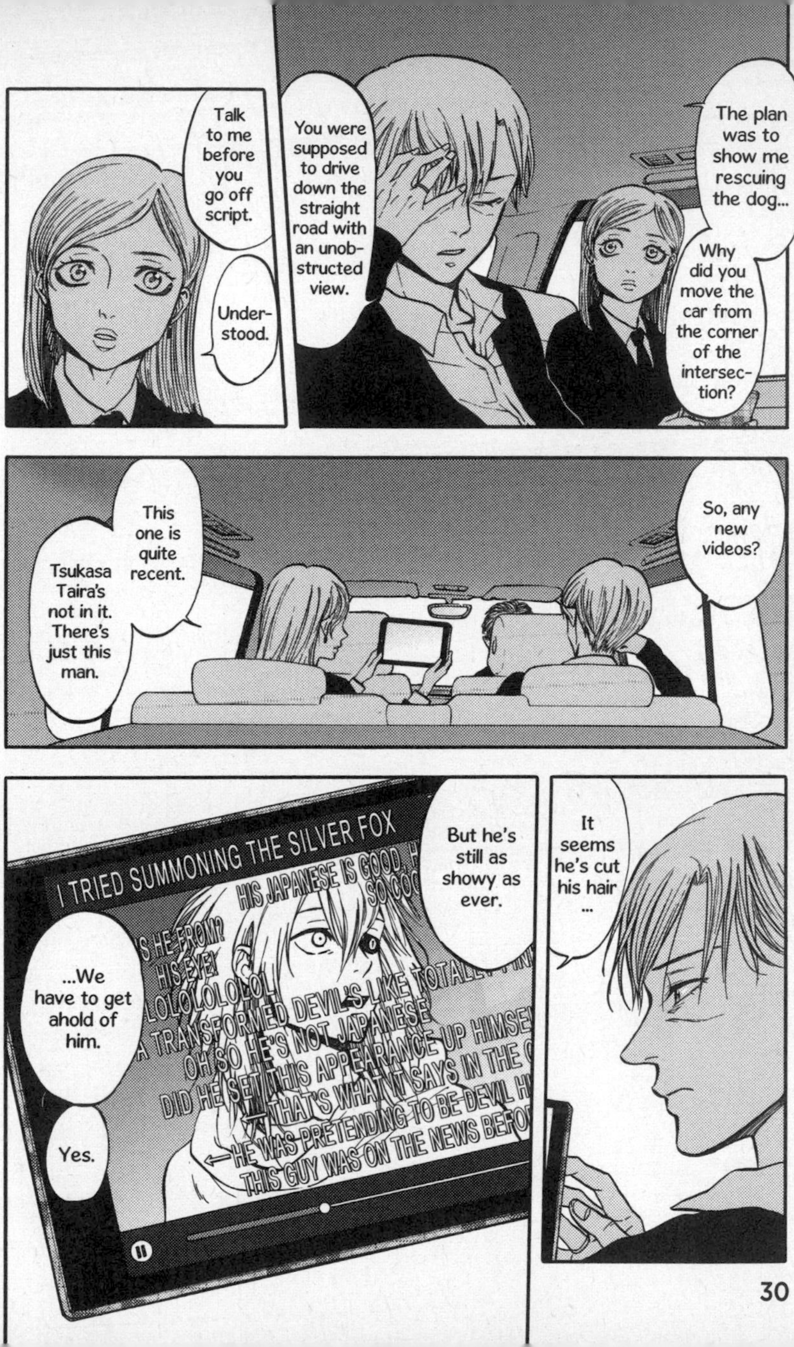

The plan was to show me rescuing the dog...
Why did you move the car from the corner of the intersection?
You were supposed to drive down the straight road with an unobstructed view.
Talk to me before you go off script.
Understood.
So, any new videos?
This one is quite recent.
Tsukasa Taira's not in it. There's just this man.
It seems he's cut his hair ...
I TRIED SUMMONING THE SILVER FOX
OH SO HE'S NOT JAPANESE
But he's still as showy as ever.
...We have to get ahold of him.
Yes.

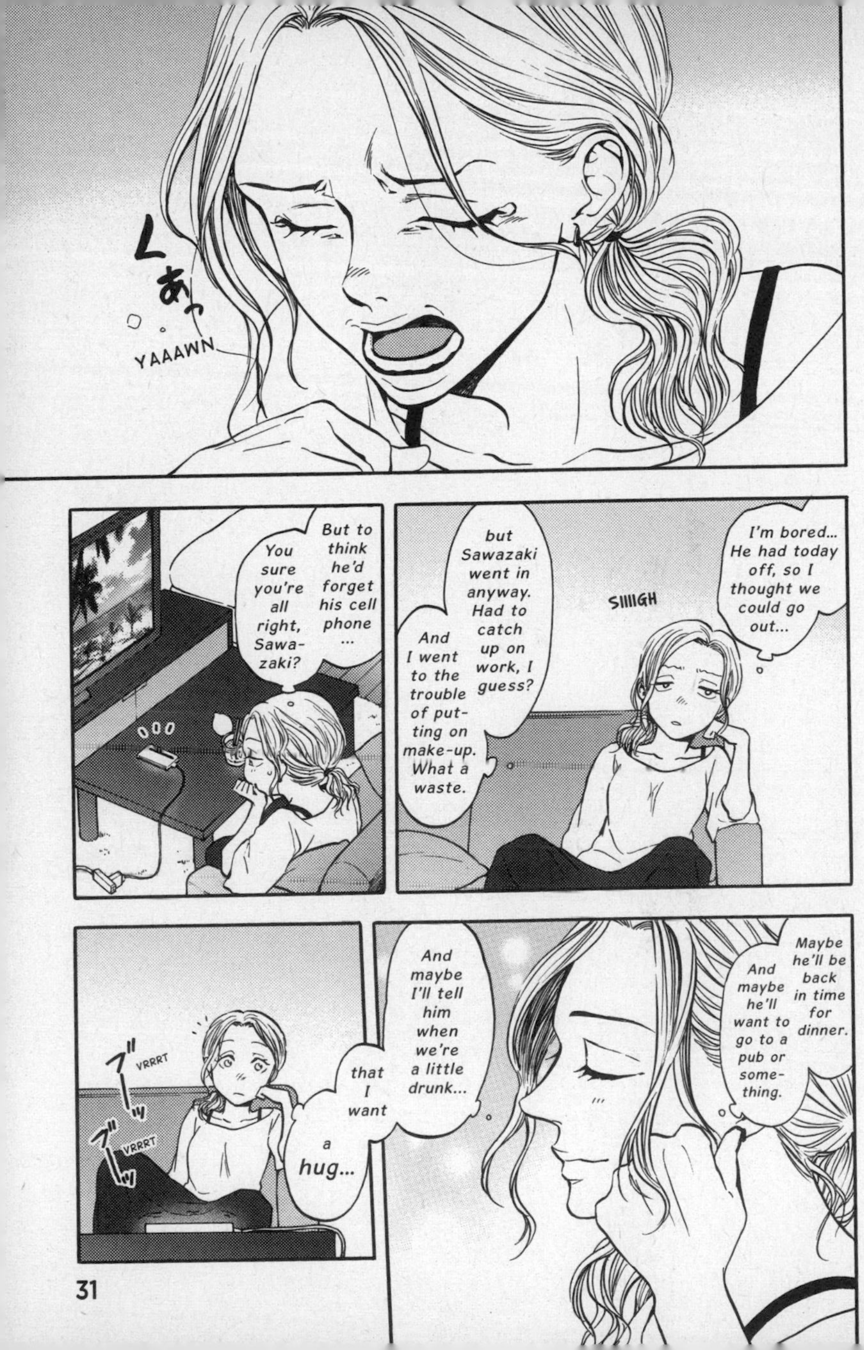
くあっ
YAAAWN
I'm bored... He had today off, so I thought we could go out...
SIIIGH
but Sawazaki went in anyway. Had to catch up on work, I guess?
And I went to the trouble of putting on make-up. What a waste.
But to think he'd forget his cell phone ...
You sure you're all right, Sawazaki?
Maybe he'll be back in time for dinner.
And maybe he'll want to go to a pub or something.
And maybe I'll tell him when we're a little drunk...
that I want a hug...
ブーッ
VRRRT
ブーッ
VRRRT

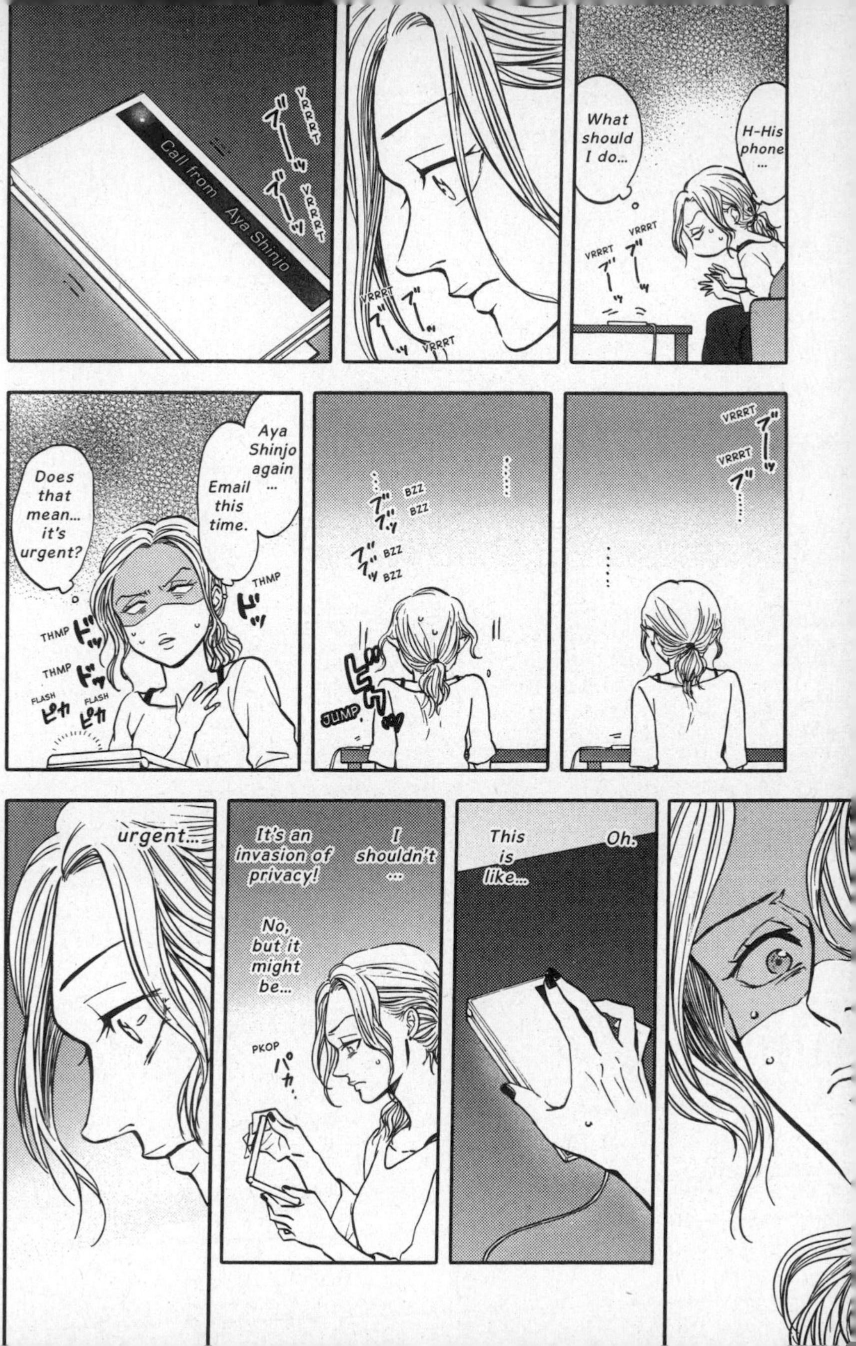

H-His phone ...
What should I do...
VRRRT
VRRRT
VRRRT
VRRRT
VRRRT
VRRRT
Call from Aya Shinjo
VRRRT
VRRRT
......
......
BZZ
BZZ
BZZ
BZZ
JUMP
Aya Shinjo again ... Email this time.
Does that mean... it's urgent?
THMP
THMP
THMP
FLASH
FLASH
Oh.
This is like...
I shouldn't ...
It's an invasion of privacy!
No, but it might be...
PKOP
urgent...

Displaying New Message

Date 2013/05/02 16:13

From Aya Shinjo

Sub It's Shinjo!

The fastest route just got shut down, so I'll be coming a different way, which means I'll be late... I'm really sorry. Please go ahead and buy the cardigan first. I think I'll manage to get there in time for the reservation at the pub! Sorry for inviting you so suddenly today. But I've really wanted to do this, so I'm happy, I'm excited to

KACHAK
KACHAK

I'm back.

B T A M

Jill, about dinner tonight.

A colleague invited me out for a drink, so...

You got a call and then an email,

Sorry...

so I thought it might be urgent, so I opened your phone...

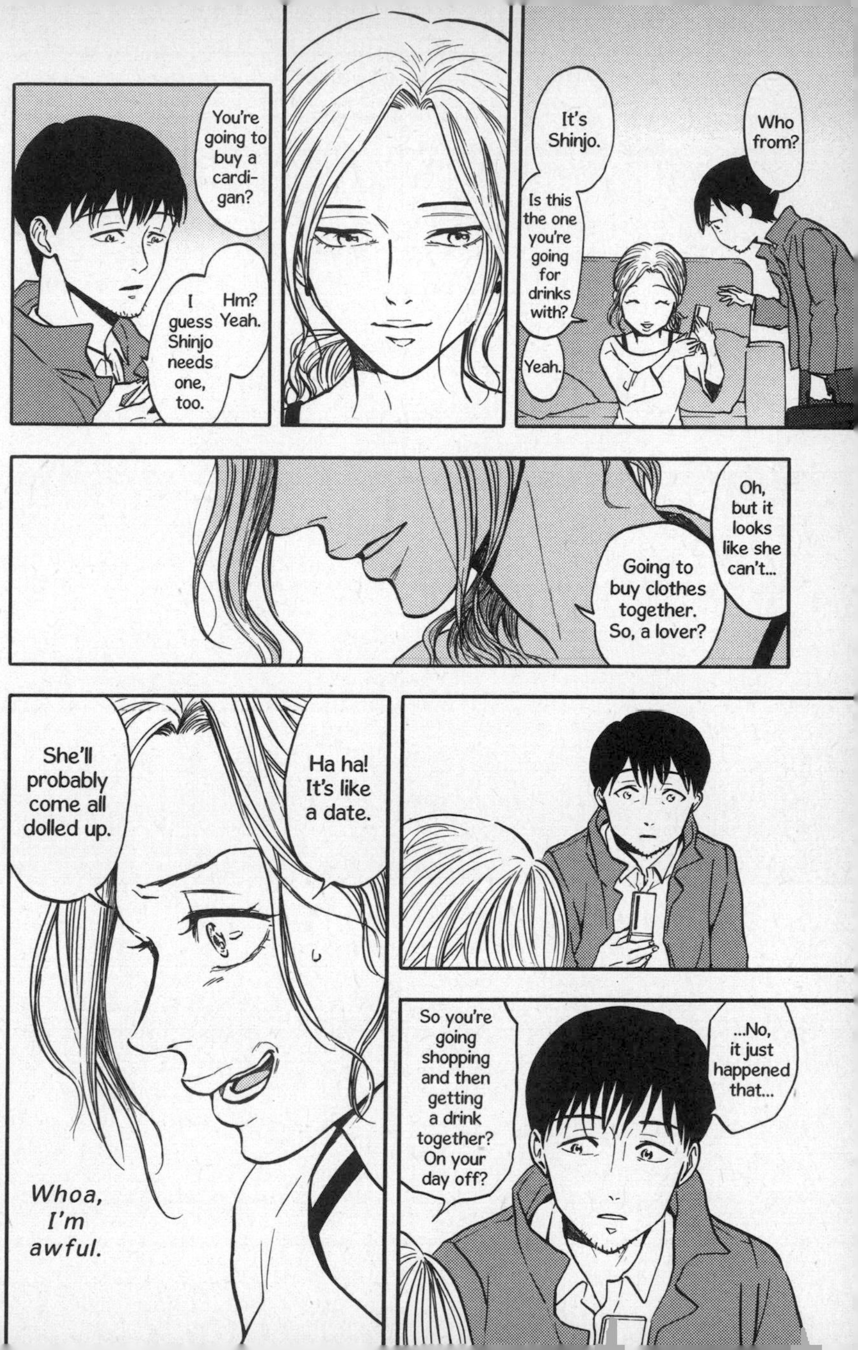
Who from?
It's Shinjo.
Is this the one you're going for drinks with?
Yeah.
You're going to buy a cardigan?
Hm? Yeah.
I guess Shinjo needs one, too.
Oh, but it looks like she can't...
Going to buy clothes together. So, a lover?
...No, it just happened that...
So you're going shopping and then getting a drink together? On your day off?
Ha ha! It's like a date.
She'll probably come all dolled up.
Whoa, I'm awful.

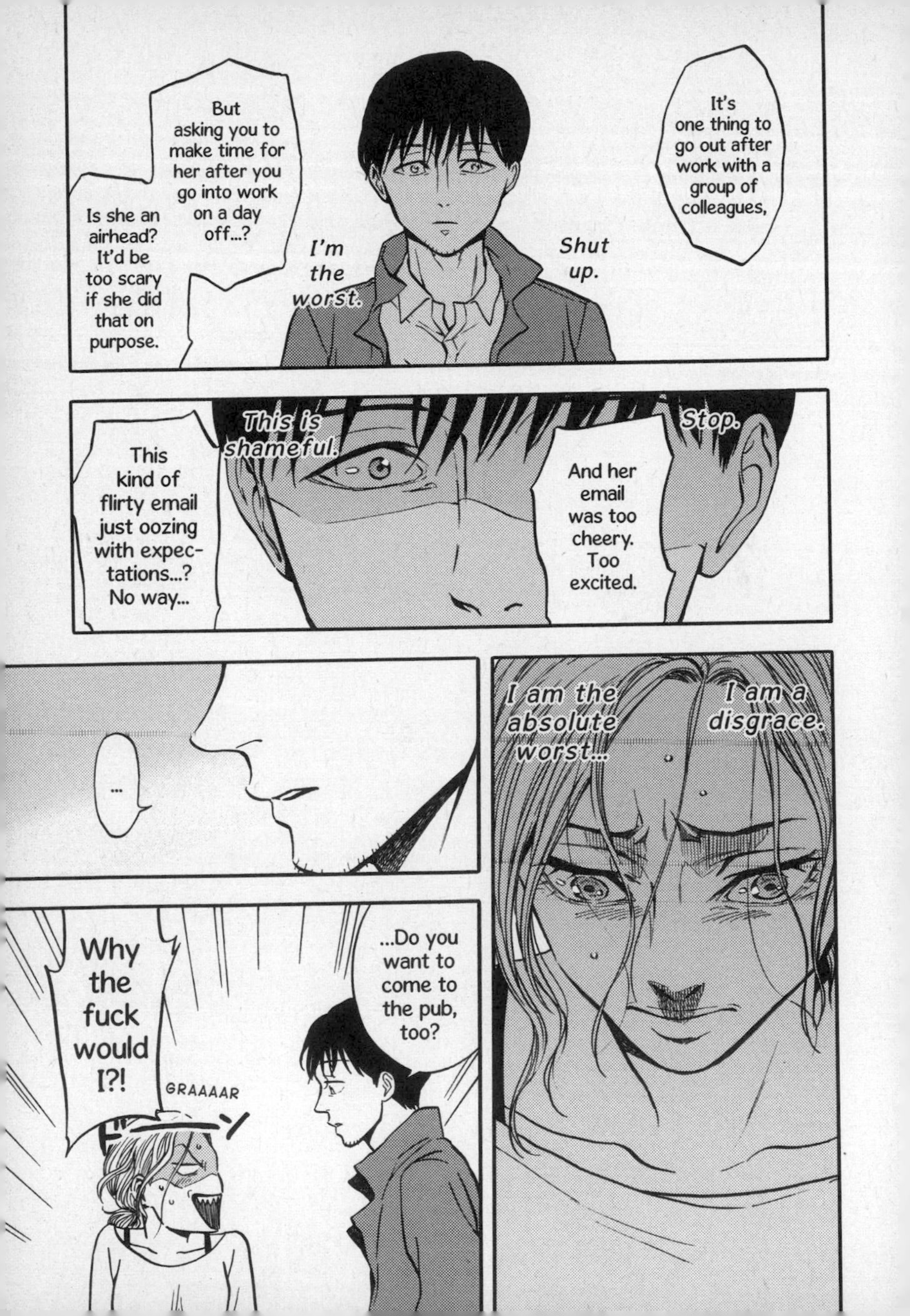
It's one thing to go out after work with a group of colleagues,
Shut up.
I'm the worst.
But asking you to make time for her after you go into work on a day off...?
Is she an airhead? It'd be too scary if she did that on purpose.
Stop.
And her email was too cheery. Too excited.
This is shameful.
This kind of flirty email just oozing with expectations...? No way...
I am a disgrace.
I am the absolute worst...
...
...Do you want to come to the pub, too?
Why the fuck would I?!
GRAAAAR

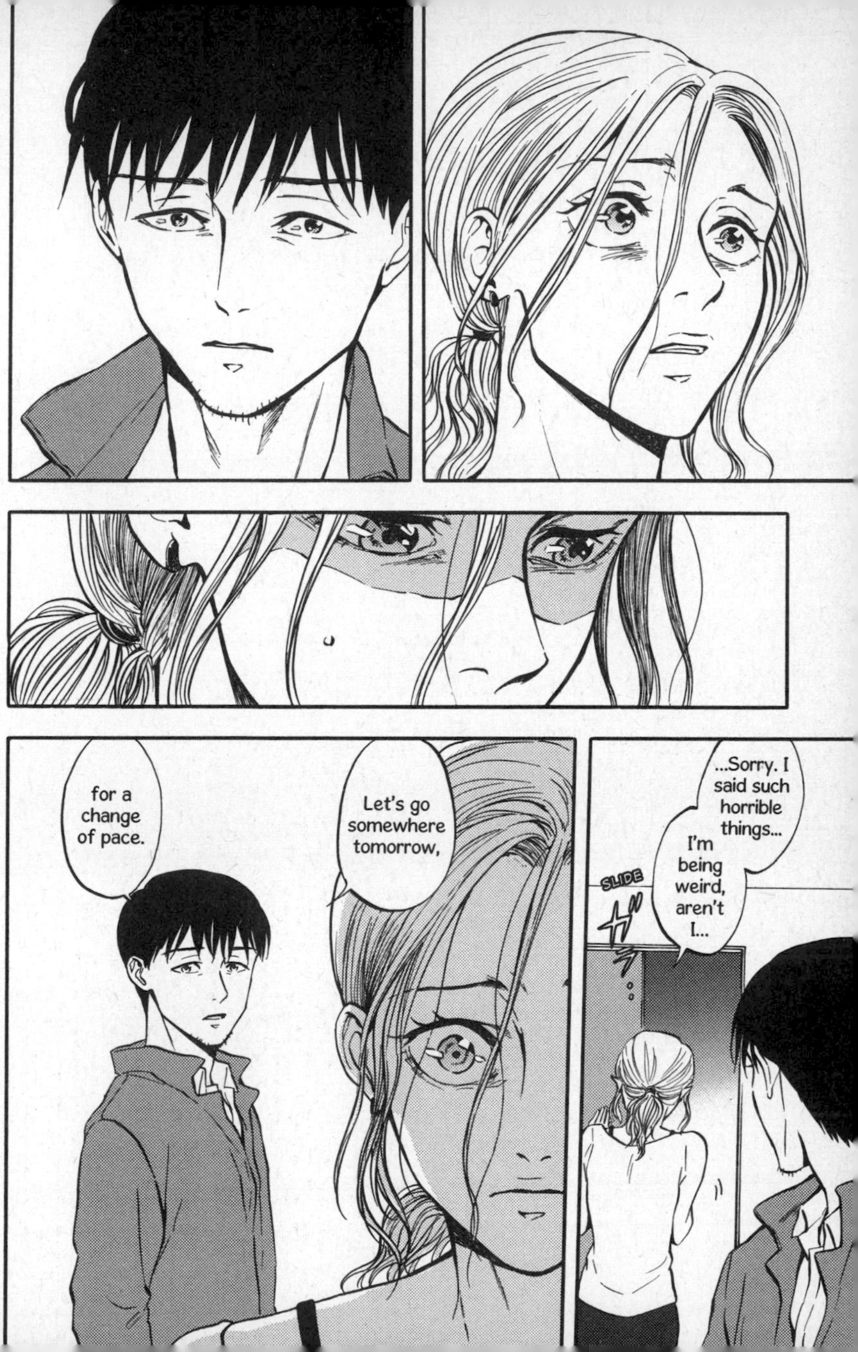
...Sorry. I said such horrible things...
I'm being weird, aren't I...
SLIDE
Let's go somewhere tomorrow,
for a change of pace.

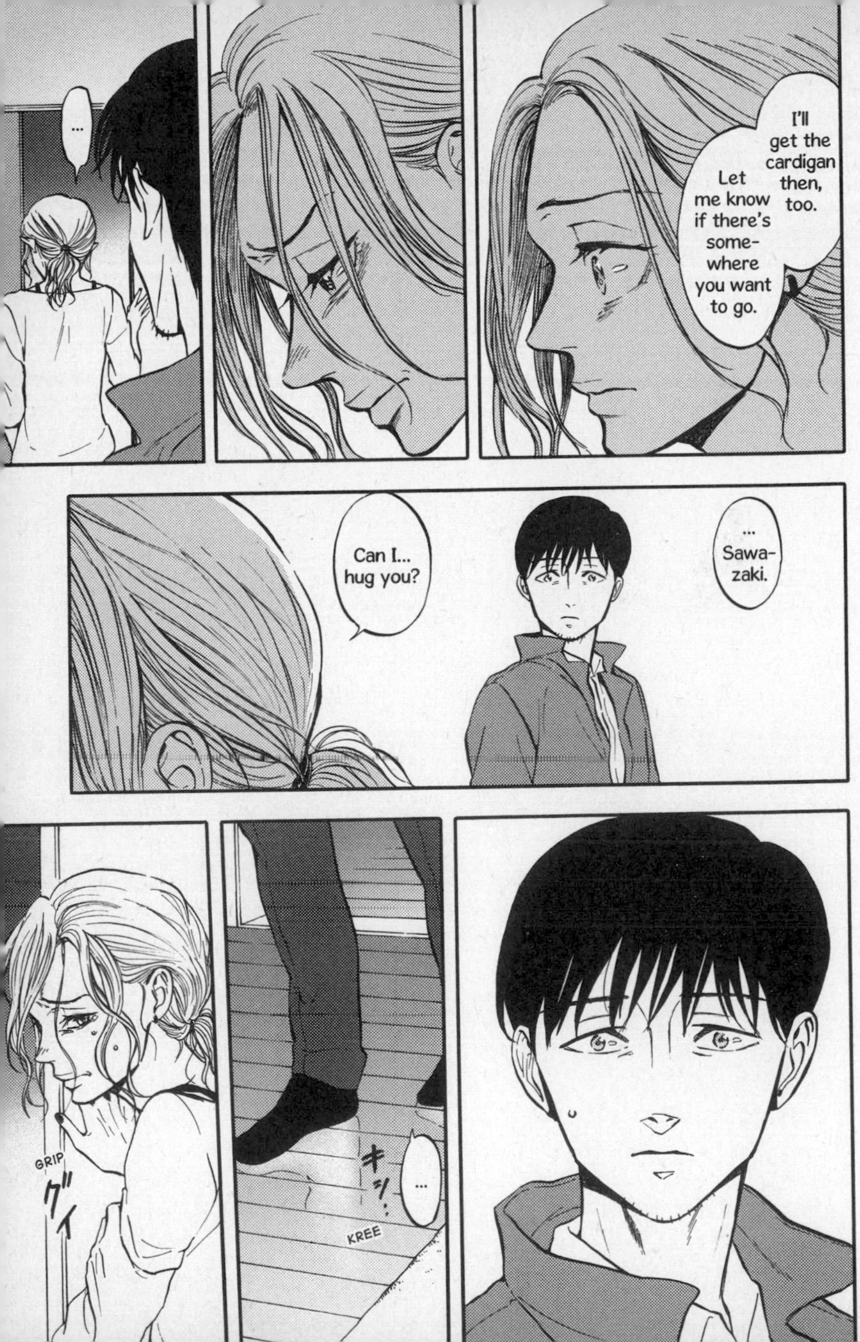
I'll get the cardigan then, too.
Let me know if there's somewhere you want to go.
...
...
Sawazaki.
Can I... hug you?
...
KREE
キシ…
GRIP
グイ

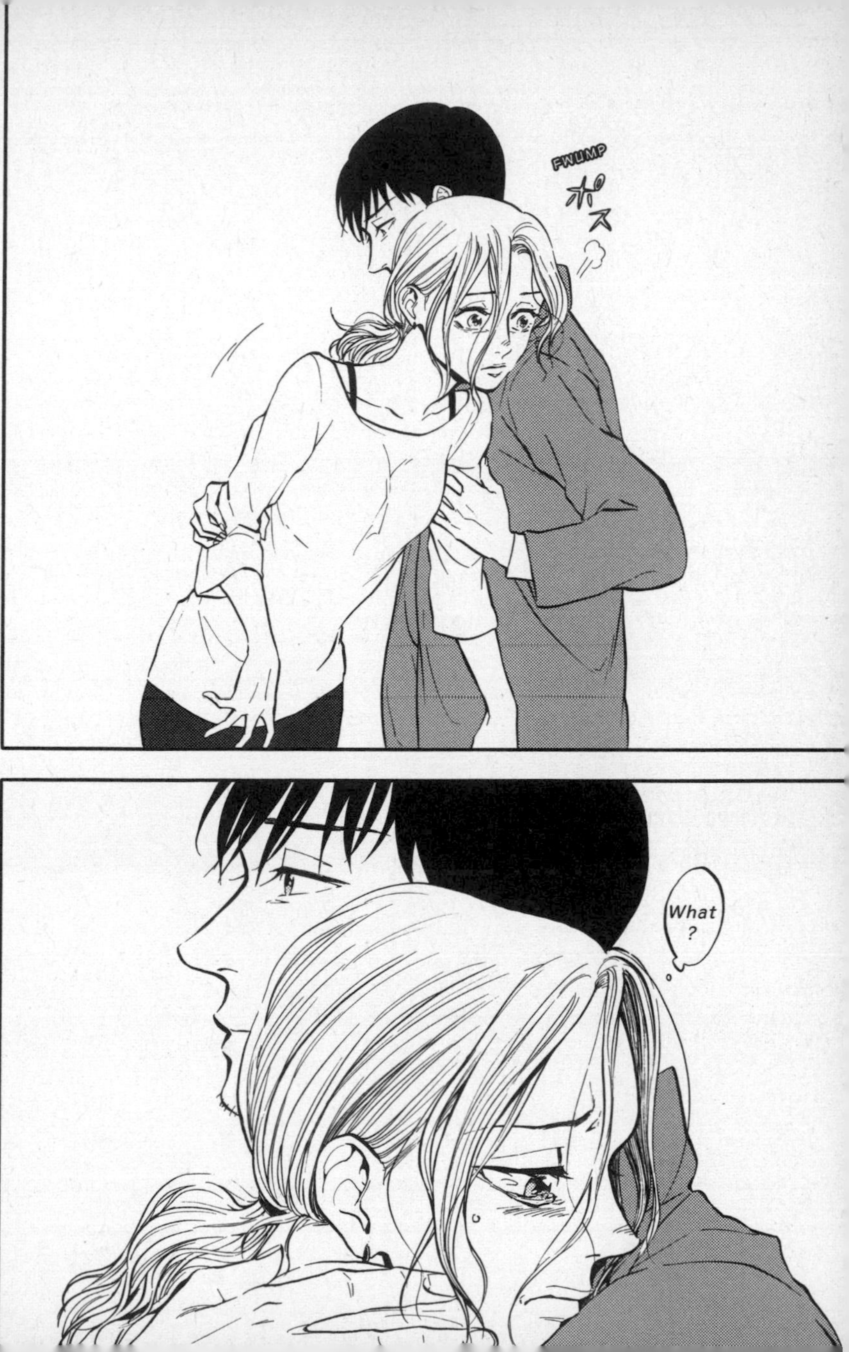
FWUMP
ポス
What ?

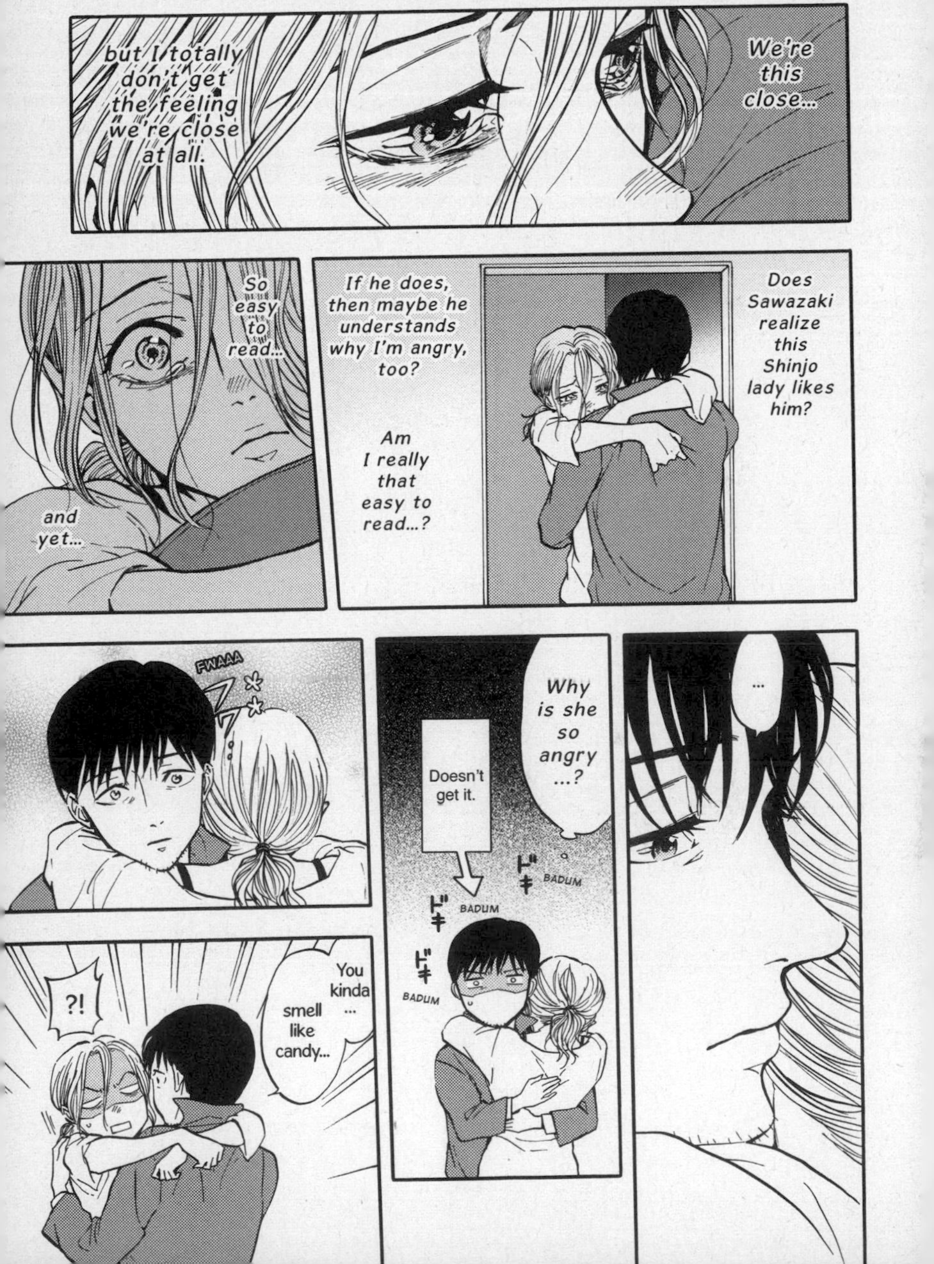
We're this close...
but I totally don't get the feeling we're close at all.
Does Sawazaki realize this Shinjo lady likes him?
If he does, then maybe he understands why I'm angry, too?
Am I really that easy to read...?
So easy to read...
and yet...
...
Why is she so angry ...?
Doesn't get it.
ドキ BADUM
ドキ BADUM
ドキ BADUM
FWAAA
You kinda ...
smell like candy...
?!

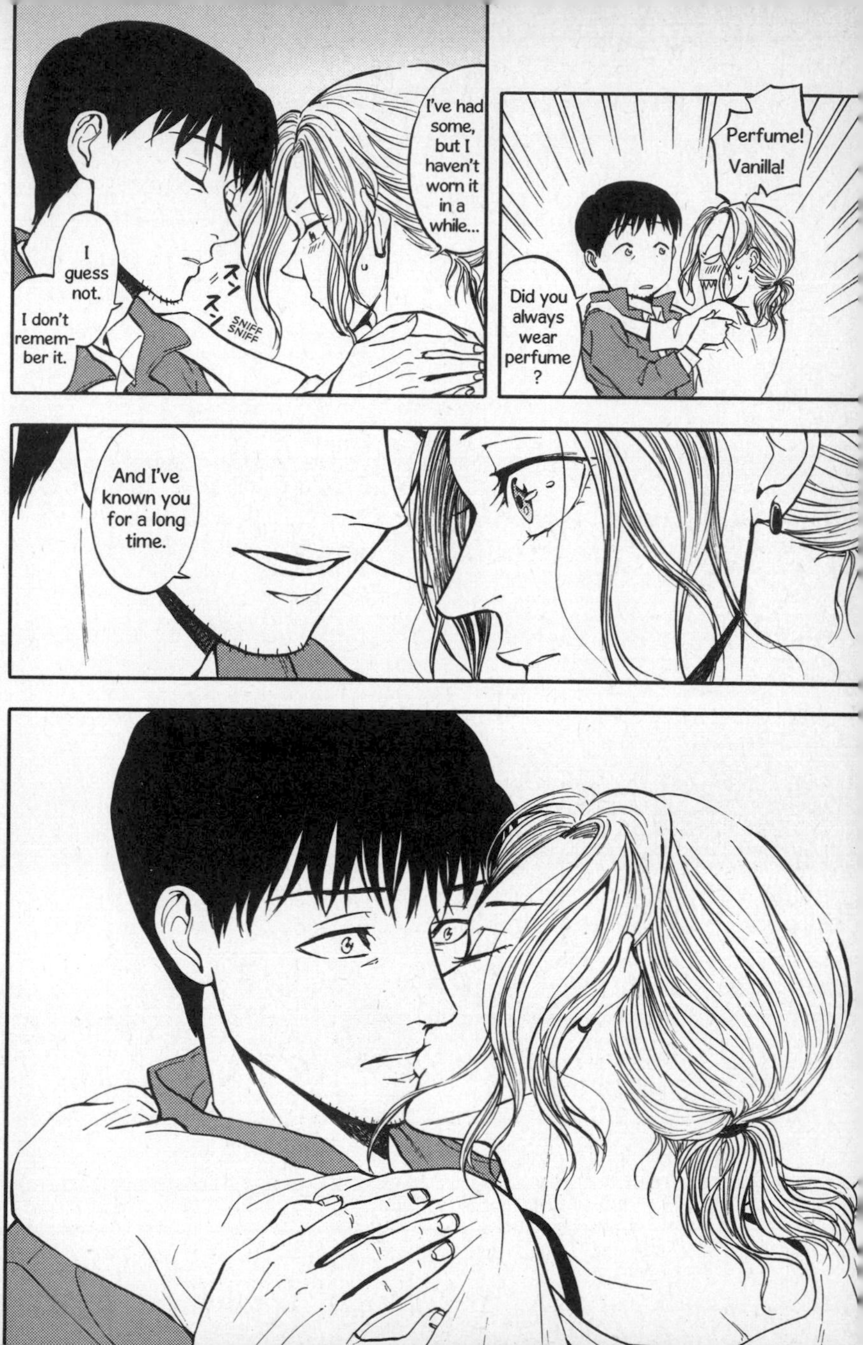
Perfume!
Vanilla!
Did you always wear perfume?
I've had some, but I haven't worn it in a while...
スン スン
SNIFF SNIFF
I guess not.
I don't remember it.
And I've known you for a long time.

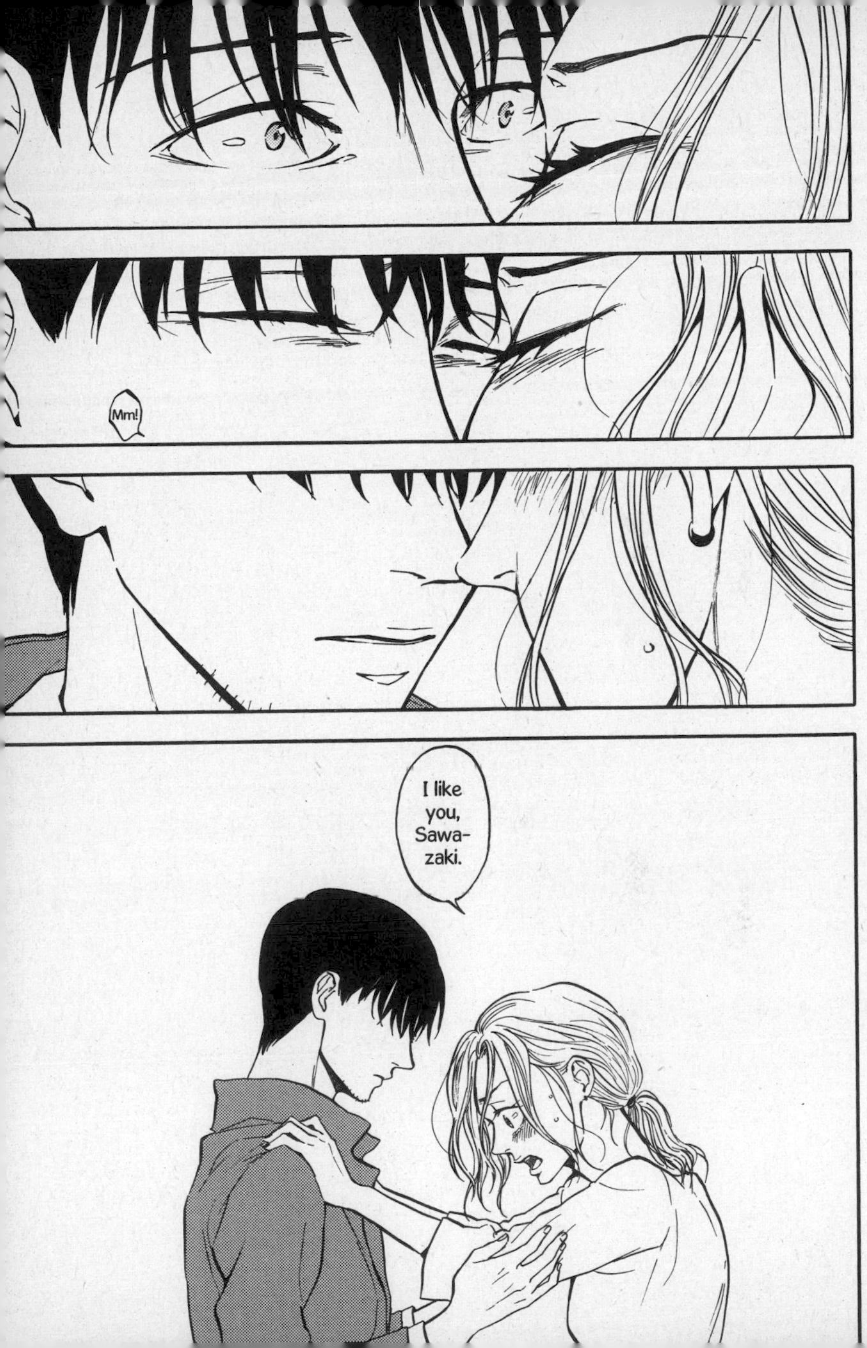
Mm!
I like you, Sawa-zaki.

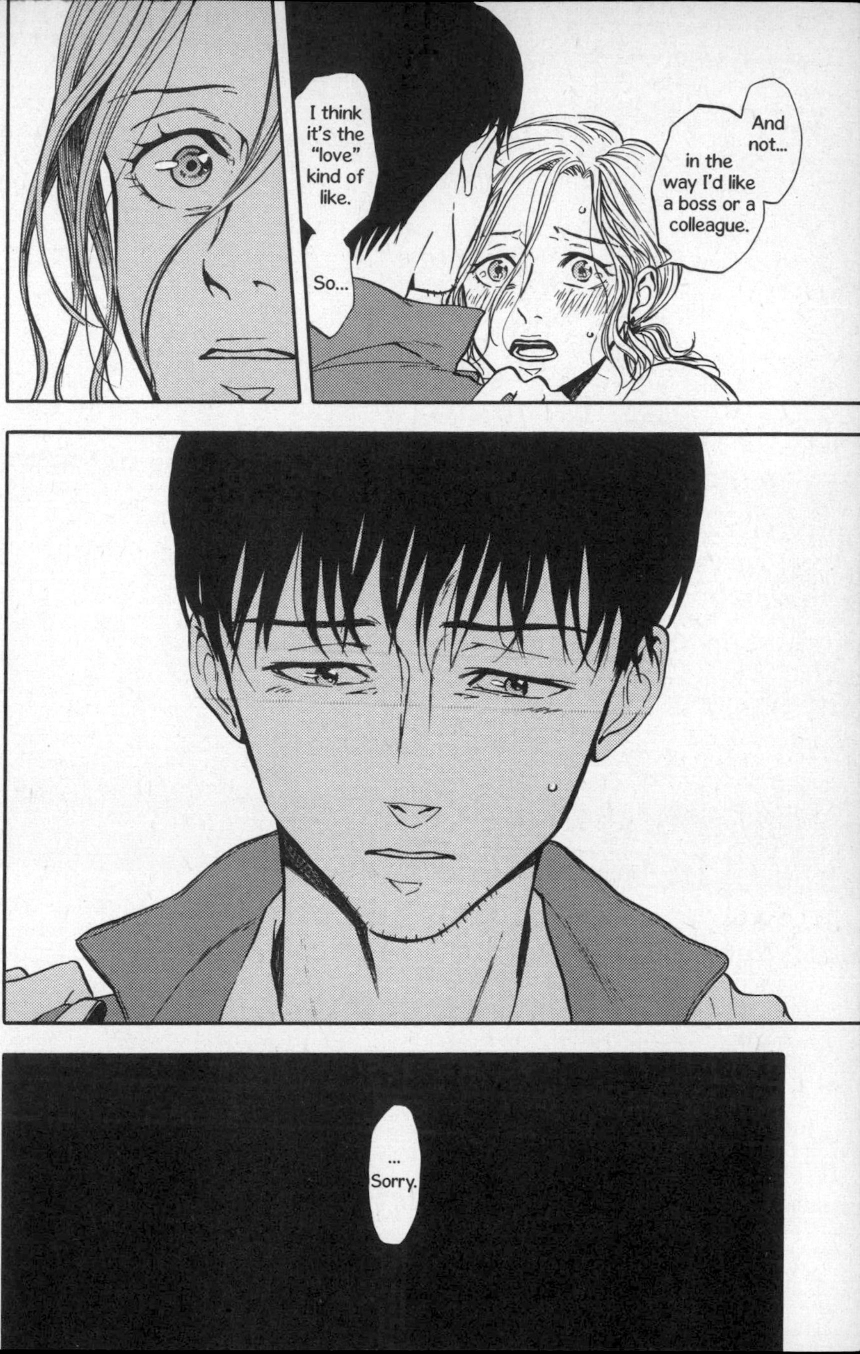
And not... in the way I'd like a boss or a colleague.
I think it's the "love" kind of like.
So...
... Sorry.

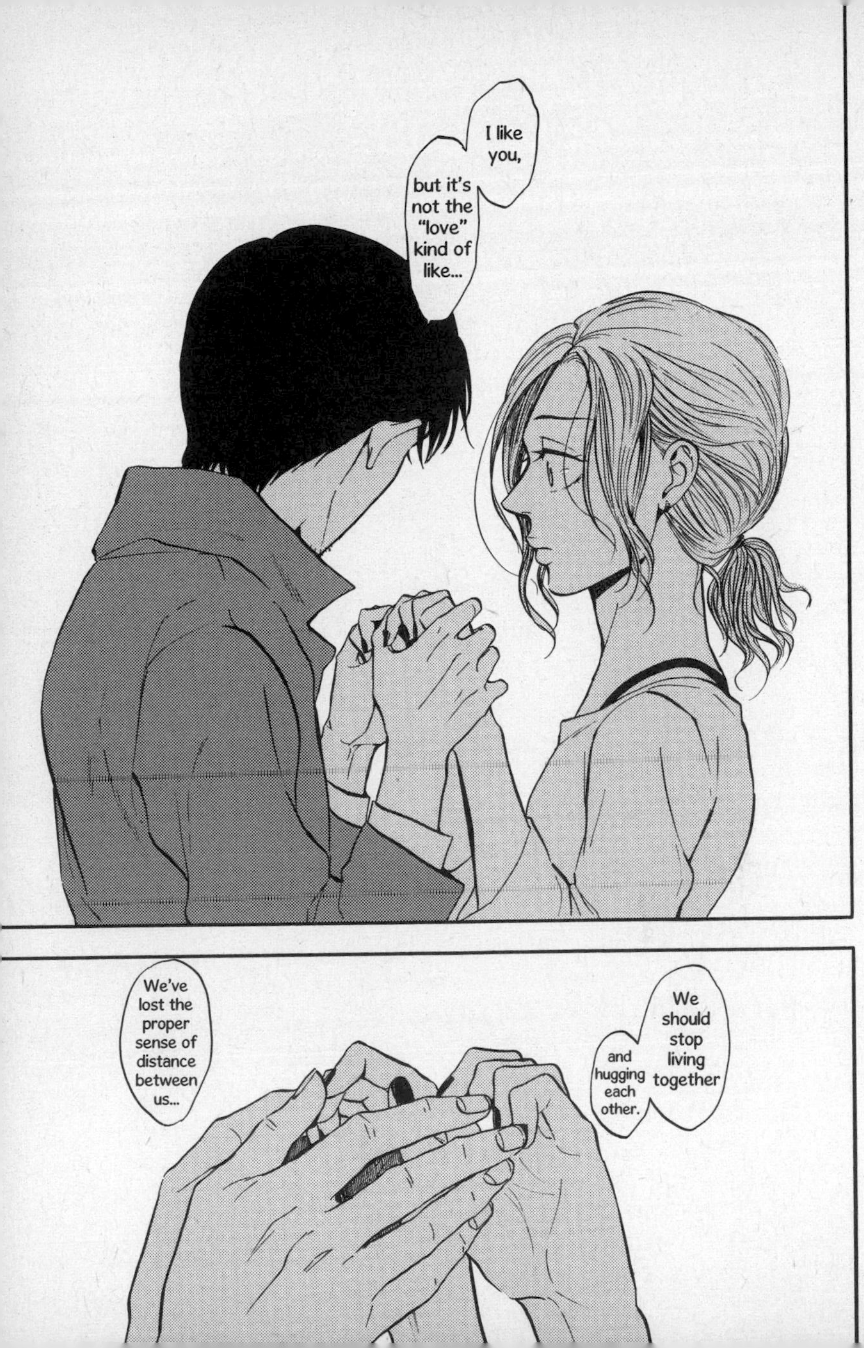
I like you,
but it's not the "love" kind of like...
We should stop living together
and hugging each other.
We've lost the proper sense of distance between us...

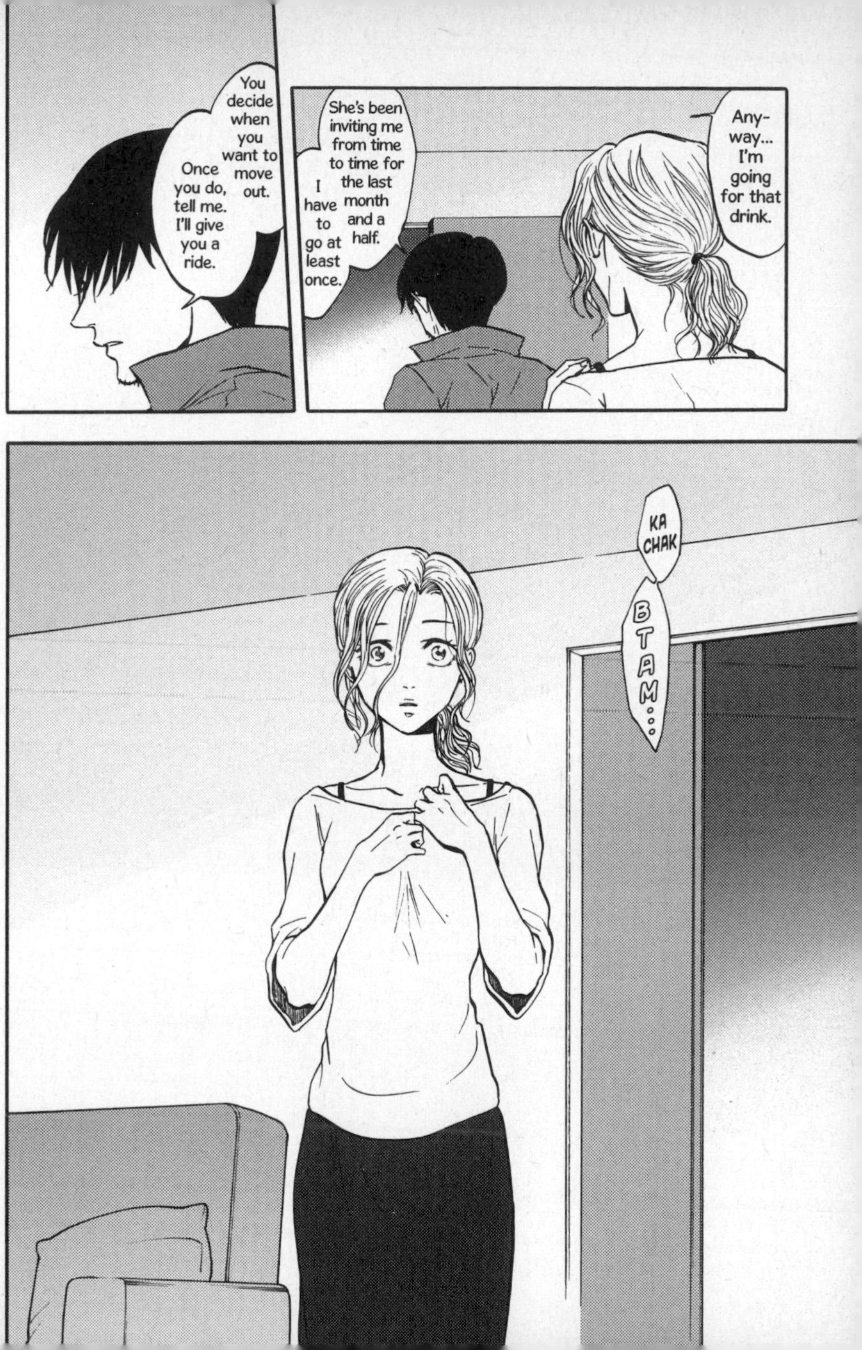
Any-way... I'm going for that drink.
She's been inviting me from time to time for the last month and a half.
I have to go at least once.
You decide when you want to move out.
Once you do, tell me. I'll give you a ride.
KA CHAK
BTAM...

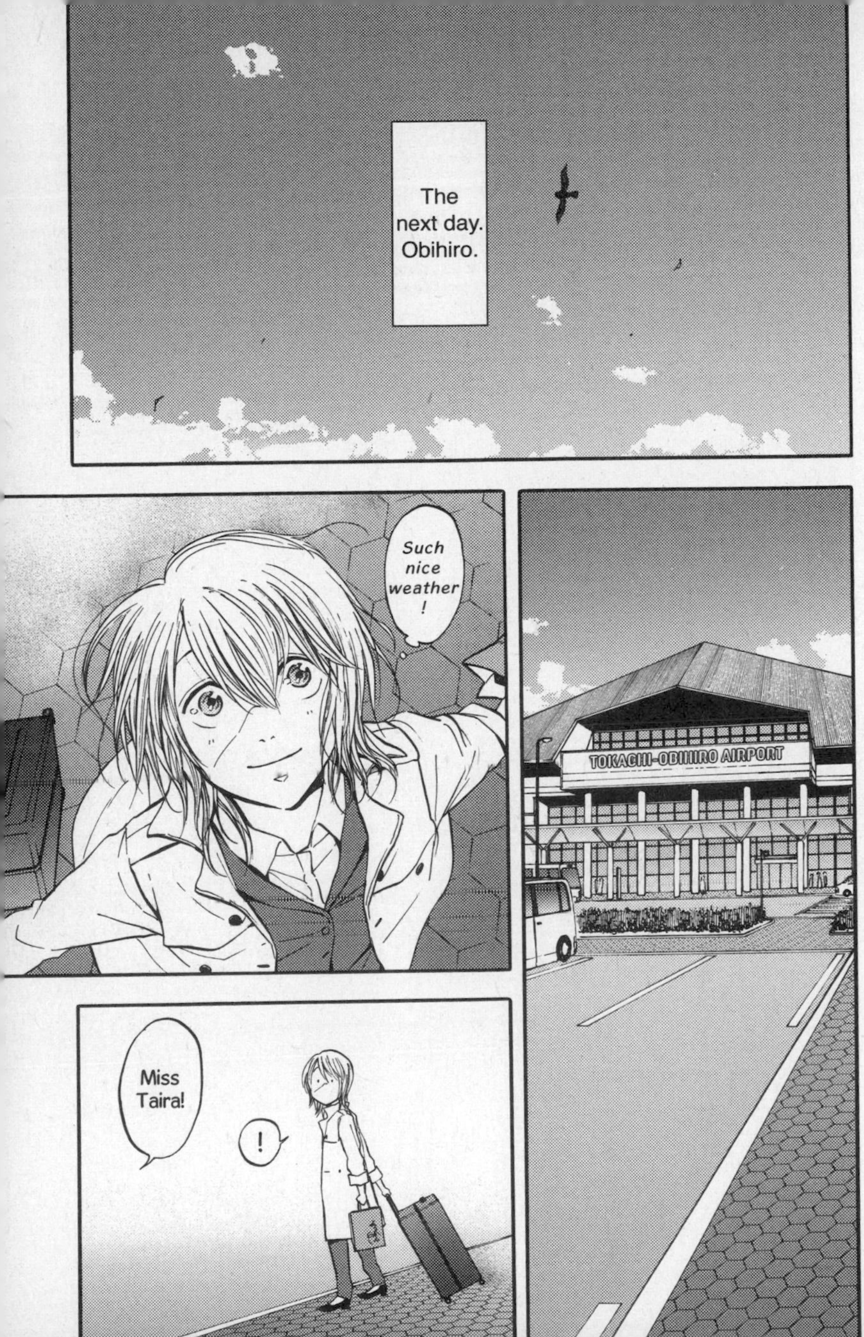
The next day. Obihiro.
TOKACHI-OBIHIRO AIRPORT
Such nice weather!
Miss Taira!
!

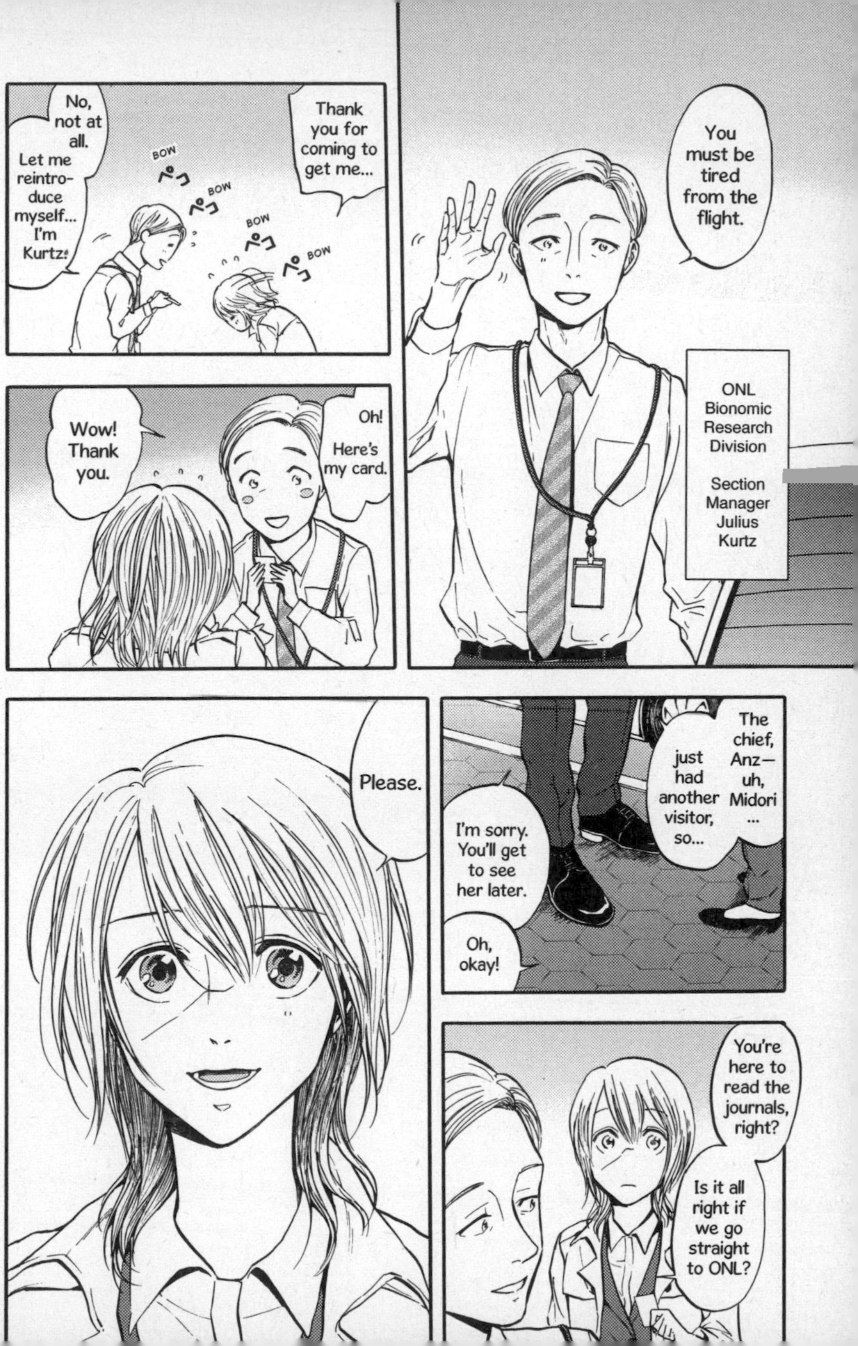

You must be tired from the flight.
ONL Bionomic Research Division
Section Manager Julius Kurtz
Thank you for coming to get me...
BOW
ペコ
BOW
ペコ
BOW
ペコ
BOW
ペコ
No, not at all.
Let me reintroduce myself... I'm Kurtz!
Oh!
Here's my card.
Wow! Thank you.
The chief, Anz— uh, Midori ...
just had another visitor, so...
I'm sorry. You'll get to see her later.
Oh, okay!
You're here to read the journals, right?
Is it all right if we go straight to ONL?
Please.

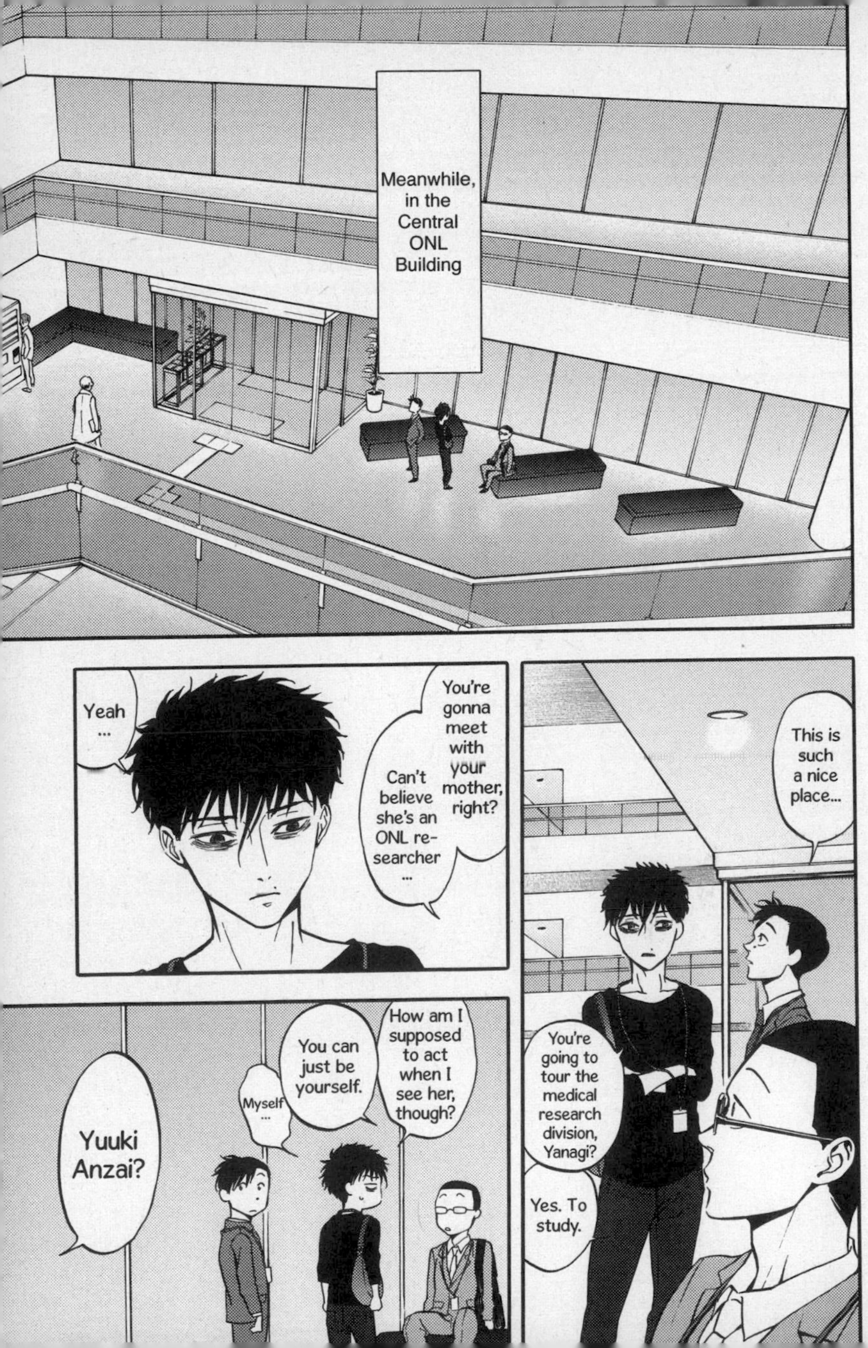
Meanwhile, in the Central ONL Building
This is such a nice place...
You're going to tour the medical research division, Yanagi?
Yes. To study.
You're gonna meet with your mother, right?
Can't believe she's an ONL researcher...
Yeah...
How am I supposed to act when I see her, though?
You can just be yourself.
Myself...
Yuuki Anzai?

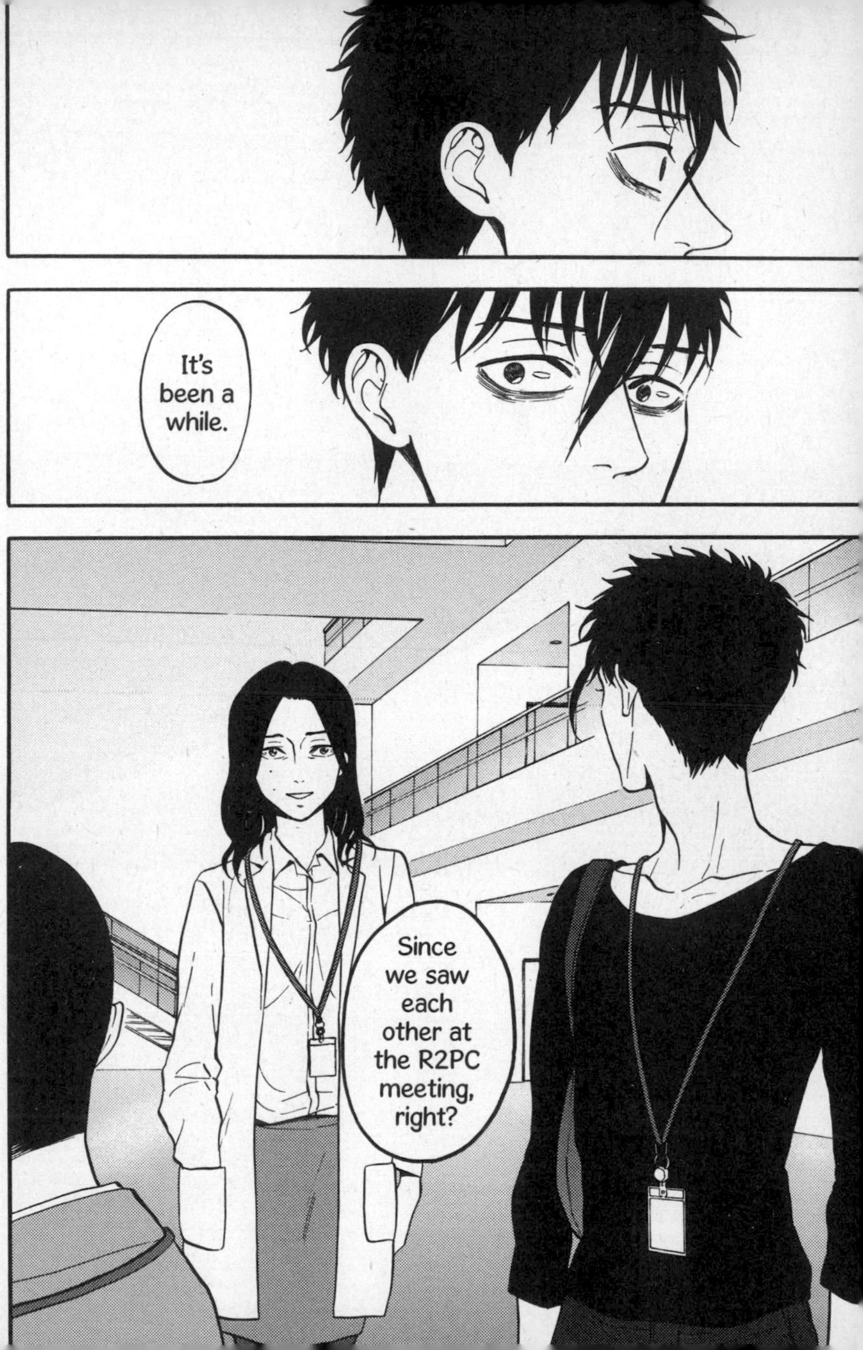
It's been a while.
Since we saw each other at the R2PC meeting, right?

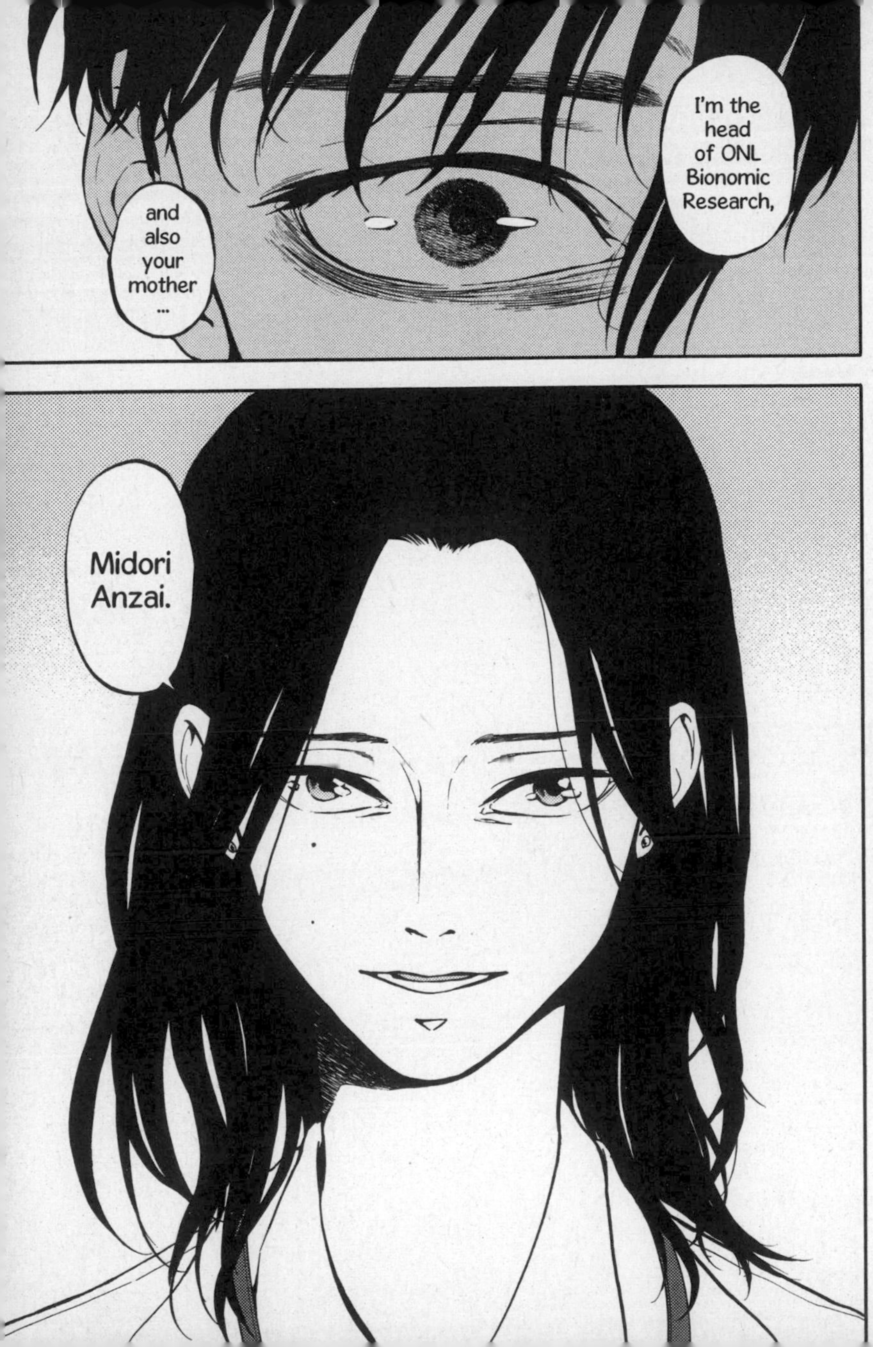
I'm the head of ONL Bionomic Research,
and also your mother ...
Midori Anzai.

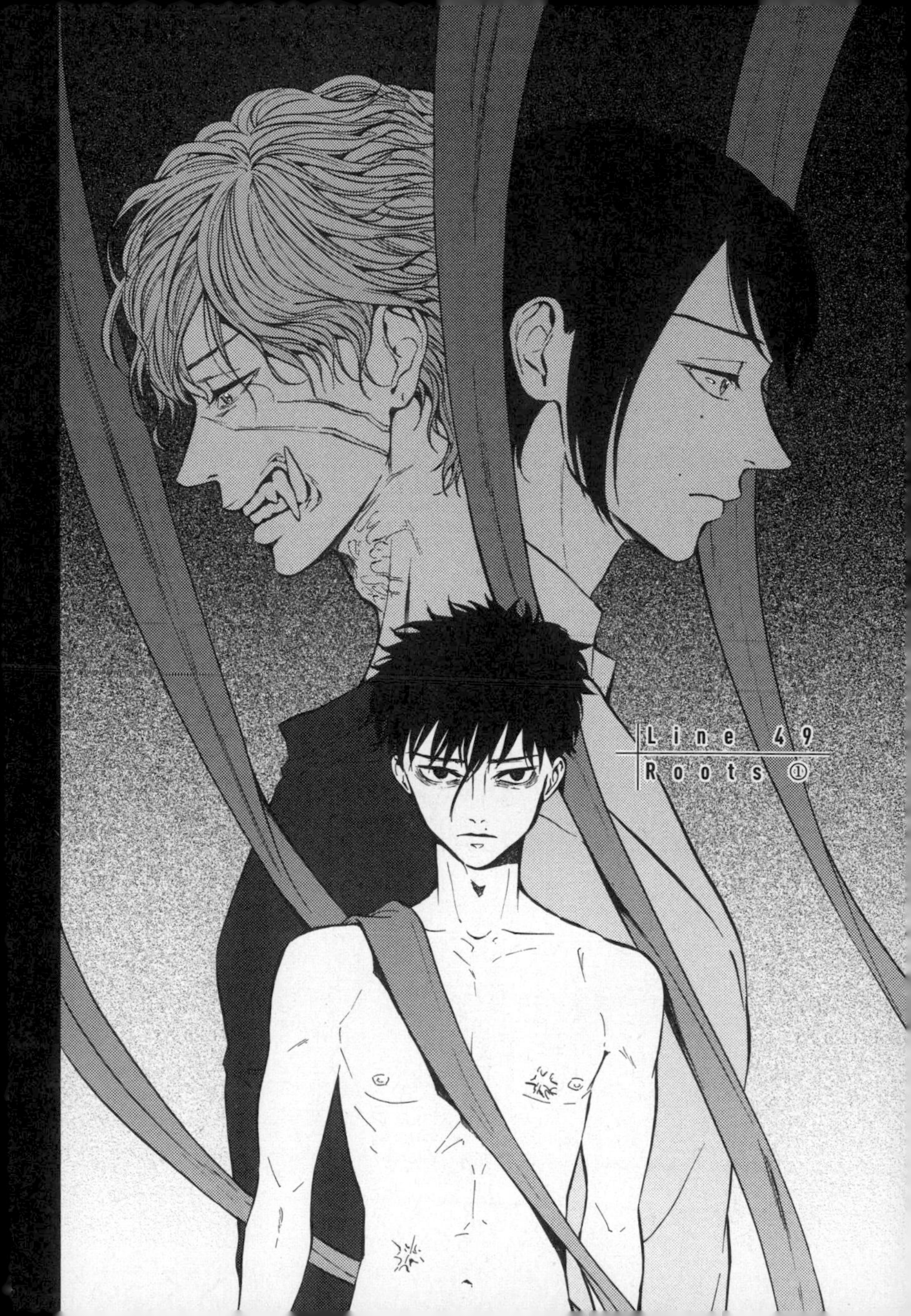
Line 49
Roots ①

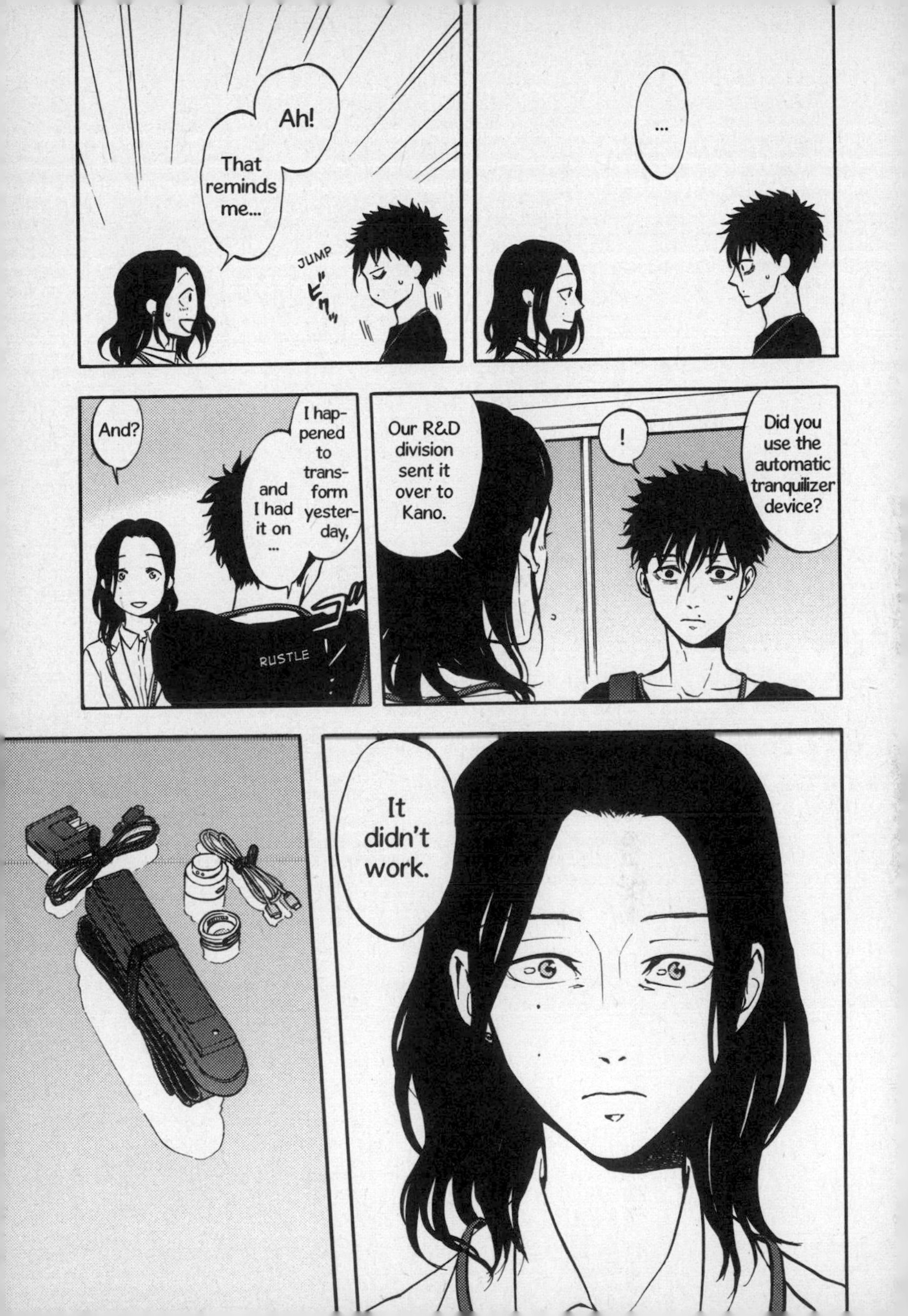
…
Ah! That reminds me…
JUMP
ビクッ
Did you use the automatic tranquilizer device?
!
Our R&D division sent it over to Kano.
I happened to transform yesterday,
and I had it on …
And?
RUSTLE
It didn't work.

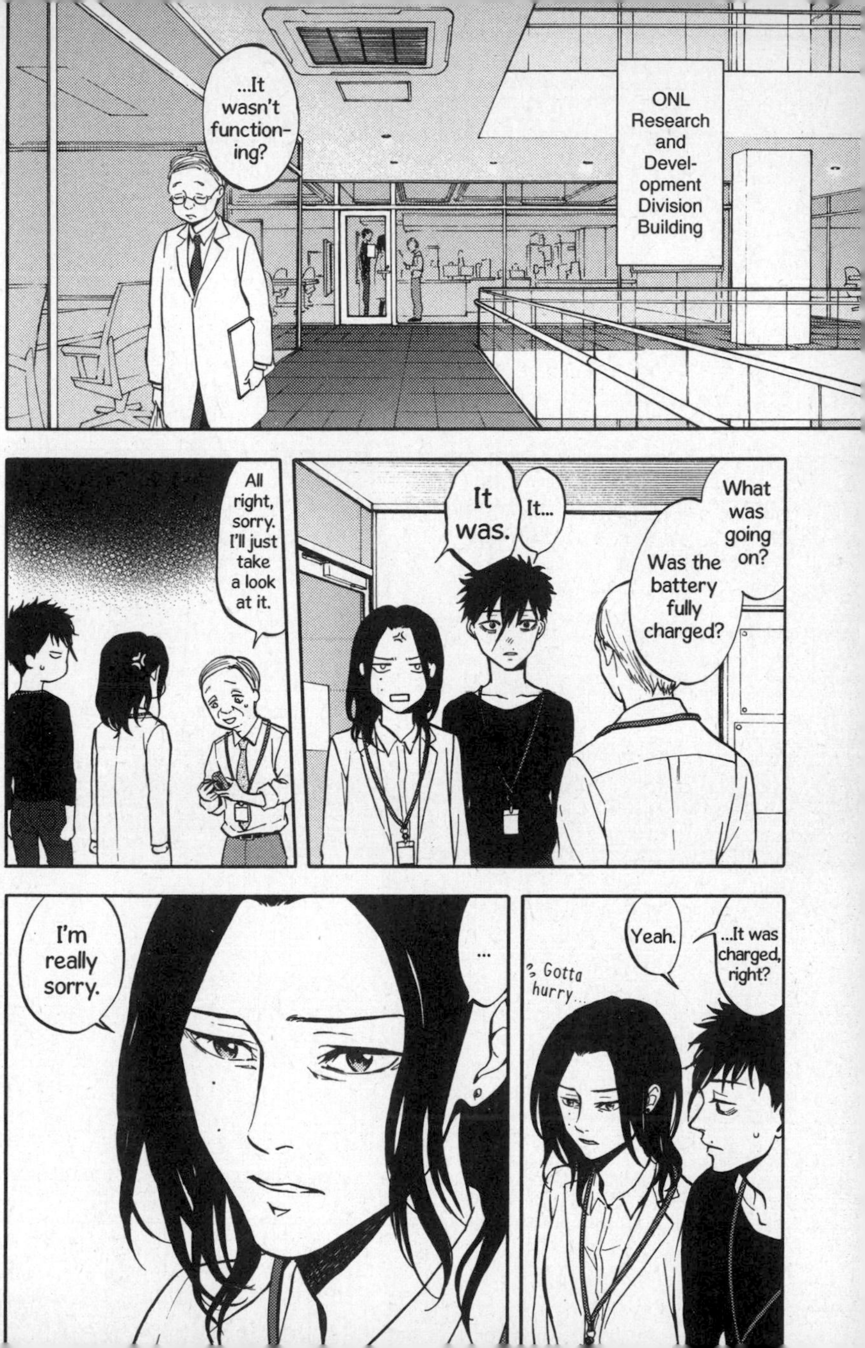
ONL Research and Development Division Building
...It wasn't functioning?
What was going on?
Was the battery fully charged?
It...
It was.
All right, sorry. I'll just take a look at it.
...It was charged, right?
Yeah.
Gotta hurry...
...
I'm really sorry.

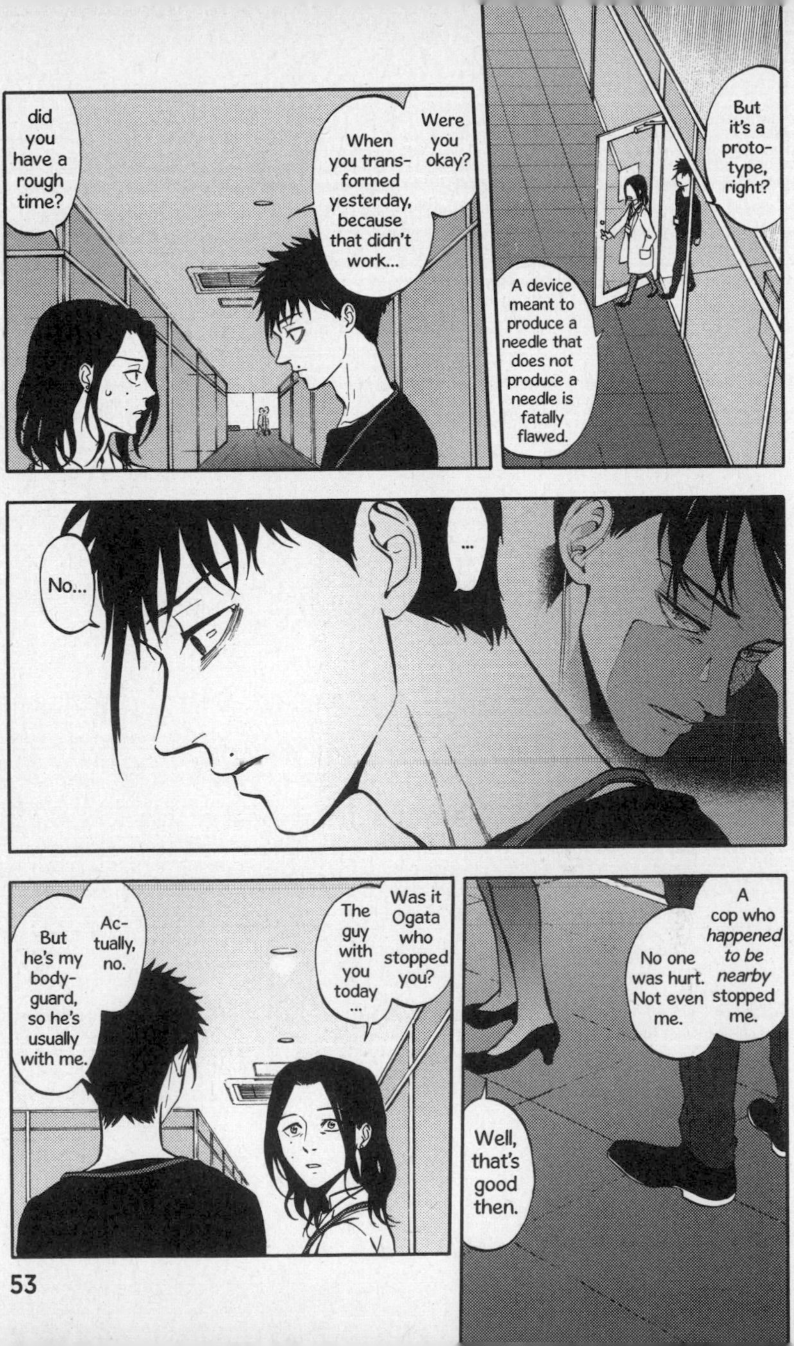
But it's a proto-type, right?
A device meant to produce a needle that does not produce a needle is fatally flawed.
Were you okay?
When you trans-formed yesterday, because that didn't work...
did you have a rough time?
...
No...
A cop who *happened to be nearby* stopped me.
No one was hurt. Not even me.
Well, that's good then.
Was it Ogata who stopped you?
The guy with you today ...
Ac-tually, no.
But he's my body-guard, so he's usually with me.

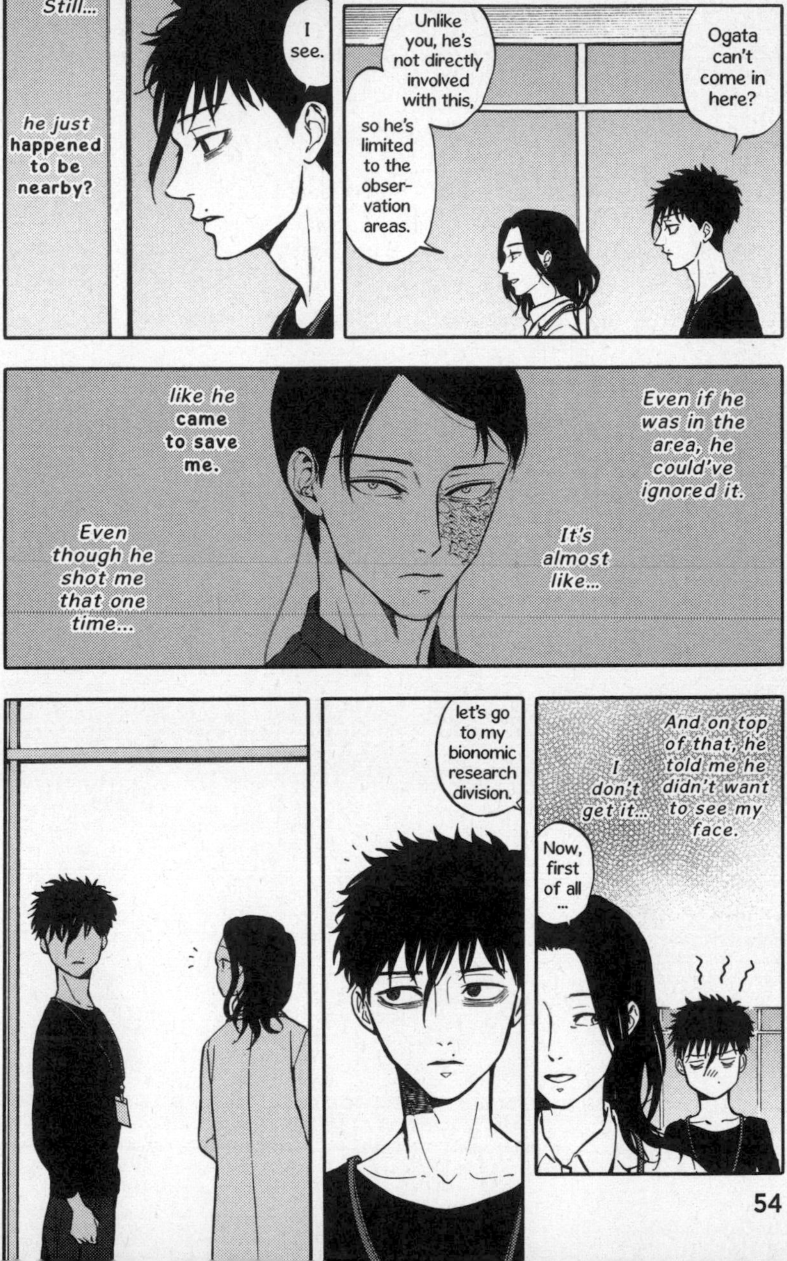
Ogata can't come in here?
Unlike you, he's not directly involved with this,
so he's limited to the obser-vation areas.
I see.
Still...
he just happened to be nearby?
Even if he was in the area, he could've ignored it.
It's almost like...
like he came to save me.
Even though he shot me that one time...
And on top of that, he told me he didn't want to see my face.
I don't get it...
Now, first of all...
let's go to my bionomic research division.

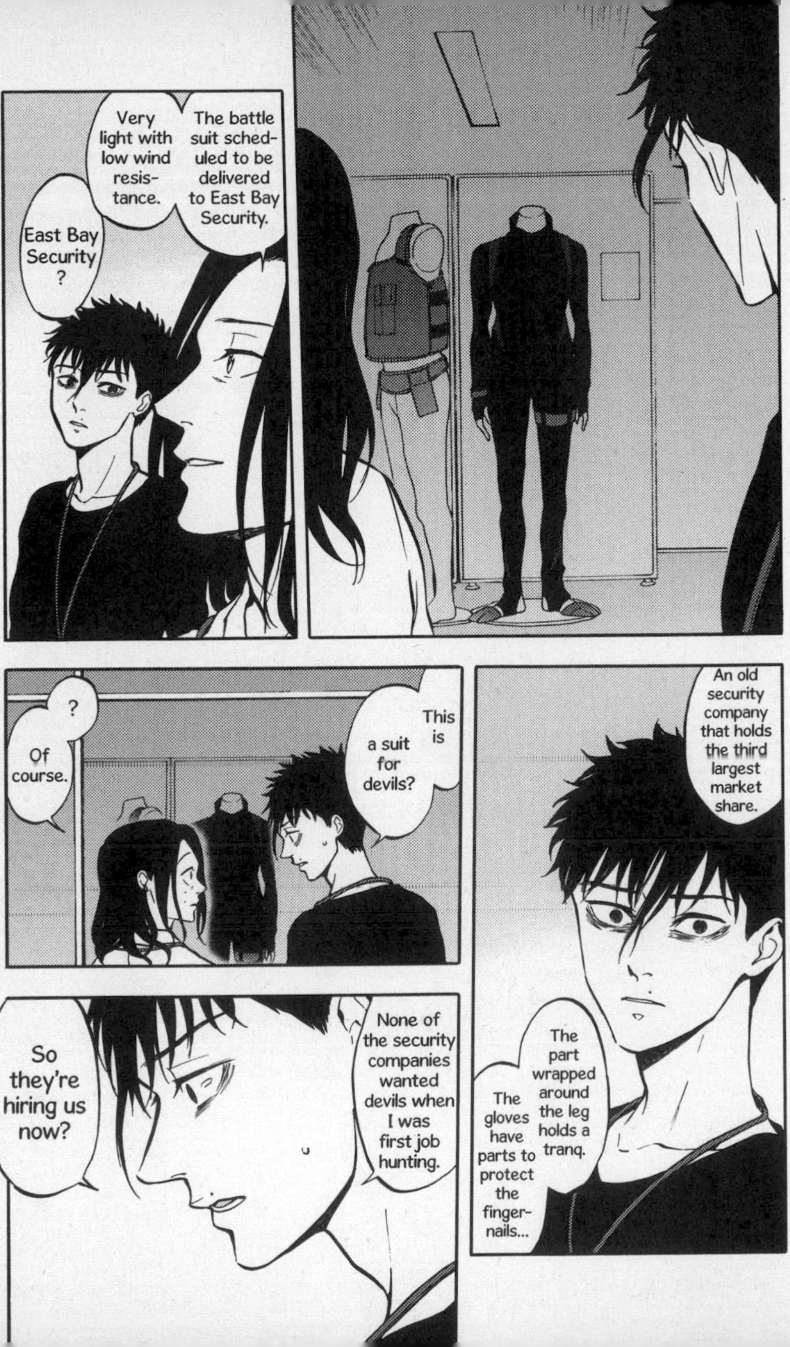
The battle suit scheduled to be delivered to East Bay Security.
Very light with low wind resistance.
East Bay Security?
An old security company that holds the third largest market share.
The part wrapped around the leg holds a tranq.
The gloves have parts to protect the finger-nails...
This is a suit for devils?
? Of course.
None of the security companies wanted devils when I was first job hunting.
So they're hiring us now?

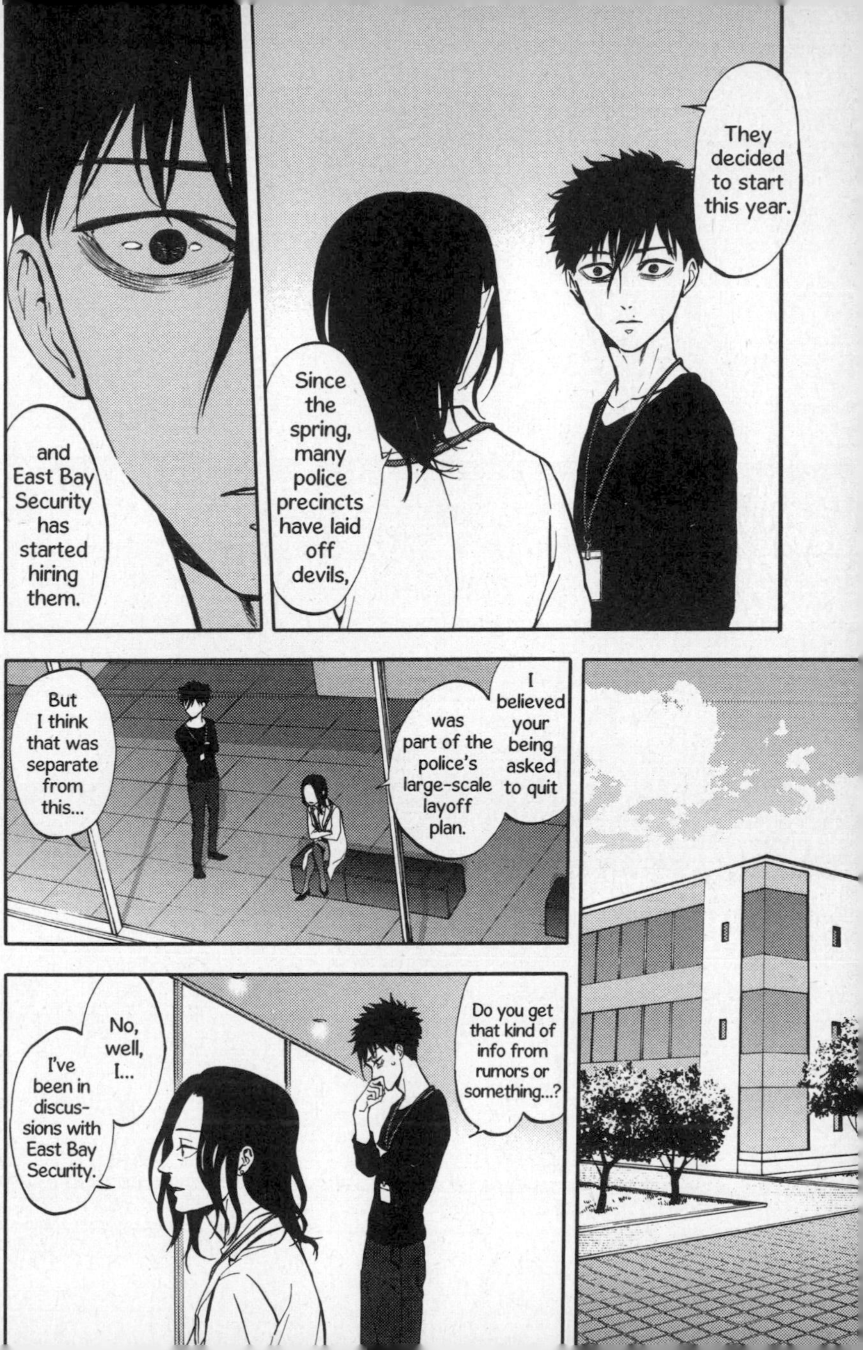
They decided to start this year.
Since the spring, many police precincts have laid off devils,
and East Bay Security has started hiring them.
I believed your being asked to quit
was part of the police's large-scale layoff plan.
But I think that was separate from this...
Do you get that kind of info from rumors or something...?
No, well, I...
I've been in discus-sions with East Bay Security.

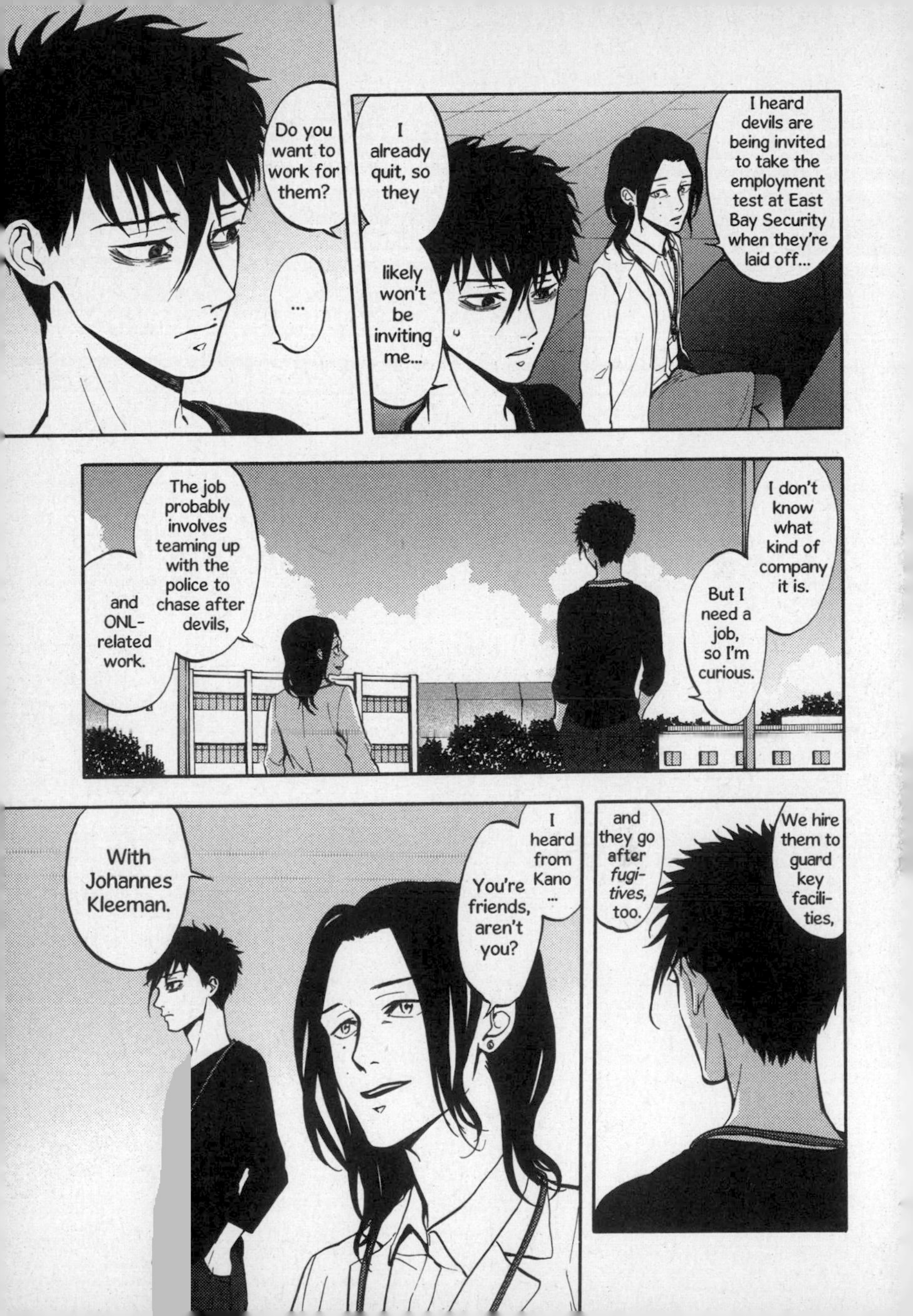
I heard devils are being invited to take the employment test at East Bay Security when they're laid off...
I already quit, so they
likely won't be inviting me...
Do you want to work for them?
...
I don't know what kind of company it is.
But I need a job, so I'm curious.
The job probably involves teaming up with the police to chase after devils,
and ONL-related work.
We hire them to guard key facili-ties,
and they go after *fugi-tives,* too.
I heard from Kano...
You're friends, aren't you?
With Johannes Kleeman.

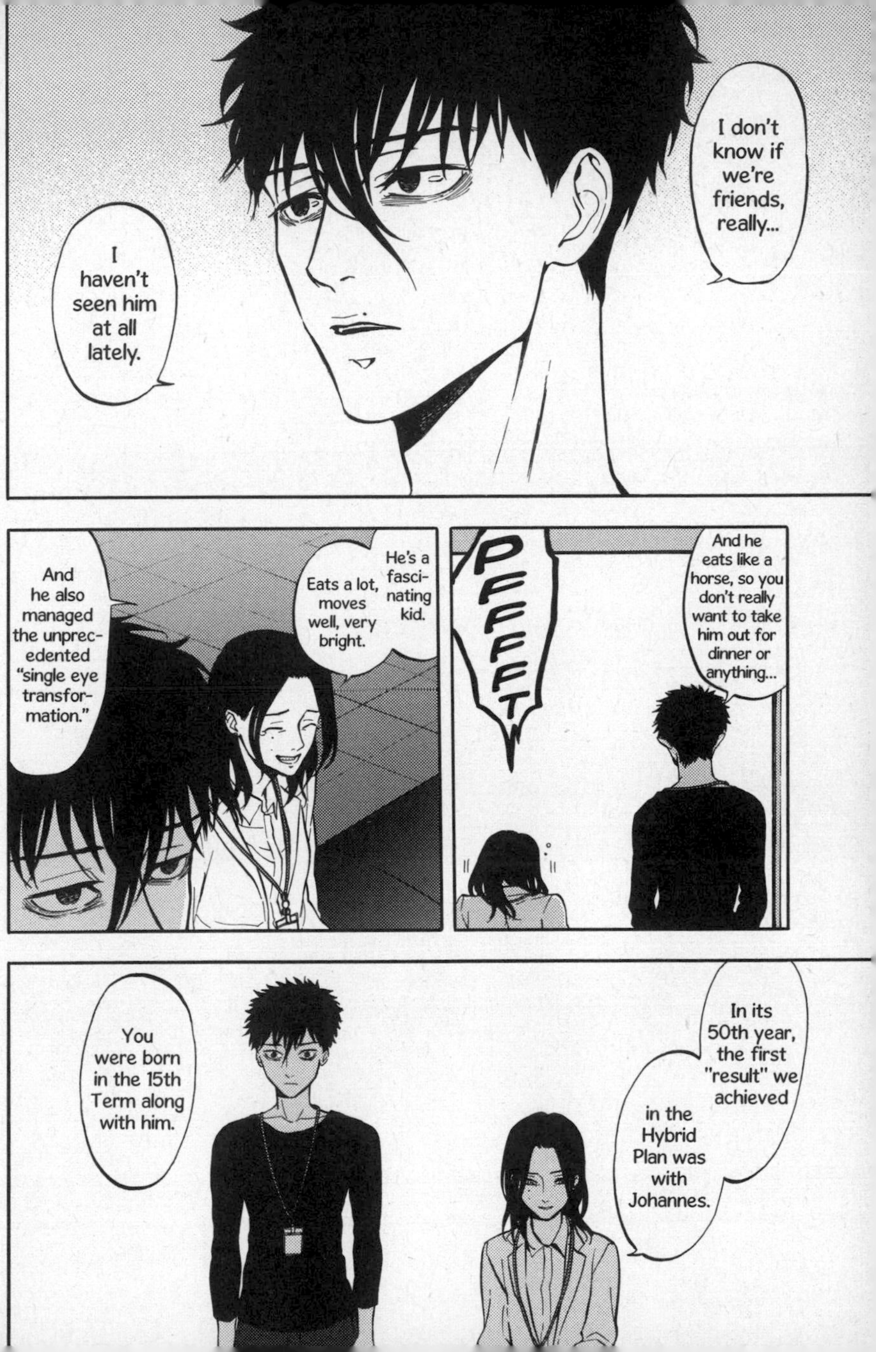
I don't know if we're friends, really...
I haven't seen him at all lately.
And he eats like a horse, so you don't really want to take him out for dinner or anything...
PFFFFT
He's a fascinating kid.
Eats a lot, moves well, very bright.
And he also managed the unprecedented "single eye transformation."
In its 50th year, the first "result" we achieved
in the Hybrid Plan was with Johannes.
You were born in the 15th Term along with him.

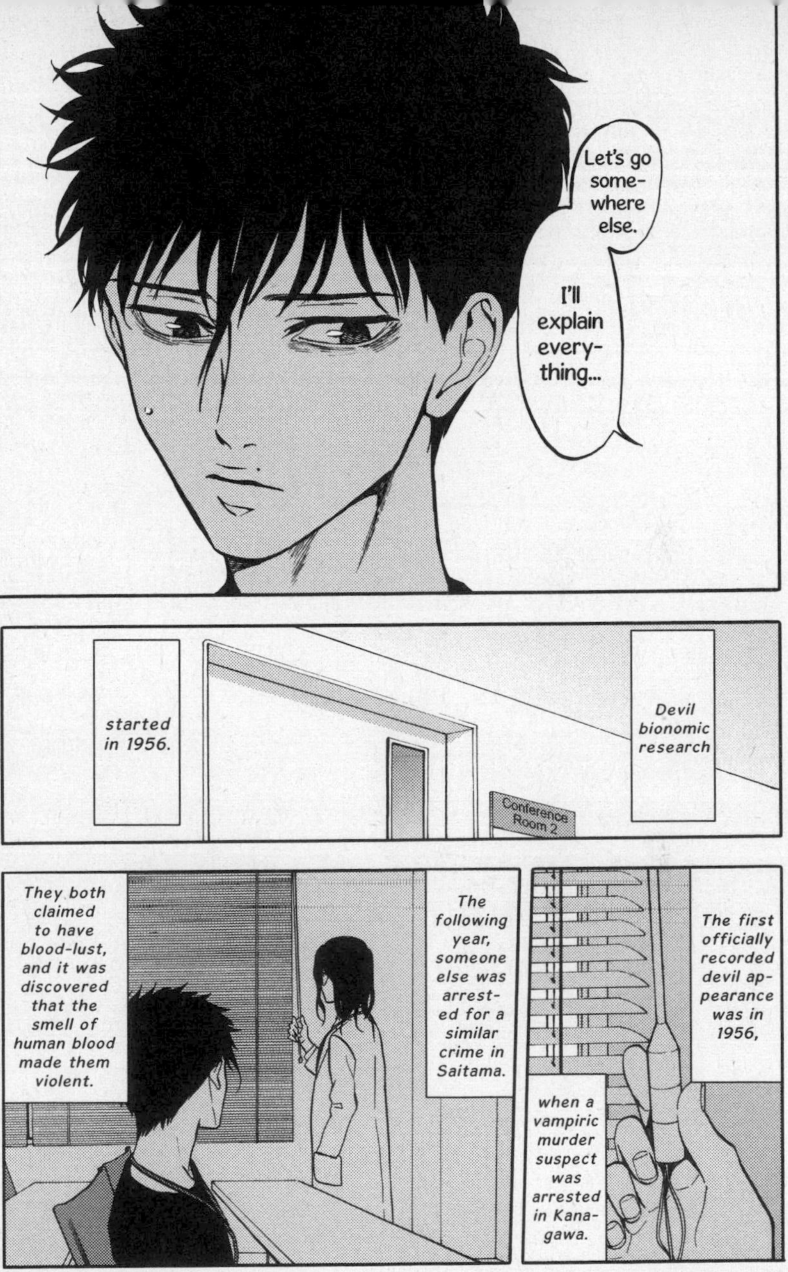
Let's go some-where else.
I'll explain every-thing...
Devil bionomic research
started in 1956.
Conference Room 2
The first officially recorded devil ap-pearance was in 1956,
when a vampiric murder suspect was arrested in Kana-gawa.
The following year, someone else was arrest-ed for a similar crime in Saitama.
They both claimed to have blood-lust, and it was discovered that the smell of human blood made them violent.

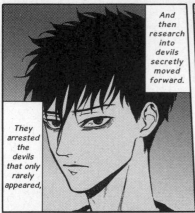

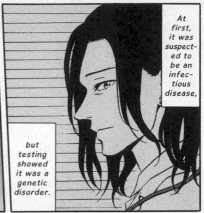

At first, it was suspected to be an infectious disease,
but testing showed it was a genetic disorder.
And then research into devils secretly moved forward.
They arrested the devils that only rarely appeared,
and researchers used them to study the physical characteristics and blood relations of devils
in order to try and understand their true nature.
At the time, devils were treated like rare beasts, even more so than now,
and their human rights were mostly ignored,
and it became particularly awful after their wound healing abilities were discovered.
The strange bionomics of devils enthralled many researchers,
and their sense of ethics became distorted.

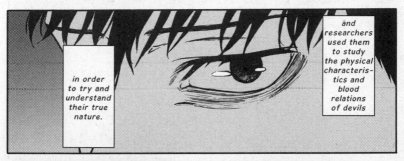

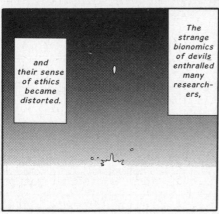

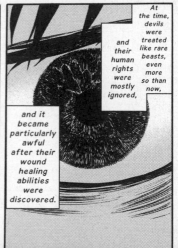

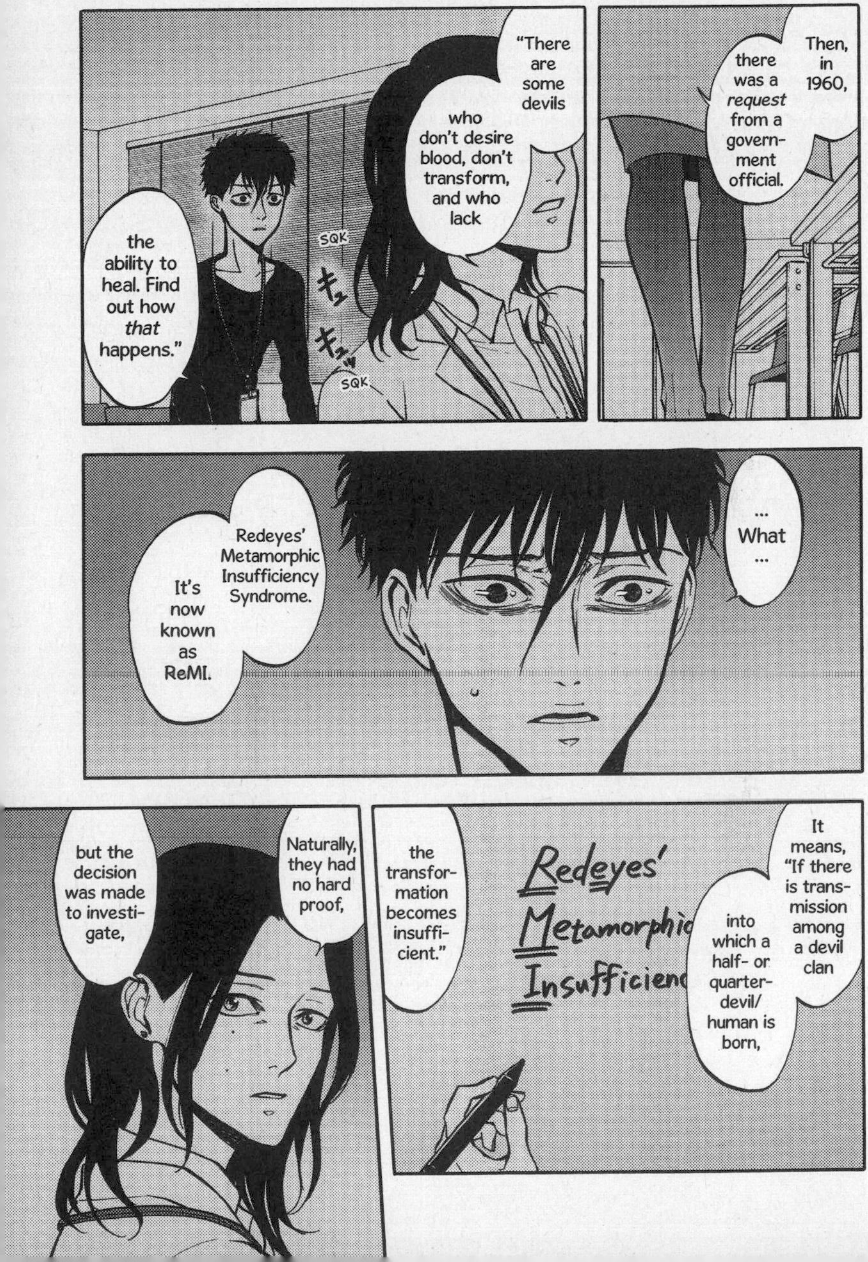
Then, in 1960,
there was a *request* from a government official.
"There are some devils
who don't desire blood, don't transform, and who lack
the ability to heal. Find out how *that* happens."
SQK
SQK
... What ...
Redeyes' Metamorphic Insufficiency Syndrome.
It's now known as ReMI.
It means, "If there is transmission among a devil clan
into which a half- or quarter-devil/human is born,
the transformation becomes insufficient."
Redeyes' Metamorphic Insufficienc
Naturally, they had no hard proof,
but the decision was made to investigate,

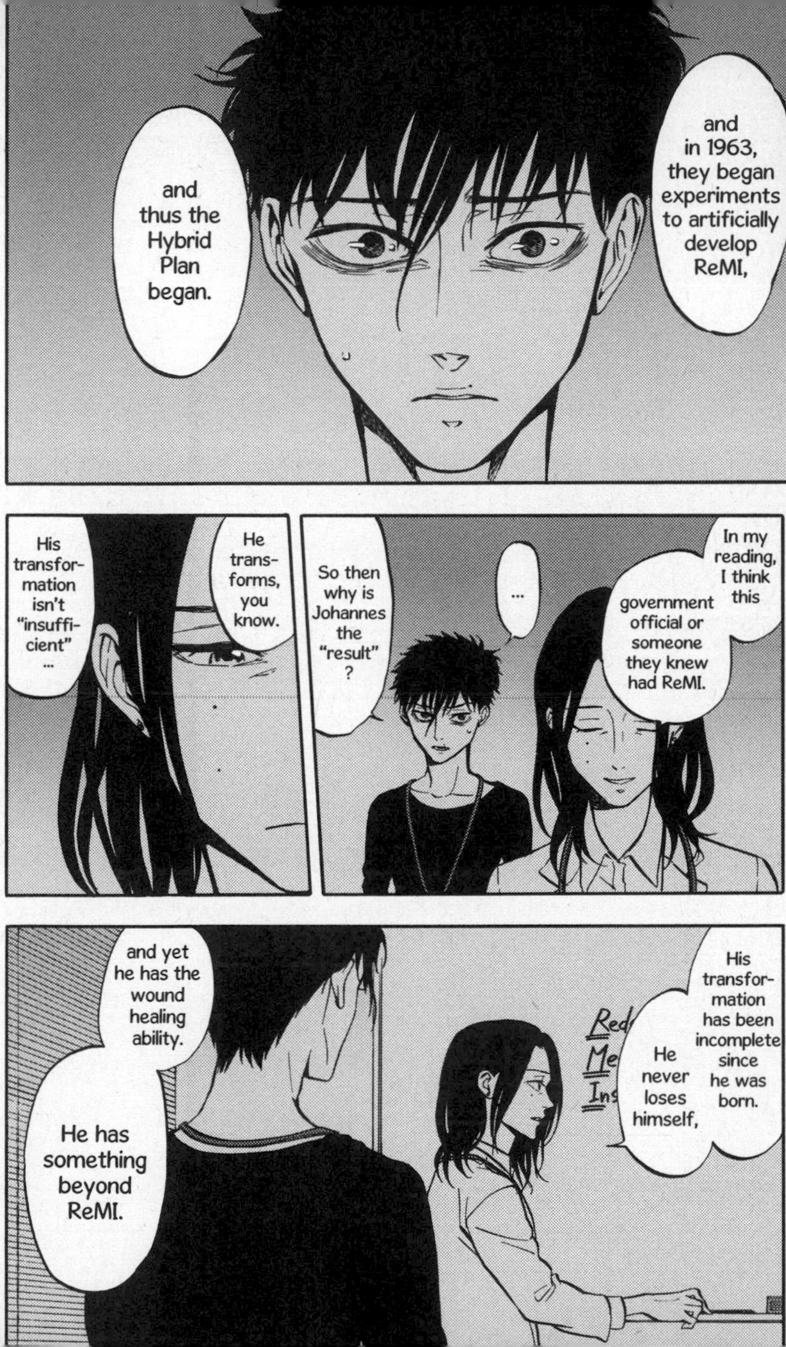
and in 1963, they began experiments to artificially develop ReMI,
and thus the Hybrid Plan began.
In my reading, I think this government official or someone they knew had ReMI.
...
So then why is Johannes the "result"?
He transforms, you know.
His transformation isn't "insufficient"...
His transformation has been incomplete since he was born.
He never loses himself,
and yet he has the wound healing ability.
He has something beyond ReMI.

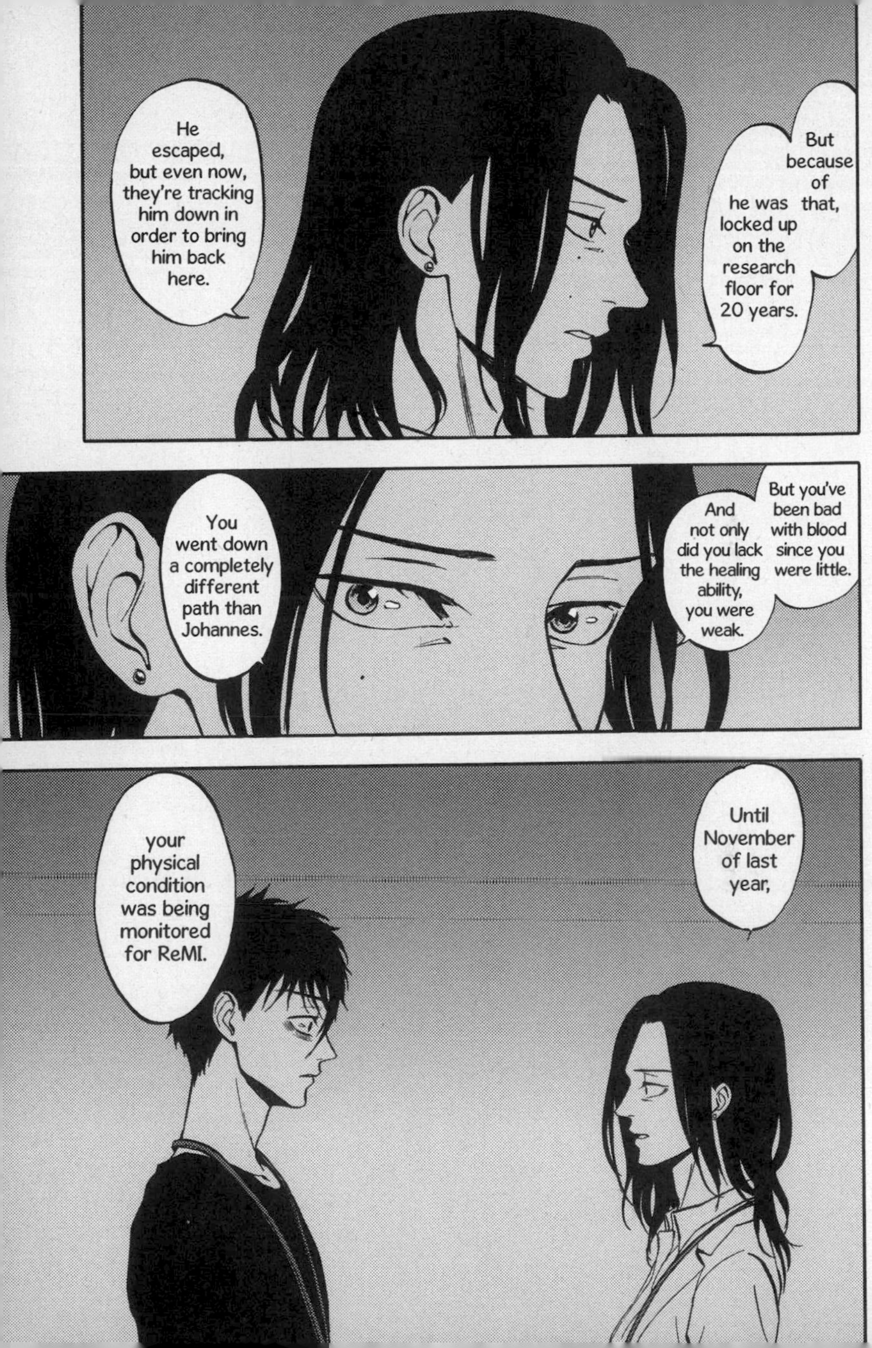
But because of that, he was locked up on the research floor for 20 years.
He escaped, but even now, they're tracking him down in order to bring him back here.
But you've been bad with blood since you were little.
And not only did you lack the healing ability, you were weak.
You went down a completely different path than Johannes.
Until November of last year,
your physical condition was being monitored for ReMI.

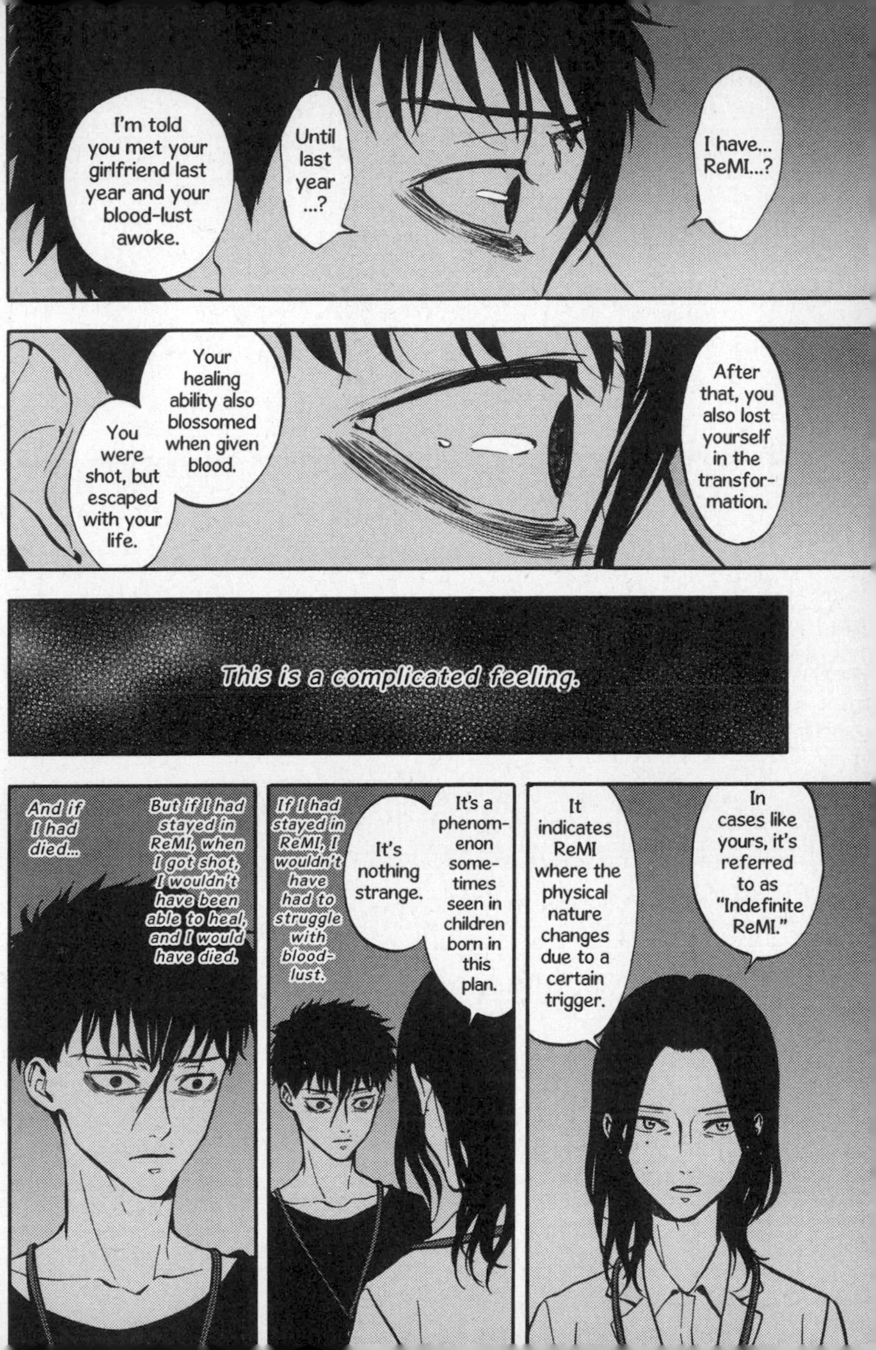
I have... ReMI...?
Until last year ...?
I'm told you met your girlfriend last year and your blood-lust awoke.
After that, you also lost yourself in the transformation.
Your healing ability also blossomed when given blood.
You were shot, but escaped with your life.
This is a complicated feeling.
In cases like yours, it's referred to as "Indefinite ReMI."
It indicates ReMI where the physical nature changes due to a certain trigger.
It's a phenomenon sometimes seen in children born in this plan.
It's nothing strange.
If I had stayed in ReMI, I wouldn't have had to struggle with blood-lust.
But if I had stayed in ReMI, when I got shot, I wouldn't have been able to heal, and I would have died.
And if I had died...

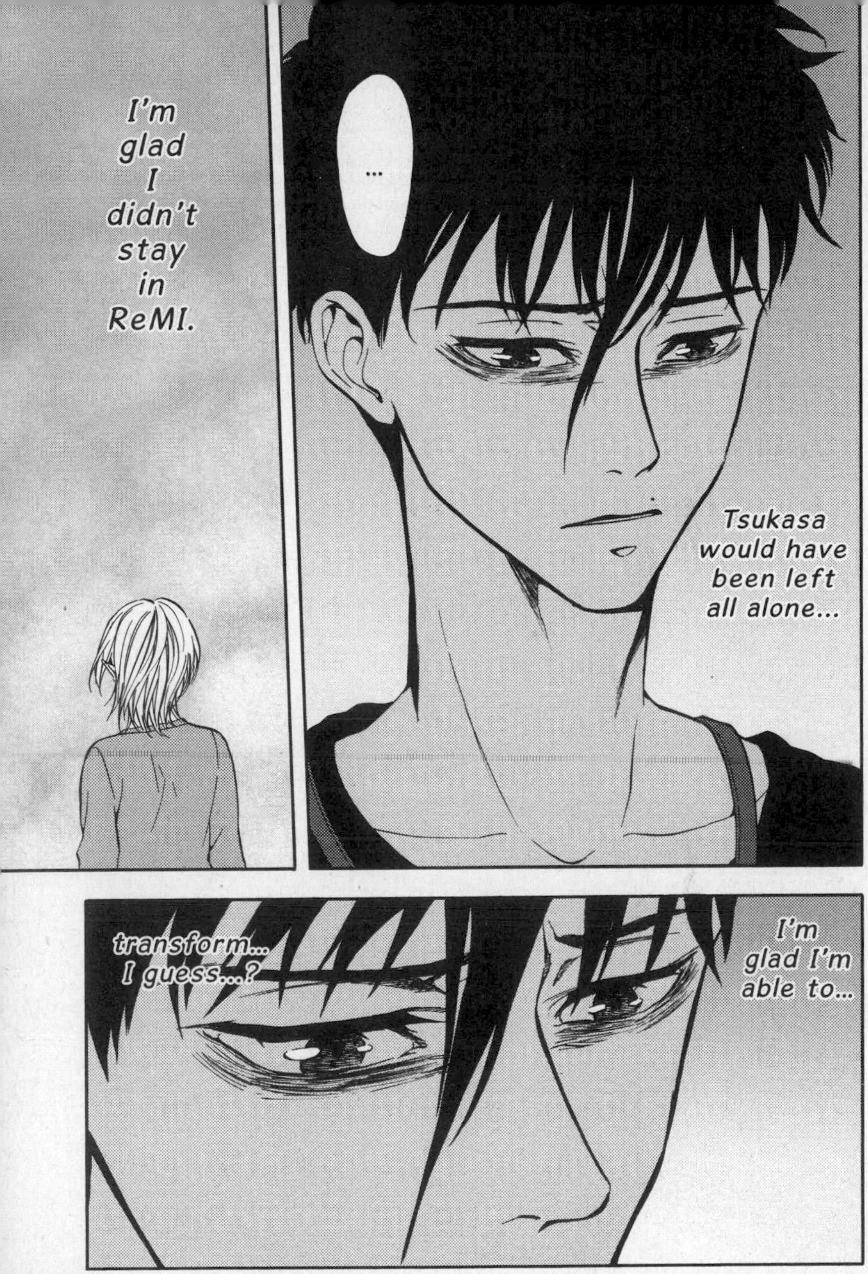
...
Tsukasa would have been left all alone...
I'm glad I didn't stay in ReMI.
I'm glad I'm able to...
transform... I guess...?

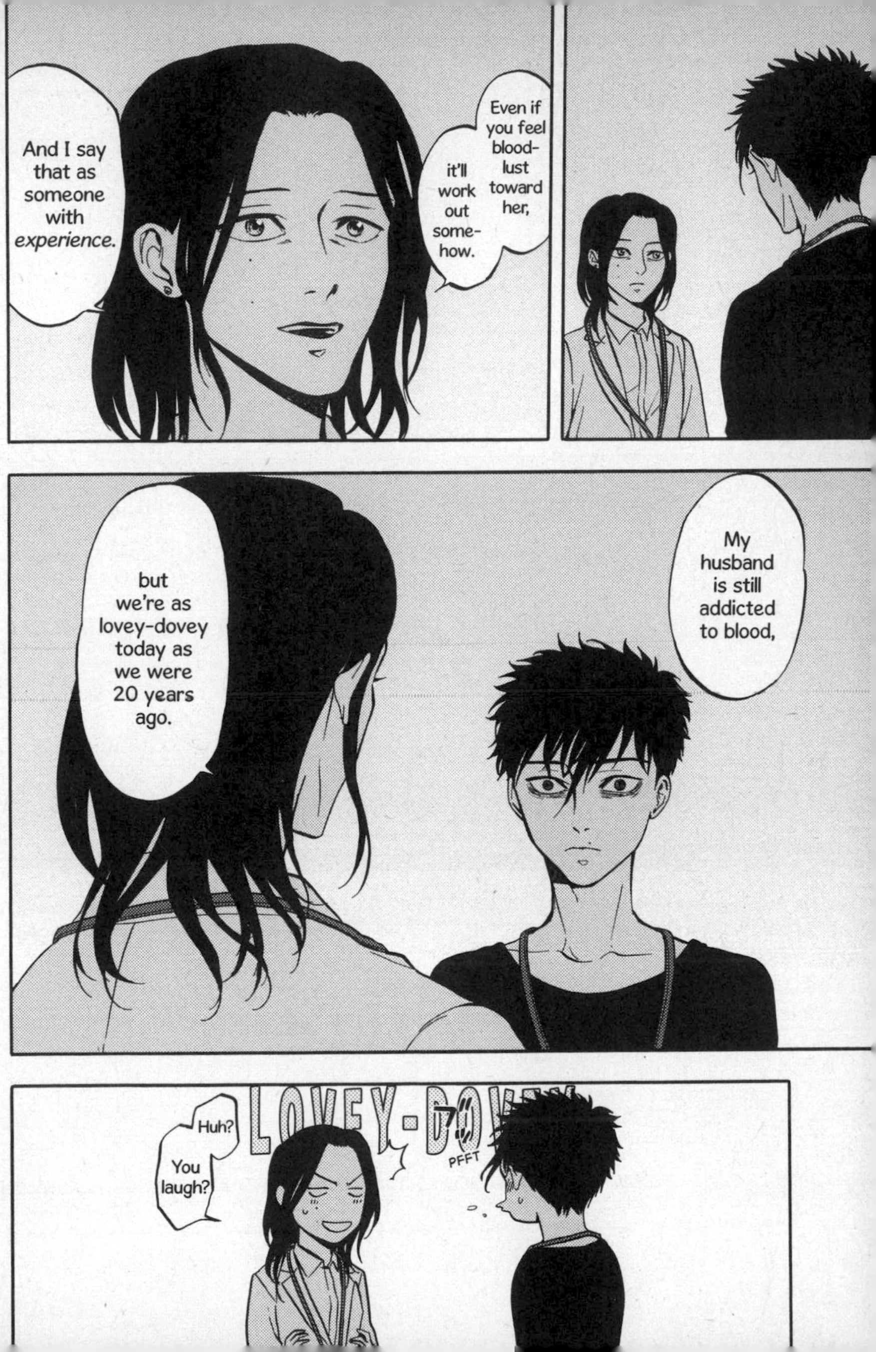
Even if you feel blood-lust toward her,
it'll work out somehow.
And I say that as someone with *experience*.
My husband is still addicted to blood,
but we're as lovey-dovey today as we were 20 years ago.
LOVEY-DO
PFFT
Huh?
You laugh?

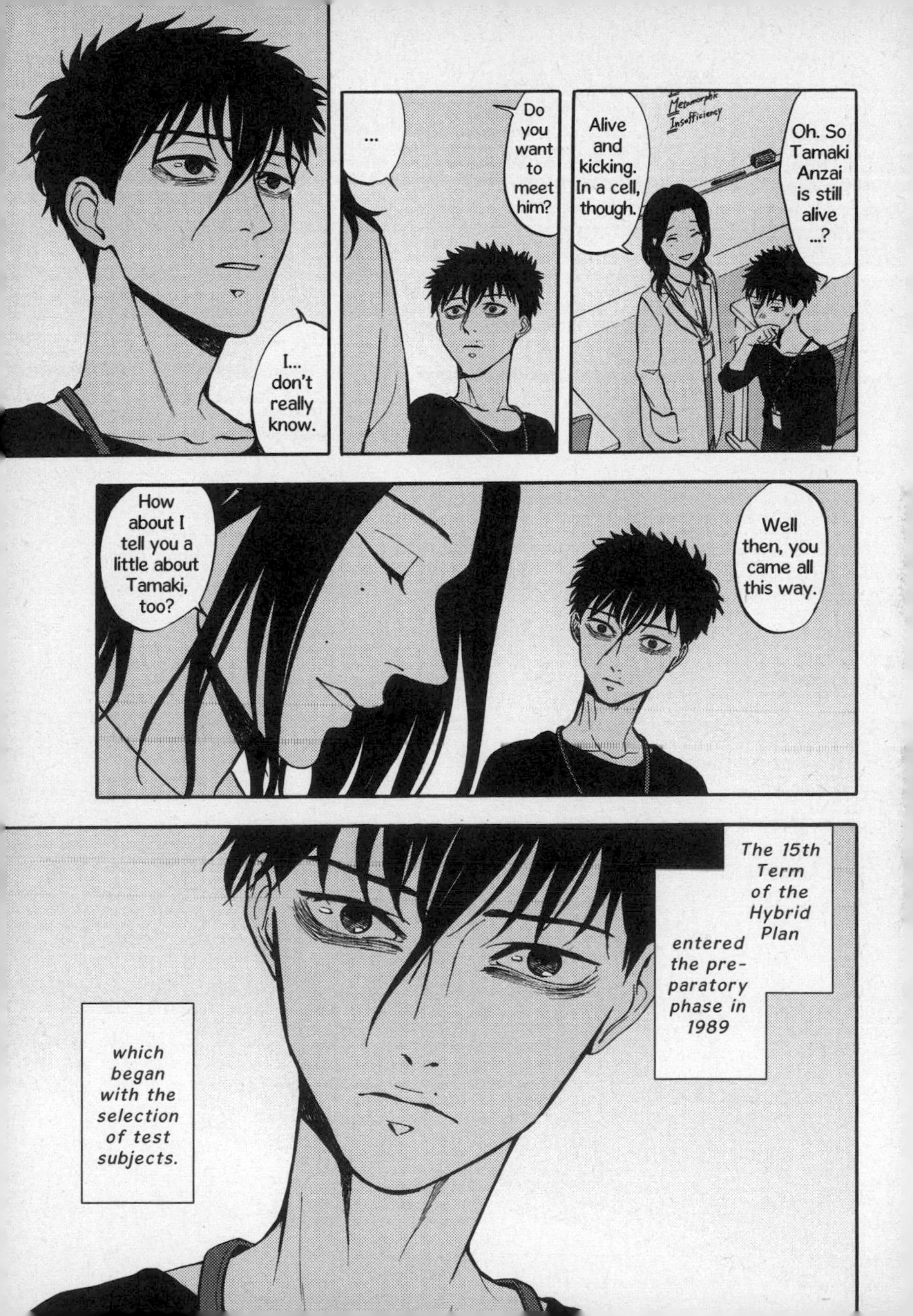
Oh. So Tamaki Anzai is still alive ...?
Metamorphic Insufficiency
Alive and kicking. In a cell, though.
Do you want to meet him?
...
I... don't really know.
Well then, you came all this way.
How about I tell you a little about Tamaki, too?
The 15th Term of the Hybrid Plan
entered the preparatory phase in 1989
which began with the selection of test subjects.

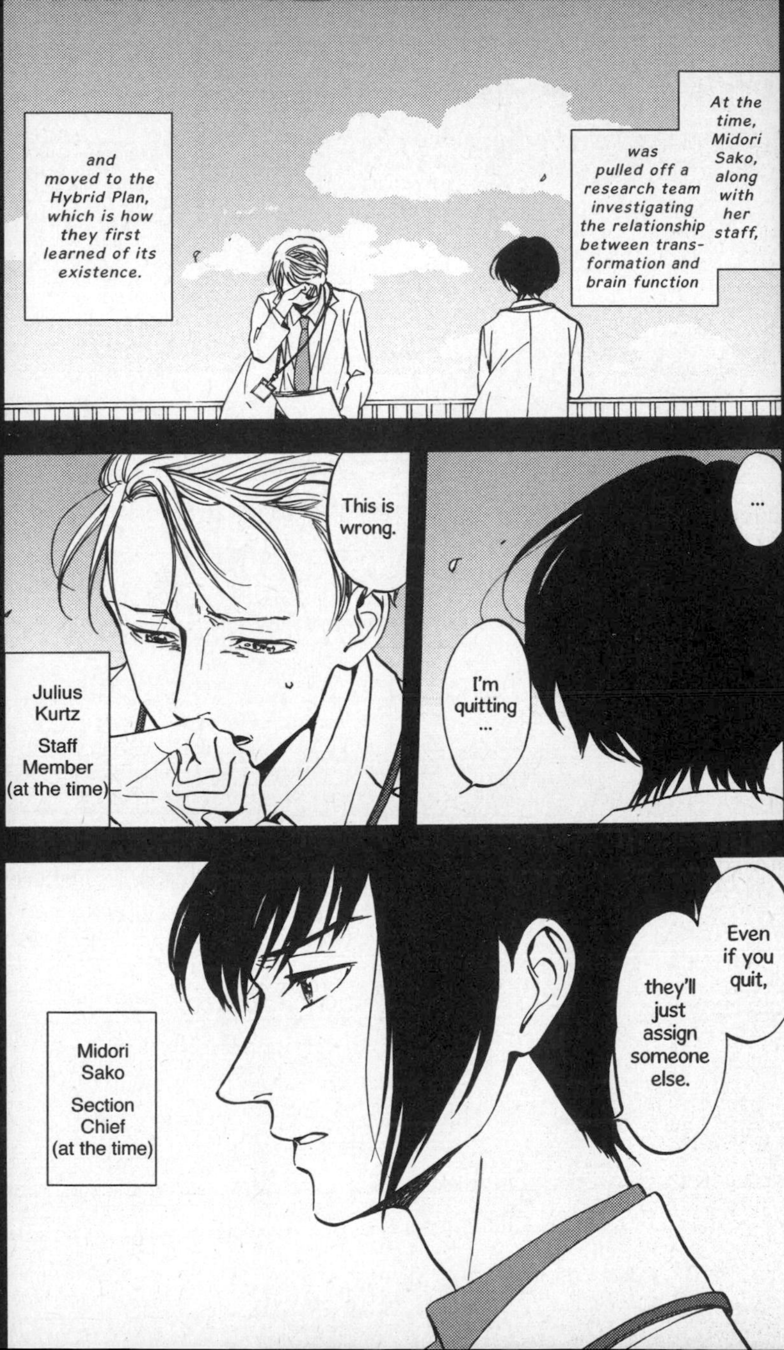
At the time, Midori Sako, along with her staff,
was pulled off a research team investigating the relationship between trans-formation and brain function
and moved to the Hybrid Plan, which is how they first learned of its existence.
...
I'm quitting ...
This is wrong.
Julius Kurtz Staff Member (at the time)
Even if you quit,
they'll just assign someone else.
Midori Sako Section Chief (at the time)

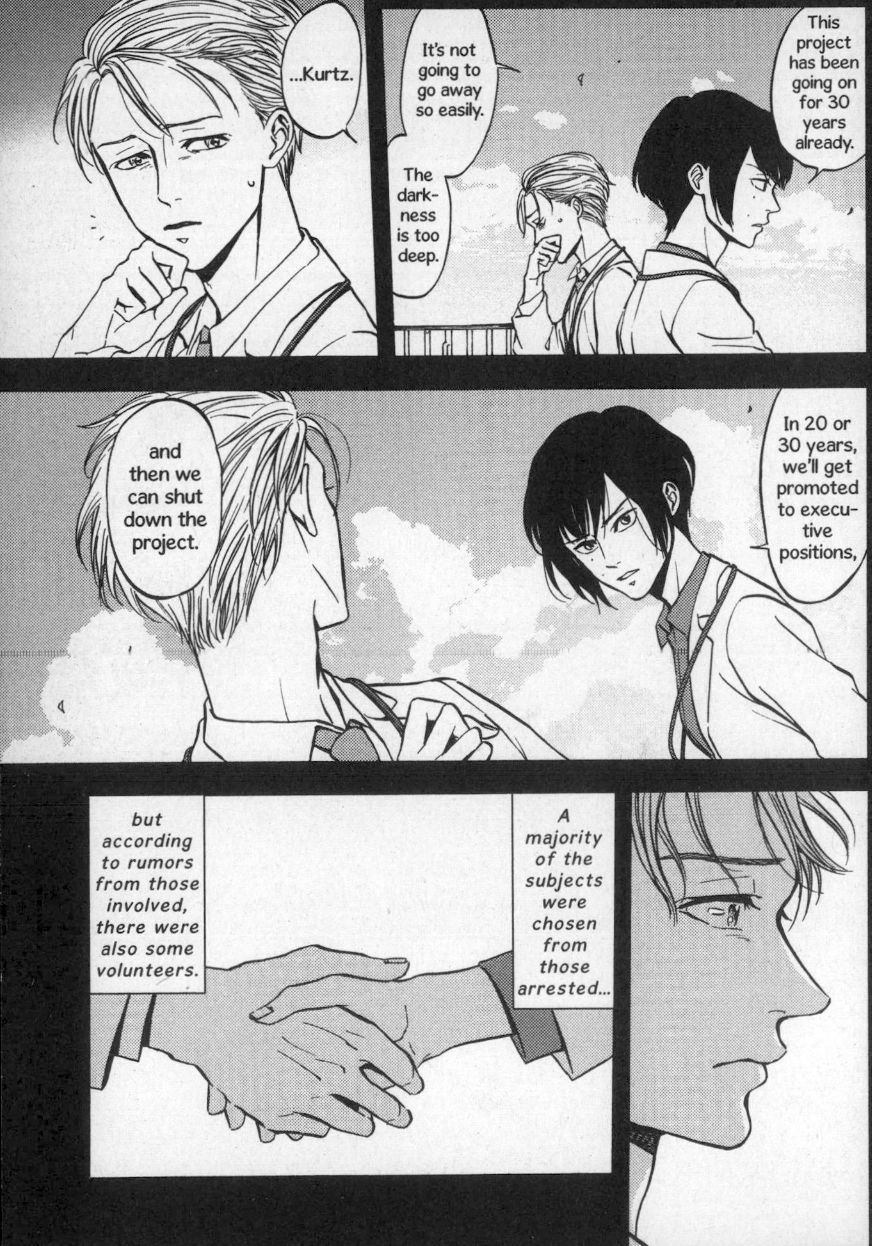
This project has been going on for 30 years already.
It's not going to go away so easily.
The darkness is too deep.
...Kurtz.
In 20 or 30 years, we'll get promoted to executive positions,
and then we can shut down the project.
A majority of the subjects were chosen from those arrested...
but according to rumors from those involved, there were also some volunteers.

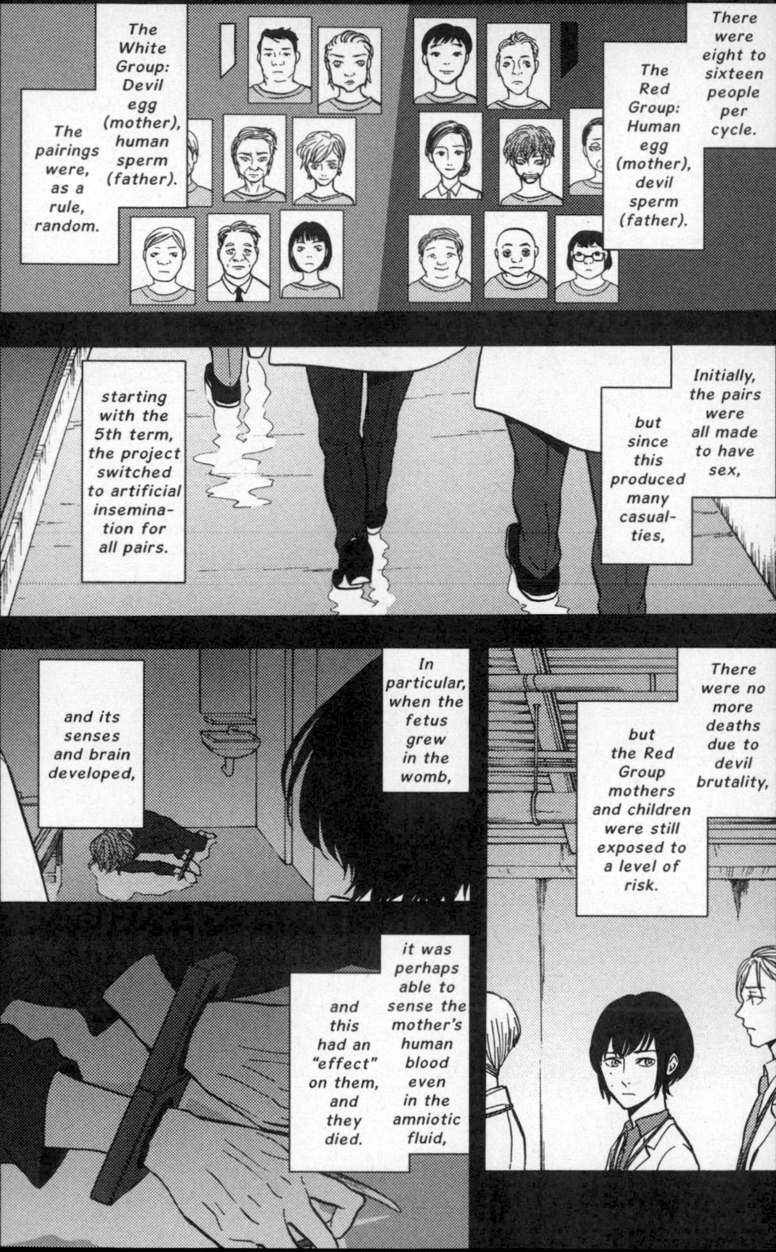
There were eight to sixteen people per cycle.
The Red Group: Human egg (mother), devil sperm (father).
The White Group: Devil egg (mother), human sperm (father).
The pairings were, as a rule, random.
Initially, the pairs were all made to have sex,
but since this produced many casualties,
starting with the 5th term, the project switched to artificial insemination for all pairs.
There were no more deaths due to devil brutality,
but the Red Group mothers and children were still exposed to a level of risk.
In particular, when the fetus grew in the womb,
and its senses and brain developed,
it was perhaps able to sense the mother's human blood even in the amniotic fluid,
and this had an "effect" on them, and they died.

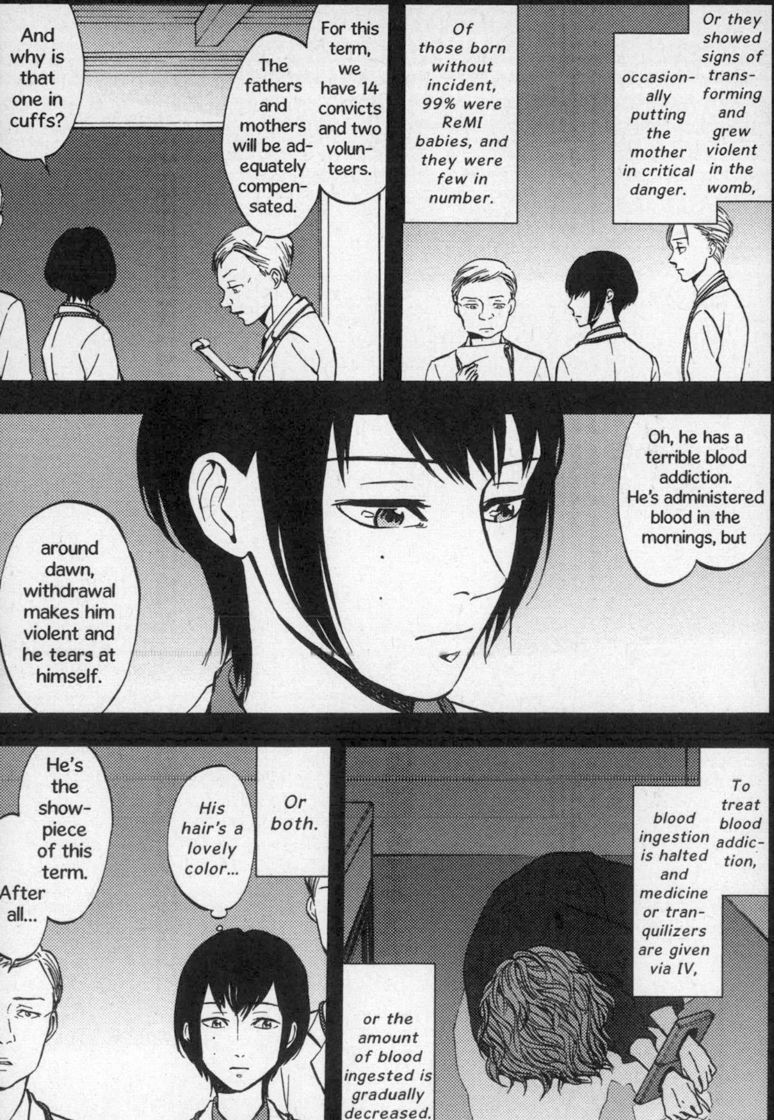
Or they showed signs of transforming and grew violent in the womb,
occasionally putting the mother in critical danger.
Of those born without incident, 99% were ReMI babies, and they were few in number.
For this term, we have 14 convicts and two volunteers.
The fathers and mothers will be adequately compensated.
And why is that one in cuffs?
Oh, he has a terrible blood addiction. He's administered blood in the mornings, but
around dawn, withdrawal makes him violent and he tears at himself.
To treat blood addiction,
blood ingestion is halted and medicine or tranquilizers are given via IV,
or the amount of blood ingested is gradually decreased.
Or both.
His hair's a lovely color...
He's the showpiece of this term. After all...

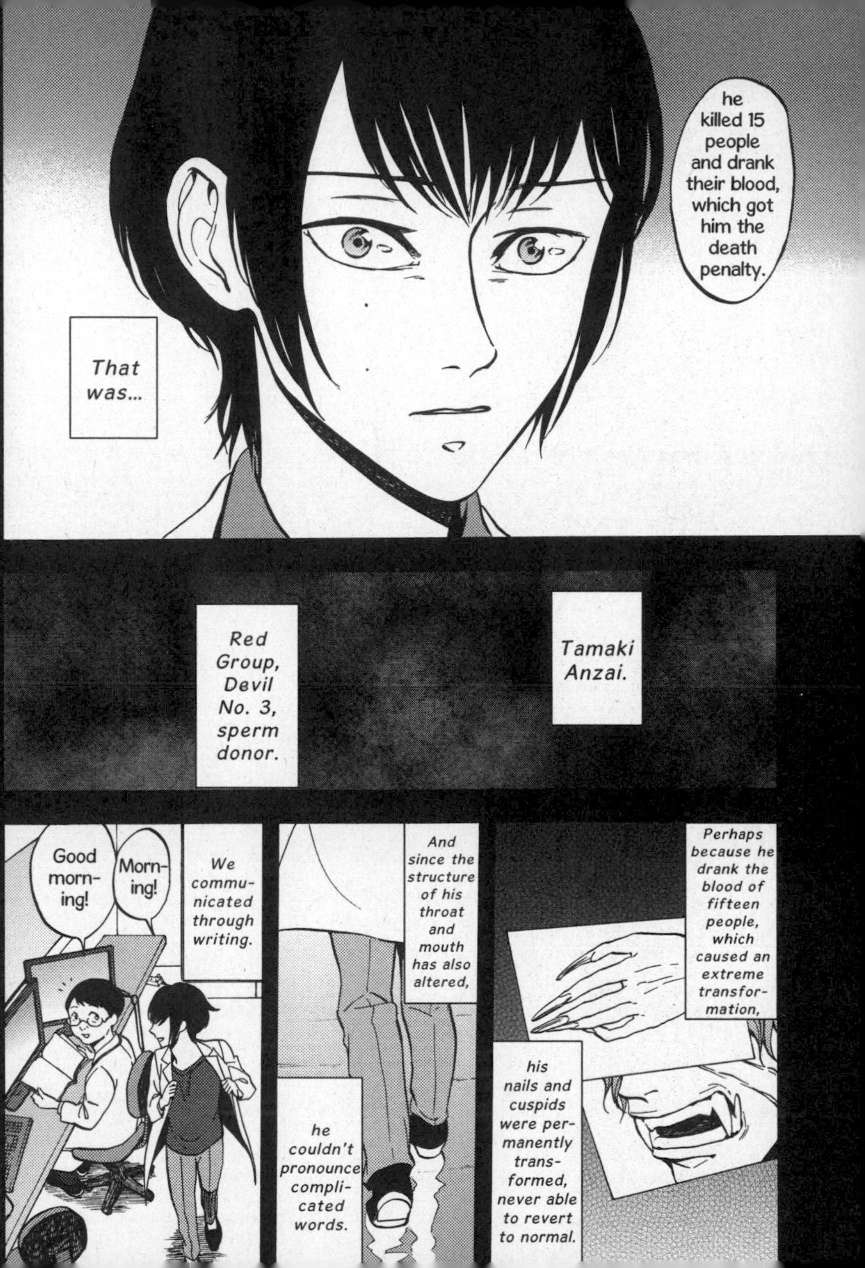

he killed 15 people and drank their blood, which got him the death penalty.
That was...
Tamaki Anzai.
Red Group, Devil No. 3, sperm donor.
Perhaps because he drank the blood of fifteen people, which caused an extreme transformation,
his nails and cuspids were permanently transformed, never able to revert to normal.
And since the structure of his throat and mouth has also altered,
he couldn't pronounce complicated words.
We communicated through writing.
Morning!
Good morning!

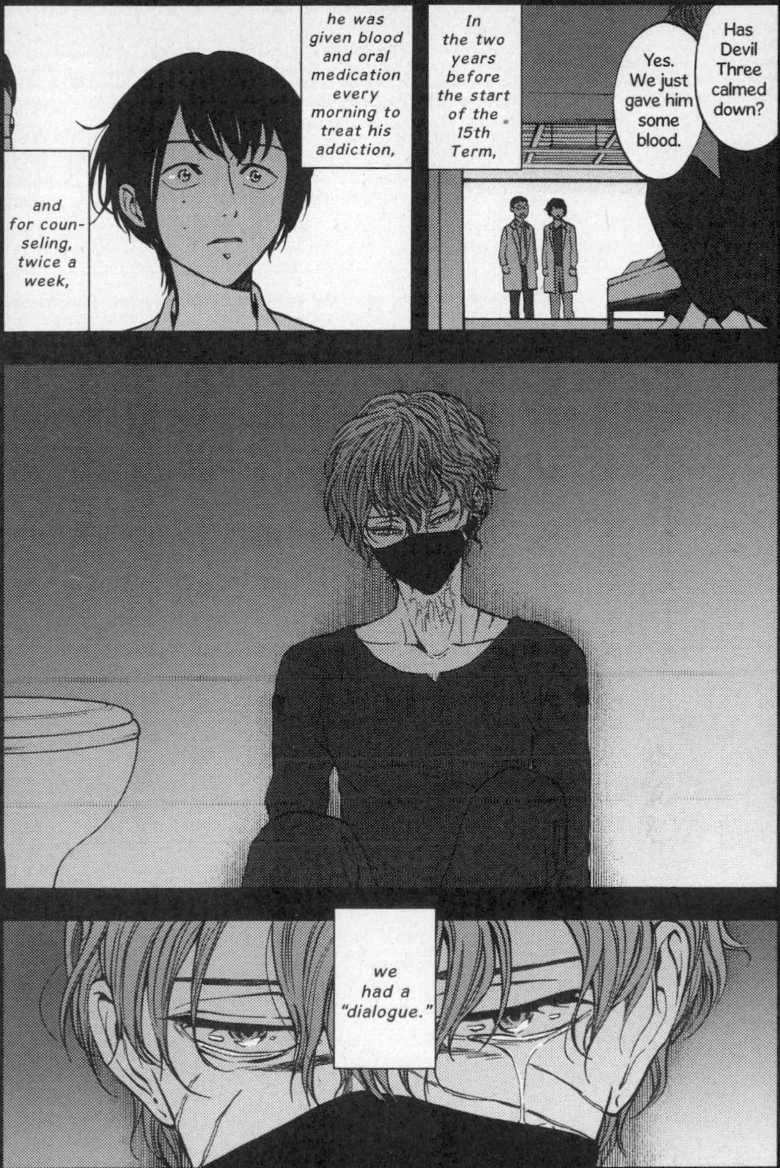

Has Devil Three calmed down?
Yes. We just gave him some blood.
In the two years before the start of the 15th Term,
he was given blood and oral medication every morning to treat his addiction,
and for counseling, twice a week,
we had a "dialogue."

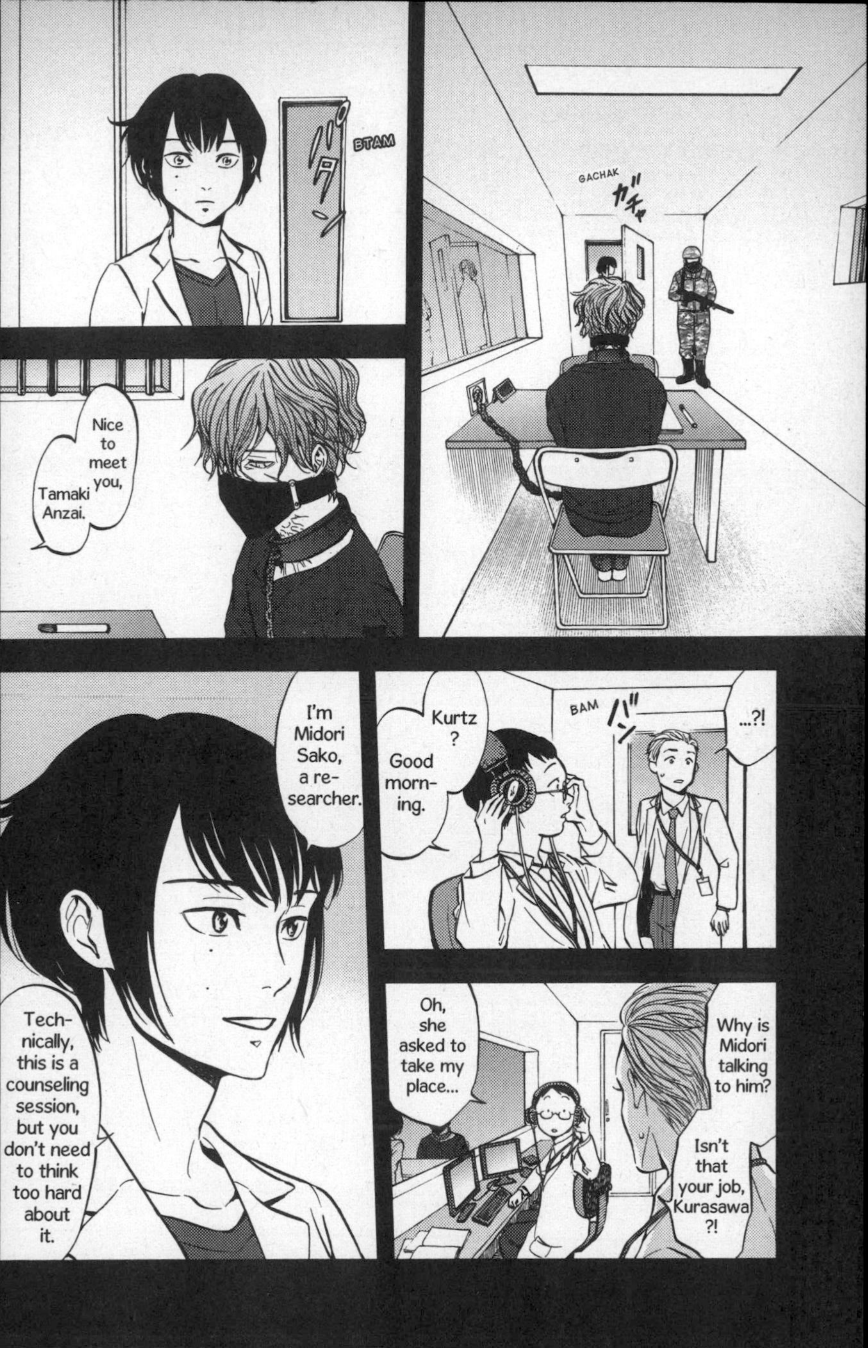
GACHAK
BTAM
Nice to meet you, Tamaki Anzai.
...?!
BAM
Kurtz?
Good morning.
Why is Midori talking to him?
Isn't that your job, Kurasawa?!
Oh, she asked to take my place...
I'm Midori Sako, a researcher.
Technically, this is a counseling session, but you don't need to think too hard about it.

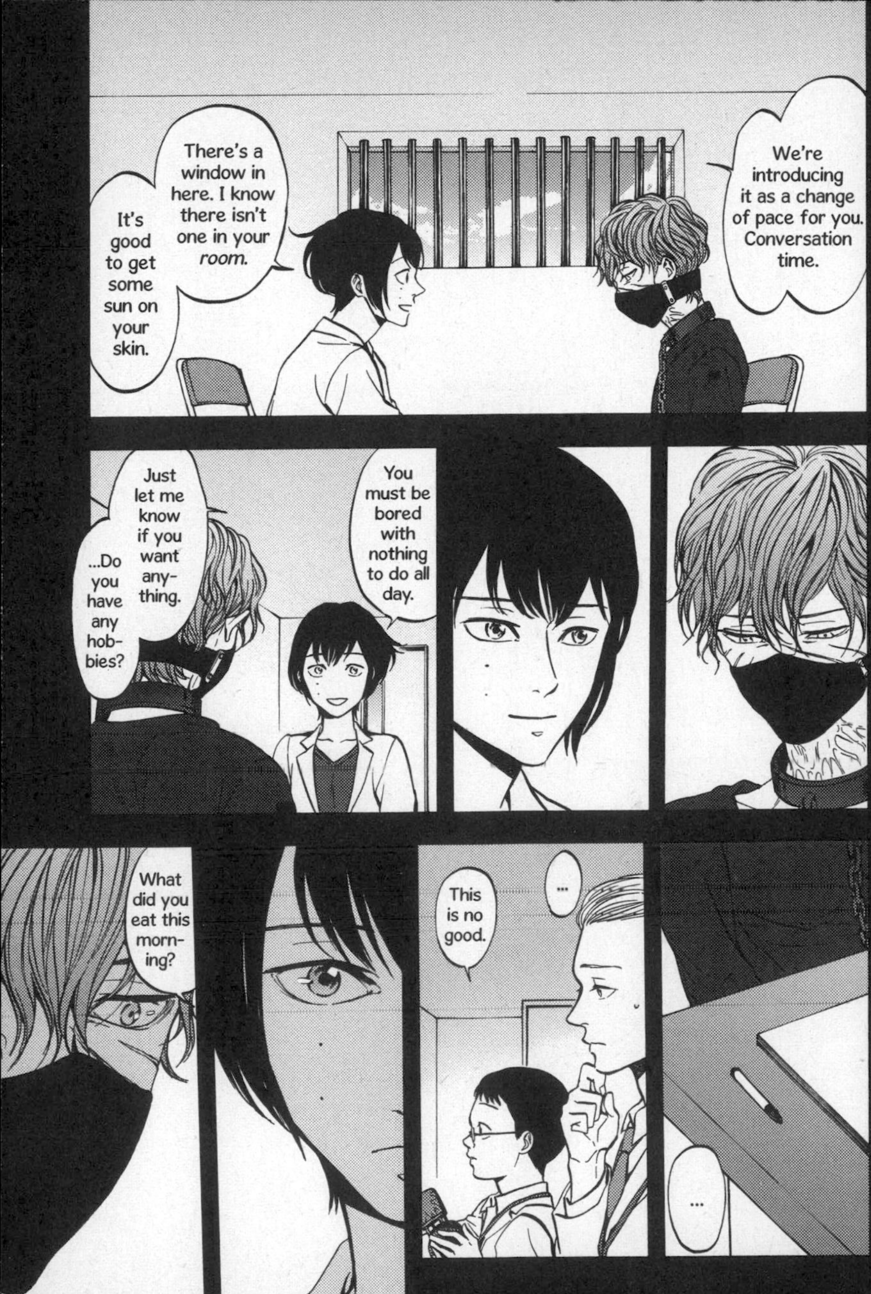
We're introducing it as a change of pace for you. Conversation time.
There's a window in here. I know there isn't one in your *room.*
It's good to get some sun on your skin.
You must be bored with nothing to do all day.
Just let me know if you want anything.
...Do you have any hobbies?
...
...
This is no good.
What did you eat this morning?

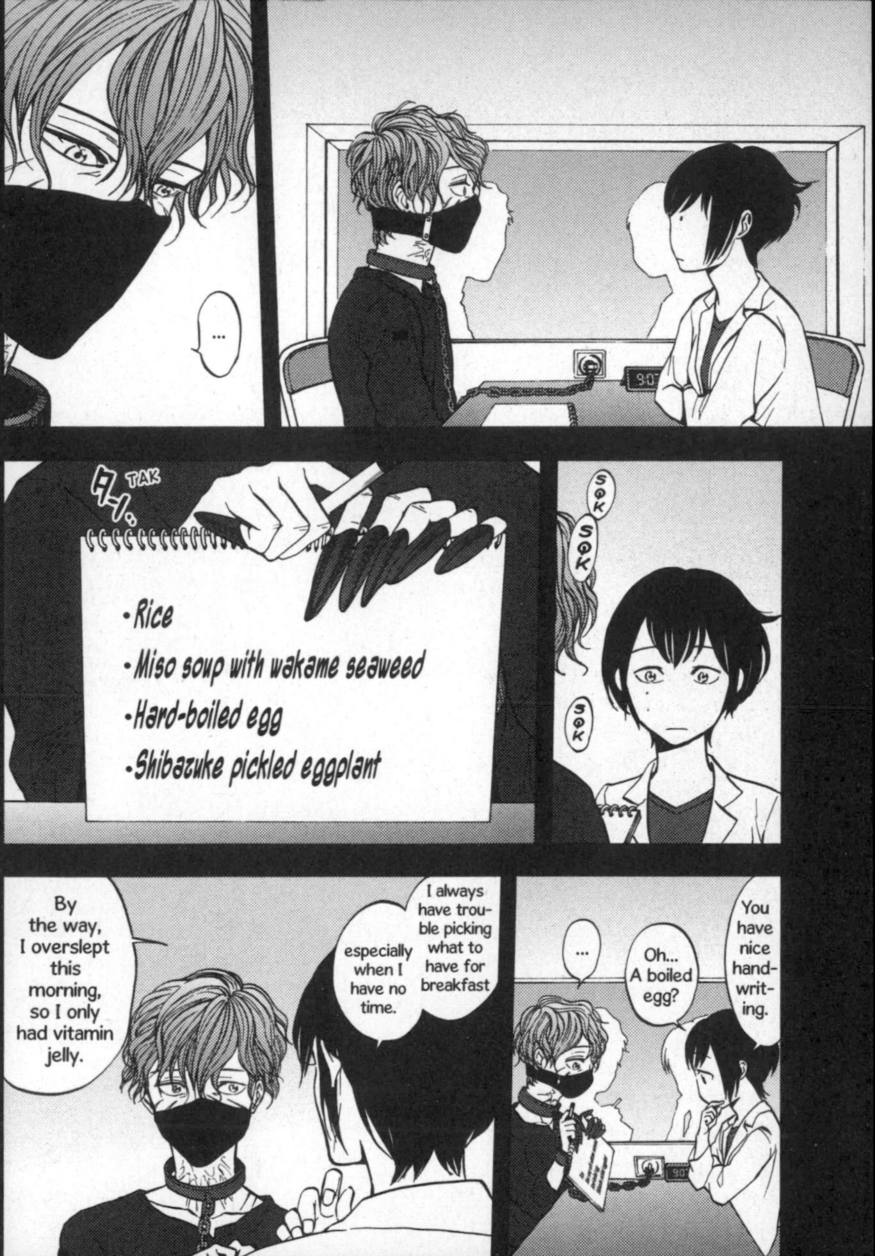
...
SQK
SQK
SQK
SQK
TAK
•Rice
•Miso soup with wakame seaweed
•Hard-boiled egg
•Shibazuke pickled eggplant
You have nice handwriting.
Oh... A boiled egg?
...
I always have trouble picking what to have for breakfast
especially when I have no time.
By the way, I overslept this morning, so I only had vitamin jelly.

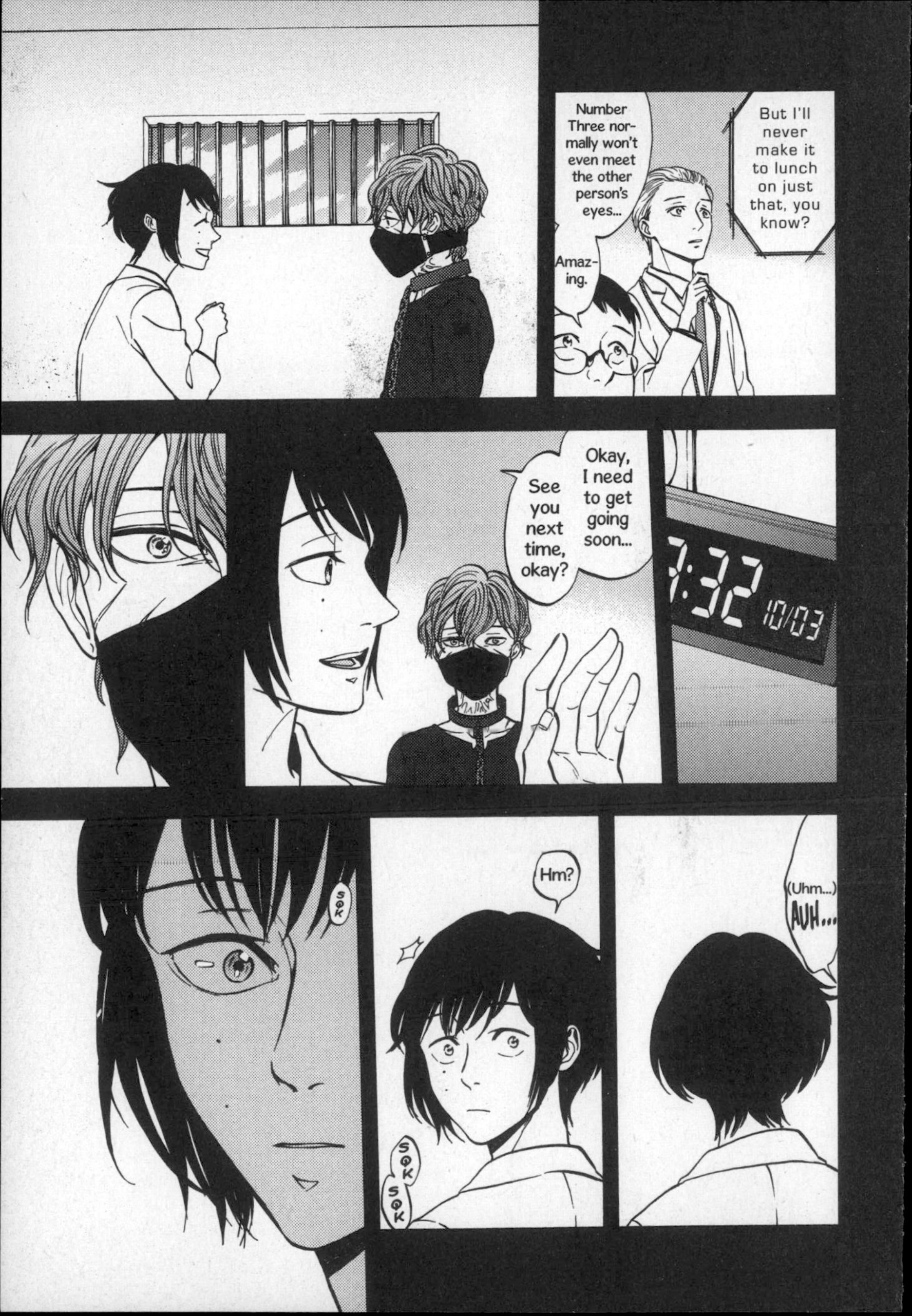
But I'll never make it to lunch on just that, you know?
Number Three normally won't even meet the other person's eyes...
Amazing.
:32 10/03
Okay, I need to get going soon...
See you next time, okay?
(Uhm...) AUH...
Hm?
SOK SOK
SOK

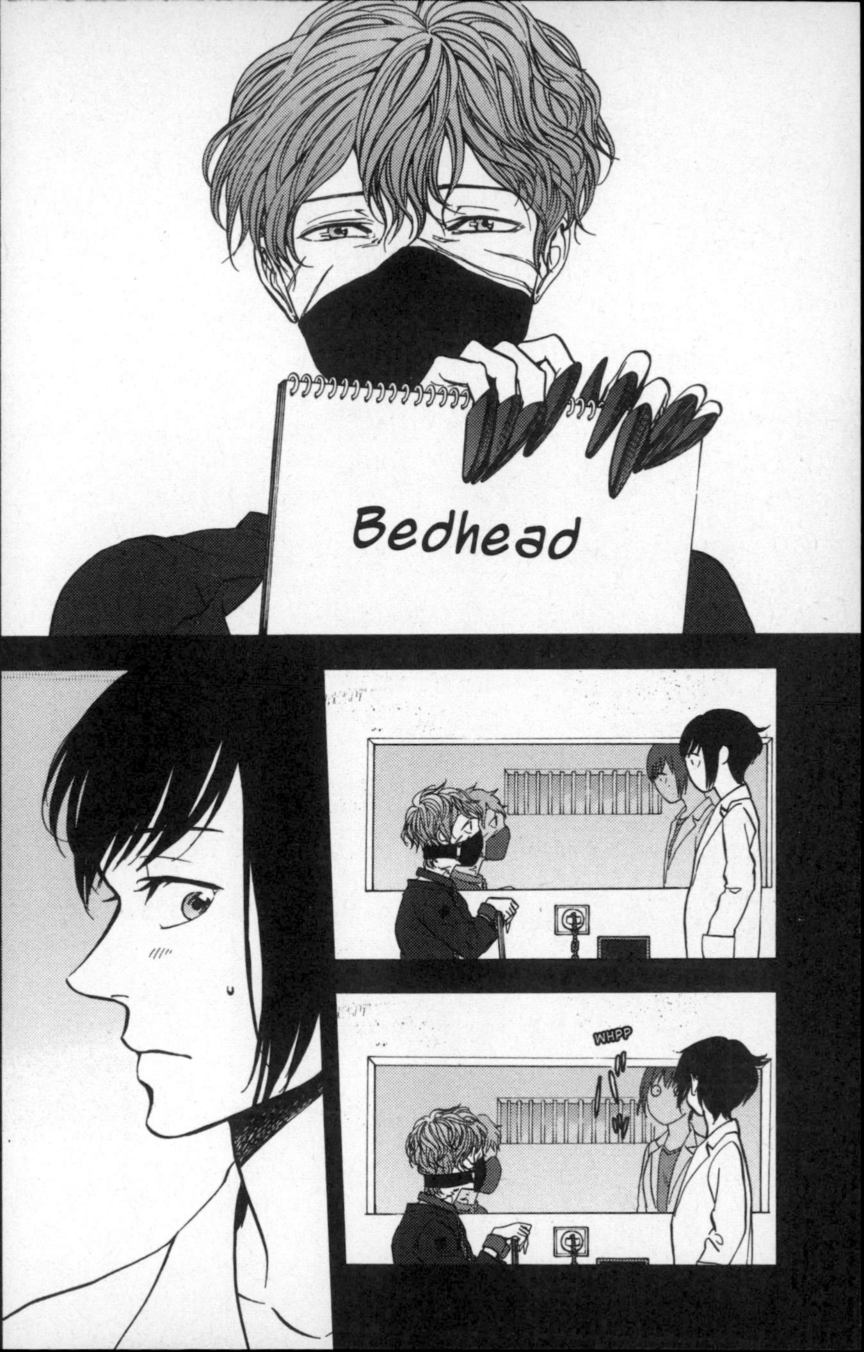
Bedhead
WHPP

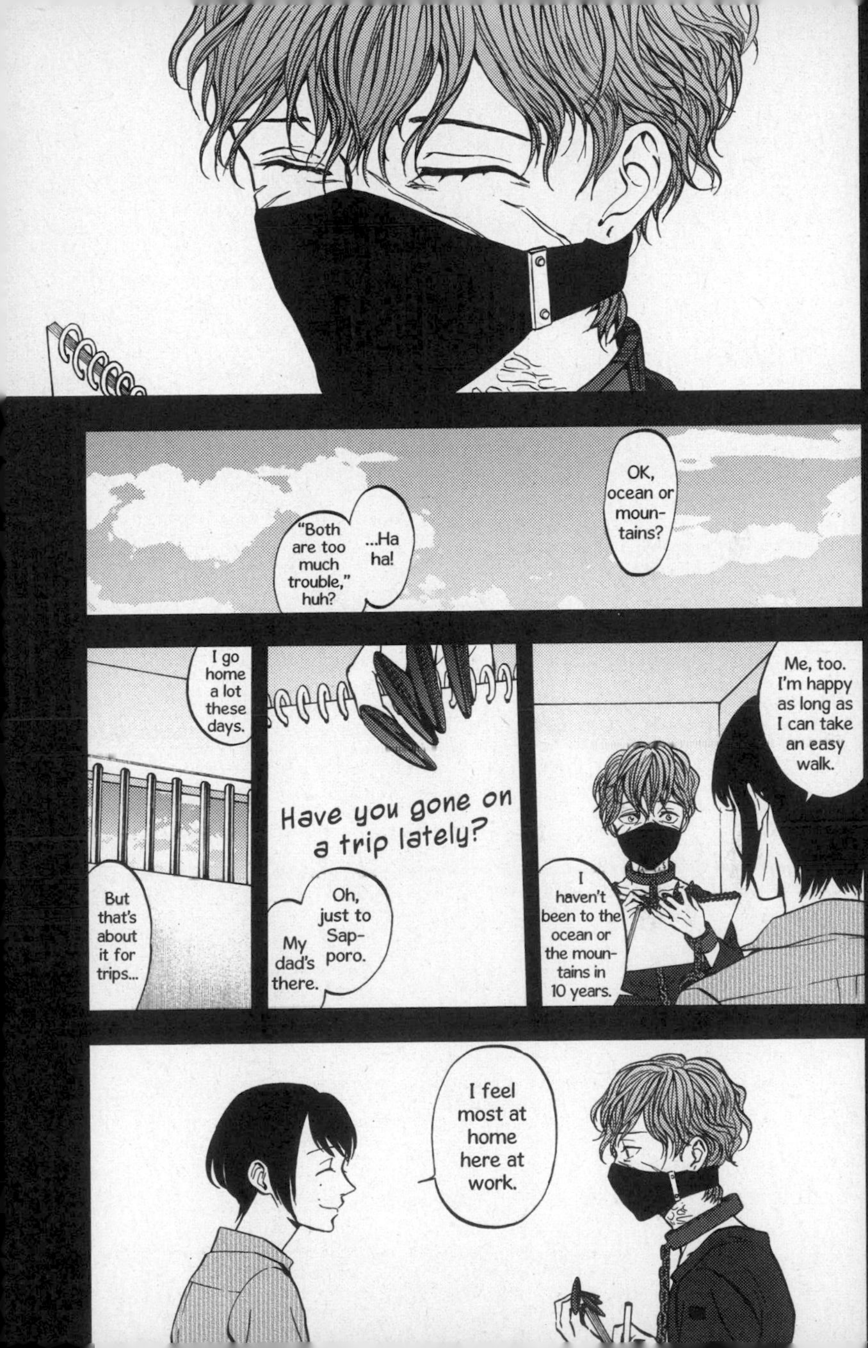
OK, ocean or moun-tains?
...Ha ha!
“Both are too much trouble,” huh?
Me, too. I'm happy as long as I can take an easy walk.
I haven't been to the ocean or the moun-tains in 10 years.
Have you gone on a trip lately?
Oh, just to Sap-poro.
My dad's there.
I go home a lot these days.
But that's about it for trips...
I feel most at home here at work.

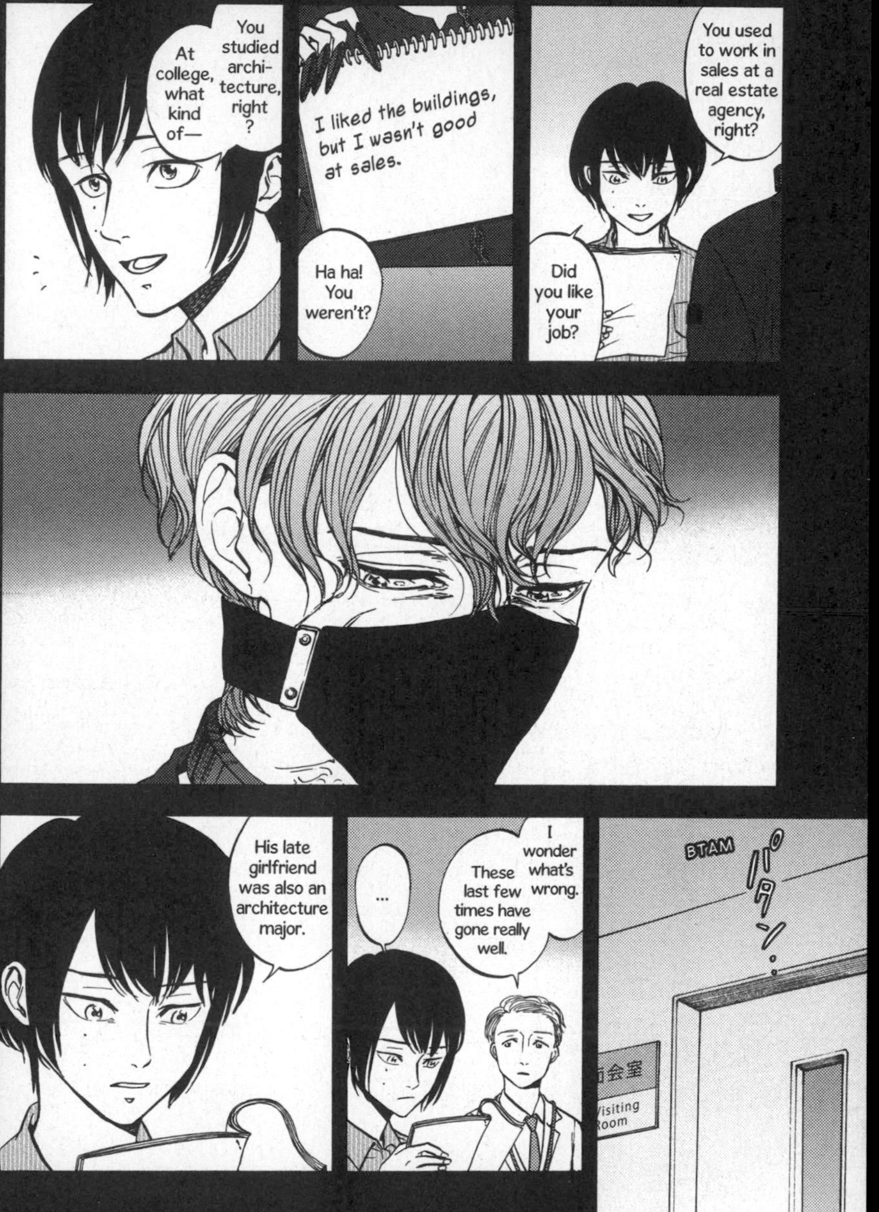
You used to work in sales at a real estate agency, right?
Did you like your job?
I liked the buildings, but I wasn't good at sales.
Ha ha! You weren't?
You studied archi-tecture, right?
At college, what kind of—
BTAM
パタン。
I wonder what's wrong.
These last few times have gone really well.
...
His late girlfriend was also an architecture major.

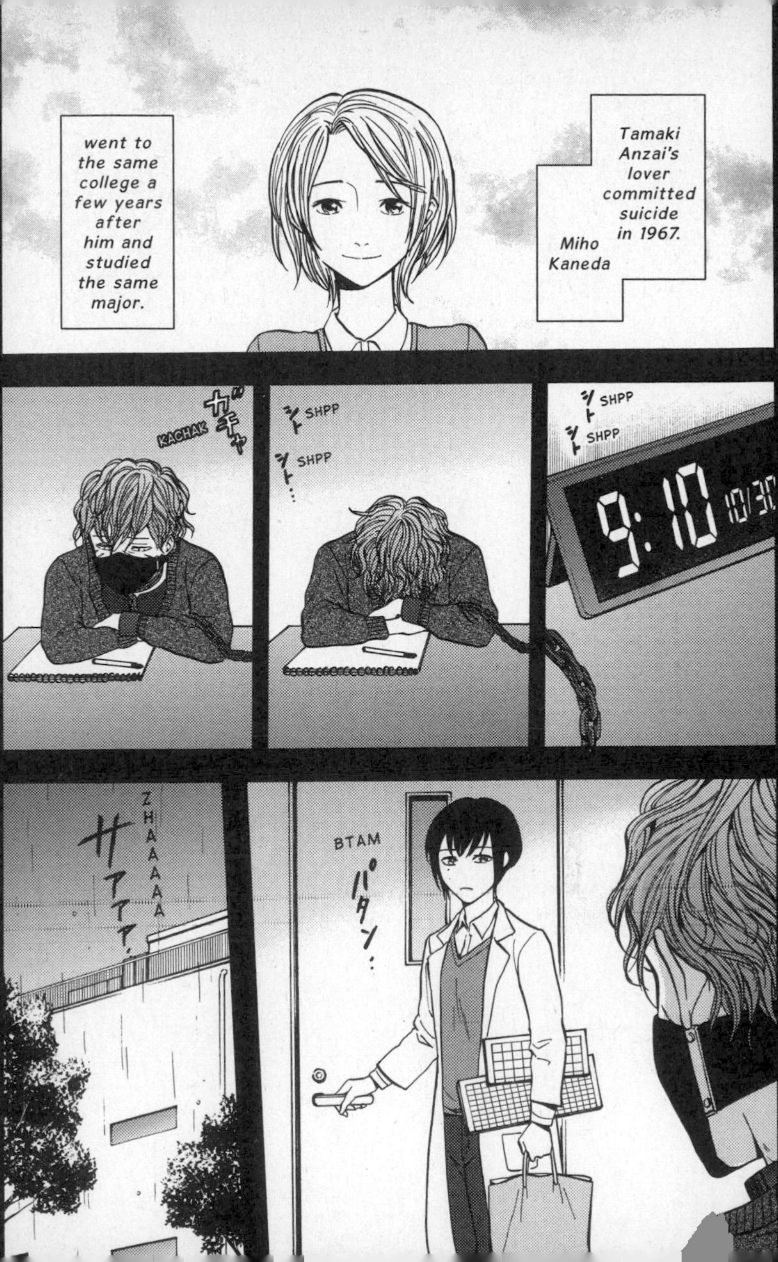
Tamaki Anzai's lover committed suicide in 1967.
Miho Kaneda
went to the same college a few years after him and studied the same major.
シト SHPP
シト SHPP
シト SHPP
シト… SHPP
9:10 10/30
ガチャ KACHAK
パタン… BTAM
サアアア… ZHAAAAA

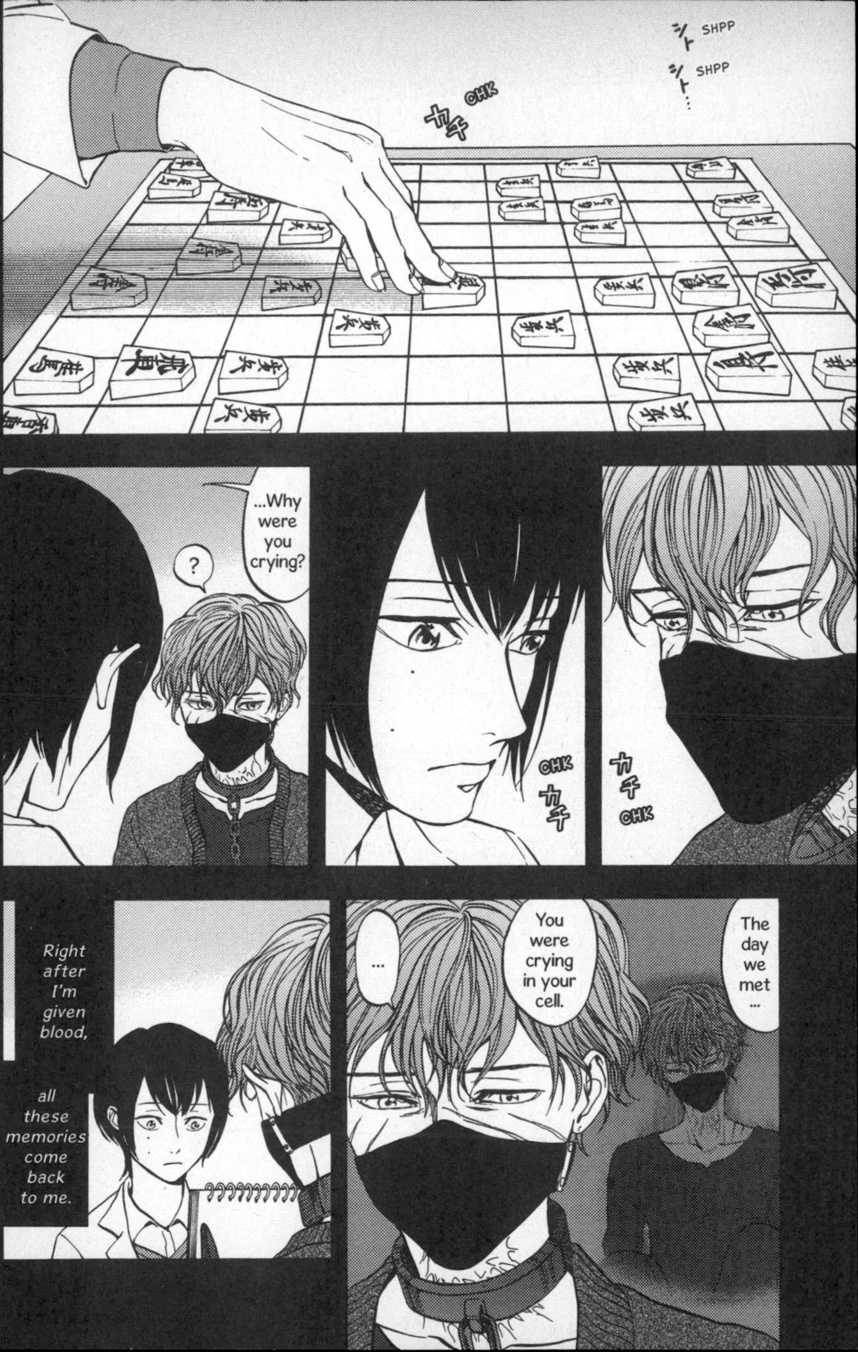

シト SHPP
シト… SHPP
カチ CHK
カチ CHK
CHK カチ
...Why were you crying?
?
The day we met ...
You were crying in your cell.
...
Right after I'm given blood,
all these memories come back to me.

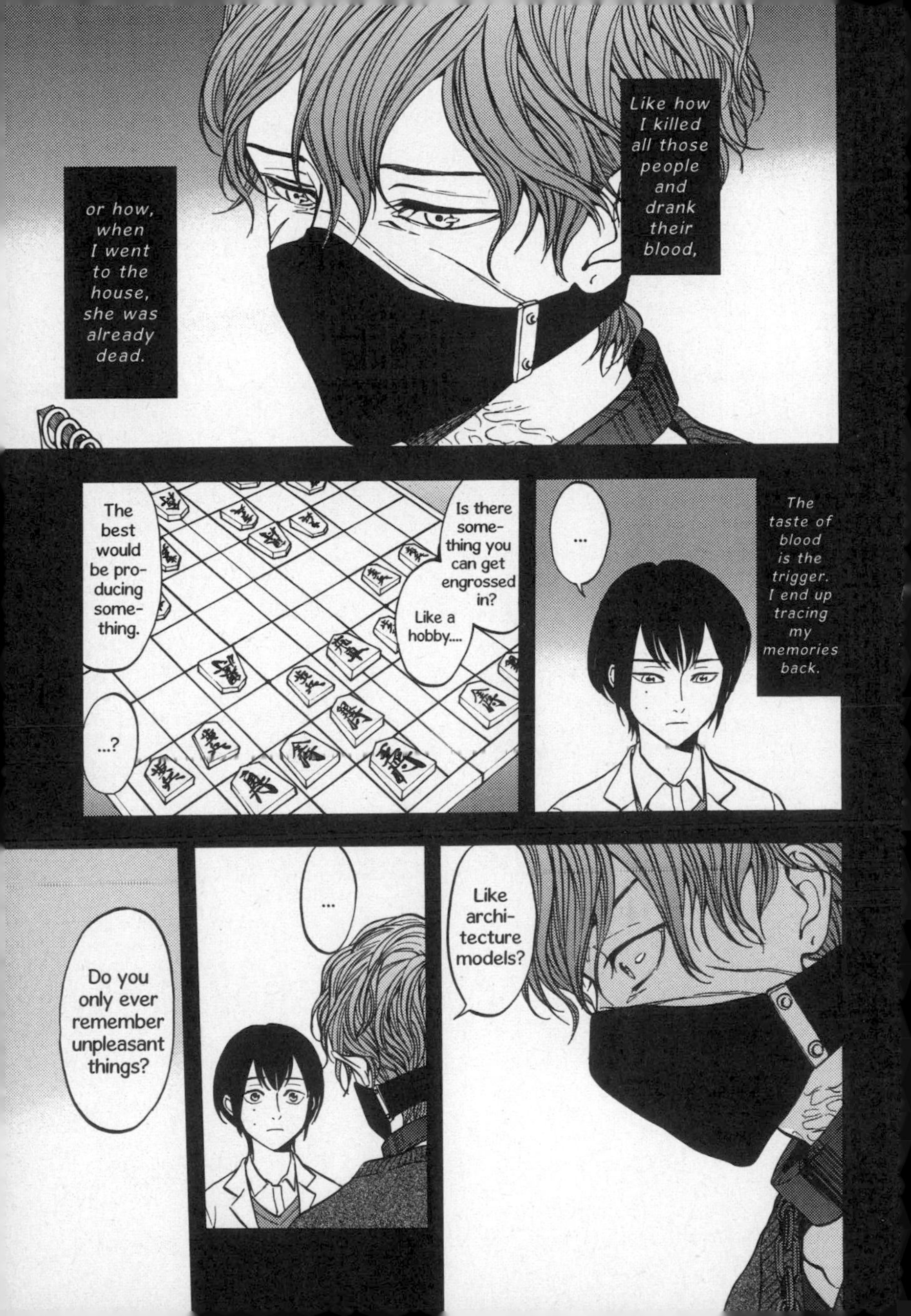
Like how I killed all those people and drank their blood,
or how, when I went to the house, she was already dead.
The taste of blood is the trigger. I end up tracing my memories back.
...
Is there some-thing you can get engrossed in?
Like a hobby....
The best would be pro-ducing some-thing.
...?
Like archi-tecture models?
...
Do you only ever remember unpleasant things?

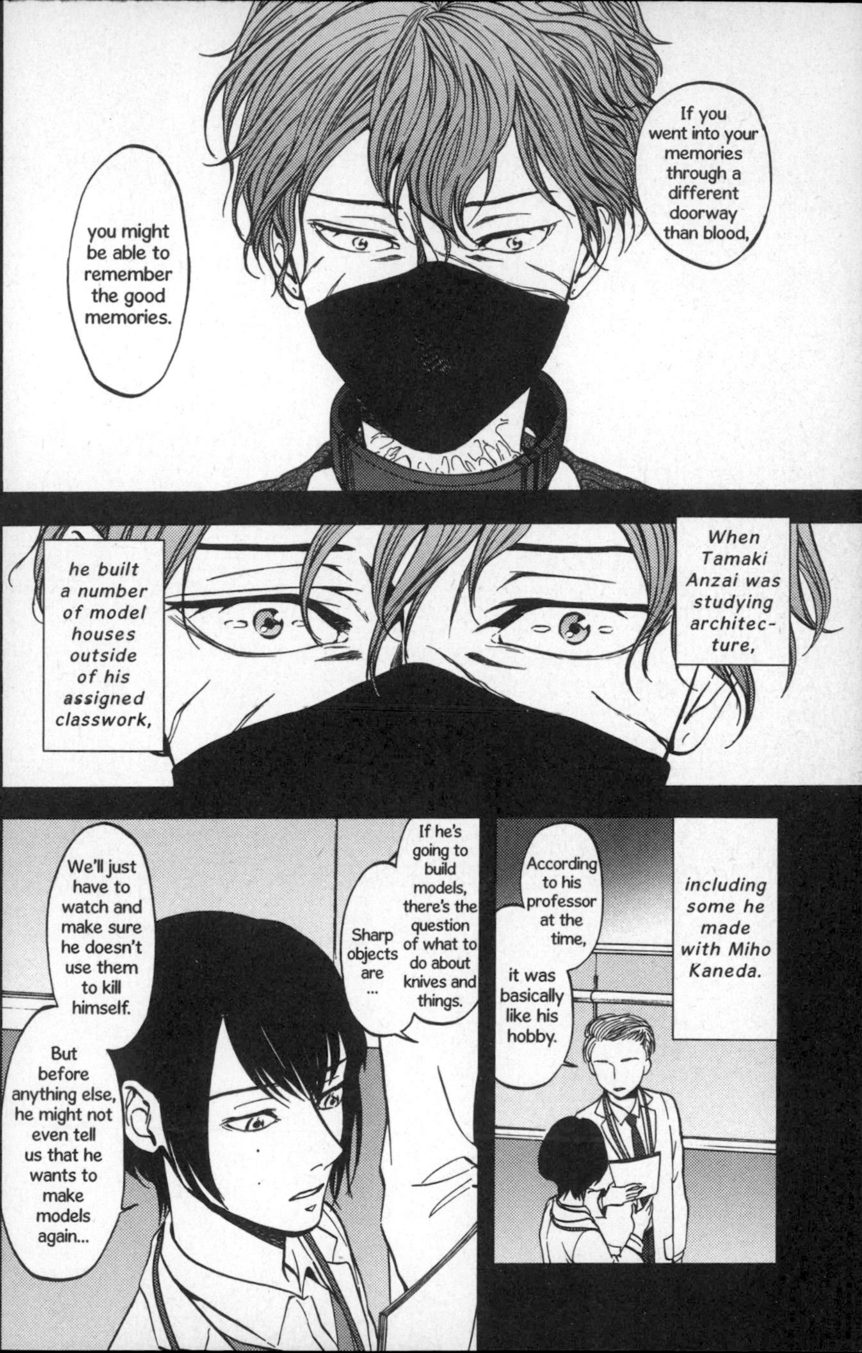
If you went into your memories through a different doorway than blood,
you might be able to remember the good memories.
When Tamaki Anzai was studying architec-ture,
he built a number of model houses outside of his assigned classwork,
including some he made with Miho Kaneda.
According to his professor at the time,
it was basically like his hobby.
If he's going to build models, there's the question of what to do about knives and things.
Sharp objects are ...
We'll just have to watch and make sure he doesn't use them to kill himself.
But before anything else, he might not even tell us that he wants to make models again...

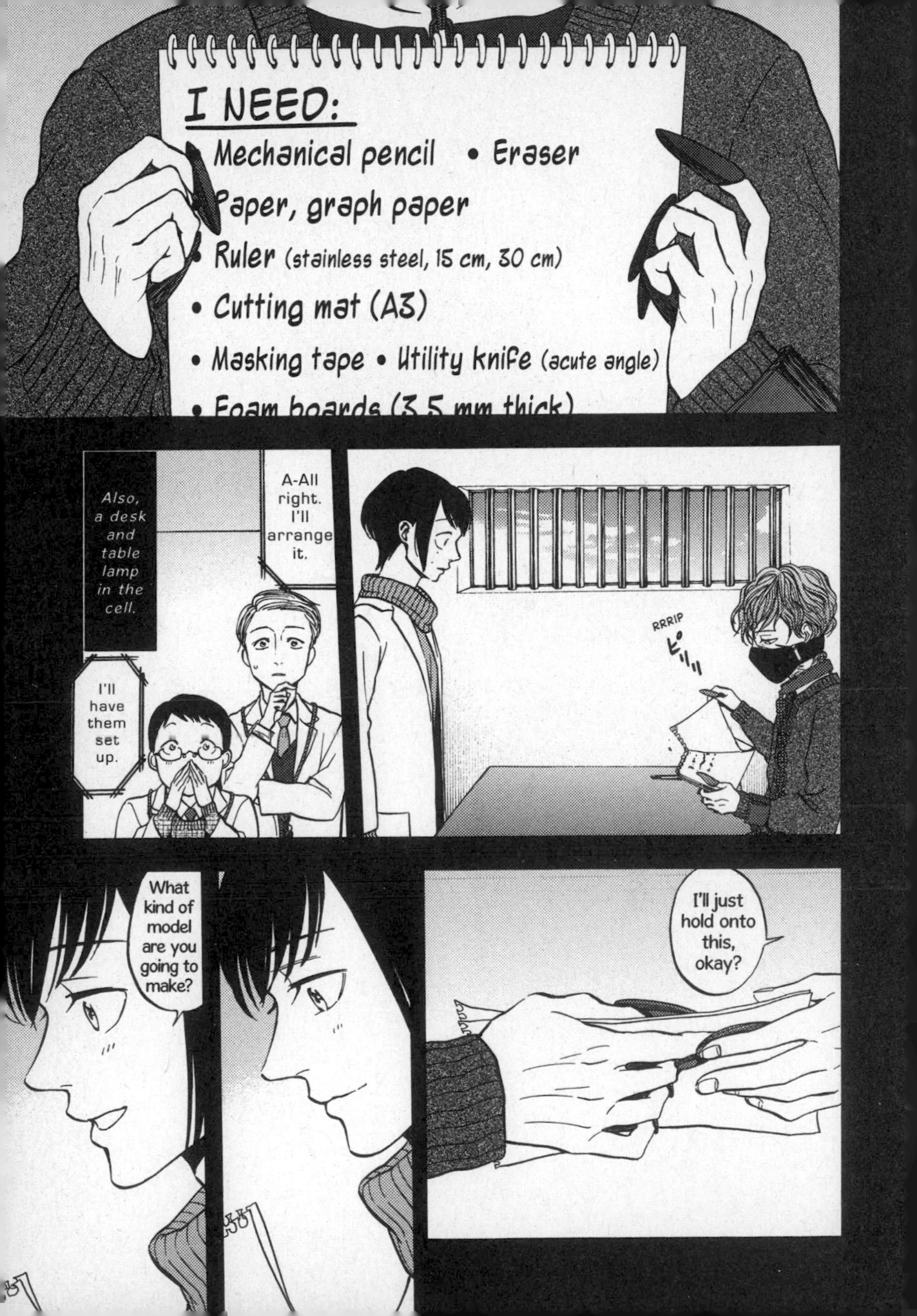
I NEED:
• Mechanical pencil • Eraser
• Paper, graph paper
• Ruler (stainless steel, 15 cm, 30 cm)
• Cutting mat (A3)
• Masking tape • Utility knife (acute angle)
• Foam boards (3.5 mm thick)
RRRIP
Also, a desk and table lamp in the cell.
A-All right. I'll arrange it.
I'll have them set up.
I'll just hold onto this, okay?
What kind of model are you going to make?

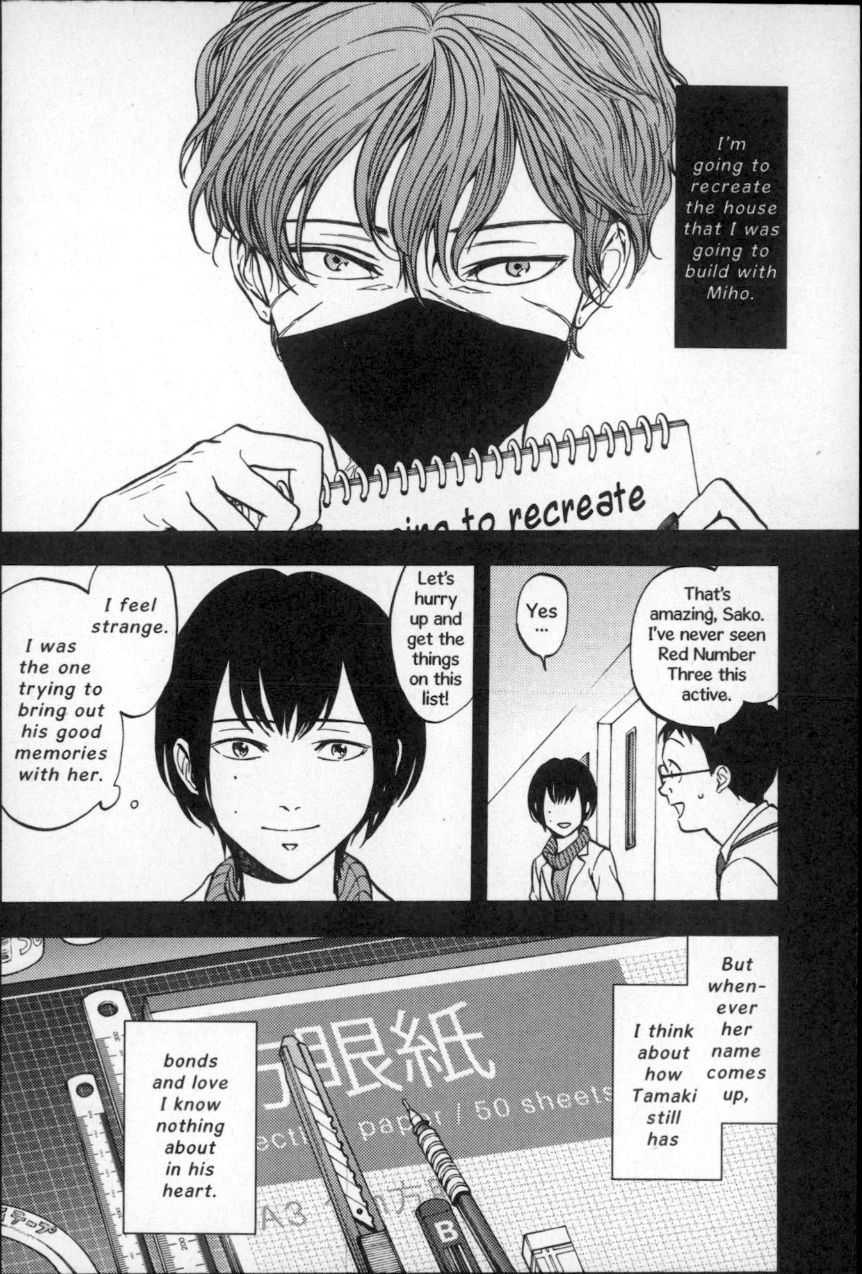
I'm going to recreate the house that I was going to build with Miho.
to recreate
That's amazing, Sako. I've never seen Red Number Three this active.
Yes ...
Let's hurry up and get the things on this list!
I feel strange. I was the one trying to bring out his good memories with her.
But whenever her name comes up,
I think about how Tamaki still has
bonds and love I know nothing about in his heart.
50 sheets

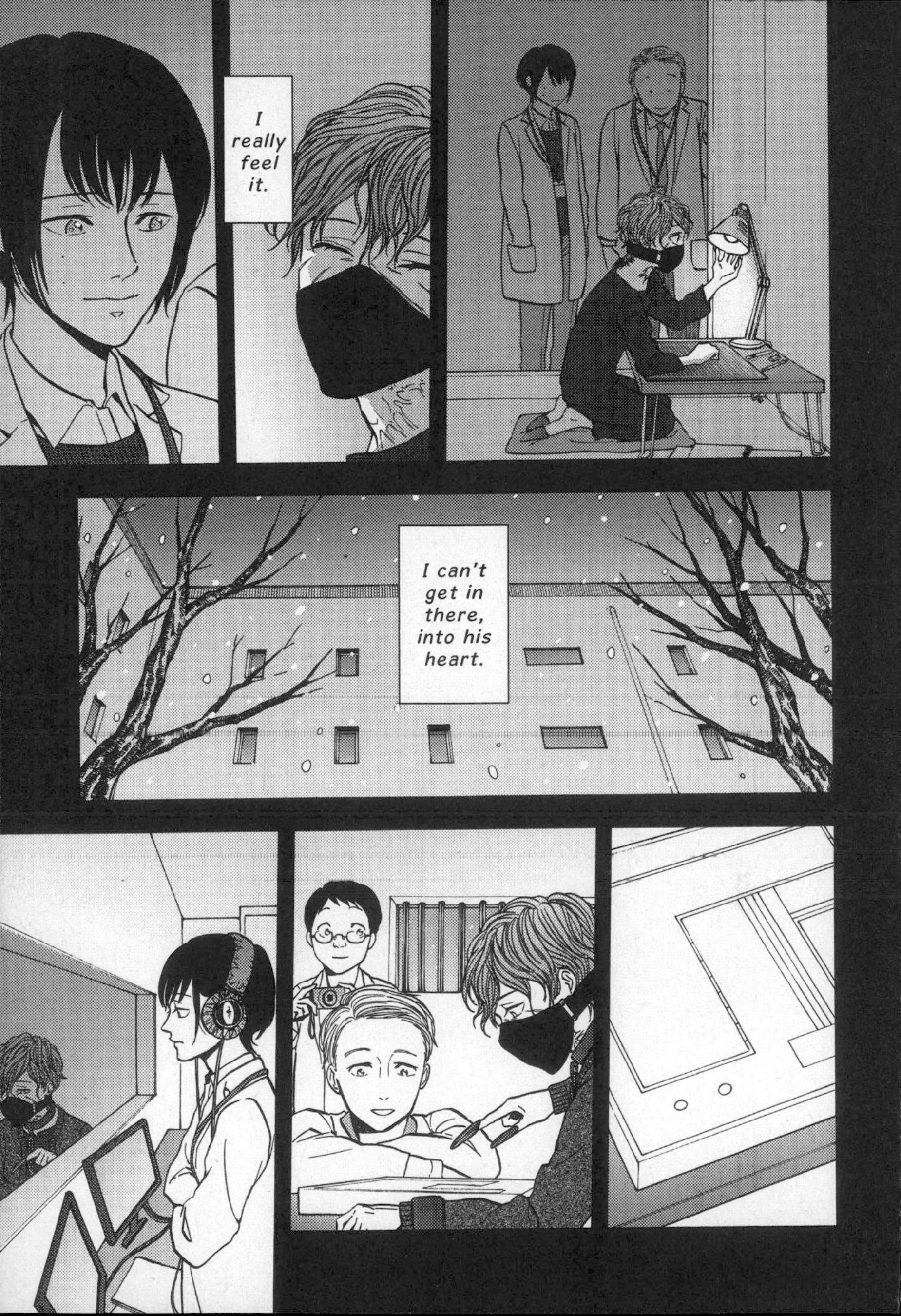
I really feel it.
I can't get in there, into his heart.

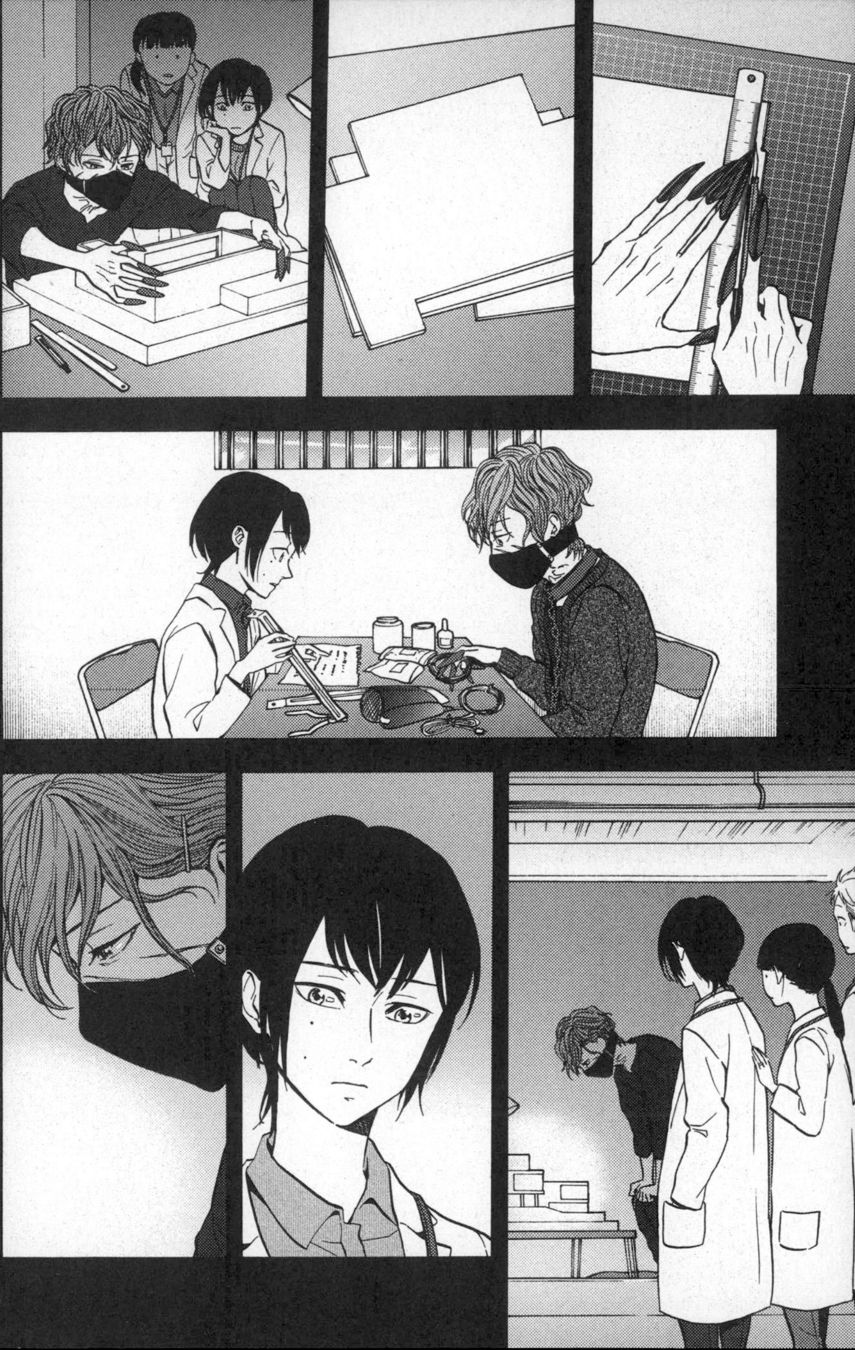

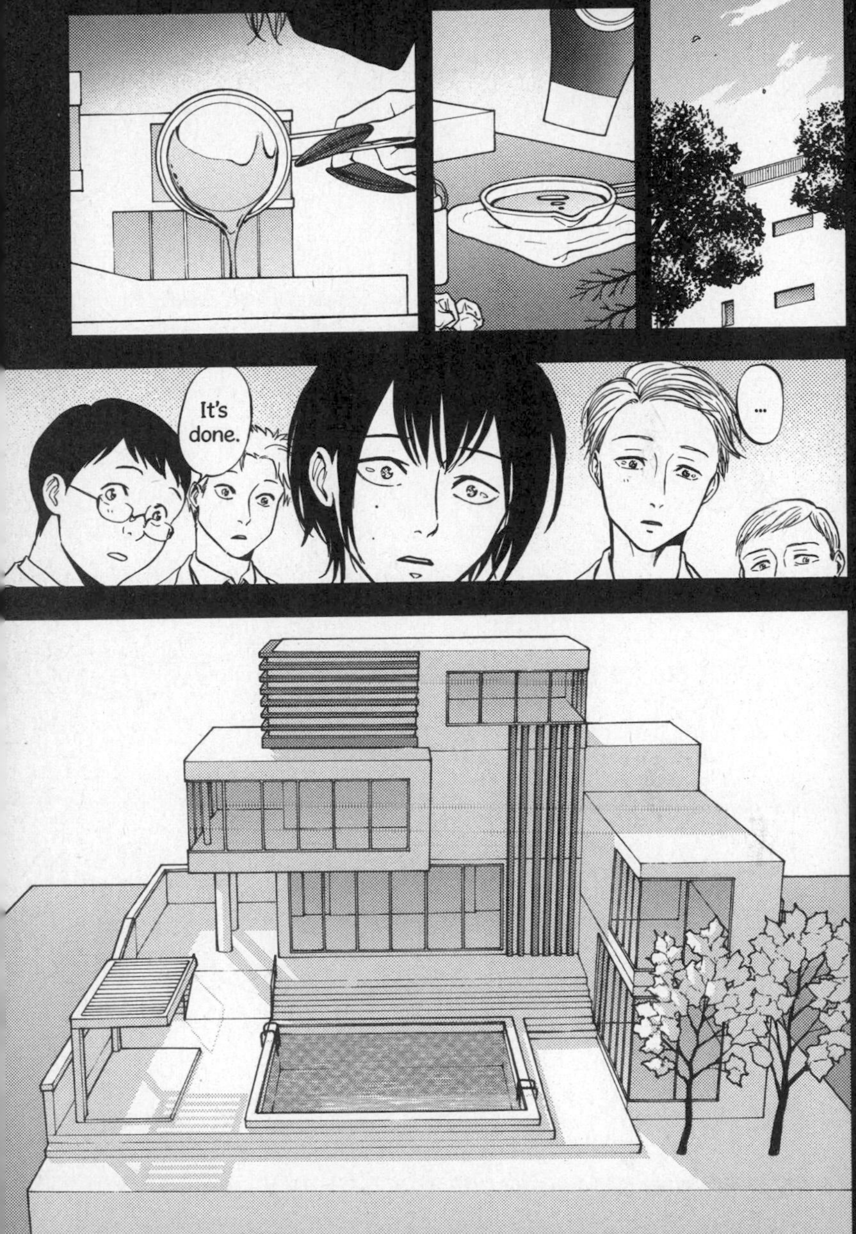
…
It's done.

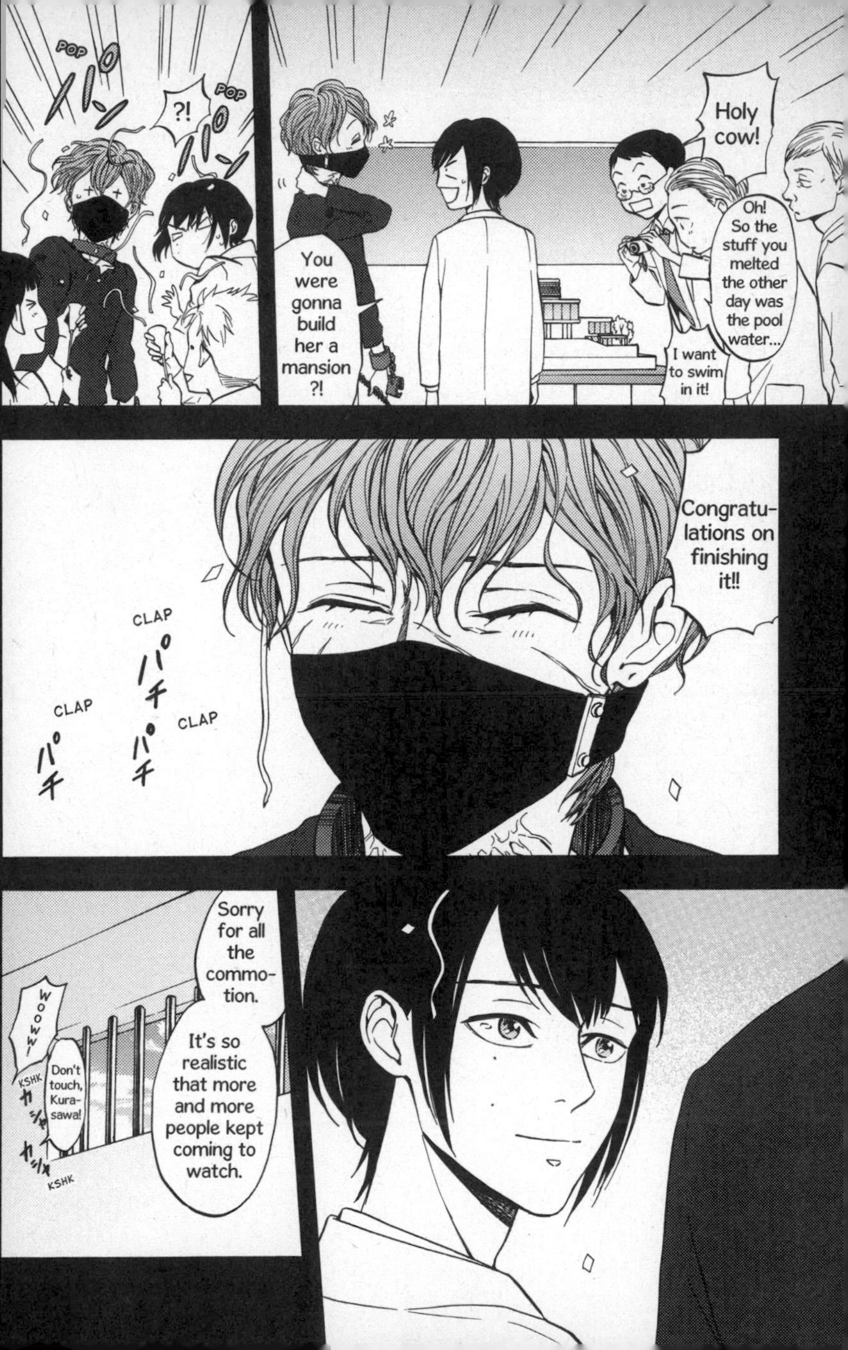
Holy cow!
Oh! So the stuff you melted the other day was the pool water...
I want to swim in it!
You were gonna build her a mansion?!
POP
?!
POP
Congratulations on finishing it!!
CLAP
パチ
パチ
CLAP
CLAP
パチ
Sorry for all the commotion.
It's so realistic that more and more people kept coming to watch.
WOOWW!
Don't touch, Kurasawa!
KSHK
KSHK

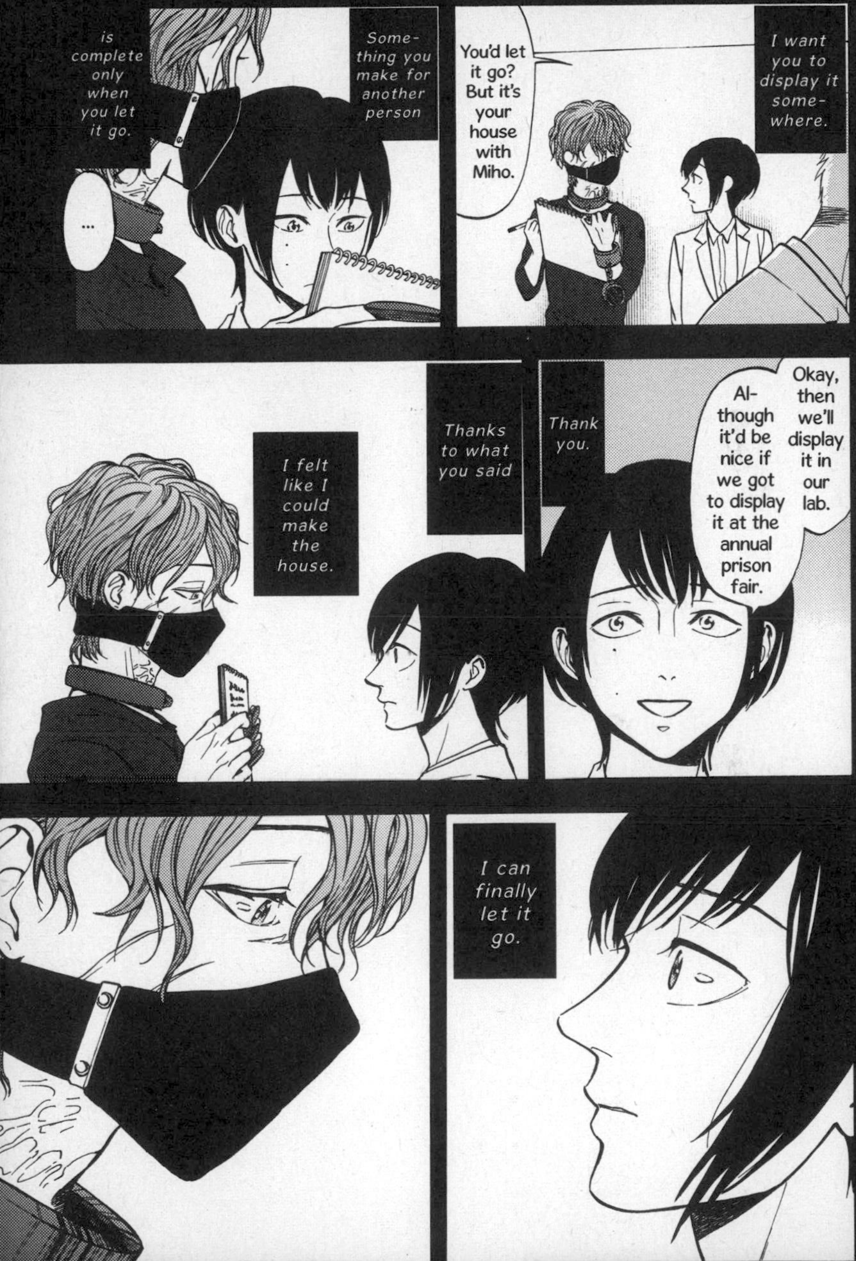
I want you to display it somewhere.
You'd let it go? But it's your house with Miho.
Something you make for another person
is complete only when you let it go.
...
Okay, then we'll display it in our lab.
Although it'd be nice if we got to display it at the annual prison fair.
Thank you.
Thanks to what you said
I felt like I could make the house.
I can finally let it go.

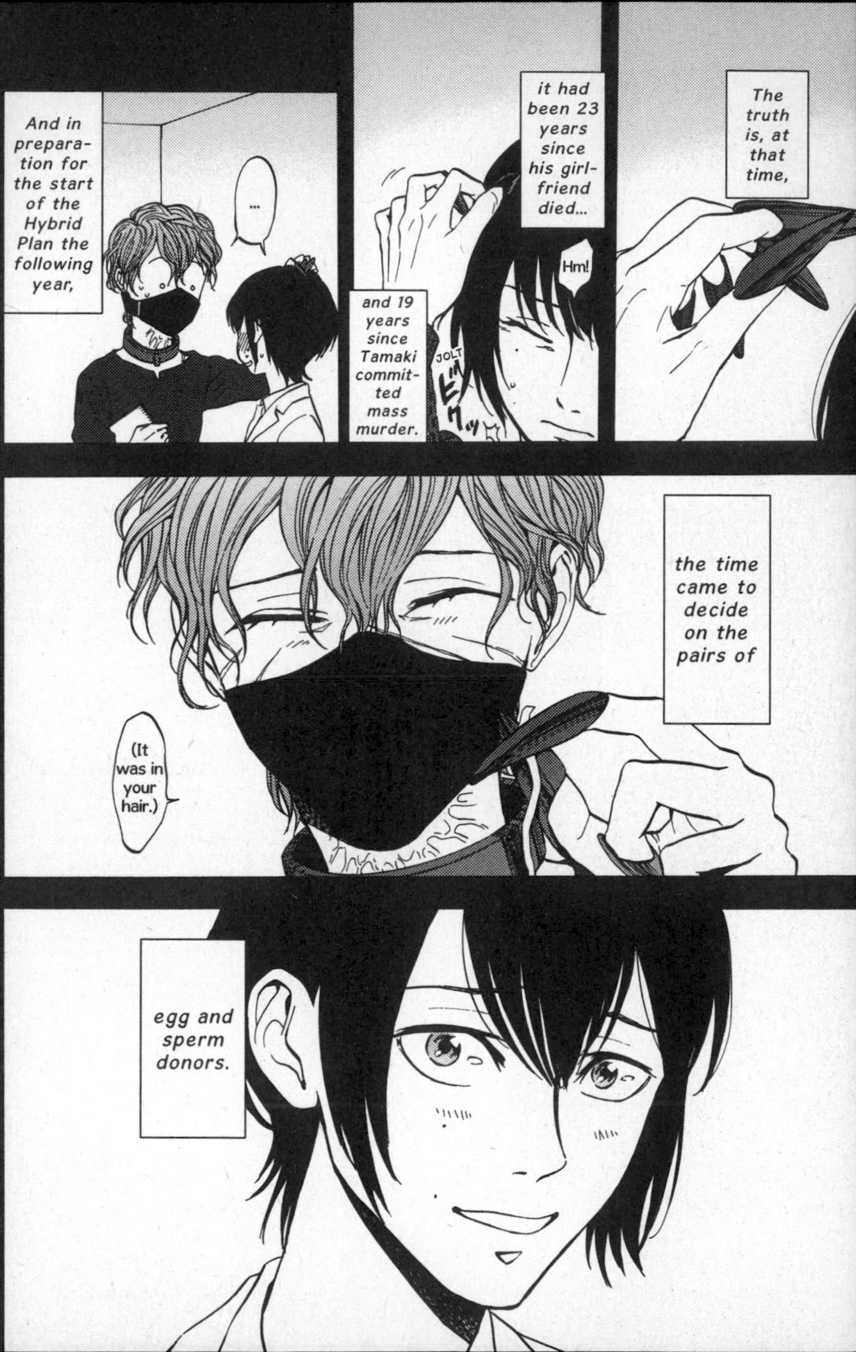
The truth is, at that time,
it had been 23 years since his girl-friend died...
Hm!
and 19 years since Tamaki commit-ted mass murder.
JOLT
And in prepara-tion for the start of the Hybrid Plan the following year,
...
the time came to decide on the pairs of
(It was in your hair.)
egg and sperm donors.

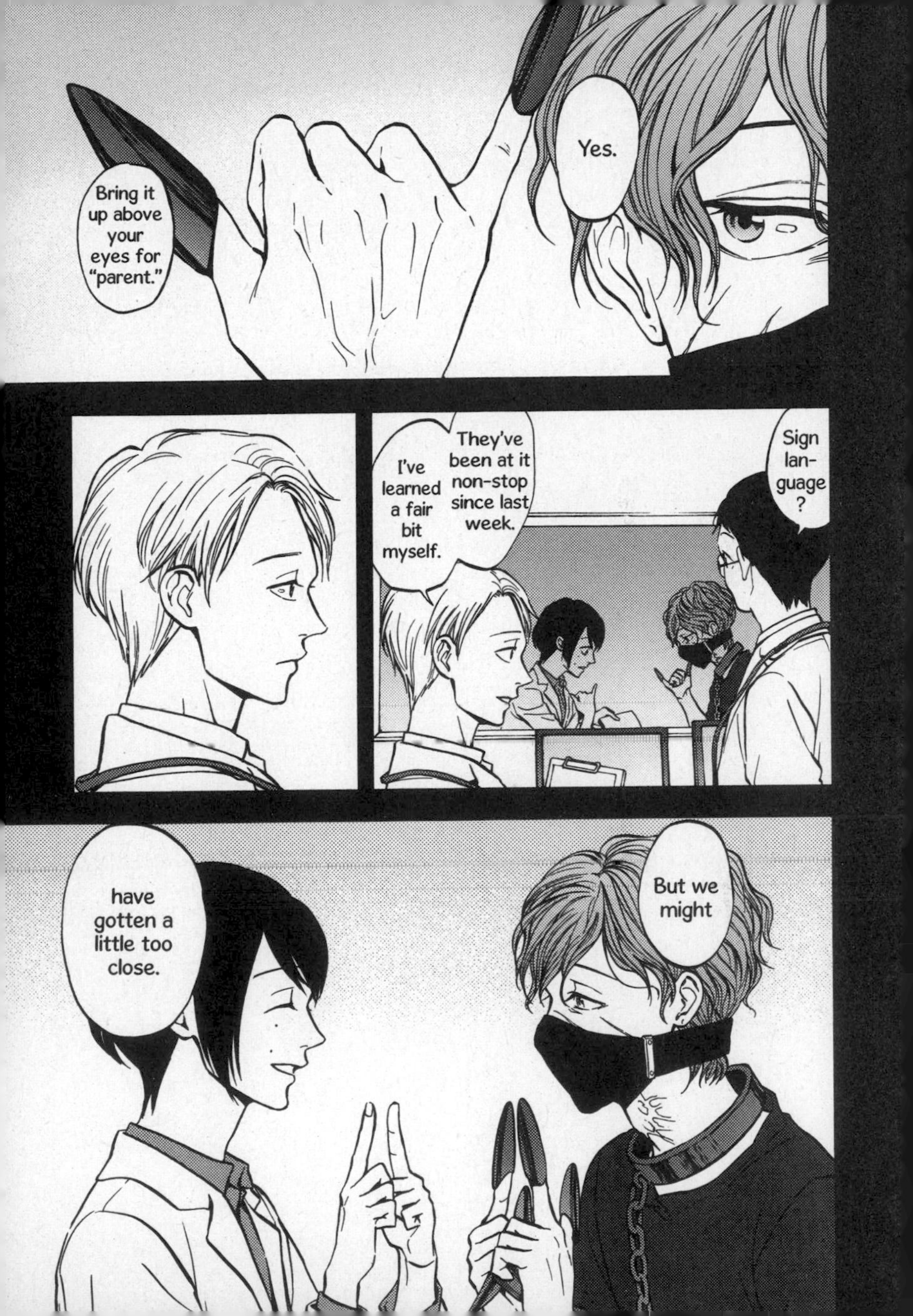
Yes.
Bring it up above your eyes for "parent."
Sign lan-guage?
They've been at it non-stop since last week.
I've learned a fair bit myself.
But we might
have gotten a little too close.

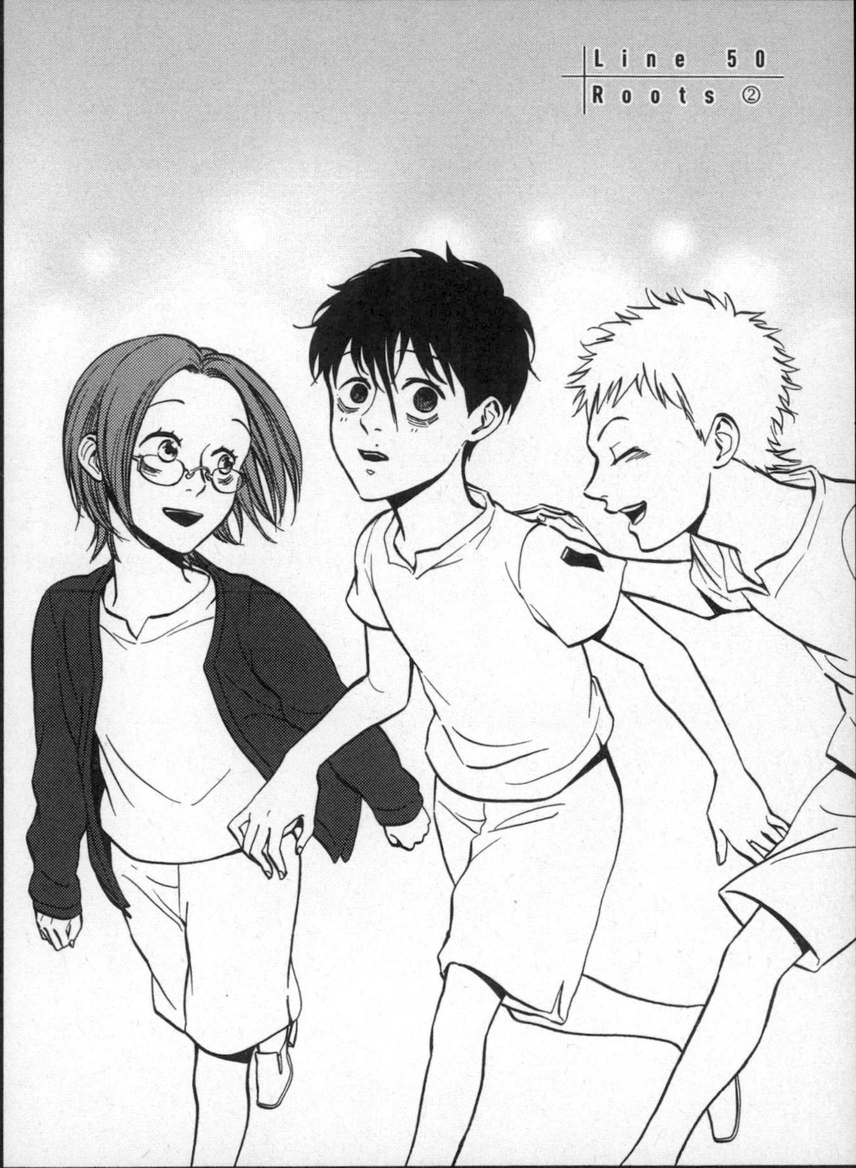
Line 50
Roots ②

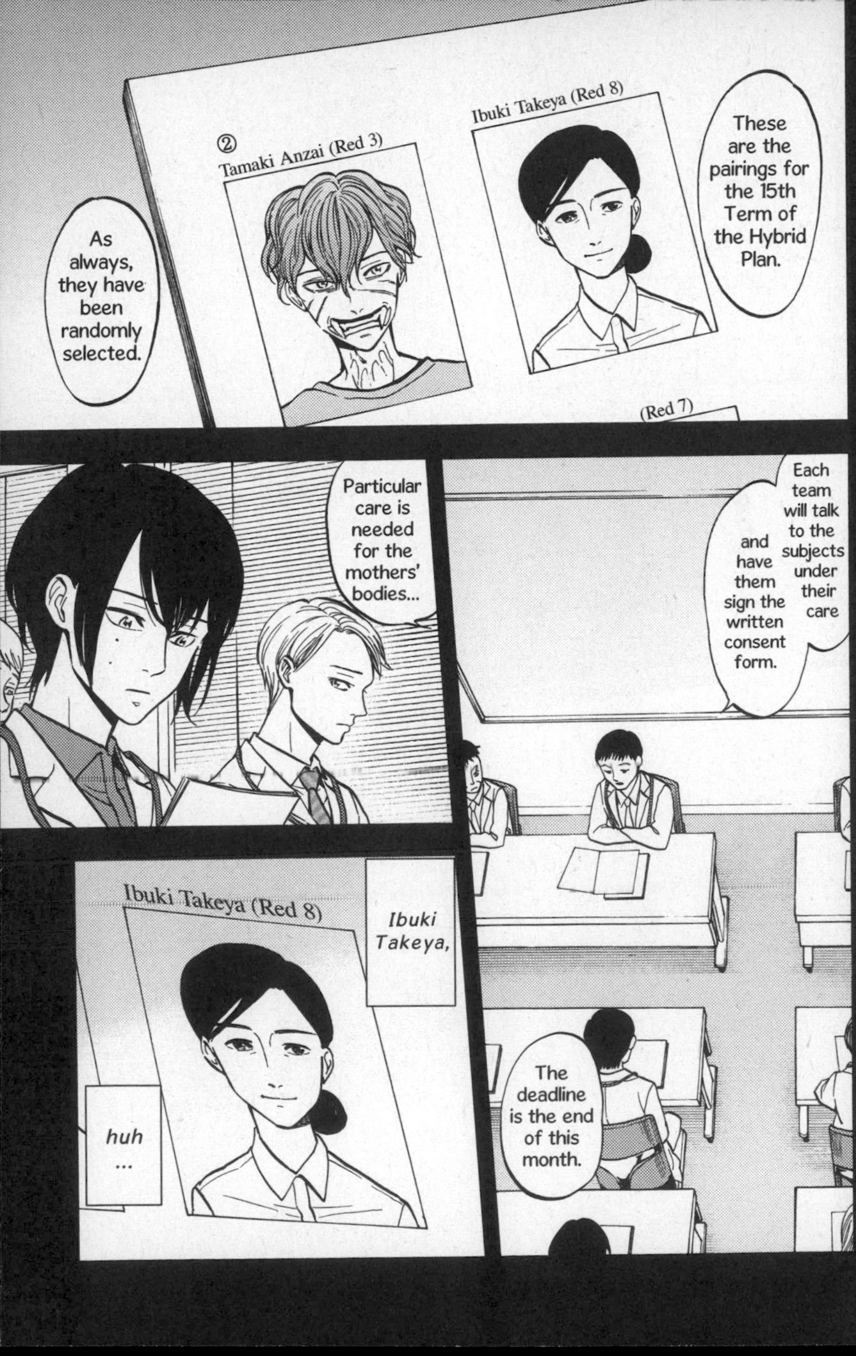
Ibuki Takeya (Red 8)
② Tamaki Anzai (Red 3)
These are the pairings for the 15th Term of the Hybrid Plan.
As always, they have been randomly selected.
(Red 7)
Each team will talk to the subjects under their care
and have them sign the written consent form.
The deadline is the end of this month.
Particular care is needed for the mothers' bodies...
Ibuki Takeya (Red 8)
Ibuki Takeya,
huh ...

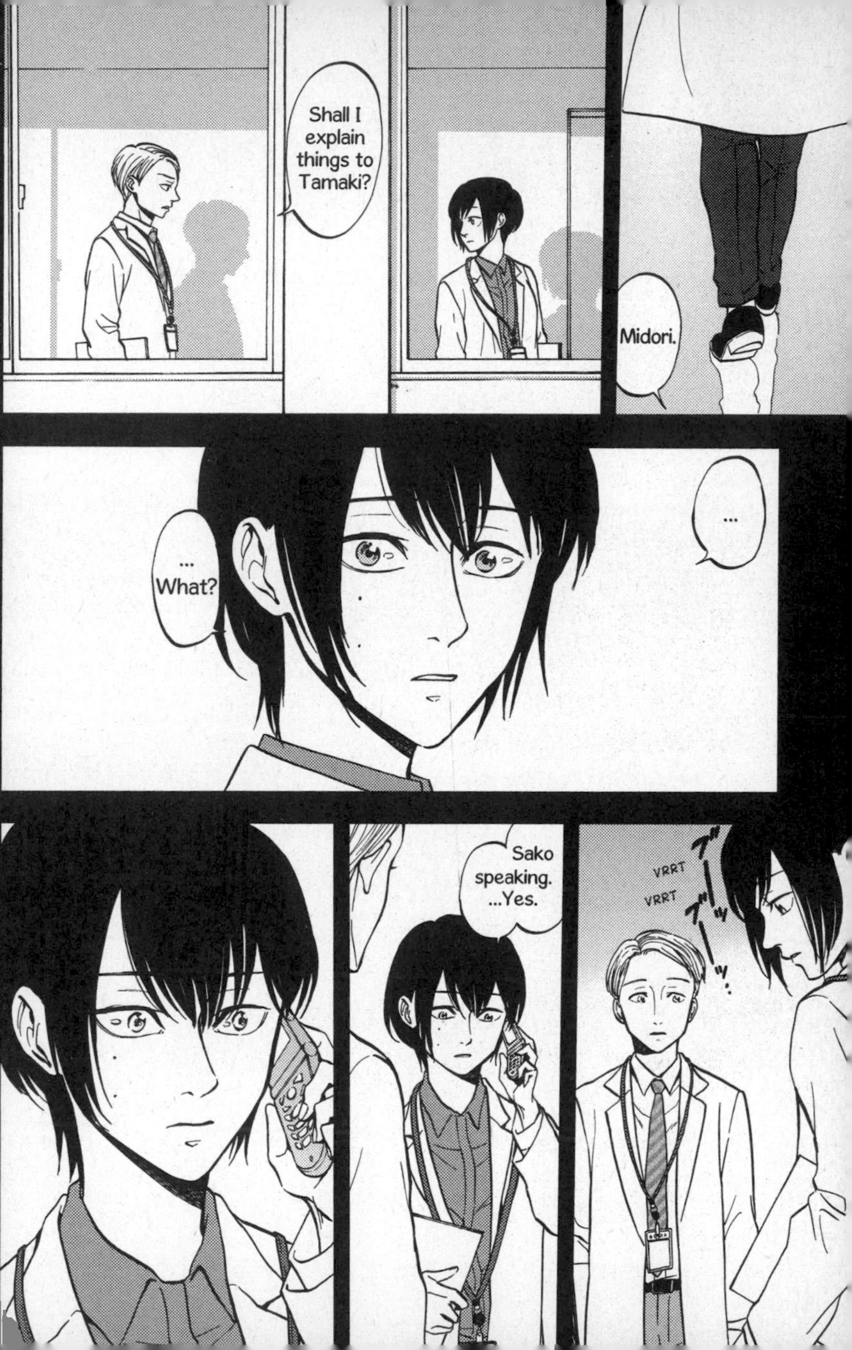
Midori.
Shall I explain things to Tamaki?
...
... What?
VRRT
VRRT
ブーッ ブーッ
Sako speaking. ...Yes.

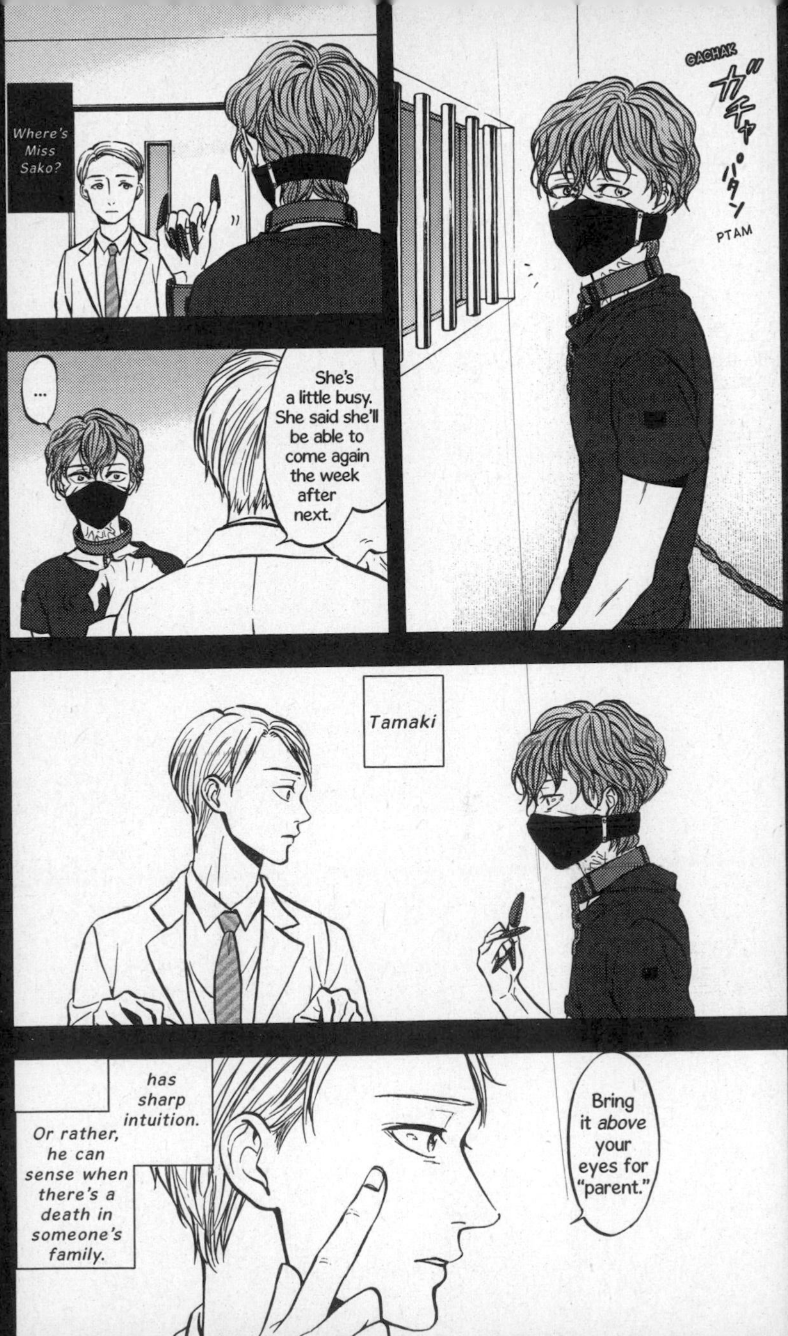
GACHAK
ガチャ
パタン
PTAM
Where's Miss Sako?
She's a little busy. She said she'll be able to come again the week after next.
...
Tamaki
Bring it *above* your eyes for "parent."
has sharp intuition.
Or rather, he can sense when there's a death in someone's family.

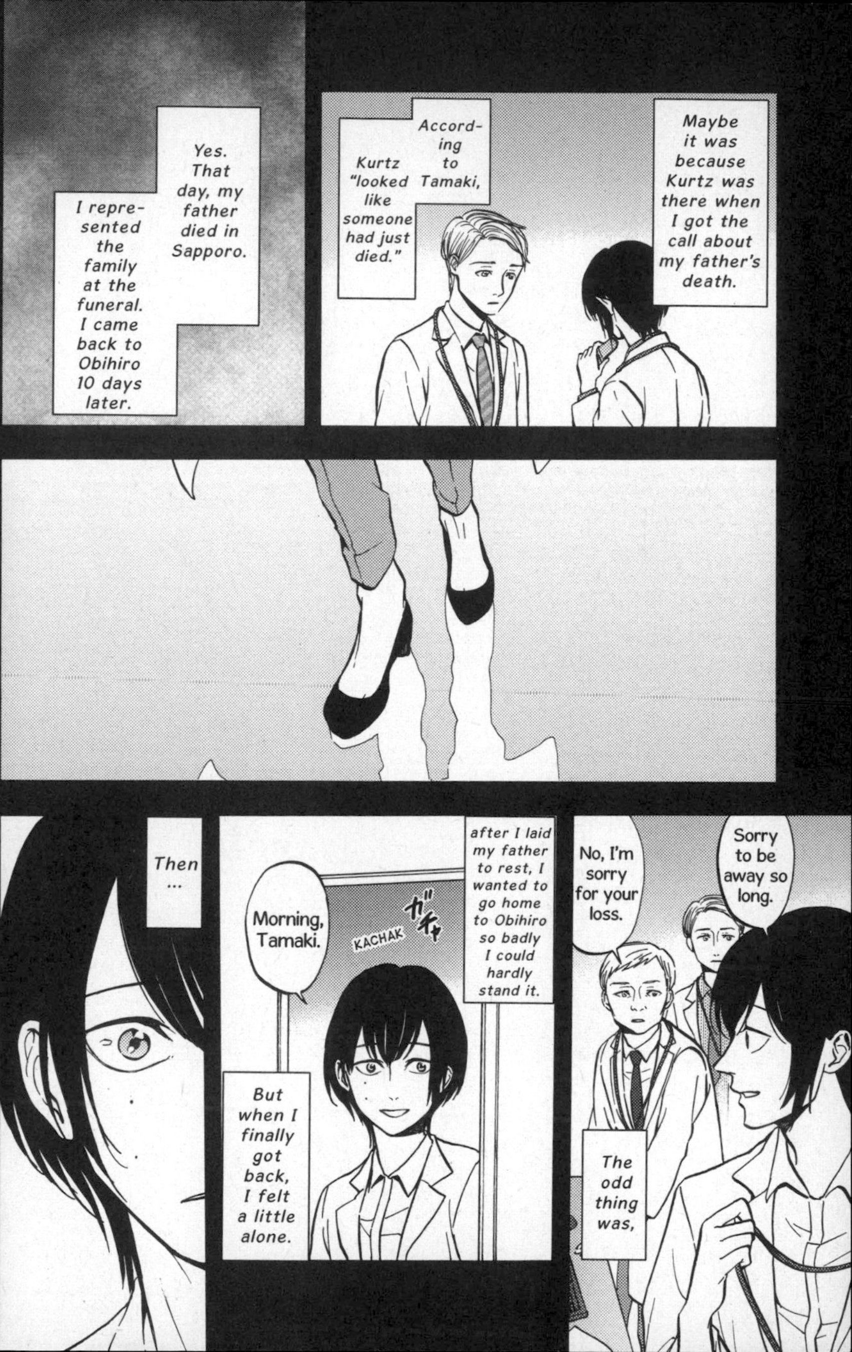
Maybe it was because Kurtz was there when I got the call about my father's death.
According to Tamaki,
Kurtz "looked like someone had just died."
Yes. That day, my father died in Sapporo.
I represented the family at the funeral. I came back to Obihiro 10 days later.
Sorry to be away so long.
No, I'm sorry for your loss.
The odd thing was,
after I laid my father to rest, I wanted to go home to Obihiro so badly I could hardly stand it.
ガチャ
KACHAK
Morning, Tamaki.
But when I finally got back, I felt a little alone.
Then ...

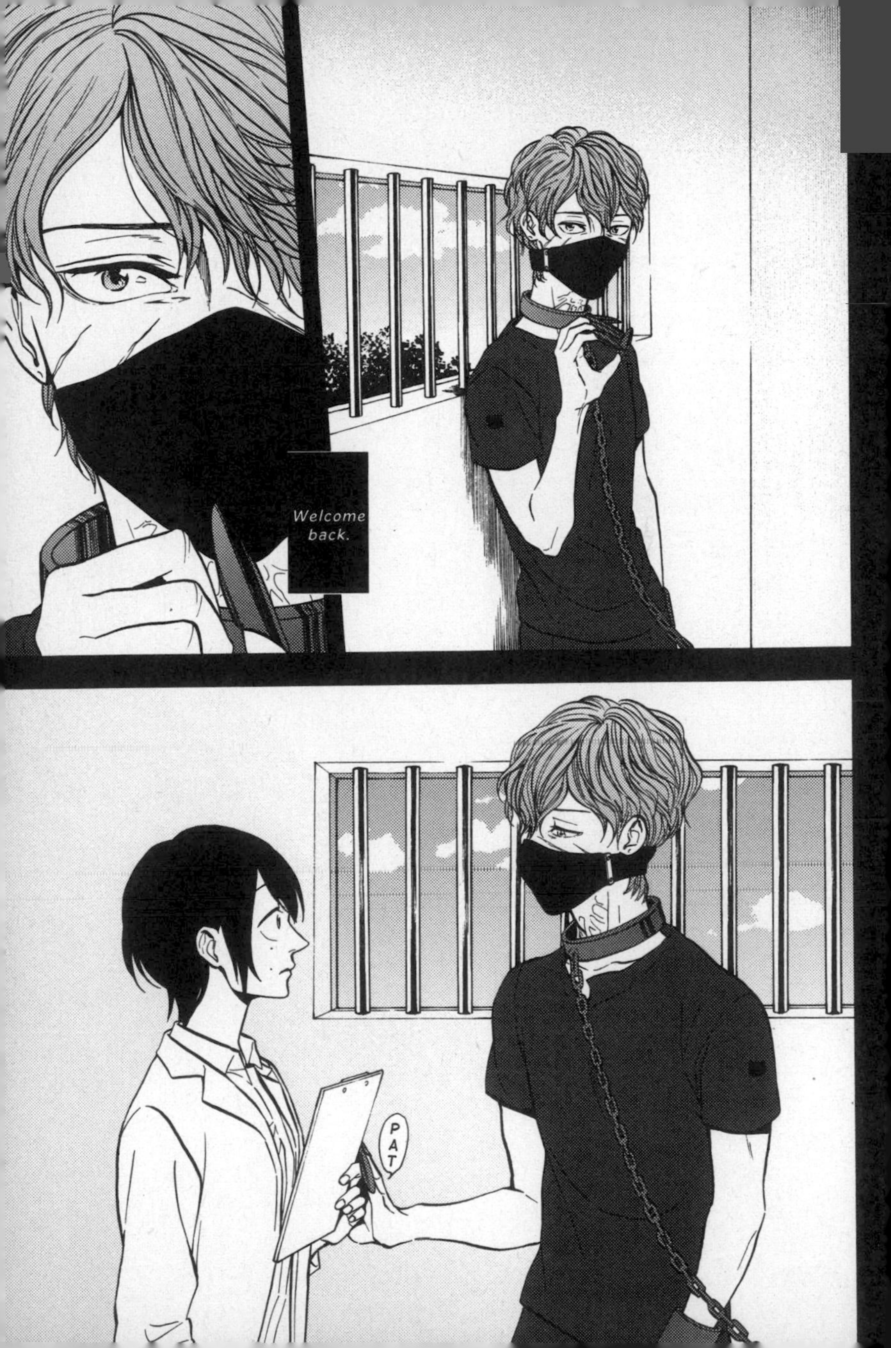
Welcome back.
PAT

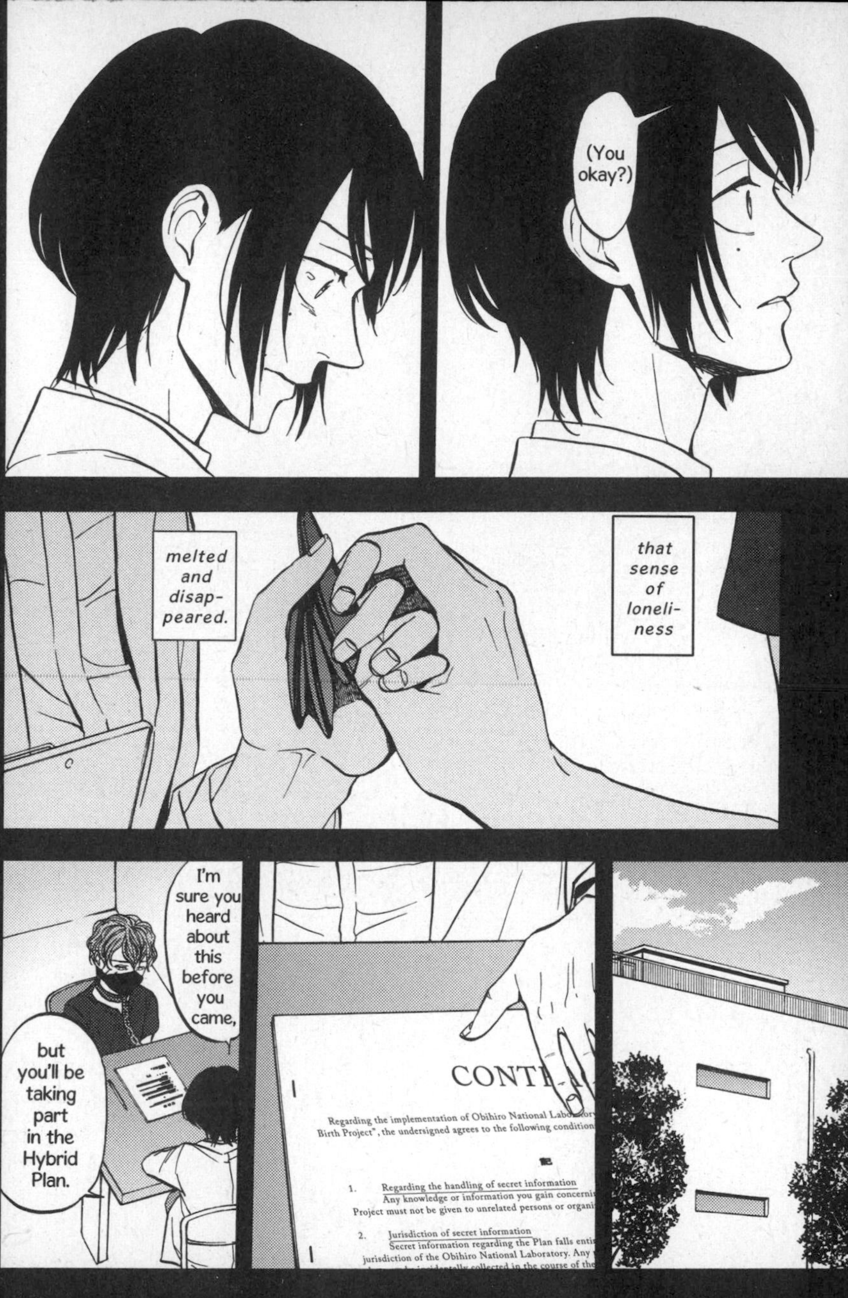
(You okay?)
that sense of loneliness
melted and disap-peared.
CONTE
Regarding the implementation of Obihiro National Laborator
Birth Project", the undersigned agrees to the following condition
1. Regarding the handling of secret information
Any knowledge or information you gain concerni
Project must not be given to unrelated persons or organi
2. Jurisdiction of secret information
Secret information regarding the Plan falls enti
jurisdiction of the Obihiro National Laboratory. Any
I'm sure you heard about this before you came,
but you'll be taking part in the Hybrid Plan.

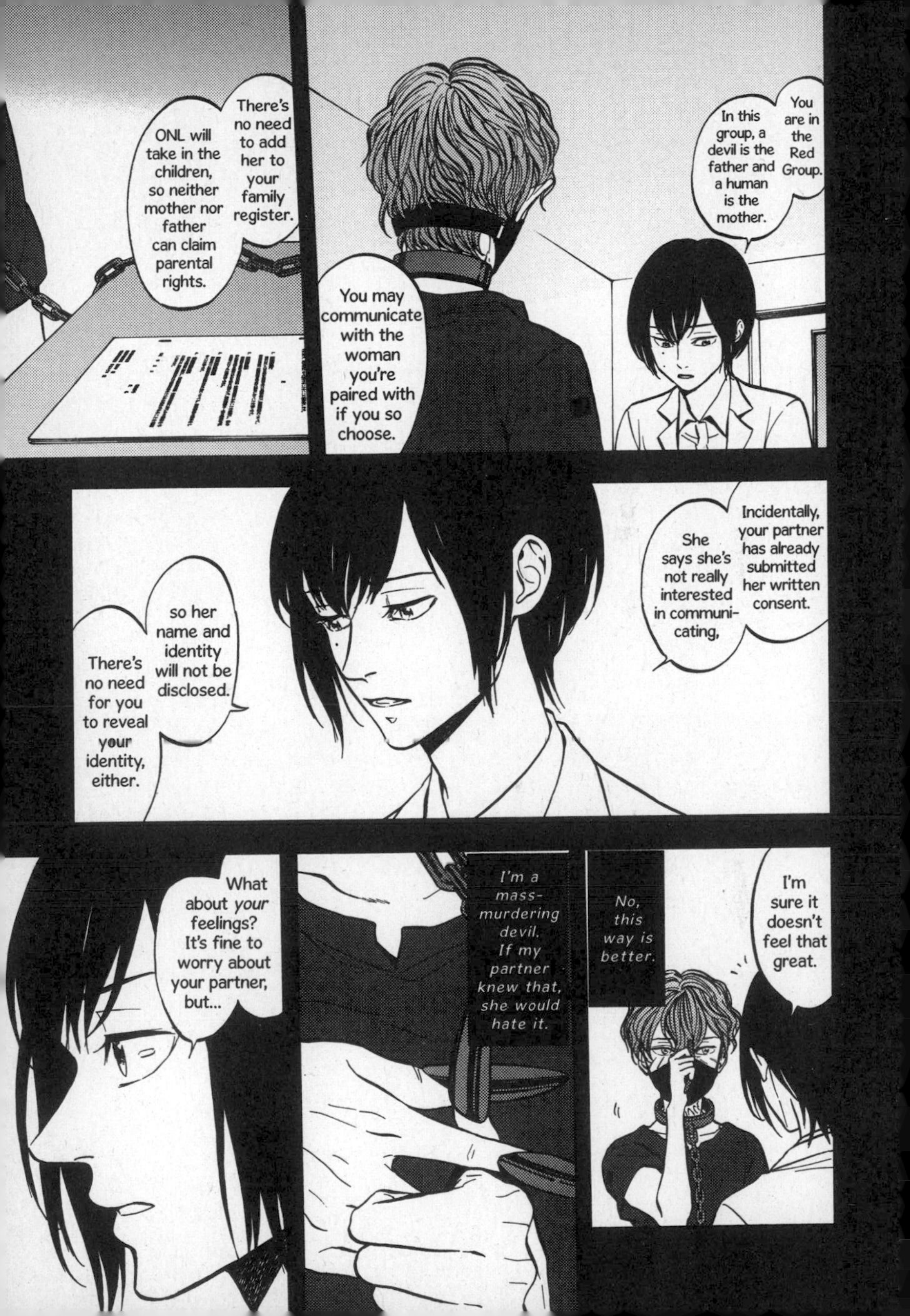
You are in the Red Group.
In this group, a devil is the father and a human is the mother.
You may communicate with the woman you're paired with if you so choose.
There's no need to add her to your family register.
ONL will take in the children, so neither mother nor father can claim parental rights.
Incidentally, your partner has already submitted her written consent.
She says she's not really interested in communicating,
so her name and identity will not be disclosed.
There's no need for you to reveal *your* identity, either.
I'm sure it doesn't feel that great.
No, this way is better.
I'm a mass-murdering devil. If my partner knew that, she would hate it.
What about *your* feelings? It's fine to worry about your partner, but...

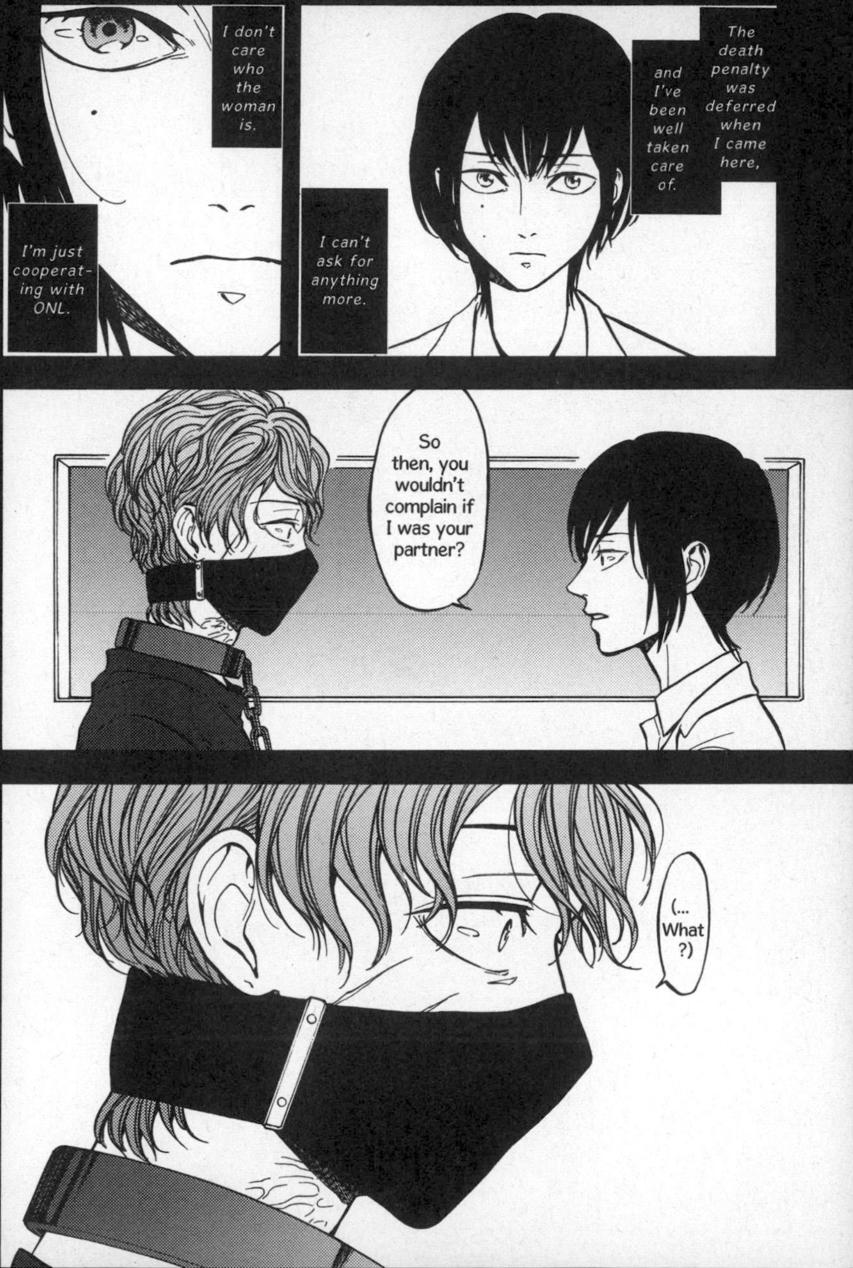
The death penalty was deferred when I came here,
and I've been well taken care of.
I can't ask for anything more.
I don't care who the woman is.
I'm just cooperating with ONL.
So then, you wouldn't complain if I was your partner?
(... What?)

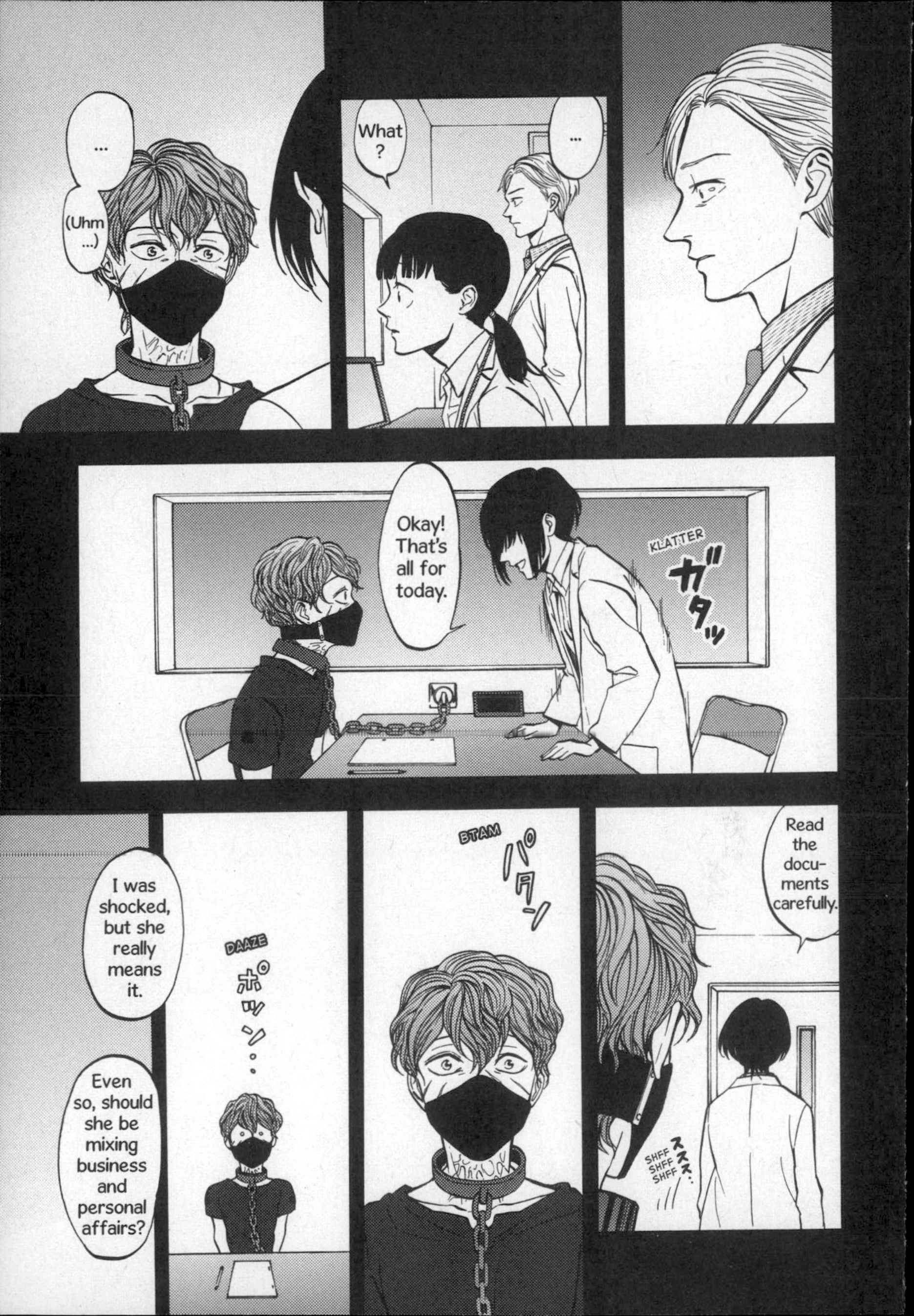
...
What?
...
(Uhm ...)
Okay! That's all for today.
KLATTER
ガタッ
Read the documents carefully.
SHFF SHFF SHFF
ススス…
BTAM
パタン
I was shocked, but she really means it.
DAAZE
ポツン。。
Even so, should she be mixing business and personal affairs?

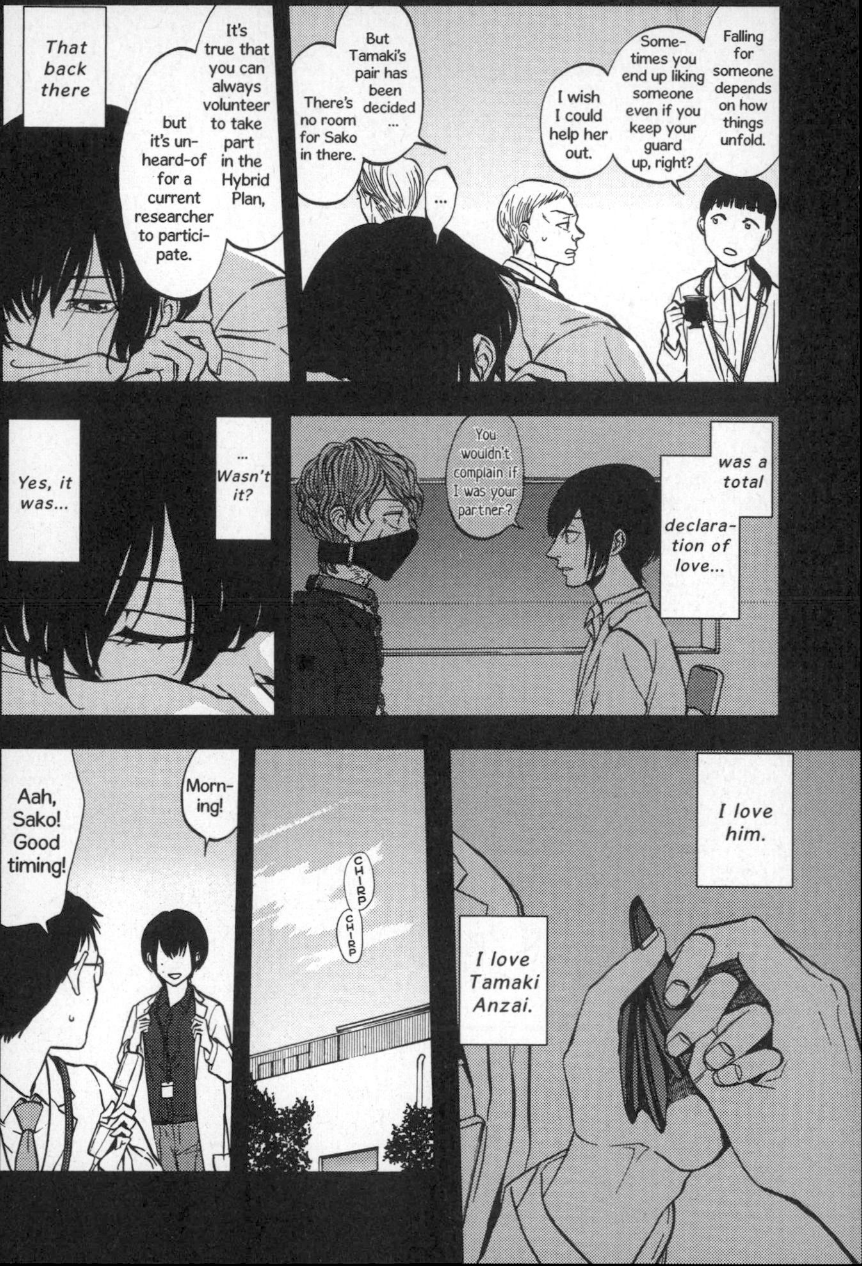

Falling for someone depends on how things unfold.
Sometimes you end up liking someone even if you keep your guard up, right?
I wish I could help her out.
But Tamaki's pair has been decided ...
There's no room for Sako in there.
...
It's true that you can always volunteer to take part in the Hybrid Plan,
but it's unheard-of for a current researcher to participate.
That back there
was a total
declaration of love...
You wouldn't complain if I was your partner?
... Wasn't it?
Yes, it was...
I love him.
I love Tamaki Anzai.
CHIRP
CHIRP
Morning!
Aah, Sako! Good timing!

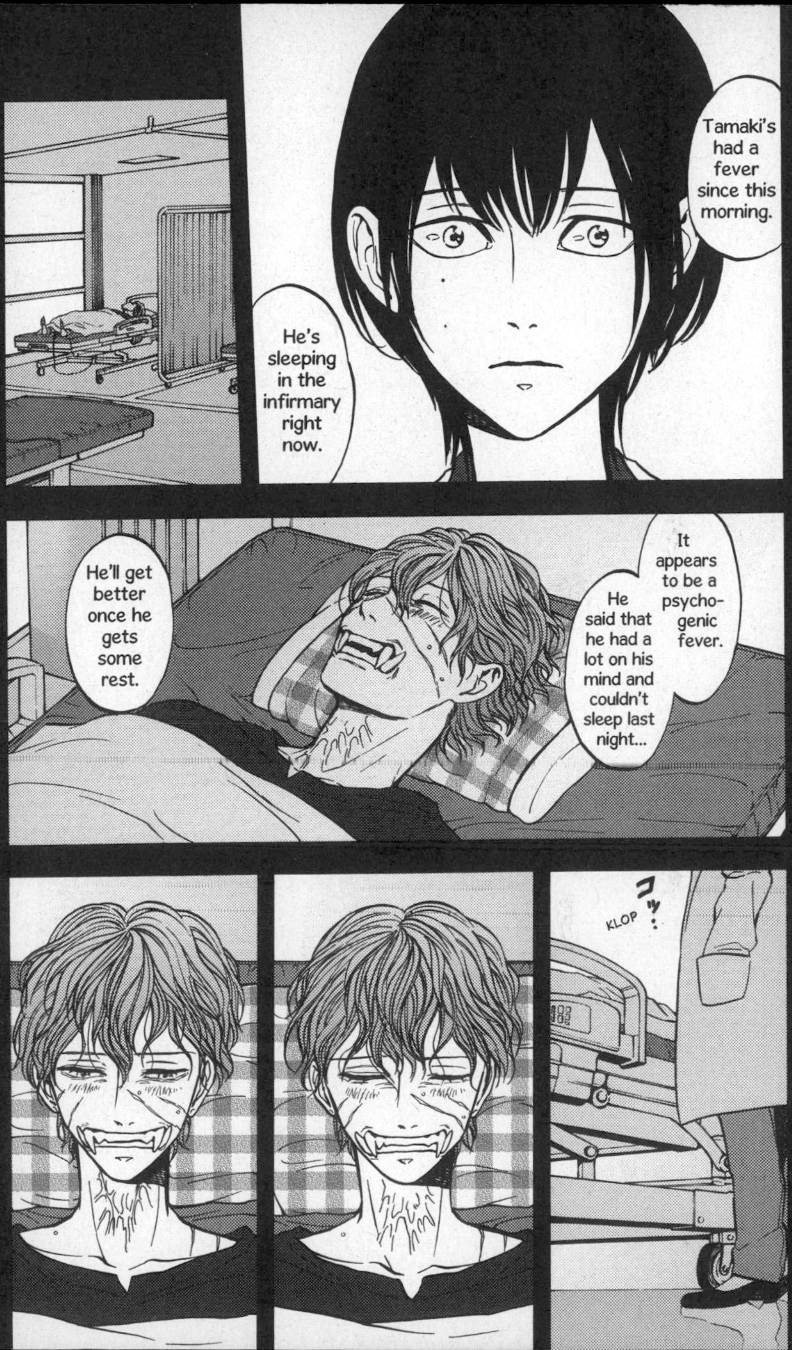
Tamaki's had a fever since this morning.
He's sleeping in the infirmary right now.
It appears to be a psycho-genic fever.
He said that he had a lot on his mind and couldn't sleep last night...
He'll get better once he gets some rest.
コッ
KLOP

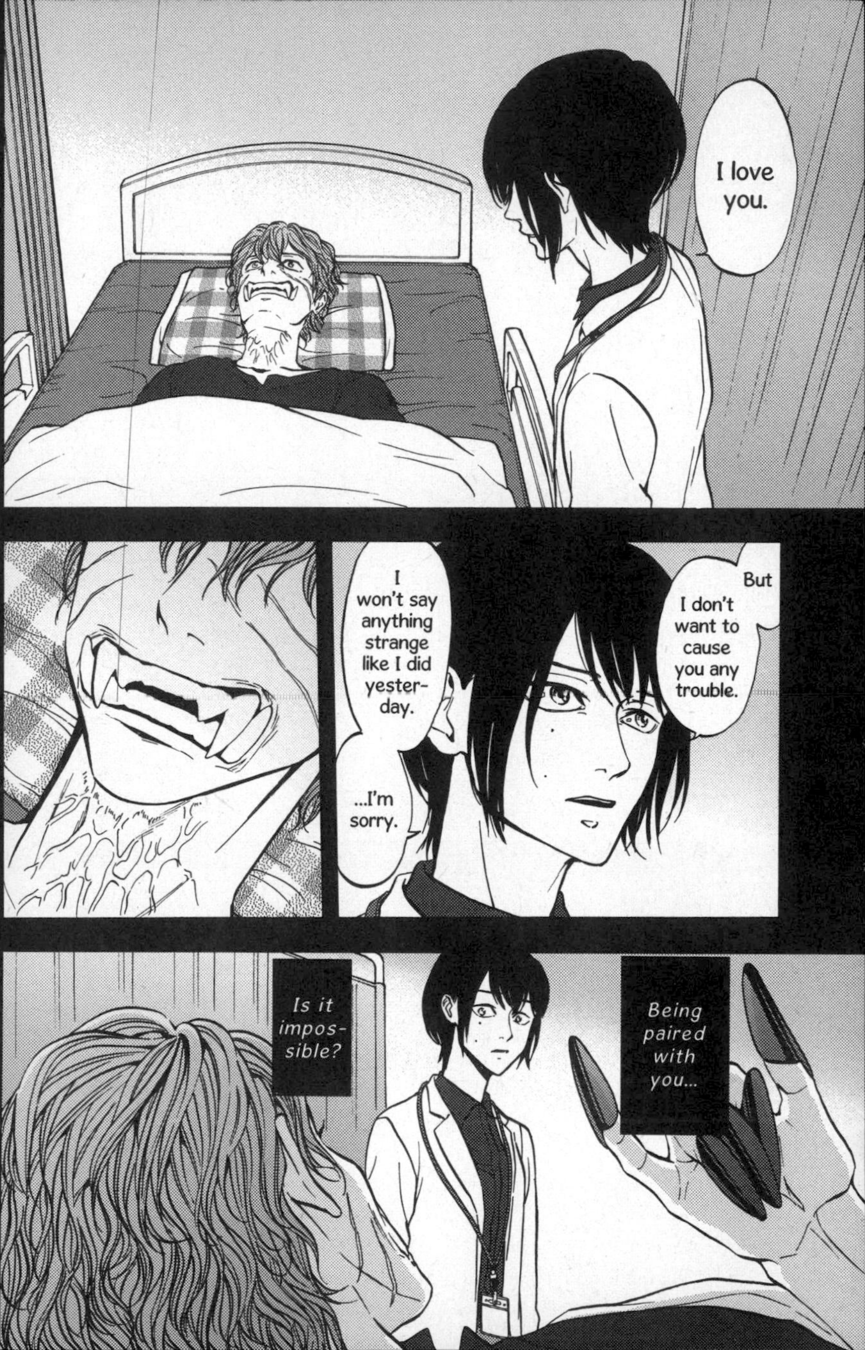

I love you.
But I don't want to cause you any trouble.
I won't say anything strange like I did yesterday.
...I'm sorry.
Being paired with you...
Is it impossible?

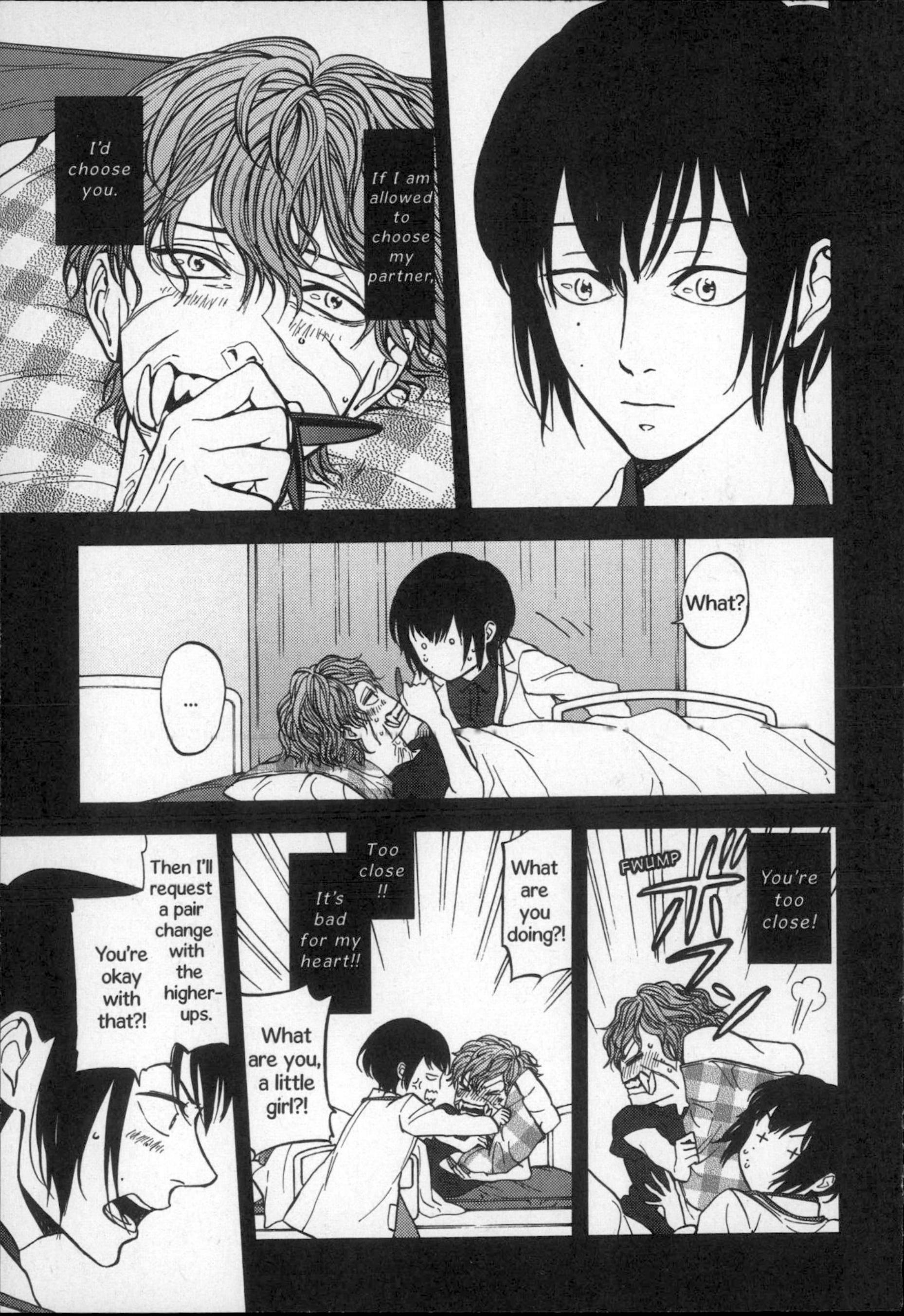
If I am allowed to choose my partner,
I'd choose you.
What?
...
You're too close!
FWUMP
What are you doing?!
Too close!!
It's bad for my heart!!
What are you, a little girl?!
Then I'll request a pair change with the higher-ups.
You're okay with that?!

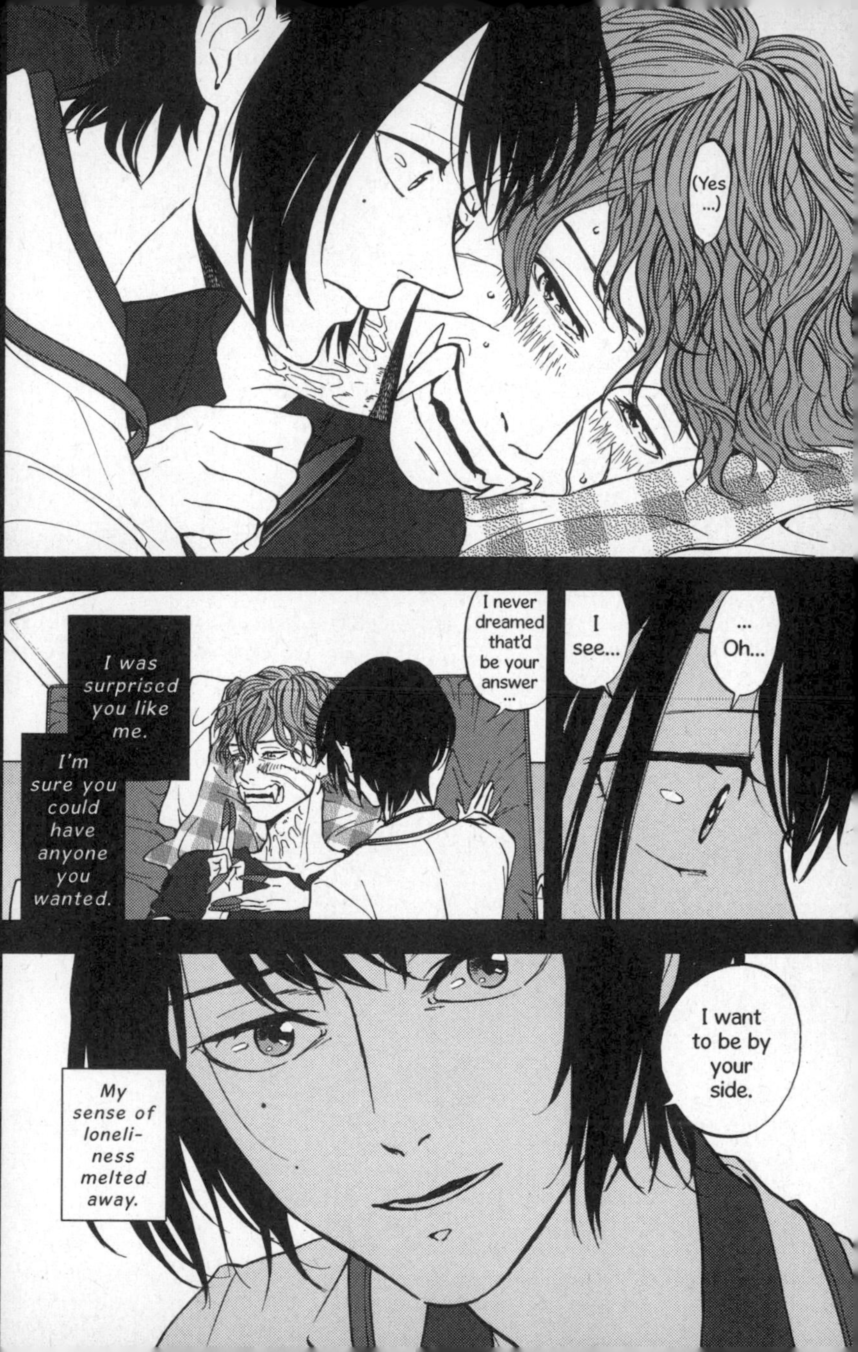
(Yes ...)
... Oh...
I see...
I never dreamed that'd be your answer ...
I was surprised you like me.
I'm sure you could have anyone you wanted.
I want to be by your side.
My sense of loneli-ness melted away.

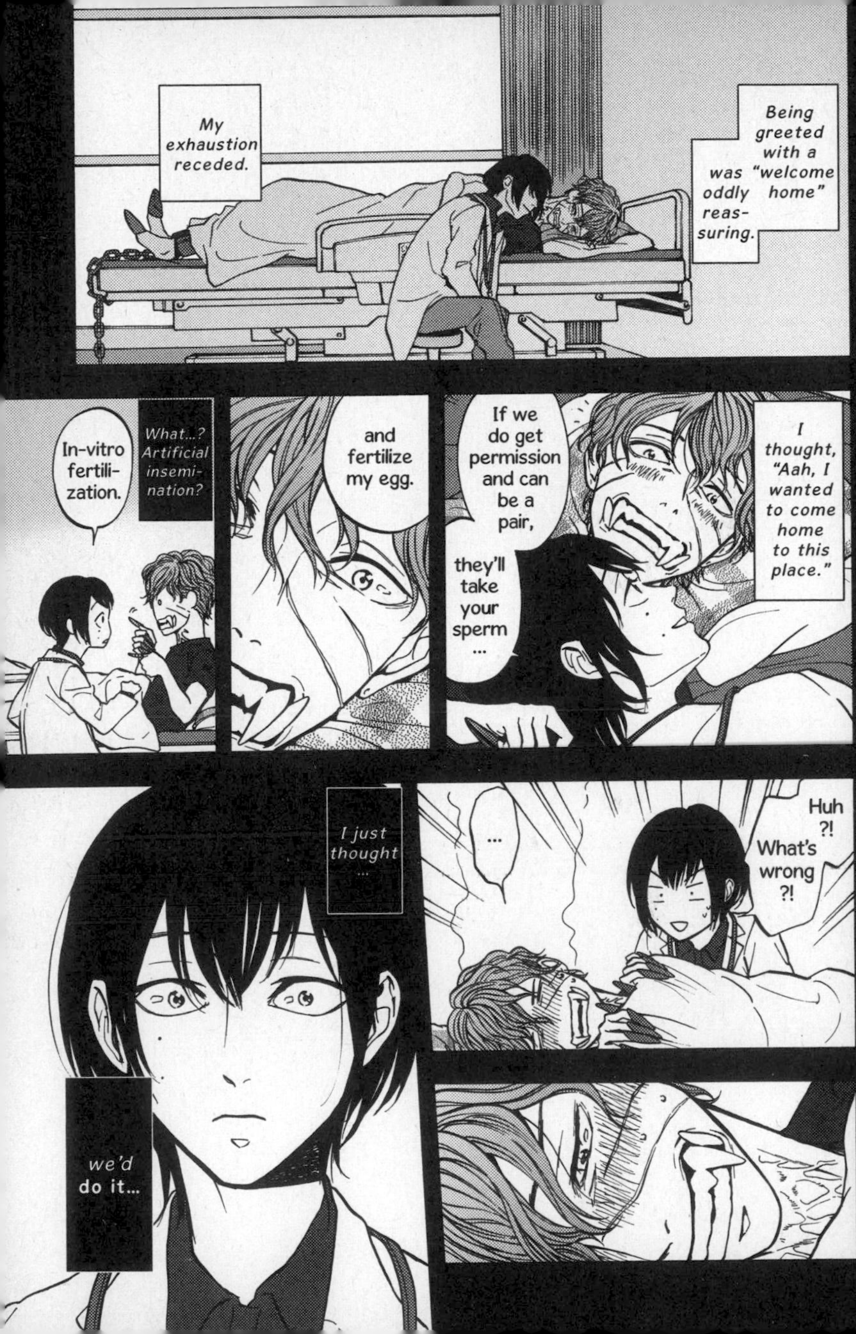
Being greeted with a "welcome home" was oddly reassuring.
My exhaustion receded.
I thought, "Aah, I wanted to come home to this place."
If we do get permission and can be a pair,
they'll take your sperm ...
and fertilize my egg.
What...? Artificial insemination?
In-vitro fertilization.
Huh?! What's wrong?!
...
I just thought ...
we'd do it...

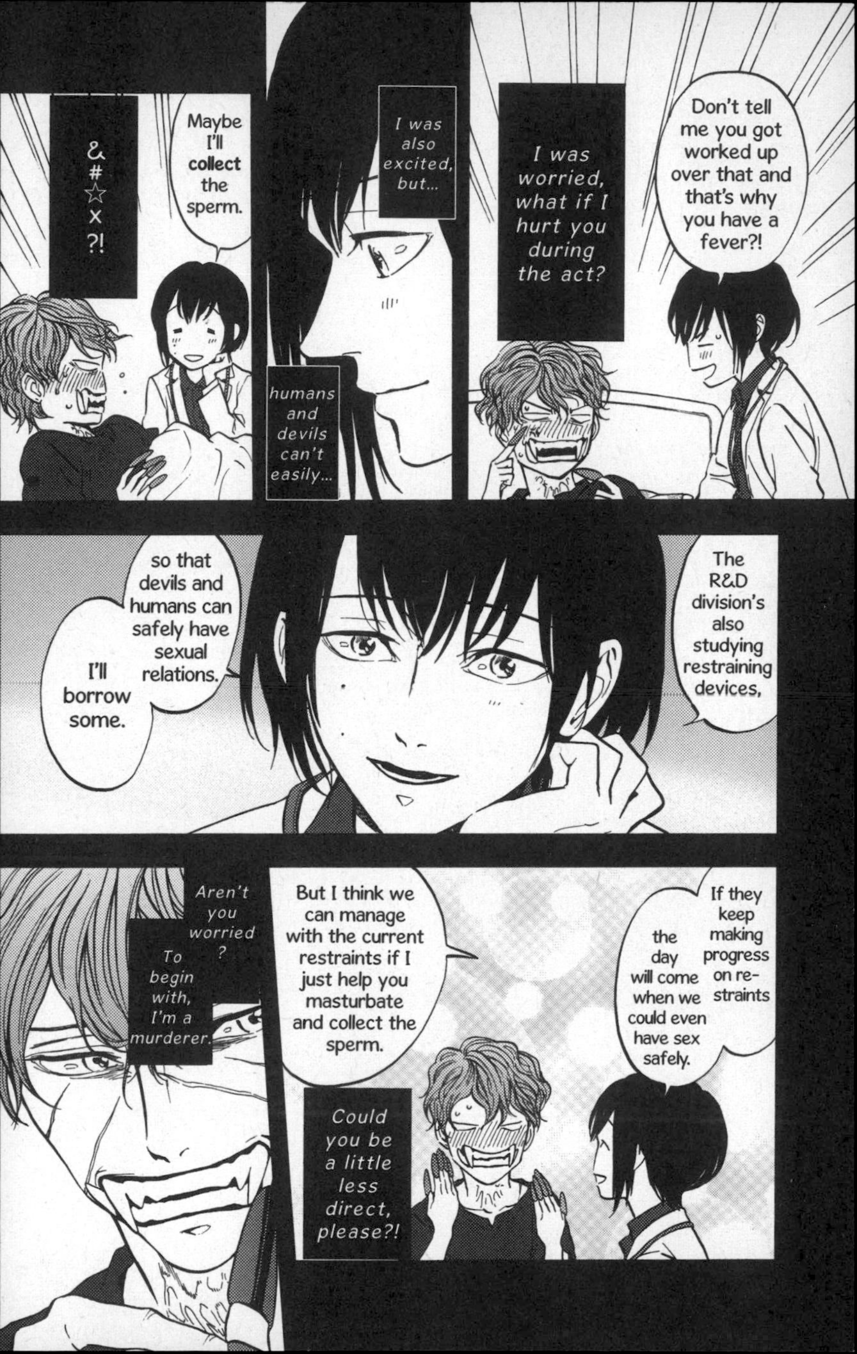
Don't tell me you got worked up over that and that's why you have a fever?!
I was worried, what if I hurt you during the act?
I was also excited, but...
humans and devils can't easily...
Maybe I'll **collect** the sperm.
&#☆×?!
The R&D division's also studying restraining devices,
so that devils and humans can safely have sexual relations.
I'll borrow some.
If they keep making progress on restraints
the day will come when we could even have sex safely.
But I think we can manage with the current restraints if I just help you masturbate and collect the sperm.
Could you be a little less direct, please?!
Aren't you worried?
To begin with, I'm a murderer.

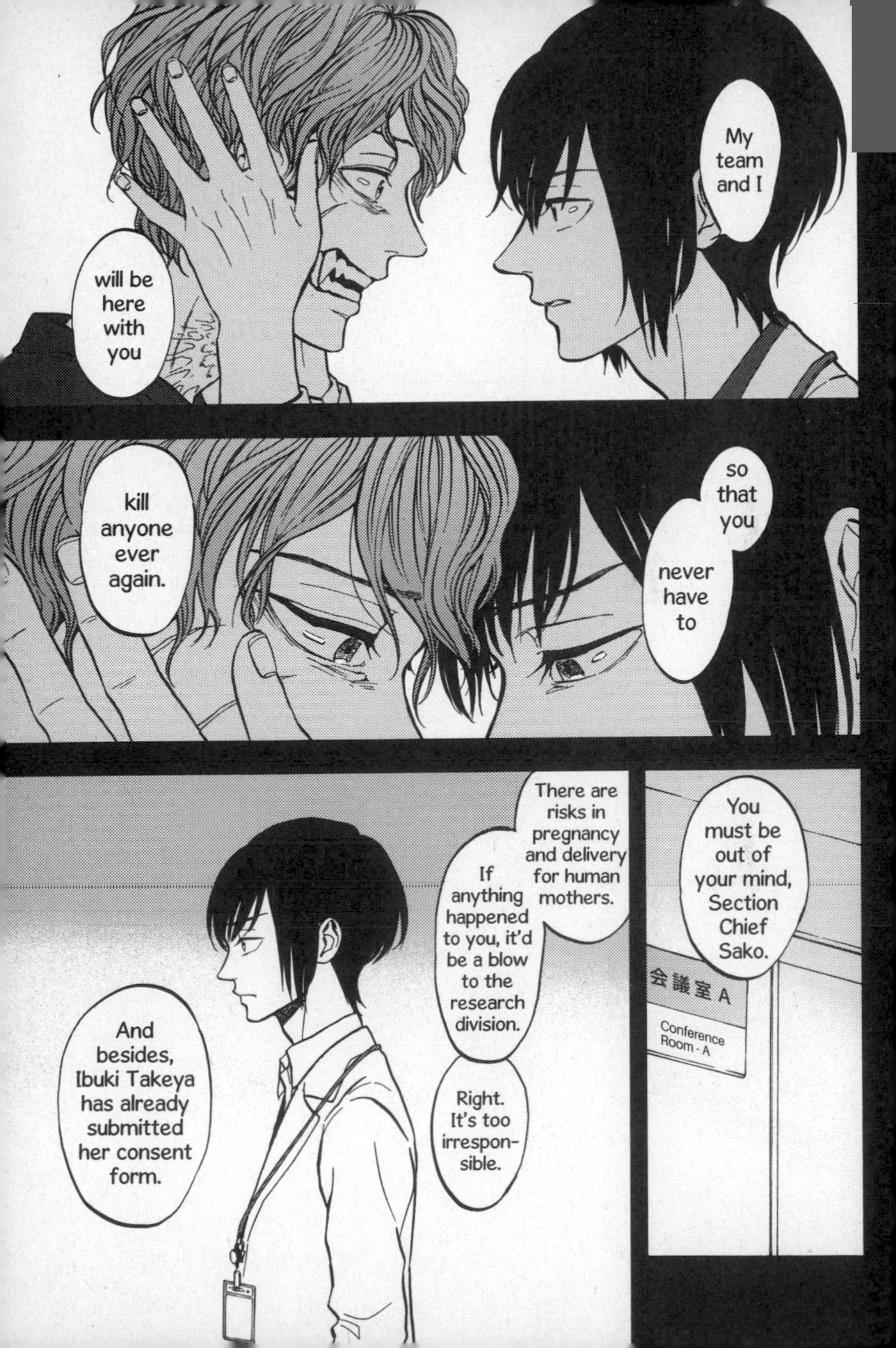
My team and I
will be here with you
so that you
never have to
kill anyone ever again.
You must be out of your mind, Section Chief Sako.
会議室A
Conference Room - A
There are risks in pregnancy and delivery for human mothers.
If anything happened to you, it'd be a blow to the research division.
Right. It's too irrespon-sible.
And besides, Ibuki Takeya has already submitted her consent form.

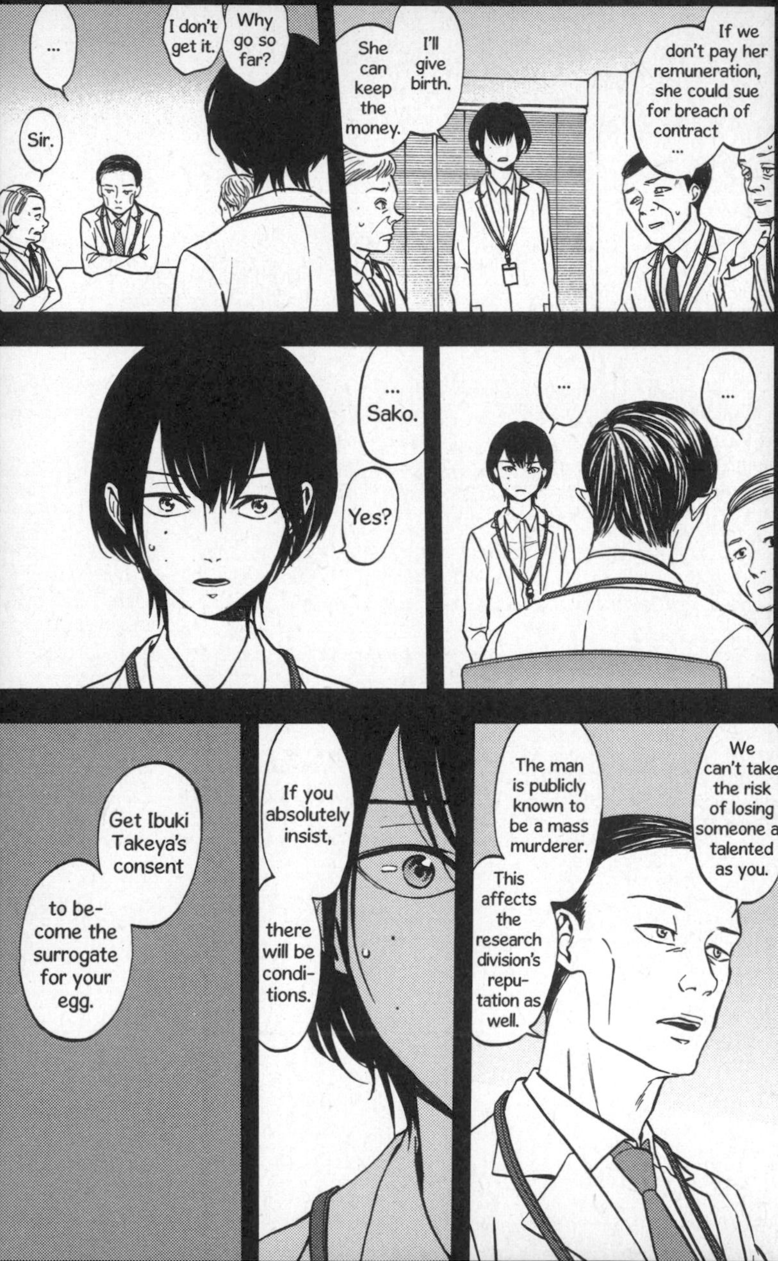
If we don't pay her remuneration, she could sue for breach of contract ...
I'll give birth.
She can keep the money.
Why go so far?
I don't get it.
...
Sir.
...
...
... Sako.
Yes?
We can't take the risk of losing someone as talented as you.
The man is publicly known to be a mass murderer.
This affects the research division's reputation as well.
If you absolutely insist,
there will be conditions.
Get Ibuki Takeya's consent
to be-come the surrogate for your egg.

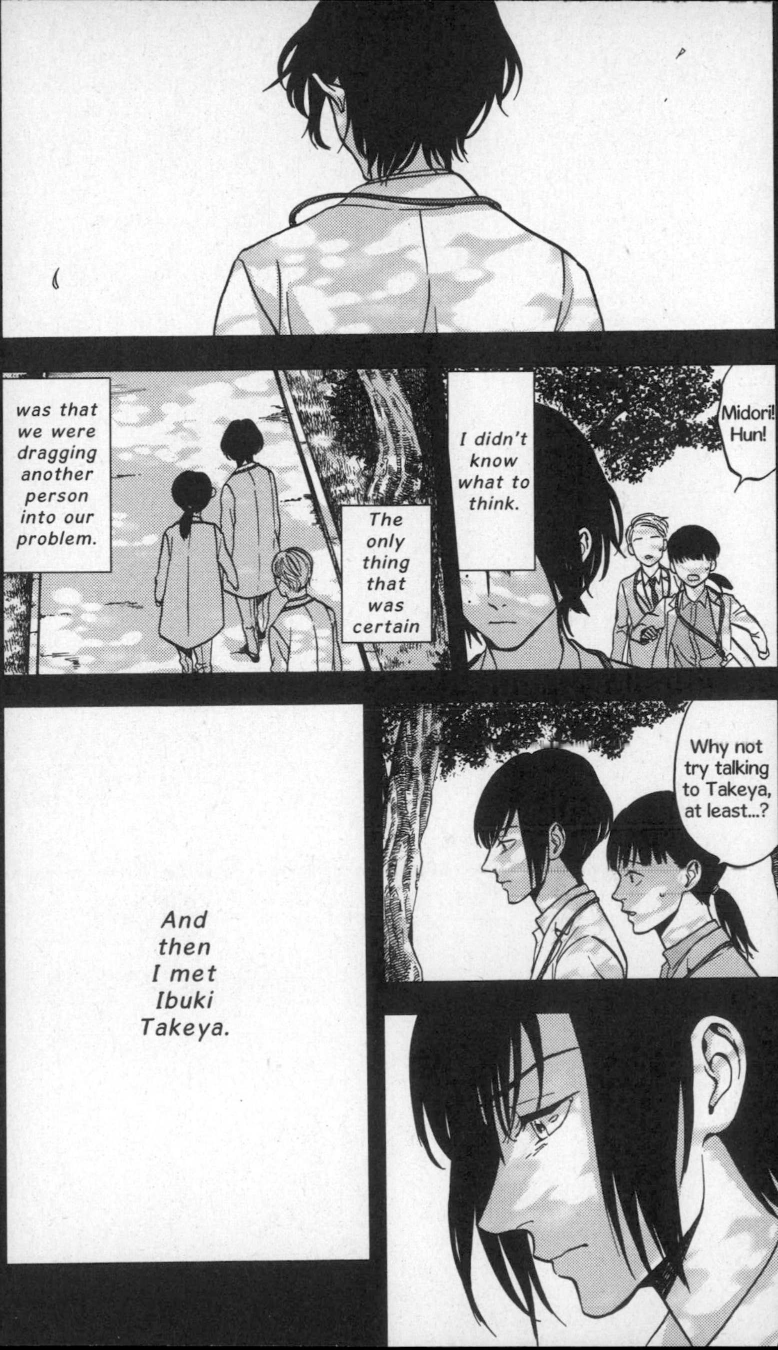

Midori! Hun!
I didn't know what to think.
The only thing that was certain
was that we were dragging another person into our problem.
Why not try talking to Takeya, at least...?
And then I met Ibuki Takeya.

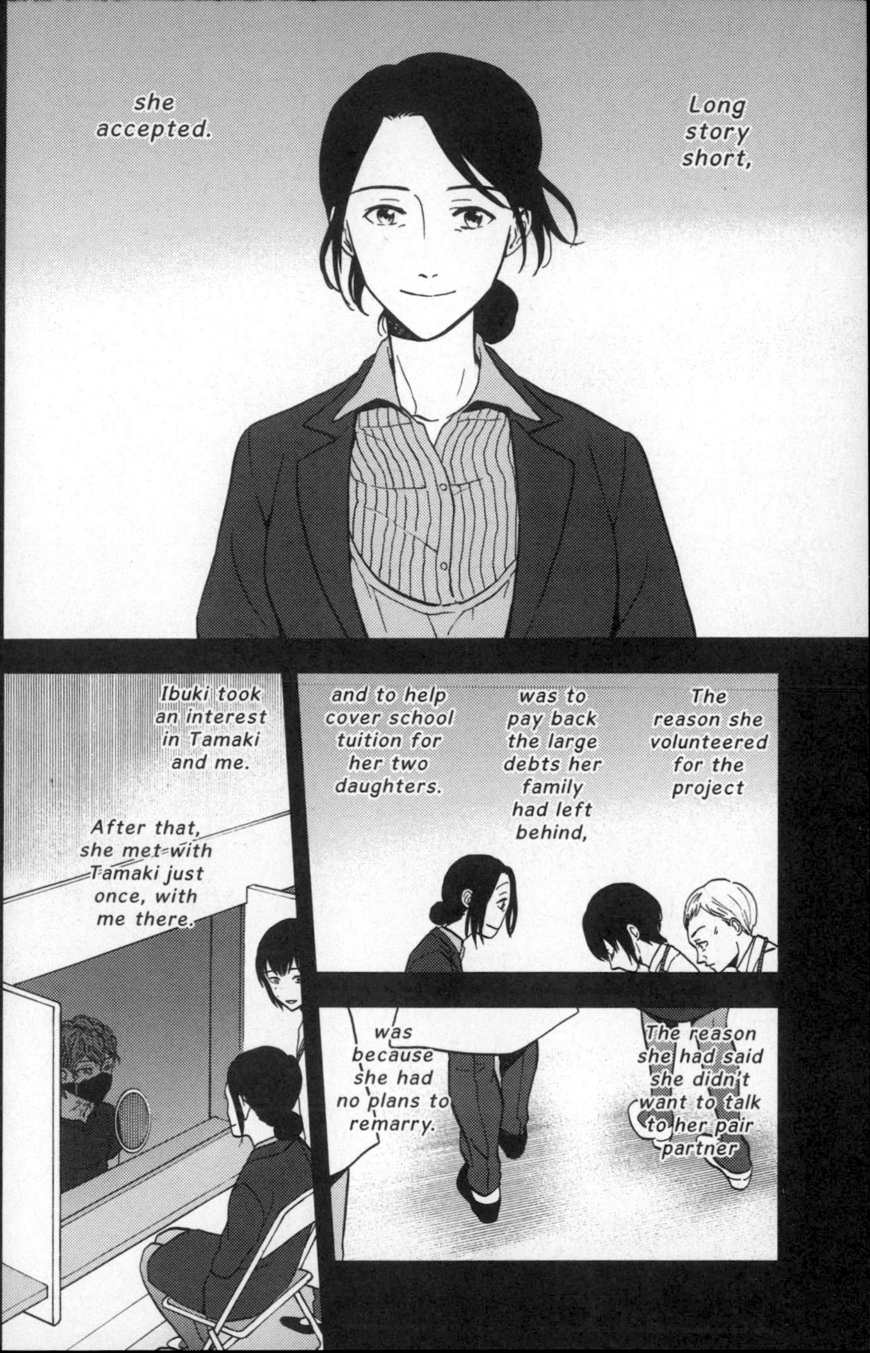
Long story short,
she accepted.
The reason she volunteered for the project
was to pay back the large debts her family had left behind,
and to help cover school tuition for her two daughters.
The reason she had said she didn't want to talk to her pair partner
was because she had no plans to remarry.
Ibuki took an interest in Tamaki and me.
After that, she met with Tamaki just once, with me there.

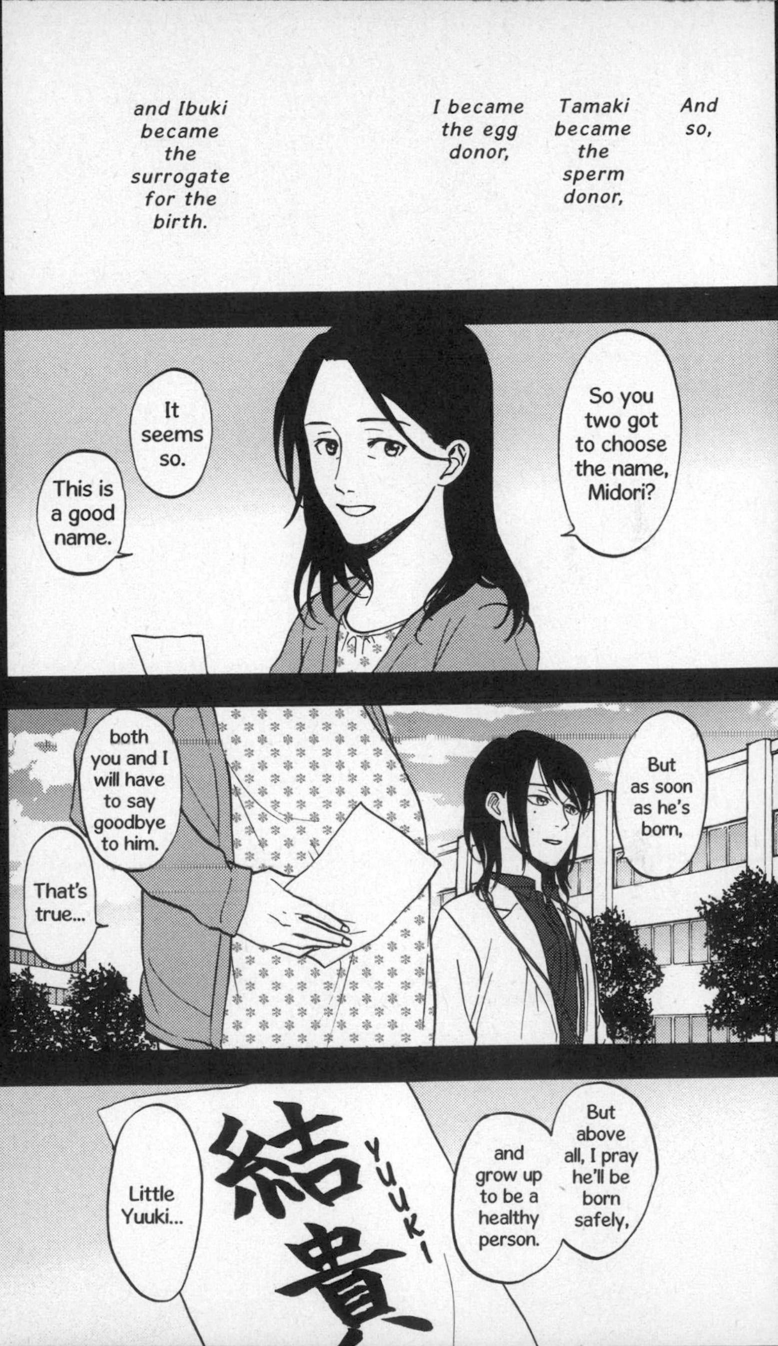
And so,
Tamaki became the sperm donor,
I became the egg donor,
and Ibuki became the surrogate for the birth.
So you two got to choose the name, Midori?
It seems so.
This is a good name.
But as soon as he's born,
both you and I will have to say goodbye to him.
That's true...
But above all, I pray he'll be born safely,
and grow up to be a healthy person.
結貴
YUUKI
Little Yuuki...

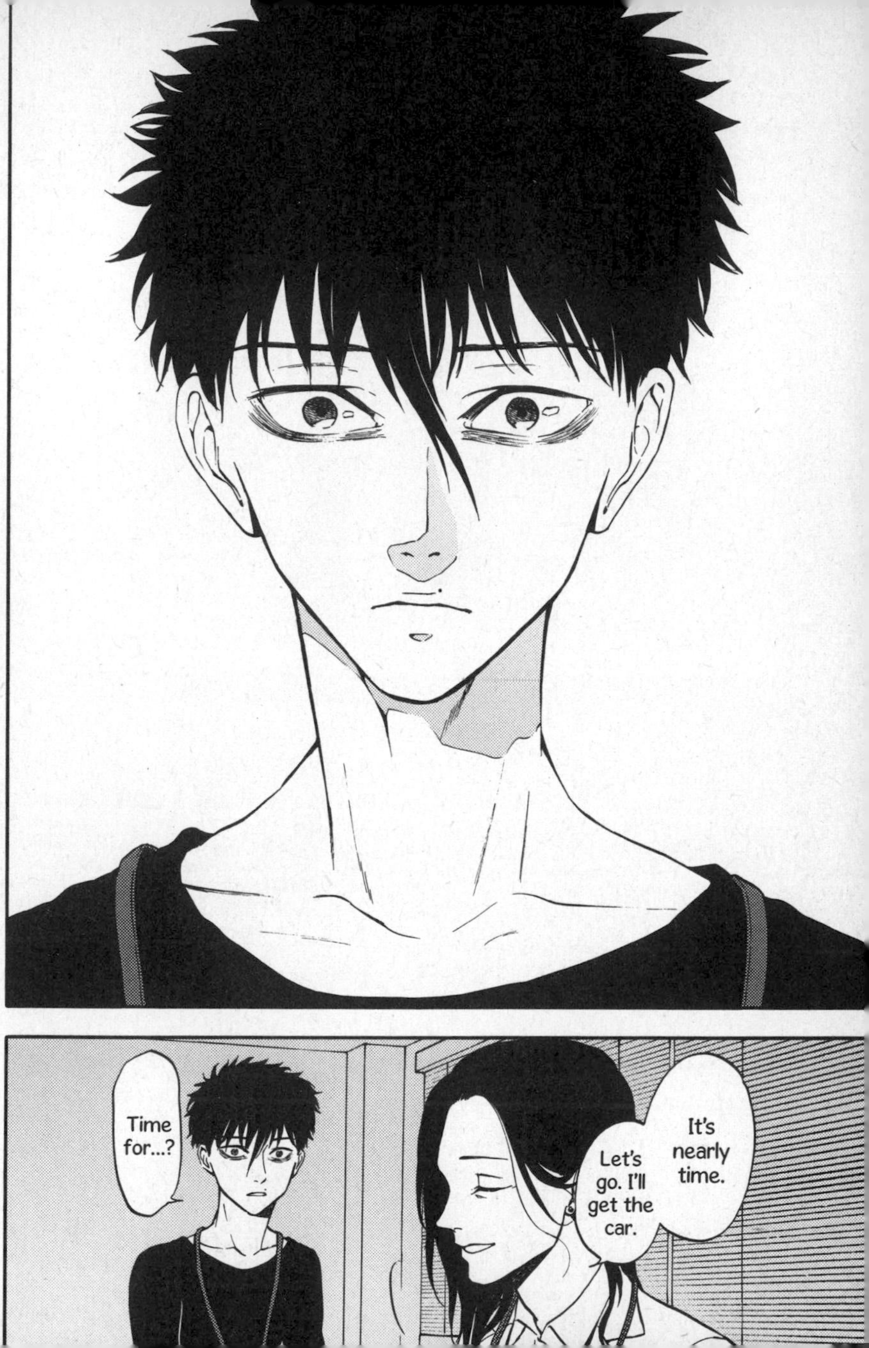
It's nearly time.
Let's go. I'll get the car.
Time for...?

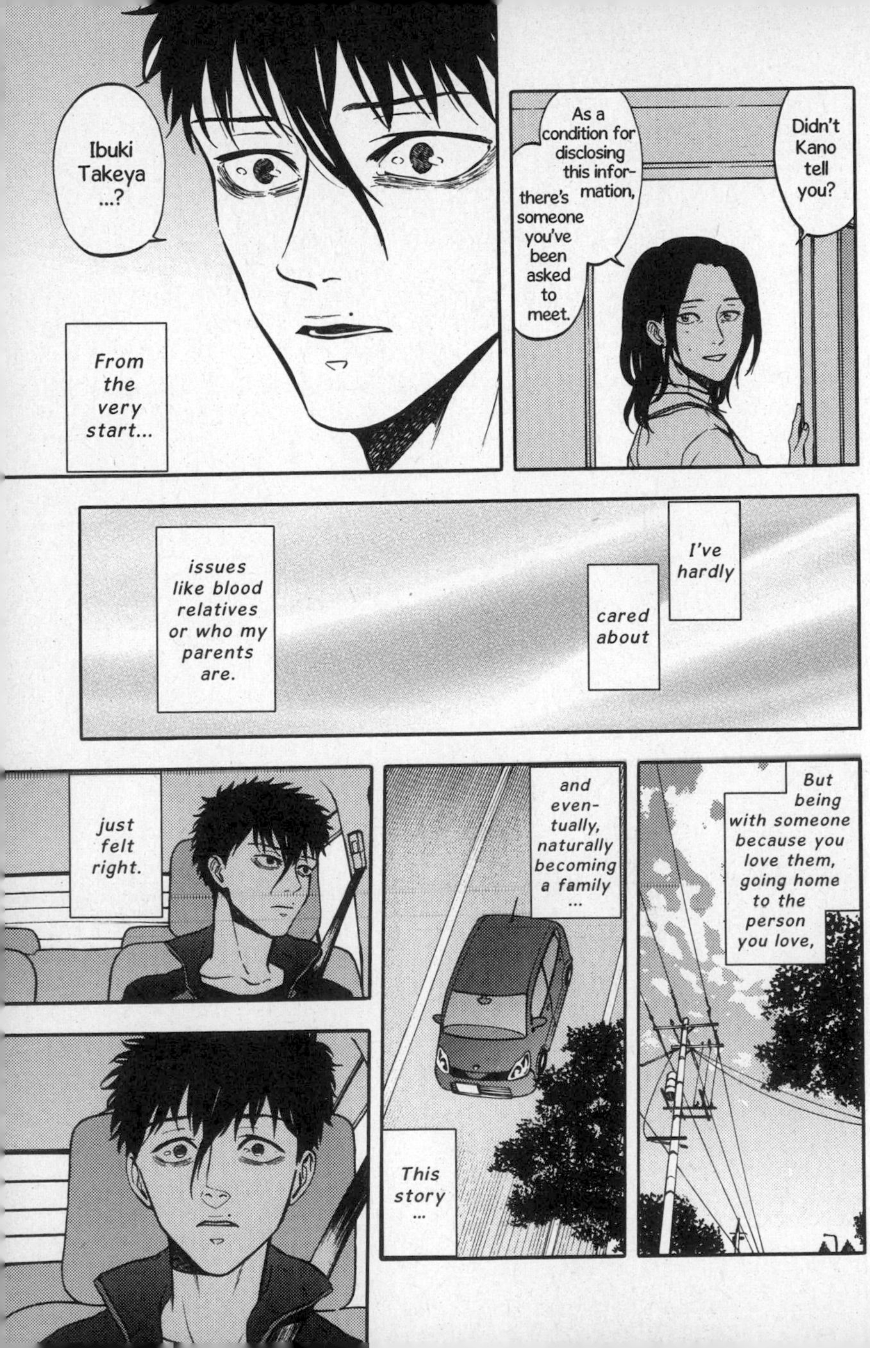
Didn't Kano tell you?
As a condition for disclosing this information, there's someone you've been asked to meet.
Ibuki Takeya ...?
From the very start...
I've hardly
cared about
issues like blood relatives or who my parents are.
But being with someone because you love them, going home to the person you love,
and eventually, naturally becoming a family ...
This story ...
just felt right.

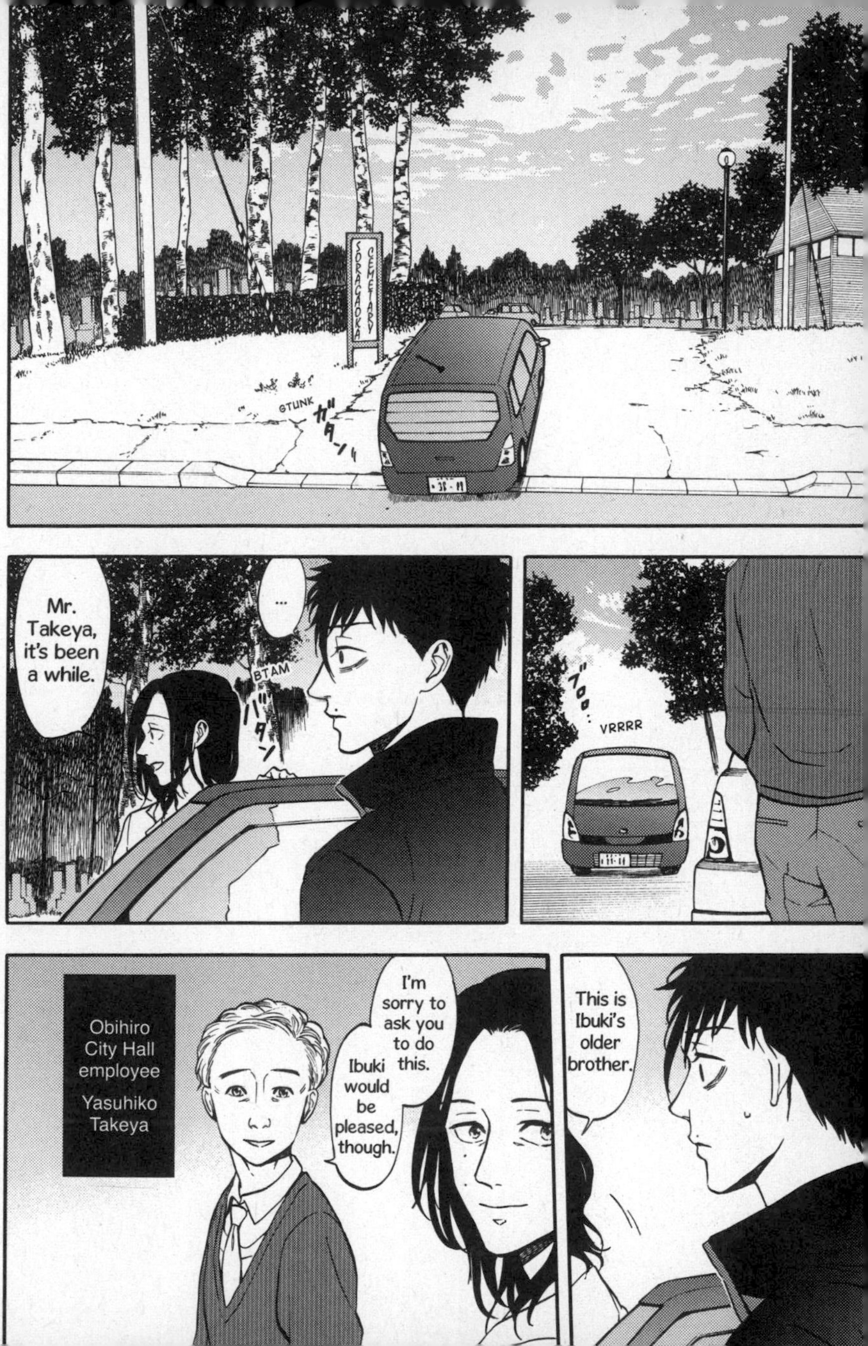
SORAGAOKA CEMETARY
GTUNK
ガタン
VRRRR
ブロロ…
...
BTAM
バタン
Mr. Takeya, it's been a while.
This is Ibuki's older brother.
I'm sorry to ask you to do this.
Ibuki would be pleased, though.
Obihiro City Hall employee
Yasuhiko Takeya

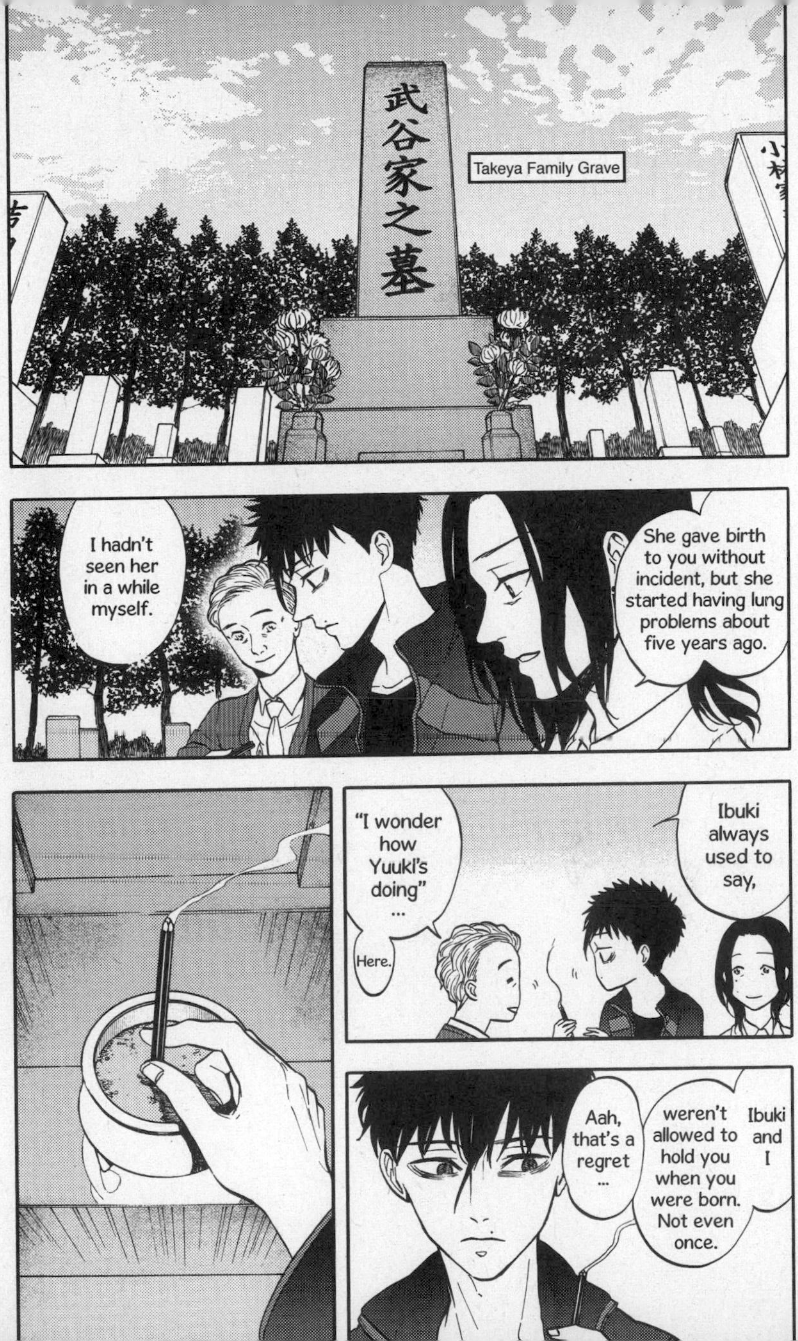
武谷家之墓
Takeya Family Grave
She gave birth to you without incident, but she started having lung problems about five years ago.
I hadn't seen her in a while myself.
Ibuki always used to say,
"I wonder how Yuuki's doing" ...
Here.
Ibuki and I
weren't allowed to hold you when you were born. Not even once.
Aah, that's a regret ...

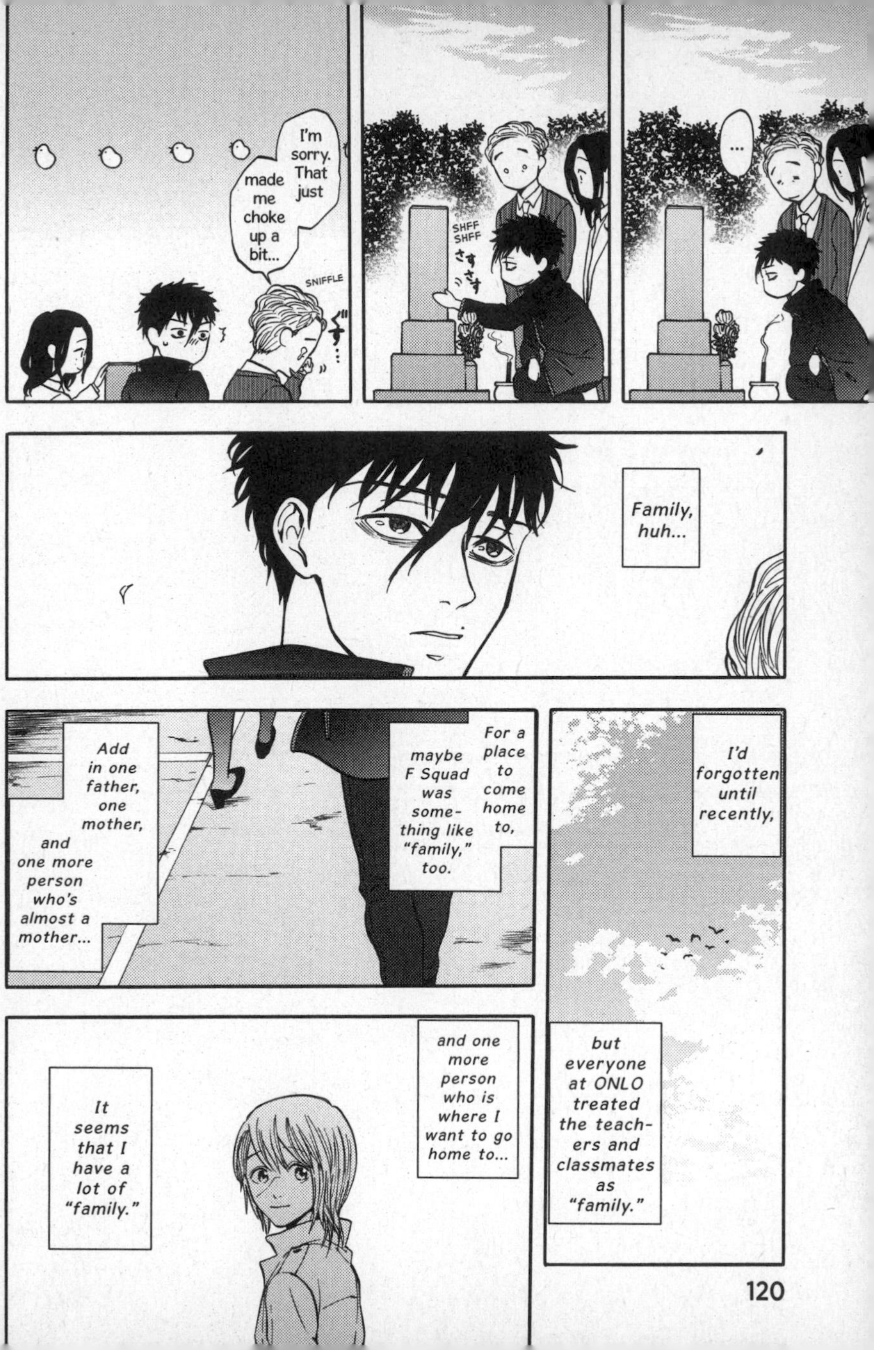
...
SHFF SHFF
さすさす
I'm sorry. That just made me choke up a bit...
SNIFFLE
ぐす...
Family, huh...
I'd forgotten until recently,
but everyone at ONLO treated the teachers and classmates as "family."
For a place to come home to,
maybe F Squad was something like "family," too.
Add in one father, one mother,
and one more person who's almost a mother...
and one more person who is where I want to go home to...
It seems that I have a lot of "family."

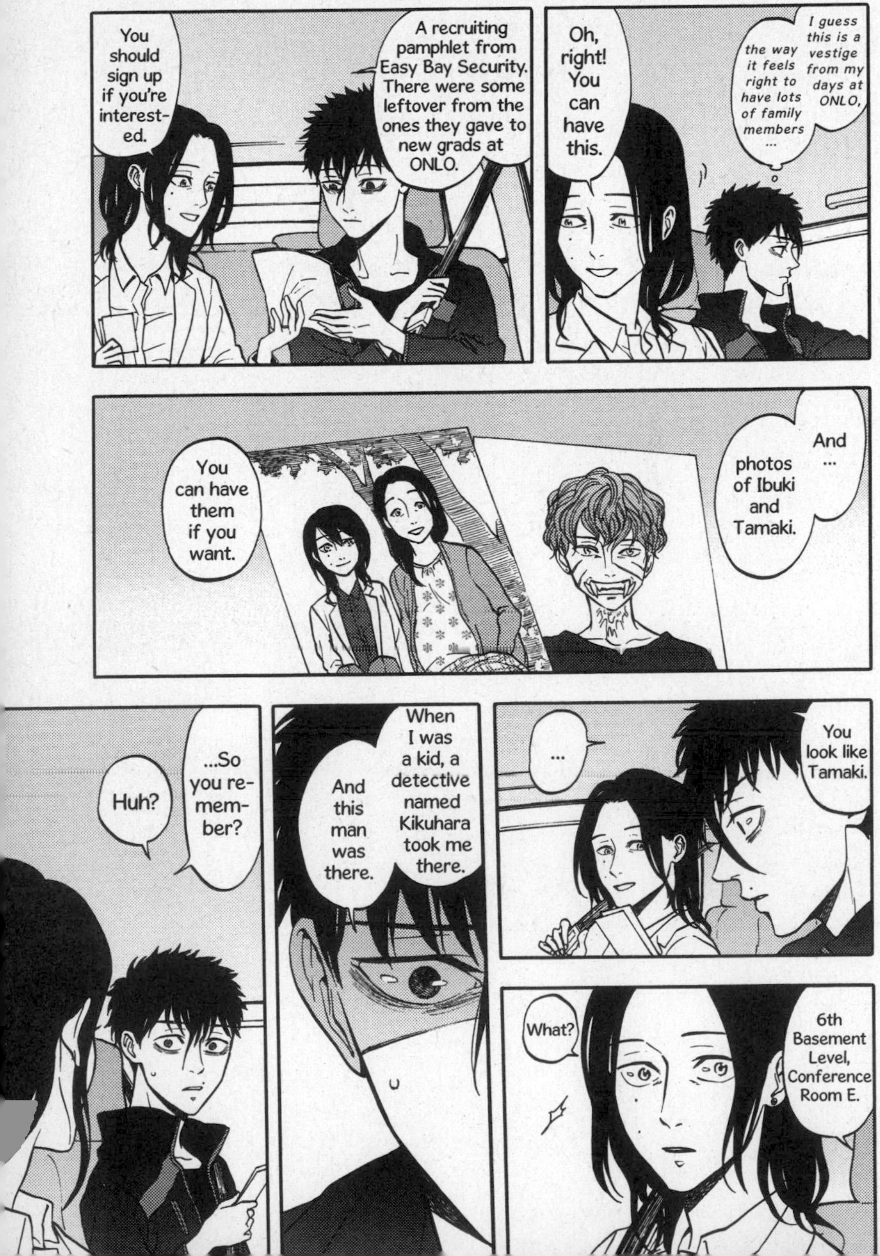
Oh, right! You can have this.
I guess this is a vestige from my days at ONLO,
the way it feels right to have lots of family members ...
A recruiting pamphlet from Easy Bay Security. There were some leftover from the ones they gave to new grads at ONLO.
You should sign up if you're interest-ed.
And ...
photos of Ibuki and Tamaki.
You can have them if you want.
You look like Tamaki.
...
6th Basement Level, Conference Room E.
What?
When I was a kid, a detective named Kikuhara took me there.
And this man was there.
...So you re-mem-ber?
Huh?

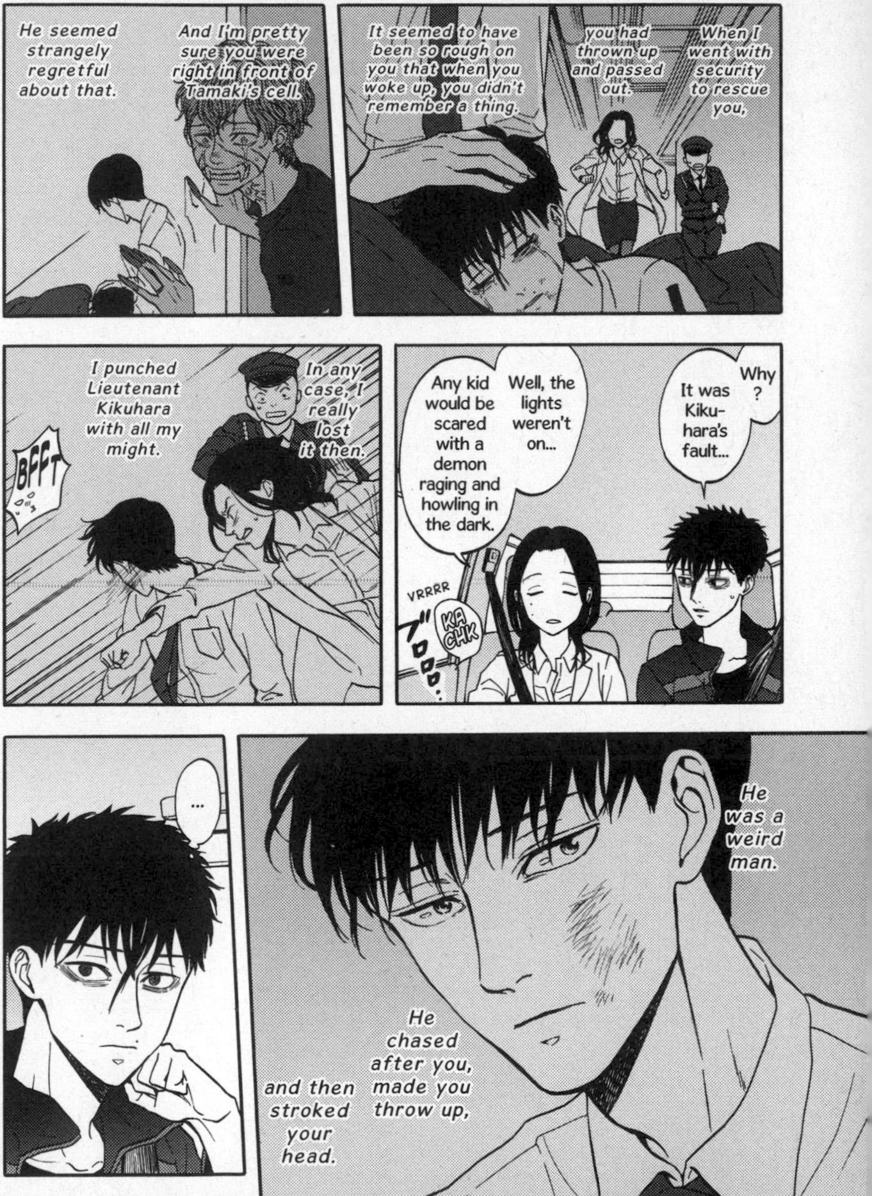
When I went with security to rescue you,
you had thrown up and passed out.
It seemed to have been so rough on you that when you woke up, you didn't remember a thing.
And I'm pretty sure you were right in front of Tamaki's cell.
He seemed strangely regretful about that.
Why?
It was Kikuhara's fault...
Well, the lights weren't on...
Any kid would be scared with a demon raging and howling in the dark.
VRRRR
KA CHK
In any case, I really lost it then.
I punched Lieutenant Kikuhara with all my might.
BFFT
He was a weird man.
He chased after you, made you throw up,
and then stroked your head.
...

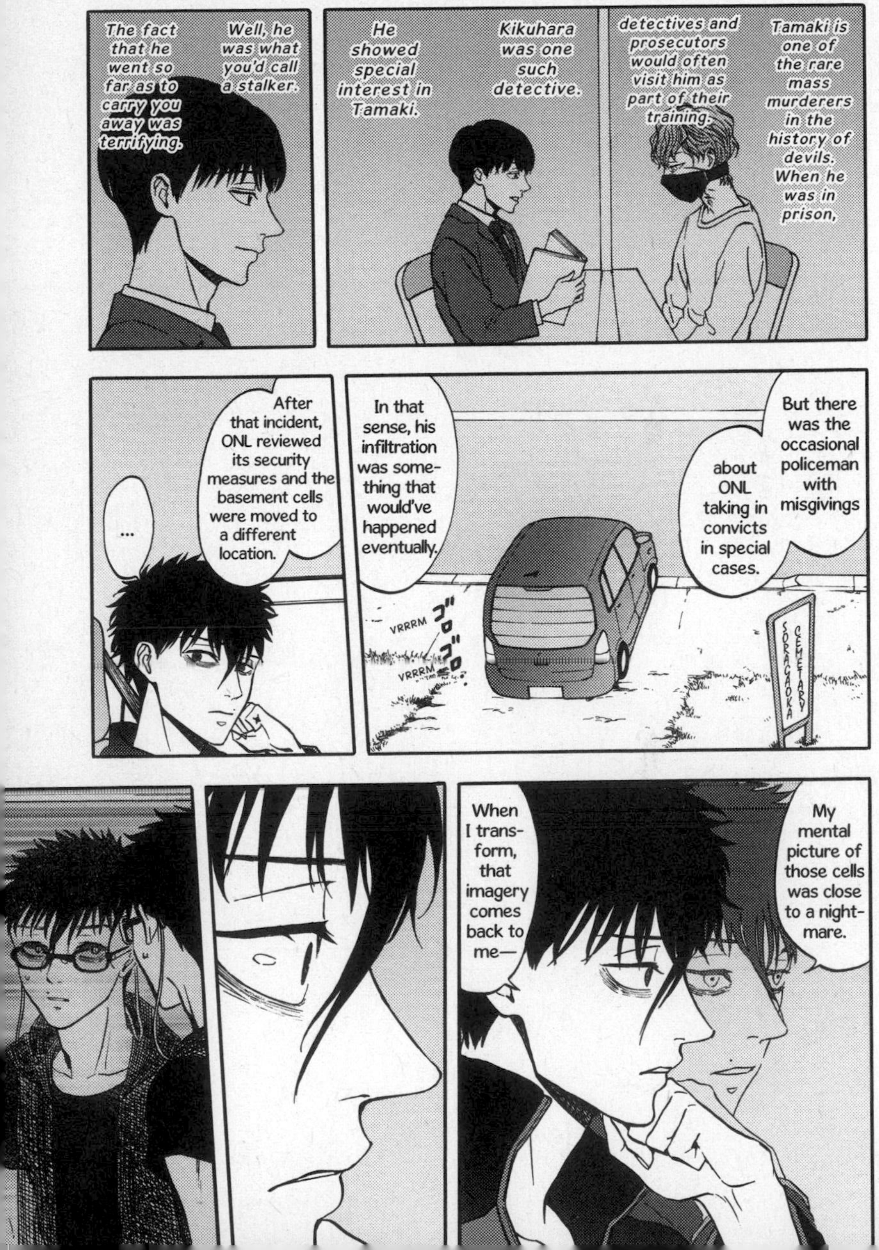
Tamaki is one of the rare mass murderers in the history of devils. When he was in prison,
detectives and prosecutors would often visit him as part of their training.
Kikuhara was one such detective.
He showed special interest in Tamaki.
Well, he was what you'd call a stalker.
The fact that he went so far as to carry you away was terrifying.
But there was the occasional policeman with misgivings
about ONL taking in convicts in special cases.
In that sense, his infiltration was some-thing that would've happened eventually.
VRRRM
VRRRM
SORAGAOKA CEMETARY
After that incident, ONL reviewed its security measures and the basement cells were moved to a different location.
...
My mental picture of those cells was close to a night-mare.
When I trans-form, that imagery comes back to me—

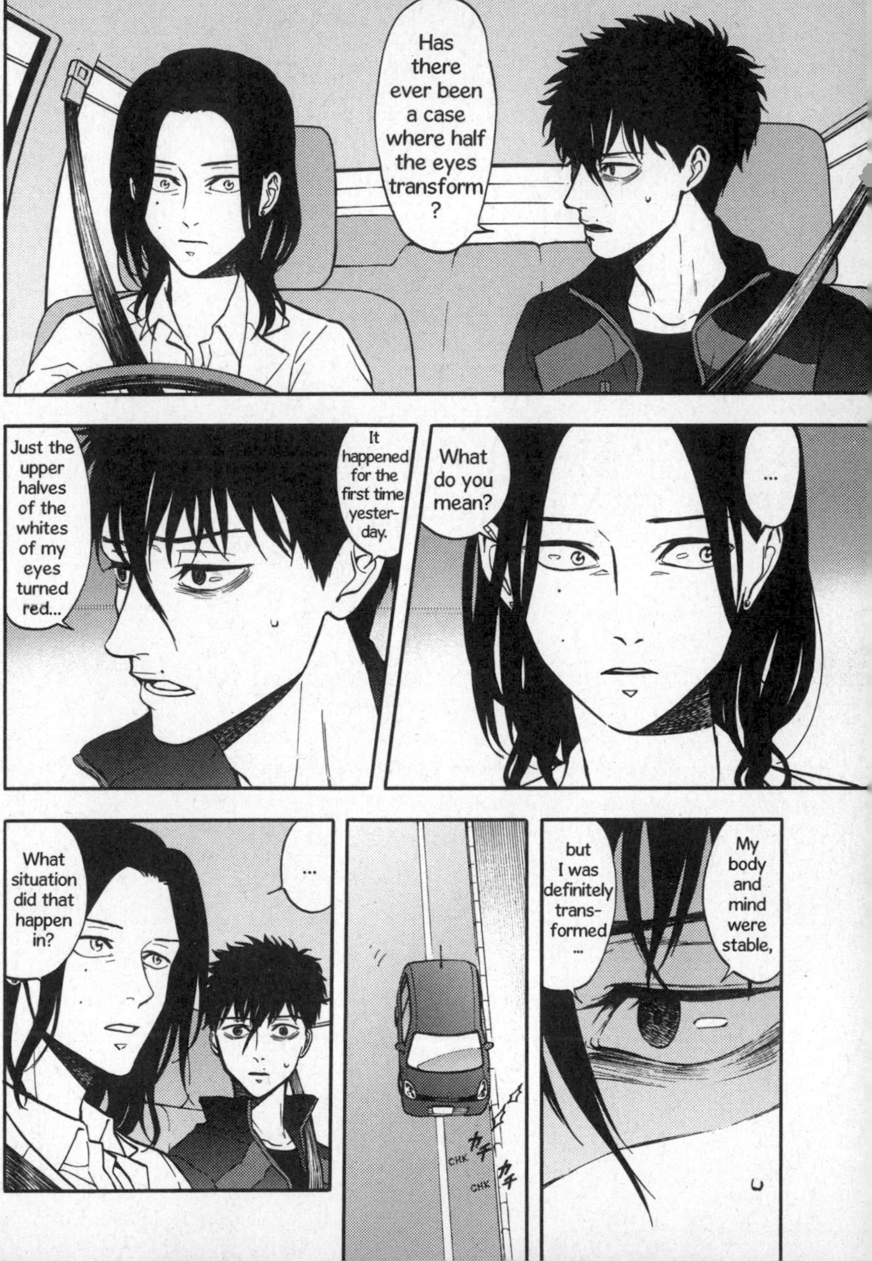
Has there ever been a case where half the eyes transform ?
...
What do you mean?
It happened for the first time yesterday.
Just the upper halves of the whites of my eyes turned red...
My body and mind were stable,
but I was definitely transformed...
カチ
CHK
カチ
CHK
...
What situation did that happen in?

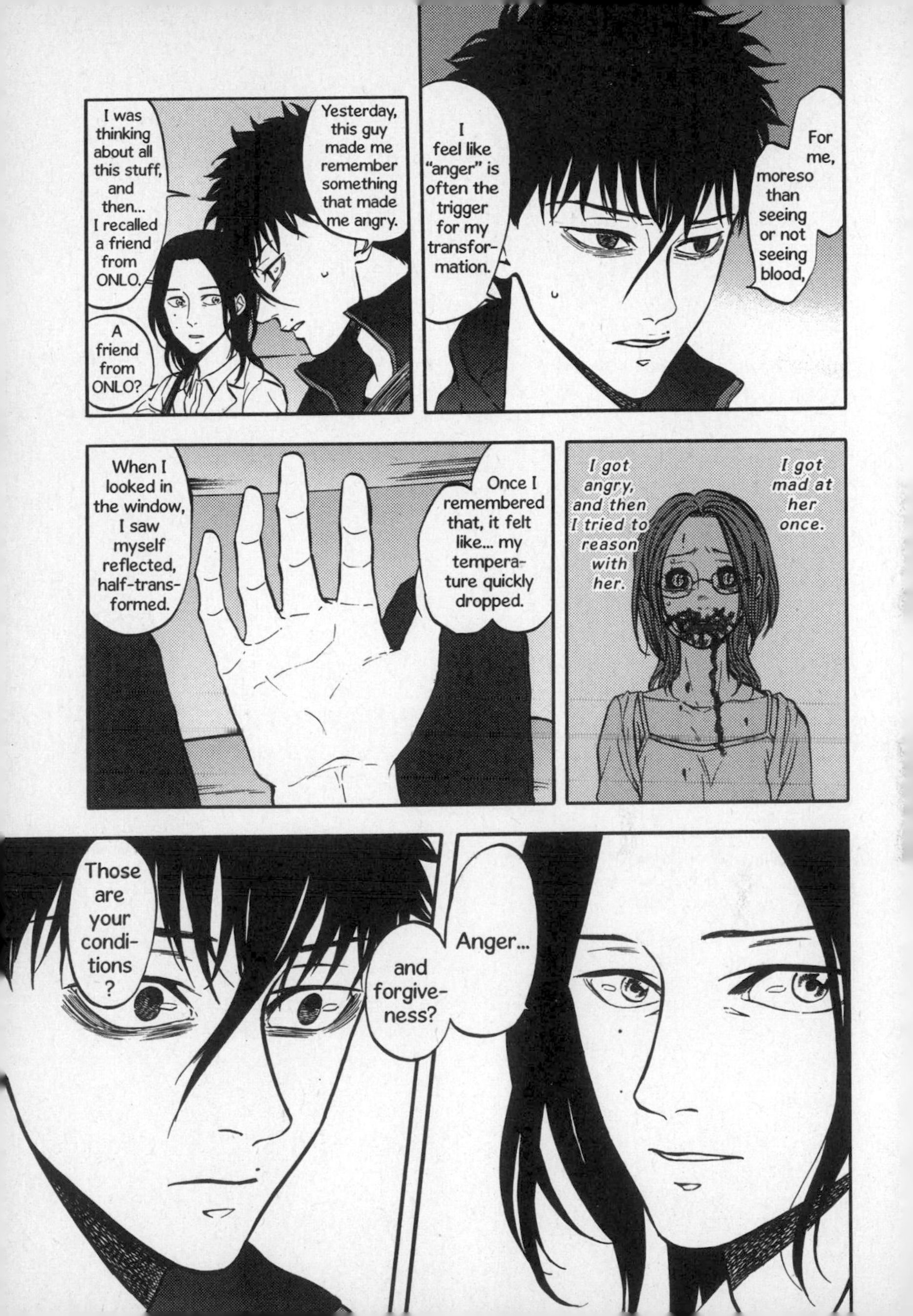
For me, moreso than seeing or not seeing blood,
I feel like "anger" is often the trigger for my transformation.
Yesterday, this guy made me remember something that made me angry.
I was thinking about all this stuff, and then... I recalled a friend from ONLO.
A friend from ONLO?
I got mad at her once.
I got angry, and then I tried to reason with her.
Once I remembered that, it felt like... my temperature quickly dropped.
When I looked in the window, I saw myself reflected, half-transformed.
Anger... and forgiveness?
Those are your conditions?

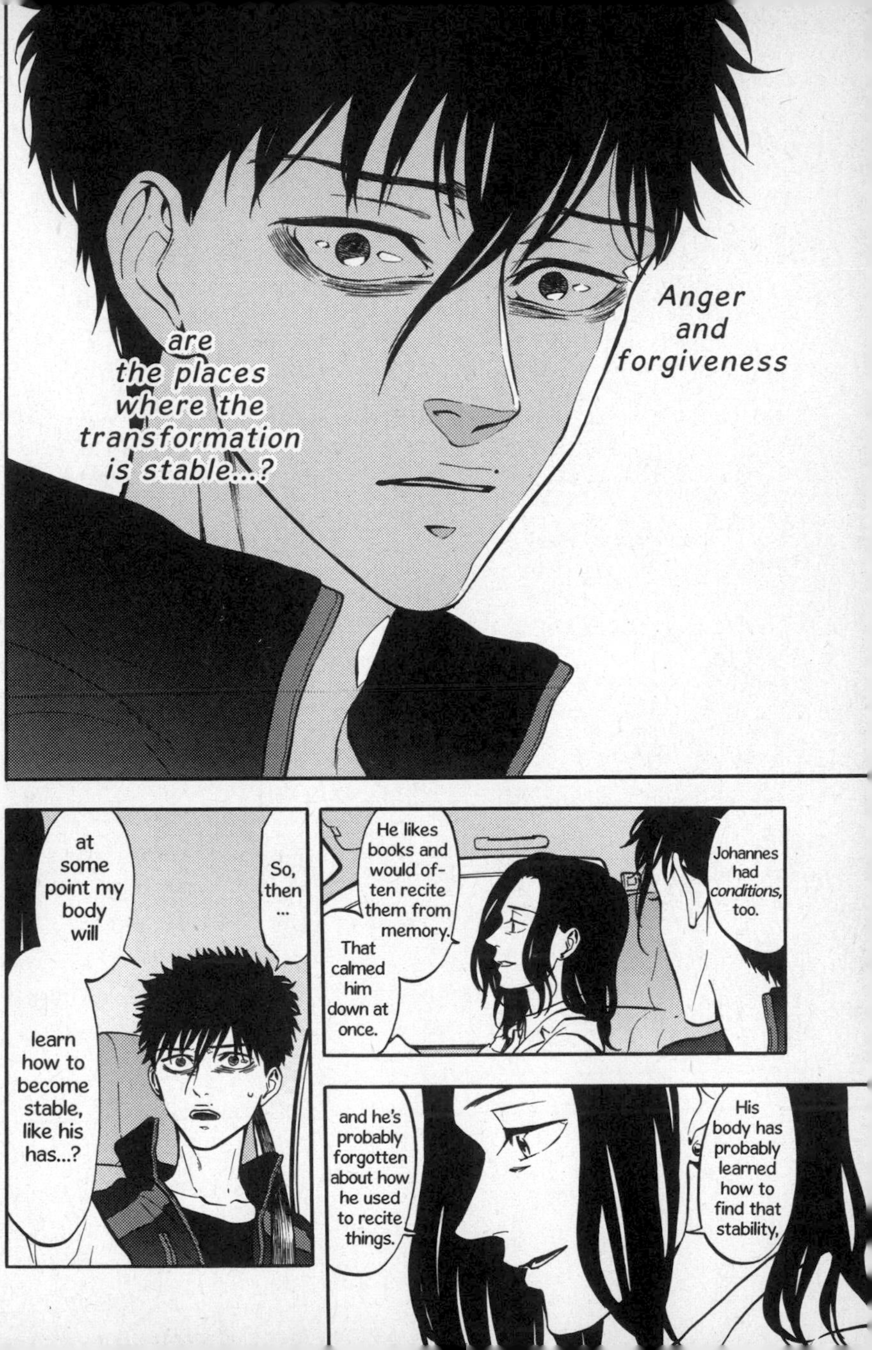
Anger and forgiveness
are the places where the transformation is stable...?
Johannes had *conditions*, too.
He likes books and would of-ten recite them from memory.
That calmed him down at once.
His body has probably learned how to find that stability,
and he's probably forgotten about how he used to recite things.
So, then ...
at some point my body will
learn how to become stable, like his has...?

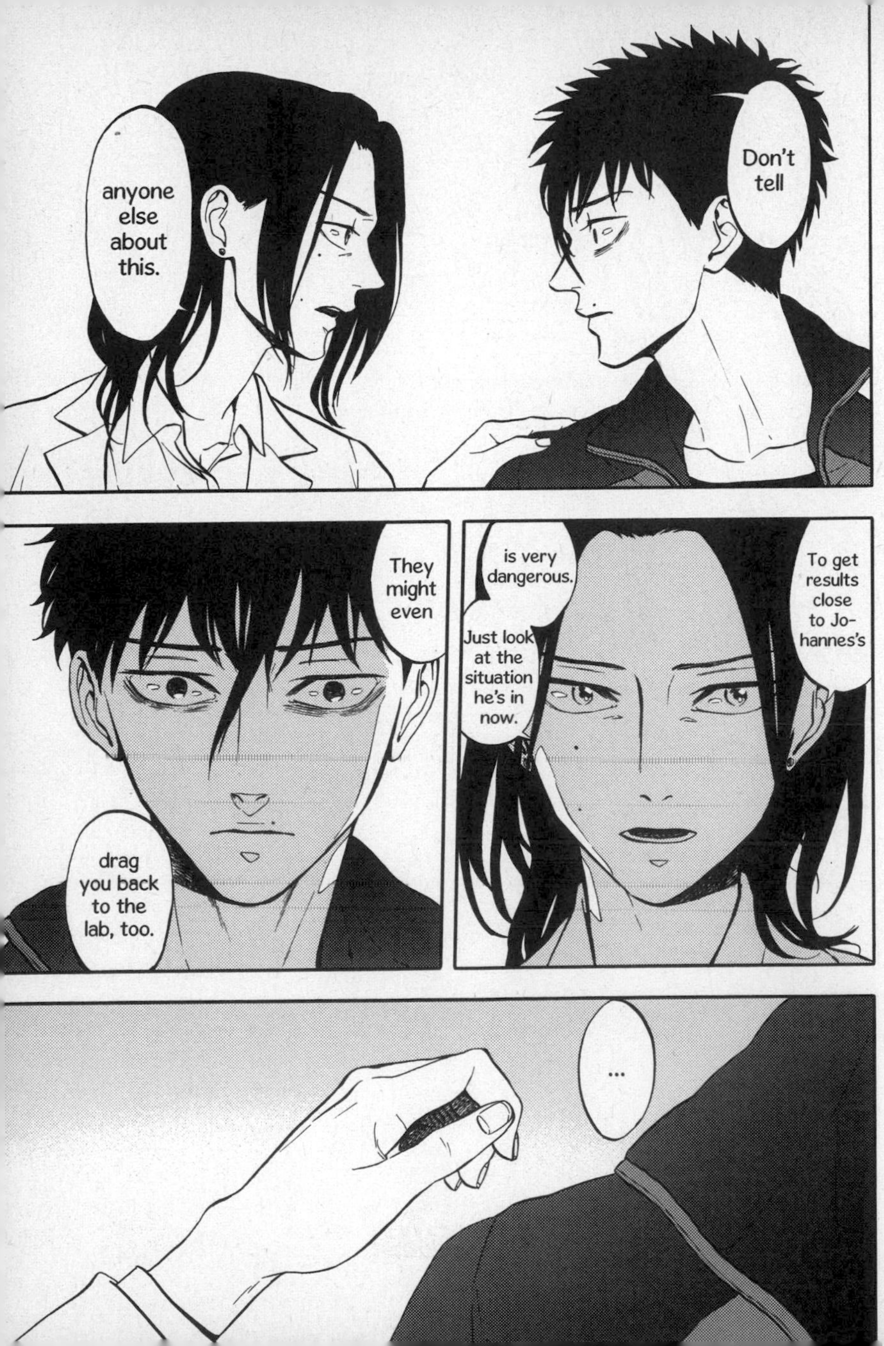
Don't tell
anyone else about this.
To get results close to Jo-hannes's
is very dangerous.
Just look at the situation he's in now.
They might even
drag you back to the lab, too.
...

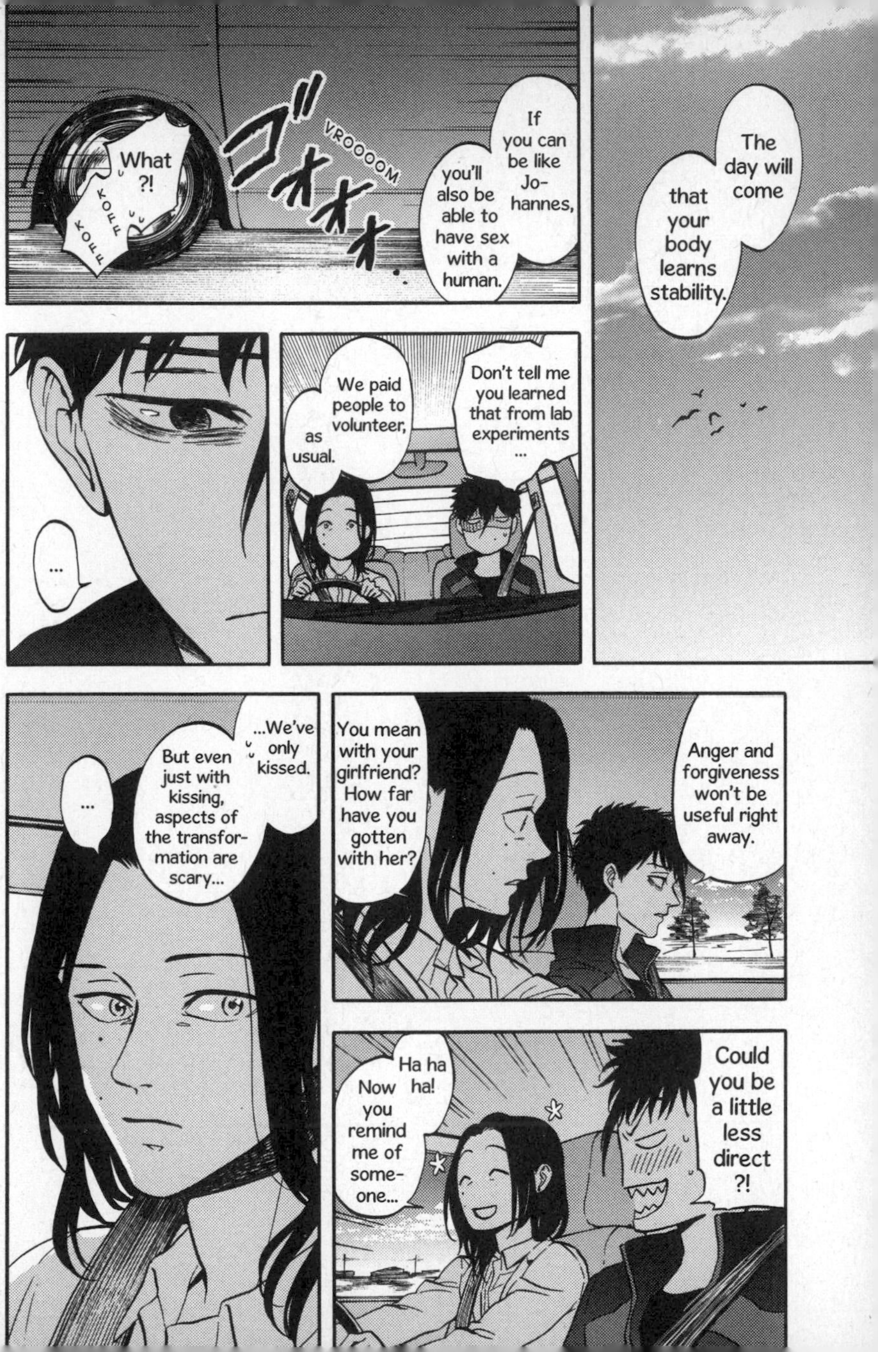
The day will come that your body learns stability.
If you can be like Johannes, you'll also be able to have sex with a human.
VROOOOM
What?!
KOFF KOFF
Don't tell me you learned that from lab experiments...
We paid people to volunteer, as usual.
...
Anger and forgiveness won't be useful right away.
You mean with your girlfriend? How far have you gotten with her?
Could you be a little less direct?!
Ha ha ha! Now you remind me of someone...
...We've only kissed.
But even just with kissing, aspects of the transformation are scary...
...

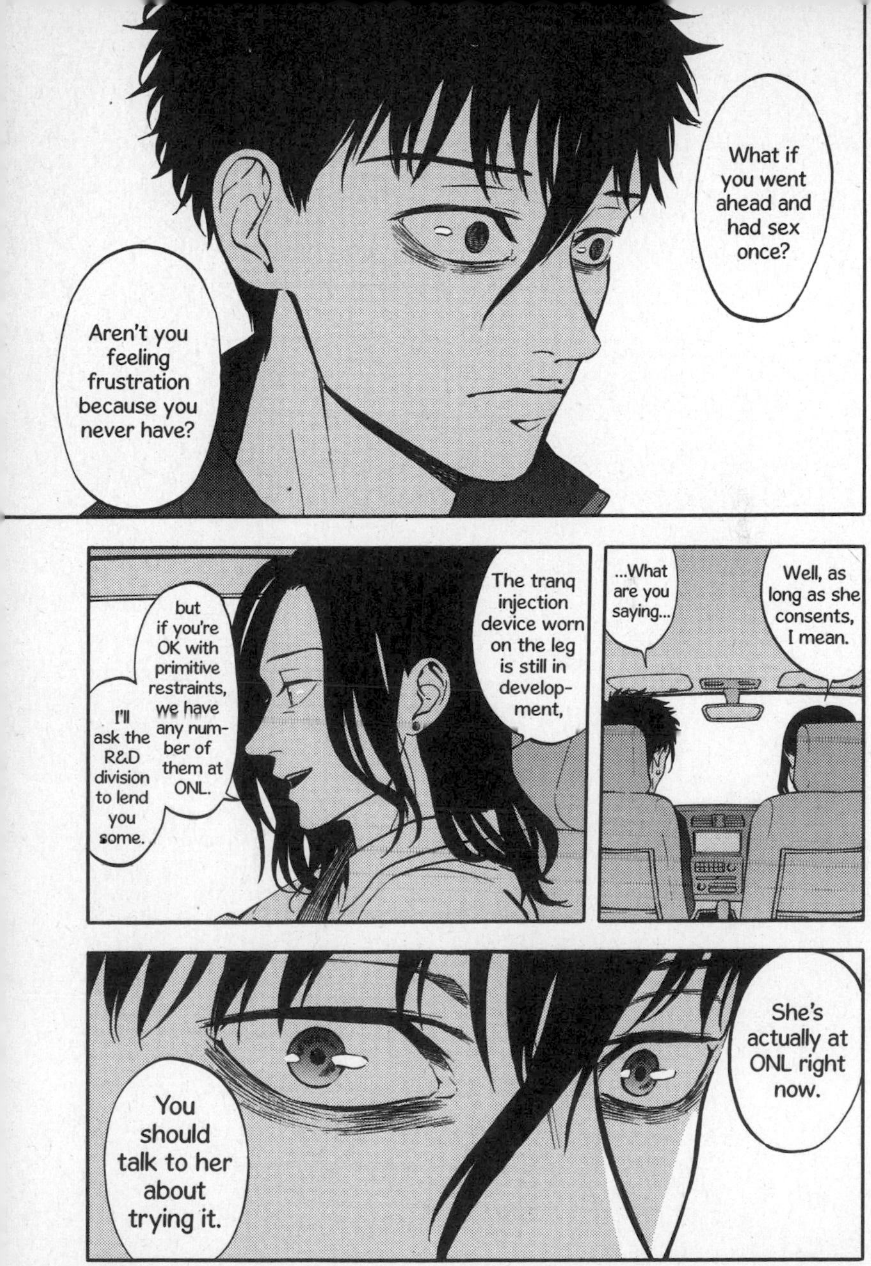
What if you went ahead and had sex once?
Aren't you feeling frustration because you never have?
Well, as long as she consents, I mean.
...What are you saying...
The tranq injection device worn on the leg is still in development,
but if you're OK with primitive restraints, we have any number of them at ONL.
I'll ask the R&D division to lend you some.
She's actually at ONL right now.
You should talk to her about trying it.

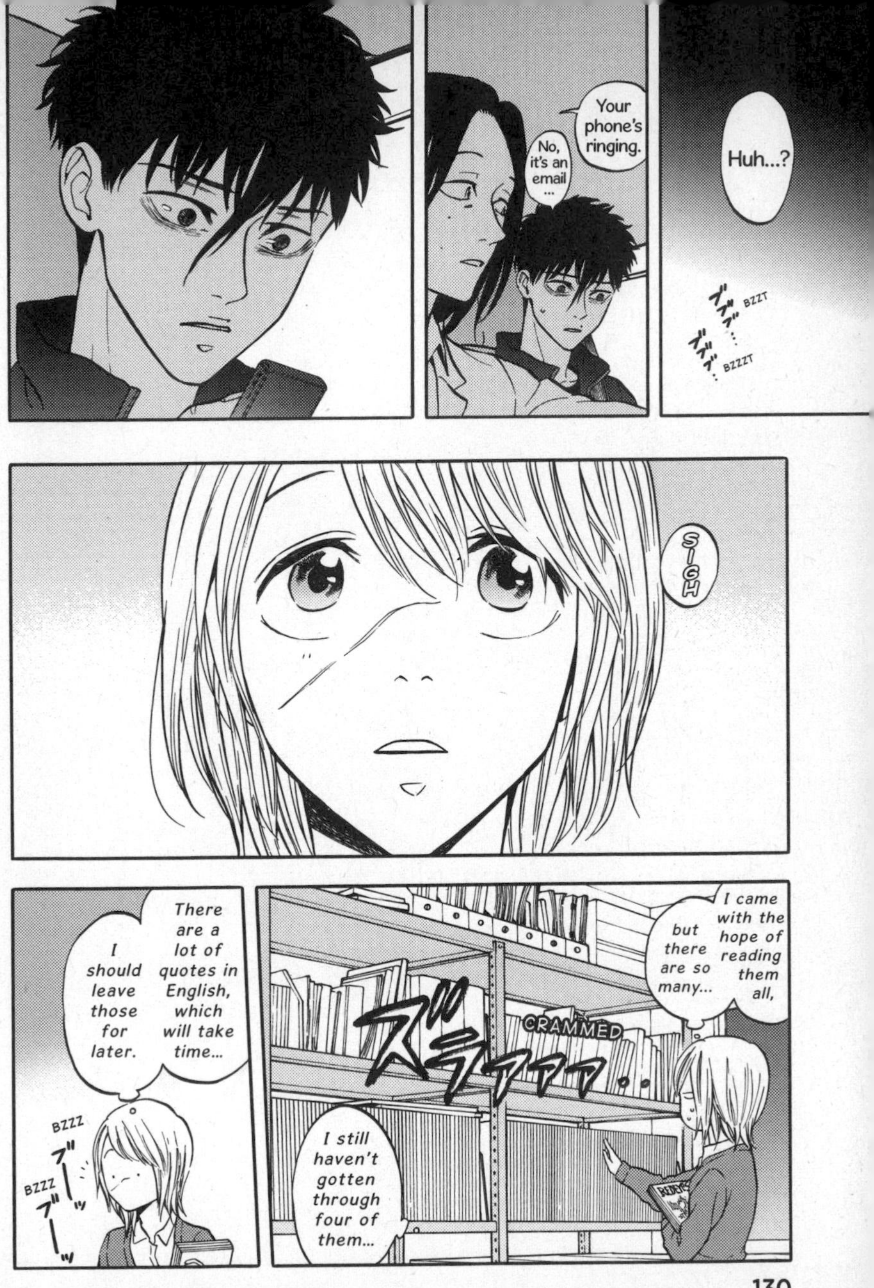
Huh...?
BZZT
BZZZT
Your phone's ringing.
No, it's an email ...
SIGH
I came with the hope of reading them all,
but there are so many...
CRAMMED
I still haven't gotten through four of them...
There are a lot of quotes in English, which will take time...
I should leave those for later.
BZZZ
BZZZ

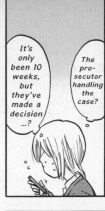

Email ...
17:01
Friday, May 3
Shomei Tojo
Who's this ...?
Oh...
Oh!!
17:01
From: Shomei Tojo
ubject: Notification of Deliberation Re
hope this finds you well
the results of the delib
The prosecutor handling the case?
It's only been 10 weeks, but they've made a decision ...?
With regard to the results of the deliberation, regarding the transfer of blood on the part of Ms. Taira, and the blood-drinking resulting in bodily injury on the part of Yuuki Anzai,
we have decided not to press charges for either incident.
Additionally, as of today, the order prohibiting contact is rescinded.
A similar notification has also been sent to Mr. Anzai.
Thank you for your cooperation.
Inbox
Shomei Tojo
Notification of Deliberation Results
I hope you're well. With regard to the results of the deliberation, regarding the transfer of blood on the part of Ms.Taira, and the blood-drinking sulting in bodily injury on the part Yuuki Anzai, we have decided o press charges for either
CLR

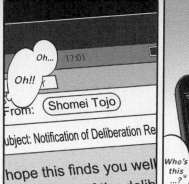

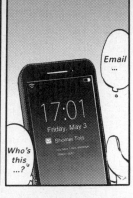

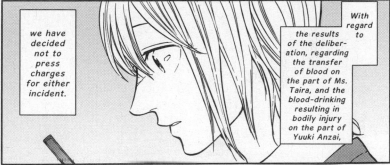

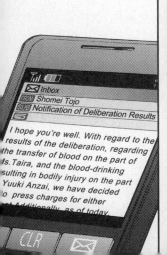

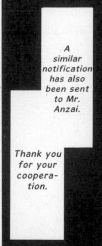

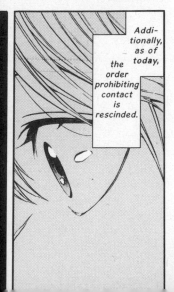

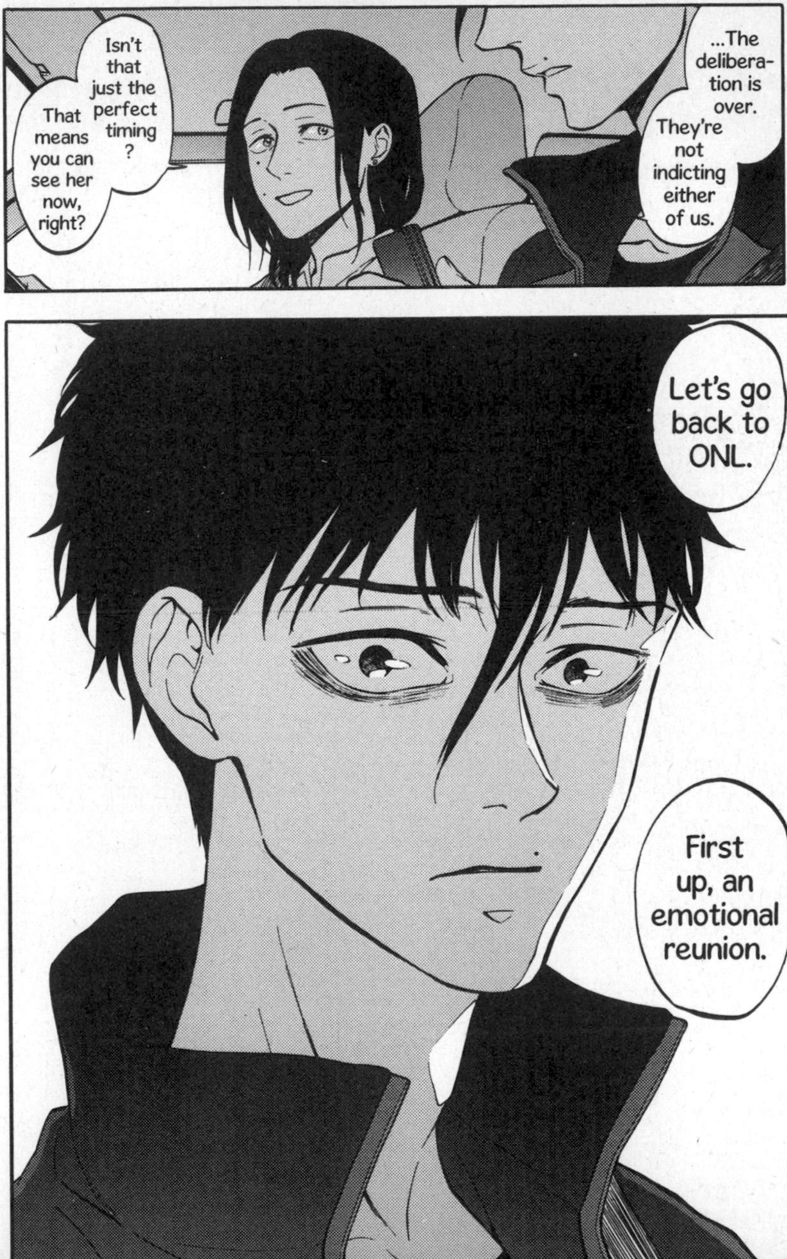
...The deliberation is over. They're not indicting either of us.
Isn't that just the perfect timing?
That means you can see her now, right?
Let's go back to ONL.
First up, an emotional reunion.

"Additionally, as of today, the order prohibiting contact is rescinded."

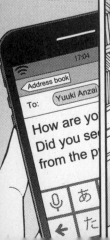

TAP
トン
TAP
トン
TAP
トン

...

What should I do? Call Anzai ...?

No, it's been a while. Maybe a text ...?

Address book
To: Yuuki Anzai
17:04
How are yo
Did you se
from the p

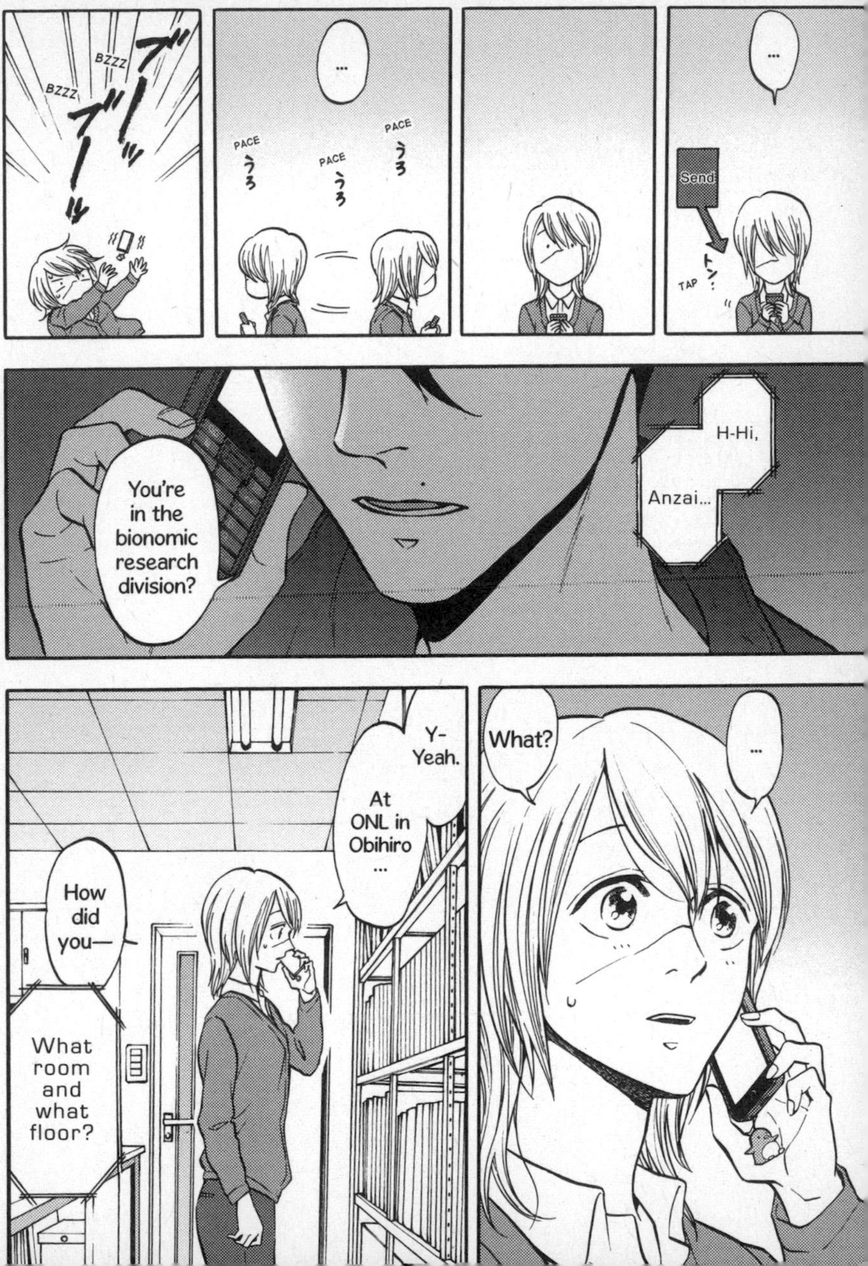
...
Send
TAP
トン
...
PACE
うろ
PACE
うろ
PACE
うろ
BZZZ
BZZZ
H-Hi,
Anzai...
You're in the bionomic research division?
...
What?
Y-Yeah.
At ONL in Obihiro ...
How did you—
What room and what floor?

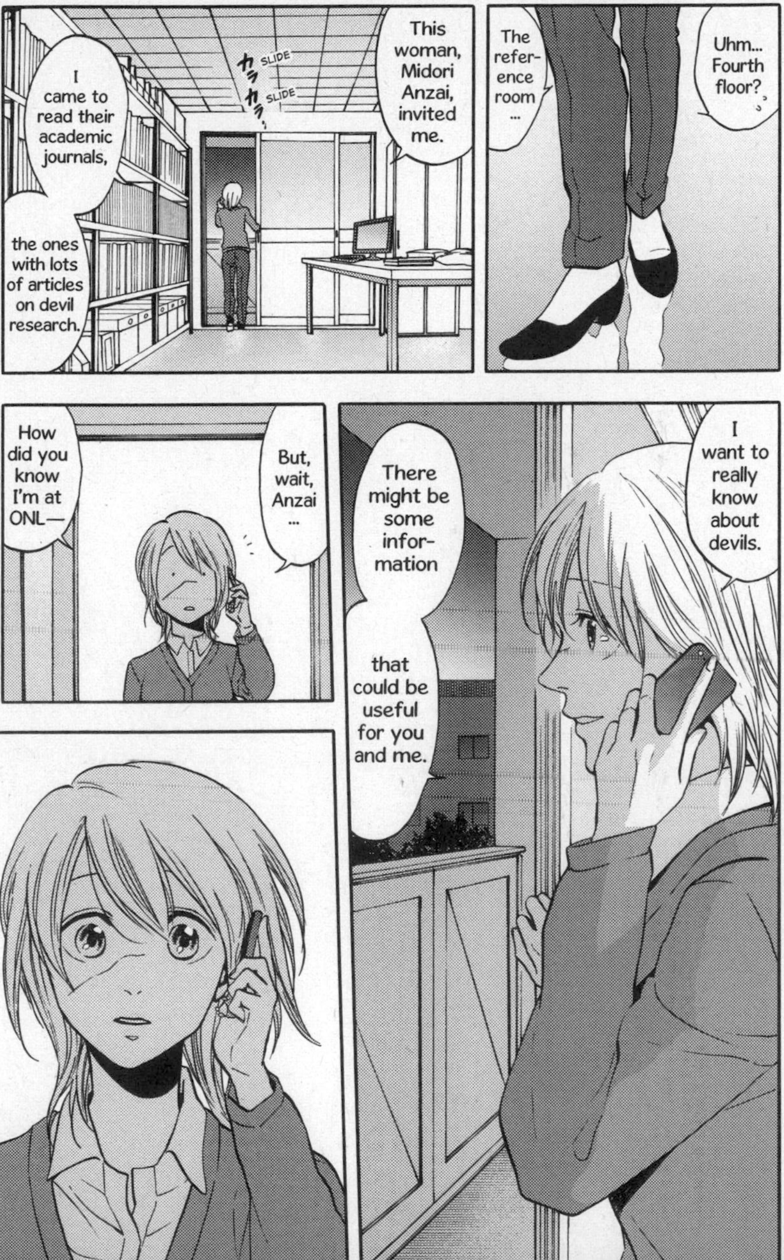
Uhm... Fourth floor?
The reference room ...
This woman, Midori Anzai, invited me.
カラ SLIDE
カラ SLIDE
I came to read their academic journals,
the ones with lots of articles on devil research.
I want to really know about devils.
There might be some information
that could be useful for you and me.
But, wait, Anzai ...
How did you know I'm at ONL—

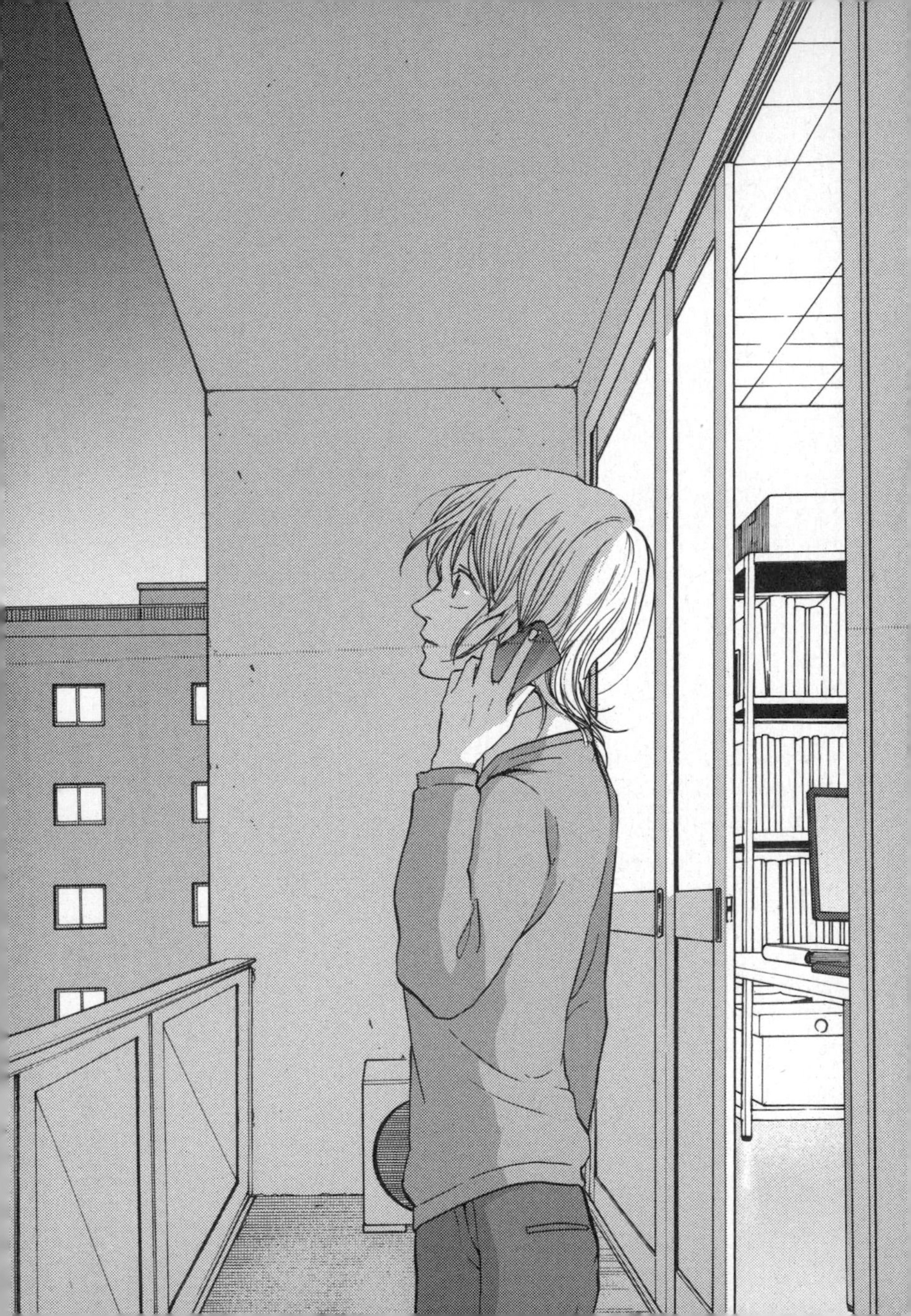

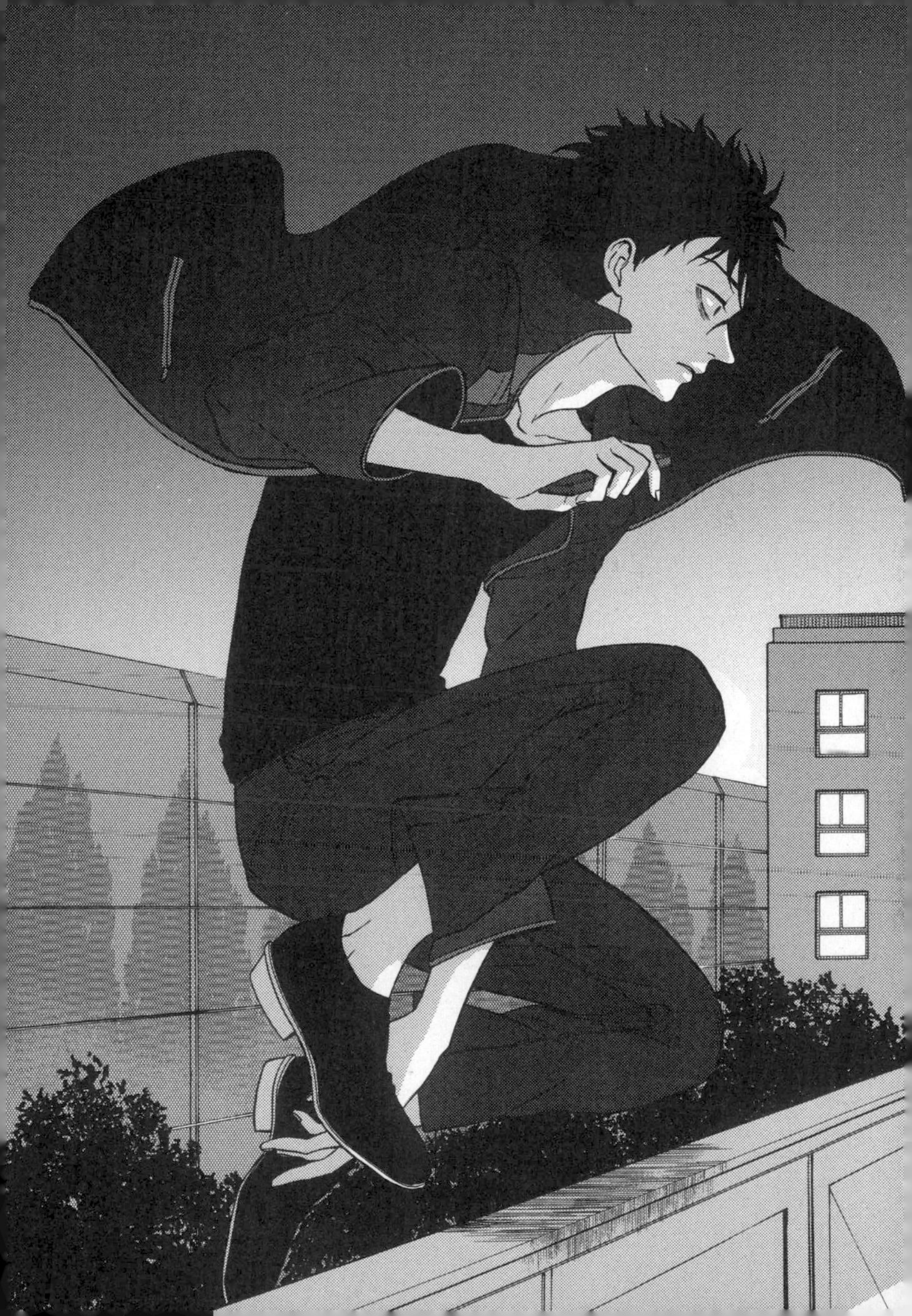

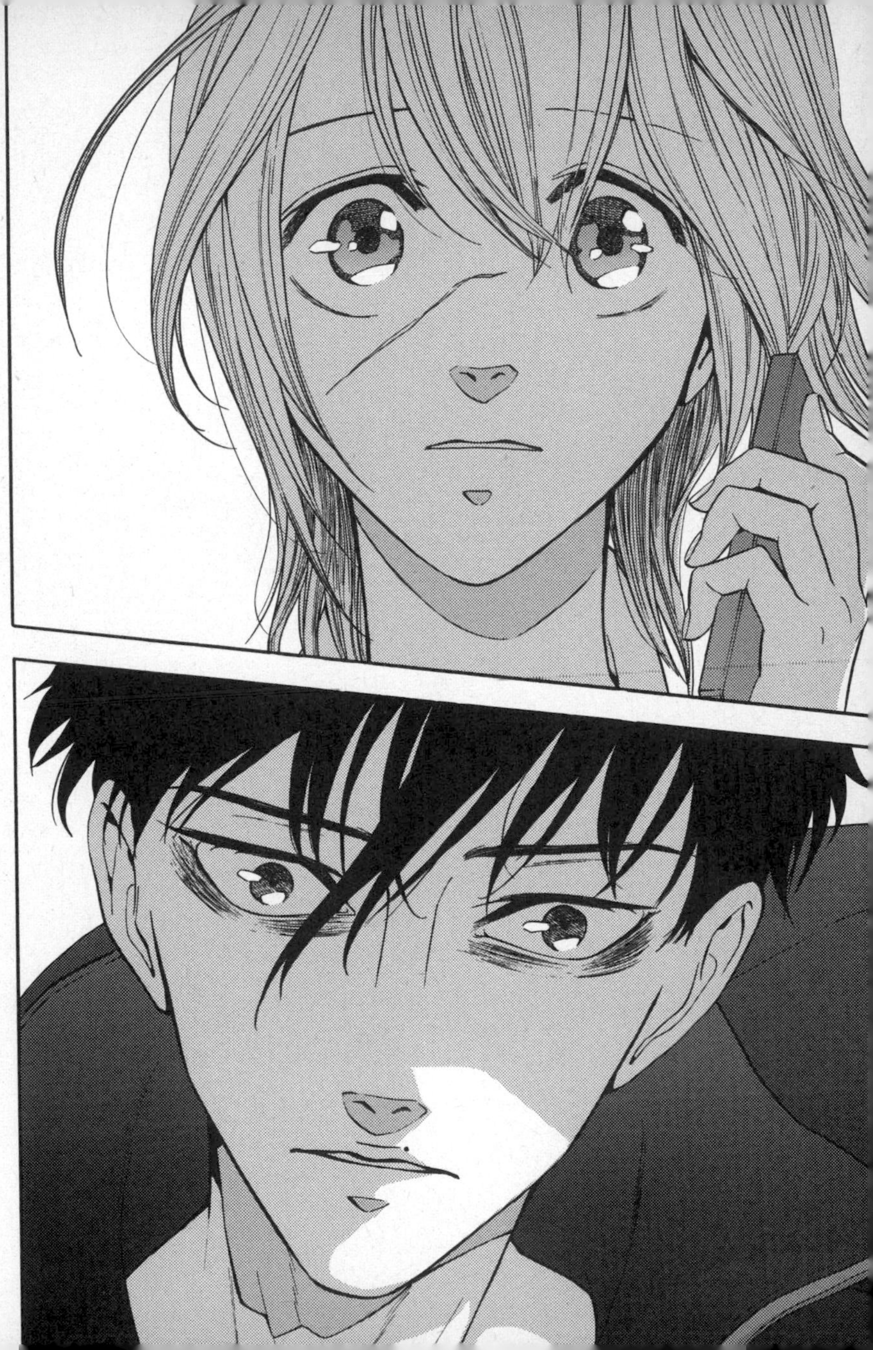

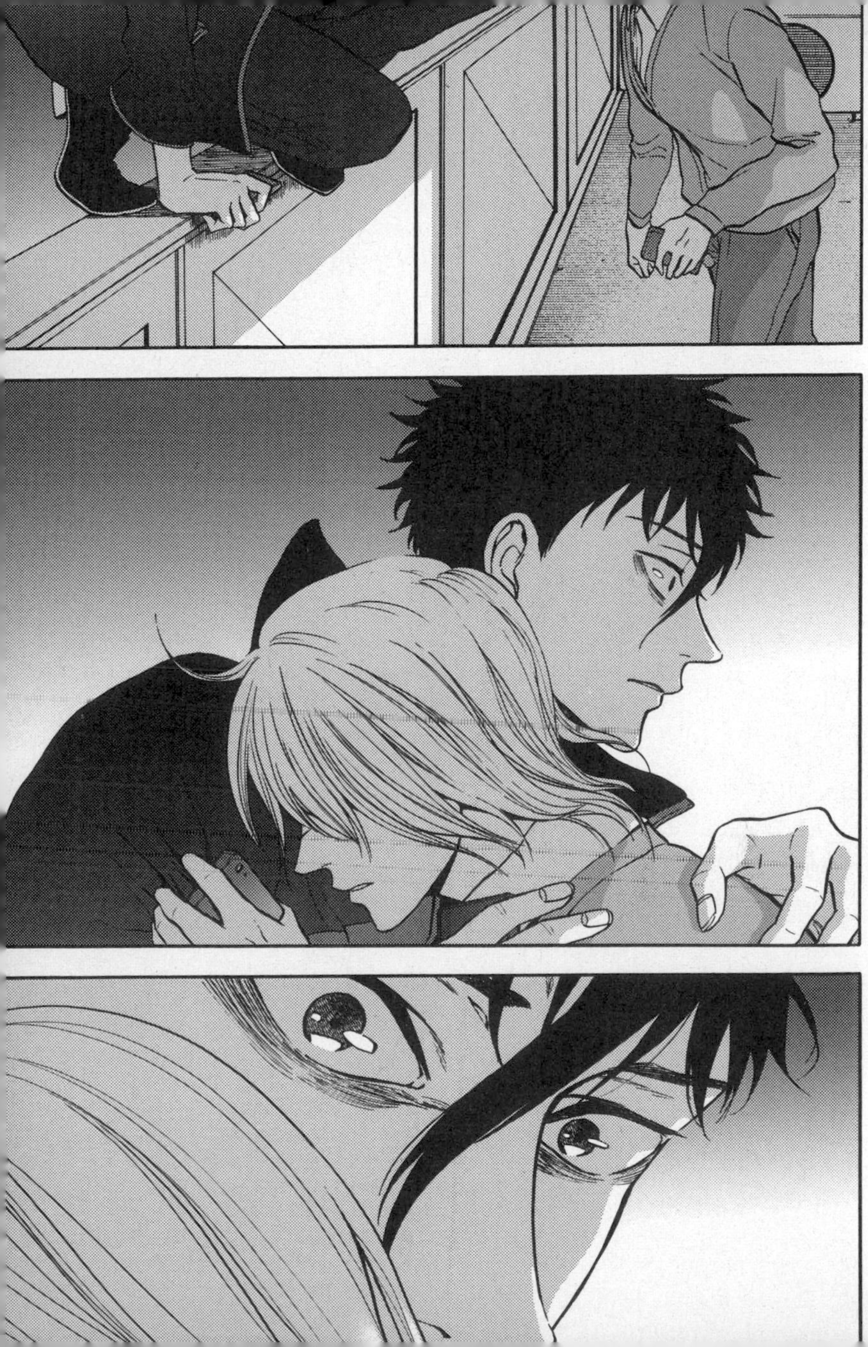

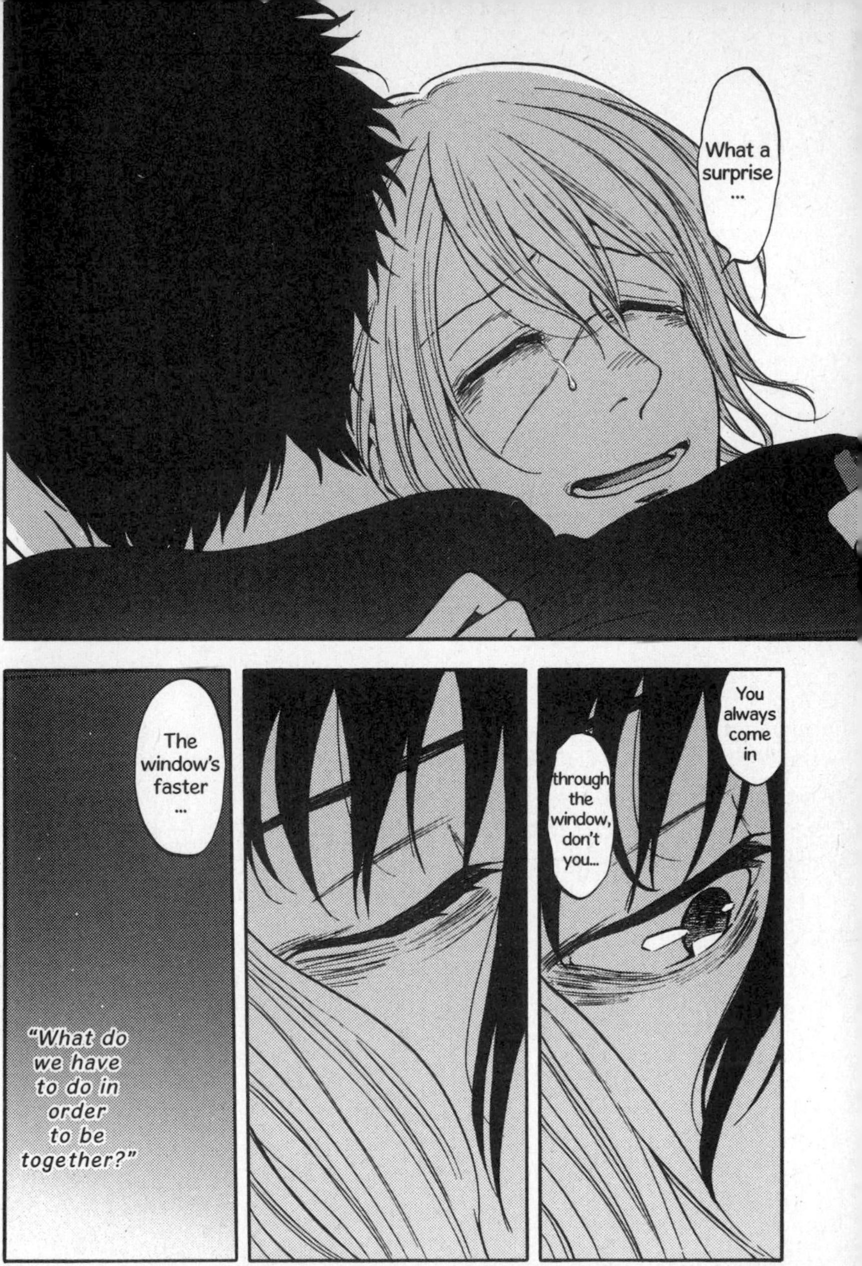
What a surprise ...
You always come in
through the window, don't you...
The window's faster ...
"What do we have to do in order to be together?"

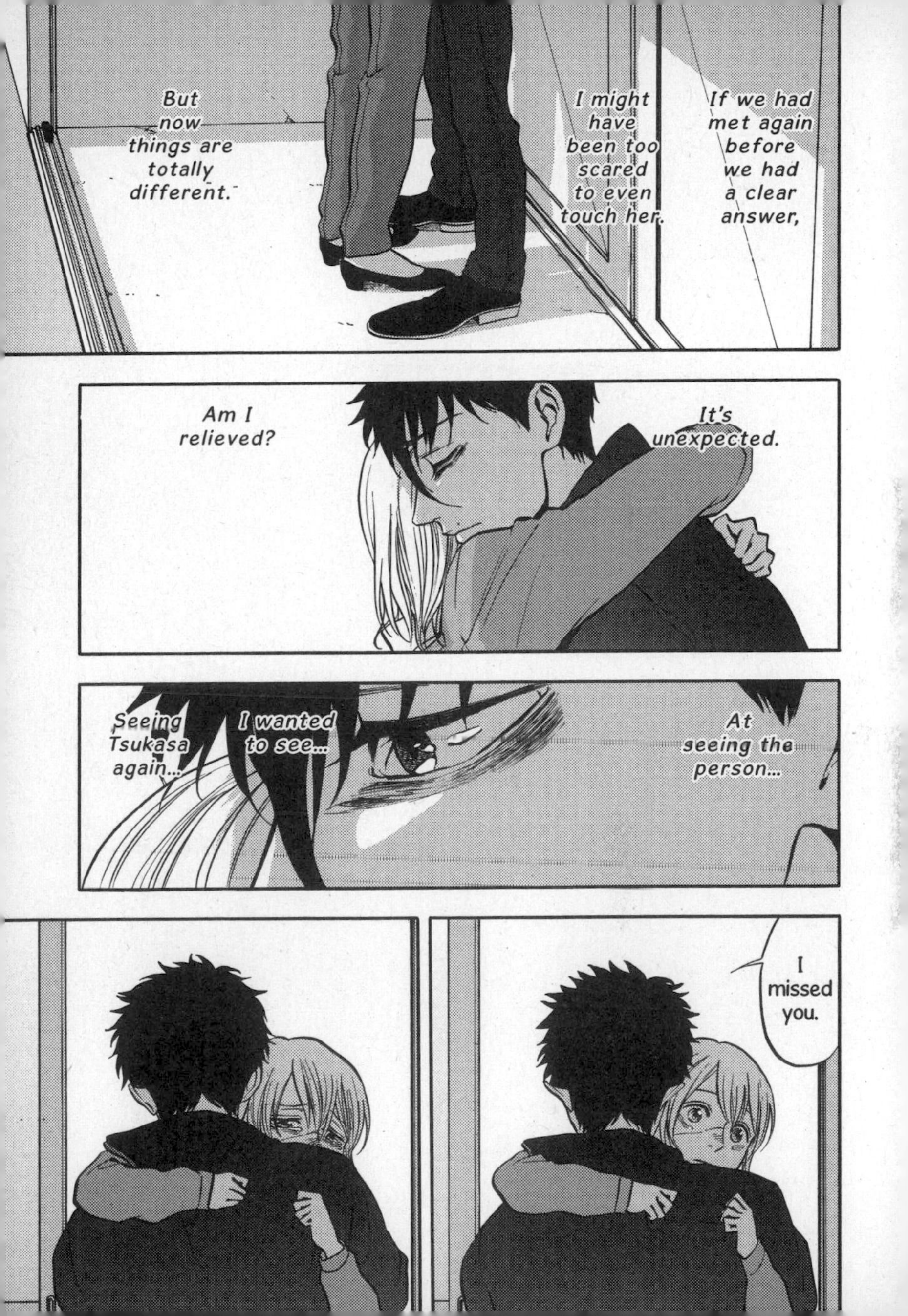
If we had met again before we had a clear answer,
I might have been too scared to even touch her.
But now things are totally different.
It's unexpected.
Am I relieved?
At seeing the person...
I wanted to see...
Seeing Tsukasa again...
I missed you.

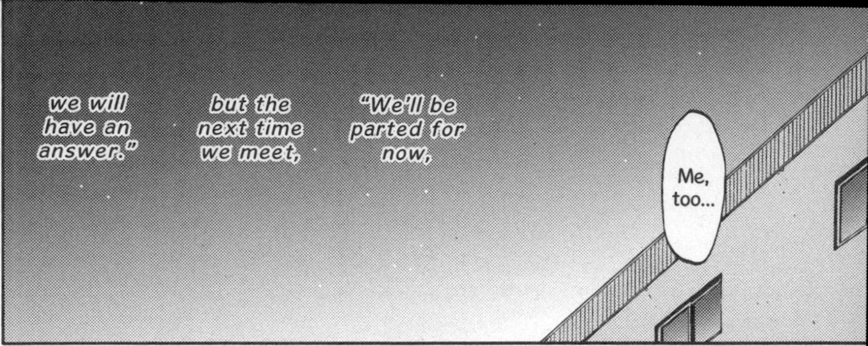
Me, too...
"We'll be parted for now,
but the next time we meet,
we will have an answer."

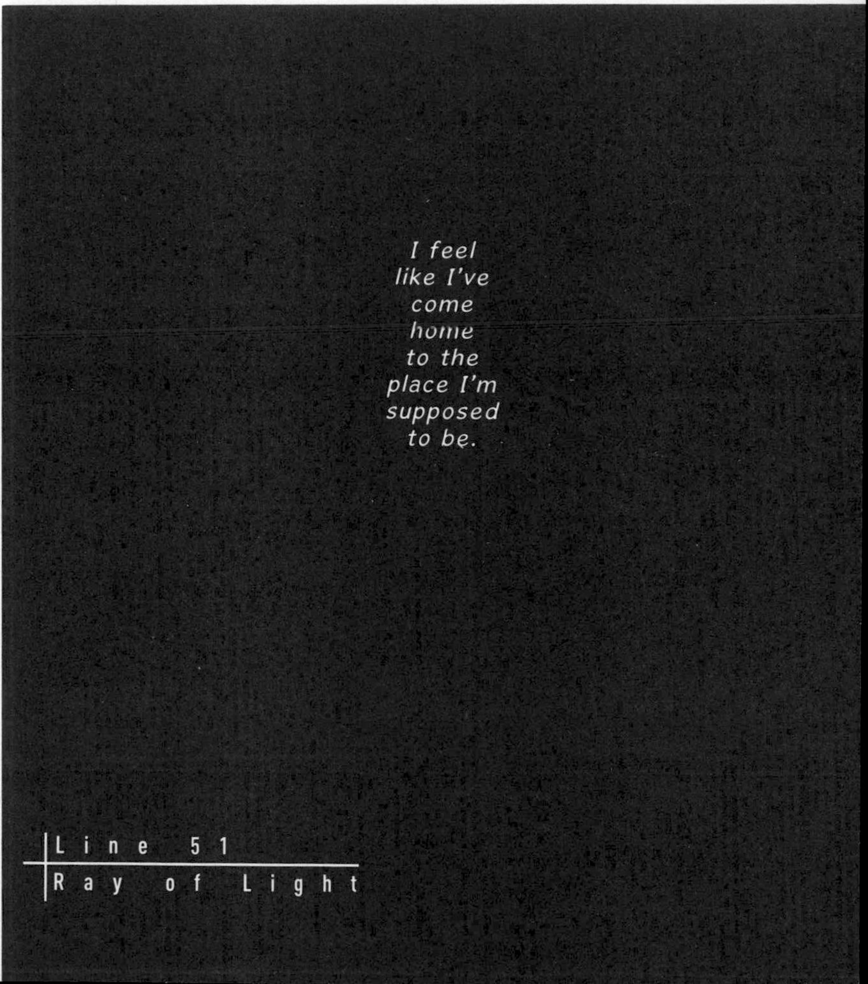
I feel like I've come home to the place I'm supposed to be.

Line 51
Ray of Light

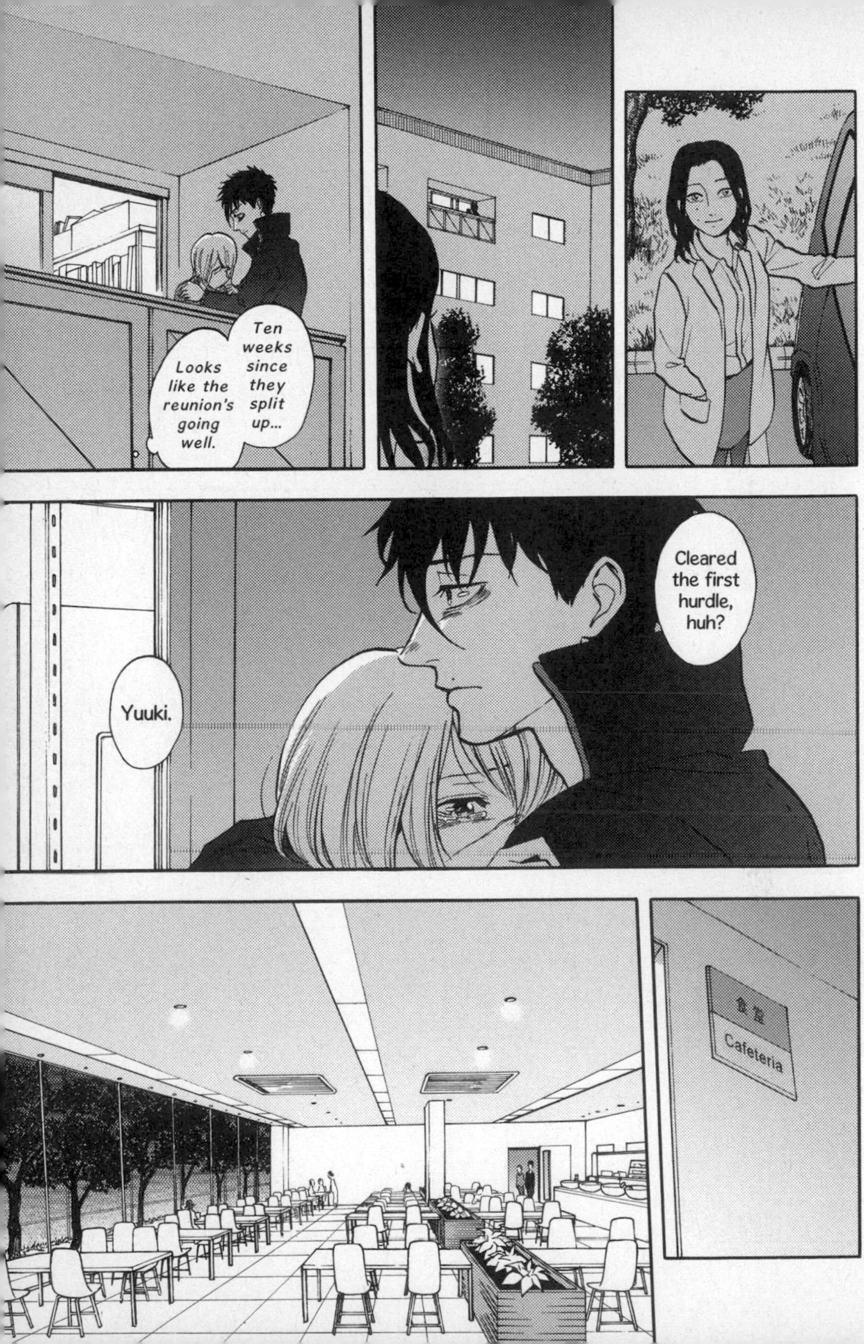
Ten weeks since they split up...
Looks like the reunion's going well.
Cleared the first hurdle, huh?
Yuuki.
Cafeteria

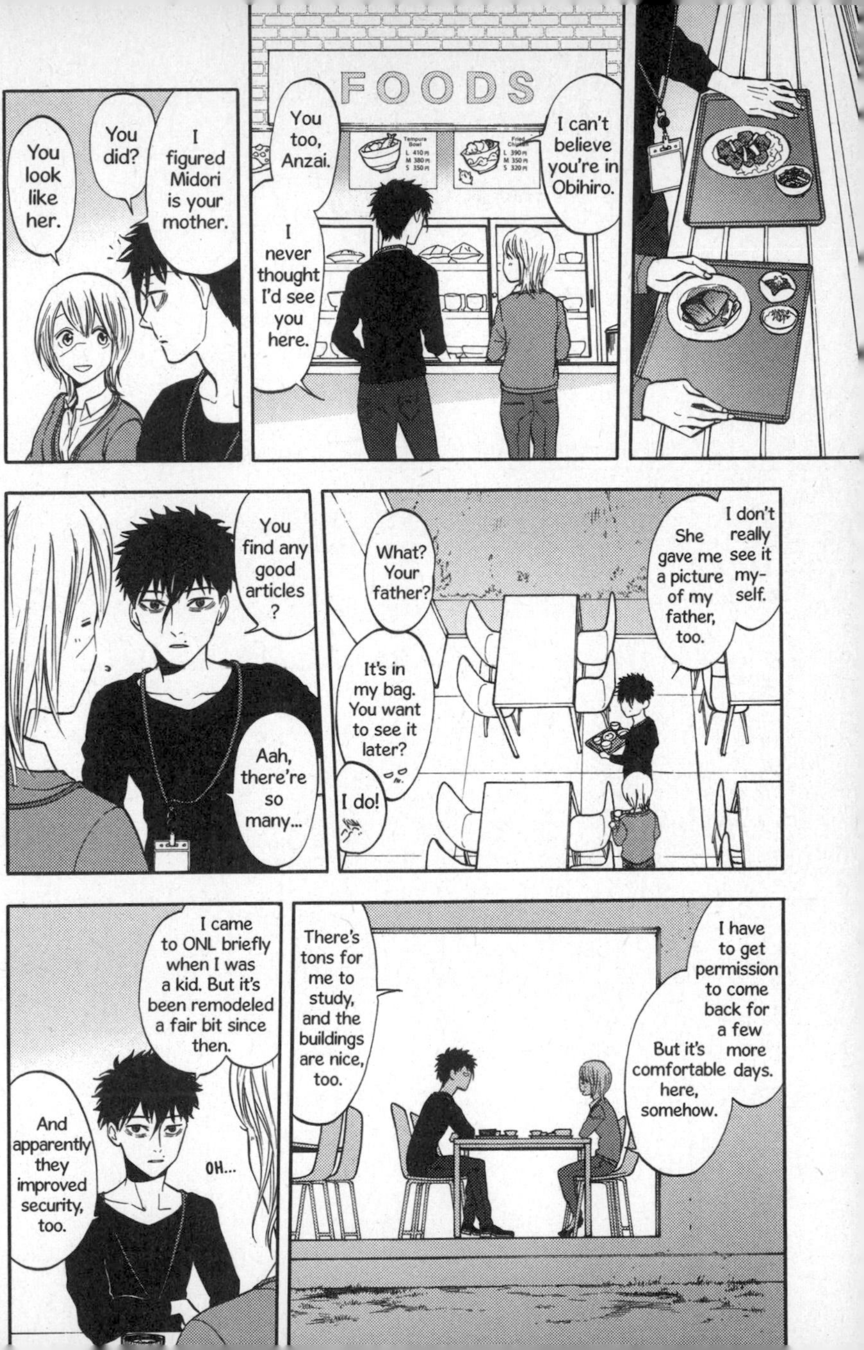
FOODS
I can't believe you're in Obihiro.
You too, Anzai.
I never thought I'd see you here.
I figured Midori is your mother.
You did?
You look like her.
I don't really see it my-self.
She gave me a picture of my father, too.
What? Your father?
It's in my bag. You want to see it later?
I do!
You find any good articles?
Aah, there're so many...
I have to get permission to come back for a few more days.
But it's comfortable here, somehow.
There's tons for me to study, and the buildings are nice, too.
I came to ONL briefly when I was a kid. But it's been remodeled a fair bit since then.
And apparently they improved security, too.
OH...

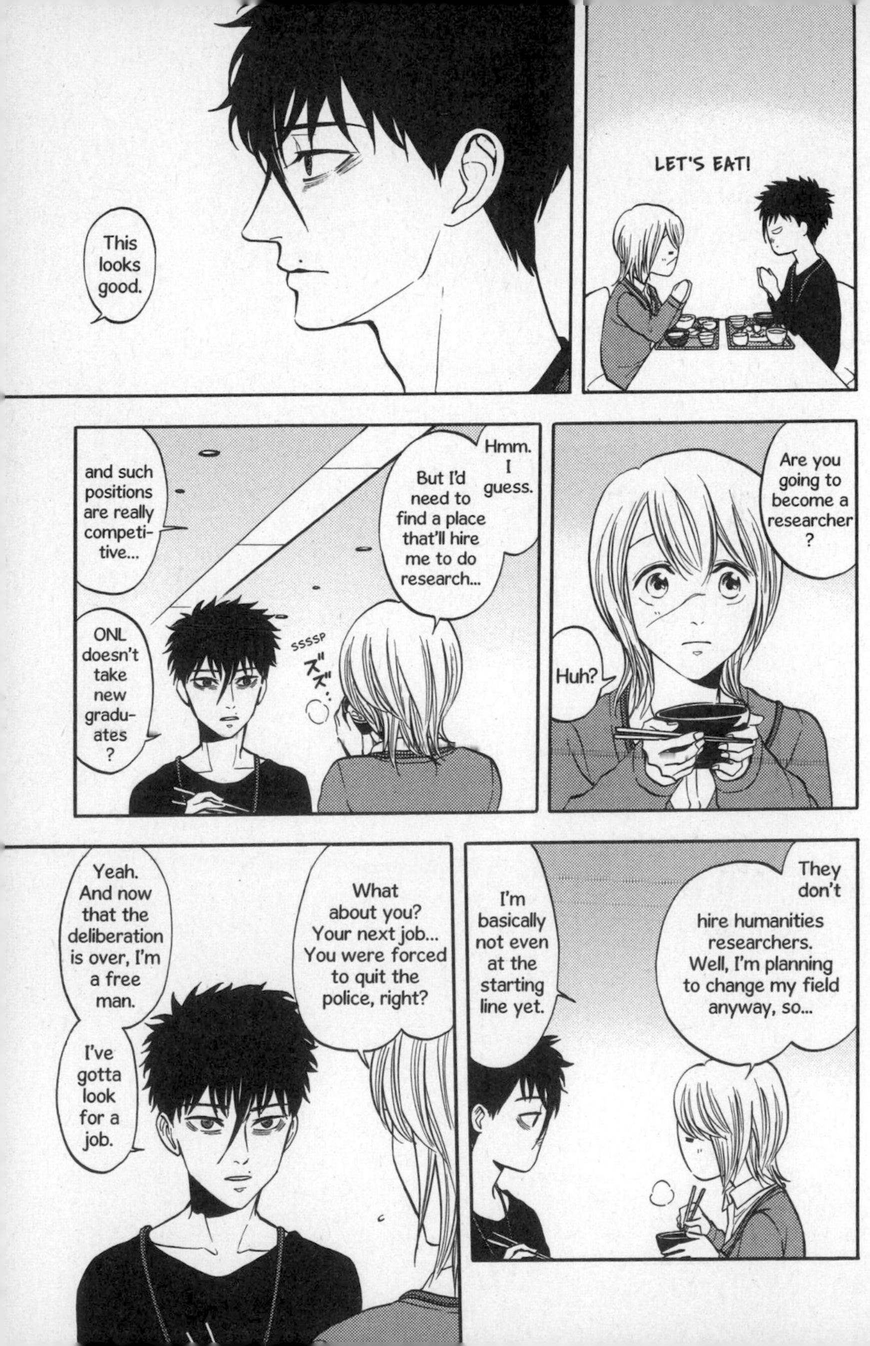
LET'S EAT!
This looks good.
Are you going to become a researcher?
Huh?
Hmm. I guess.
But I'd need to find a place that'll hire me to do research...
and such positions are really competitive...
SSSSP
ズズ
ONL doesn't take new graduates?
They don't hire humanities researchers. Well, I'm planning to change my field anyway, so...
I'm basically not even at the starting line yet.
What about you? Your next job... You were forced to quit the police, right?
Yeah. And now that the deliberation is over, I'm a free man.
I've gotta look for a job.

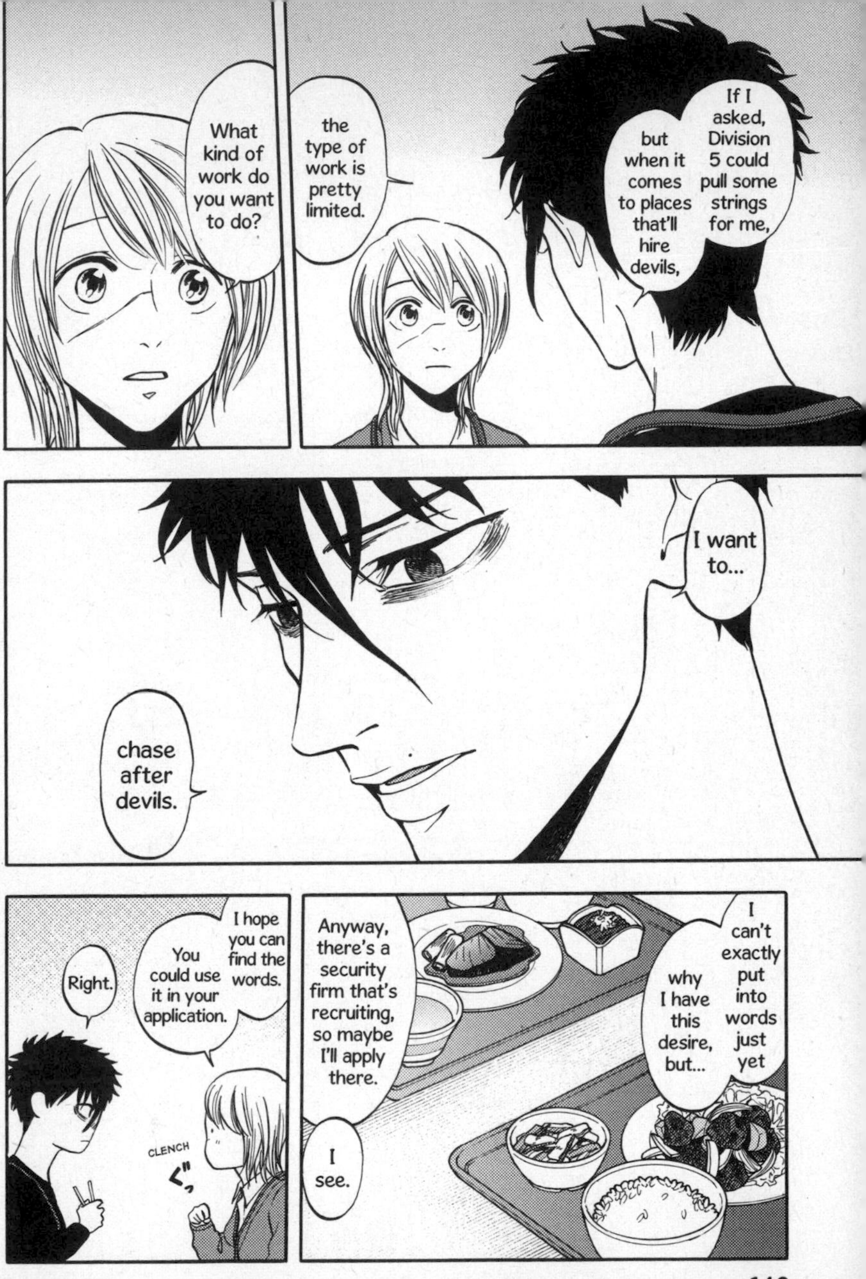
If I asked, Division 5 could pull some strings for me,
but when it comes to places that'll hire devils,
the type of work is pretty limited.
What kind of work do you want to do?
I want to...
chase after devils.
I can't exactly put into words just yet
why I have this desire, but...
Anyway, there's a security firm that's recruiting, so maybe I'll apply there.
I see.
I hope you can find the words.
You could use it in your application.
Right.
CLENCH

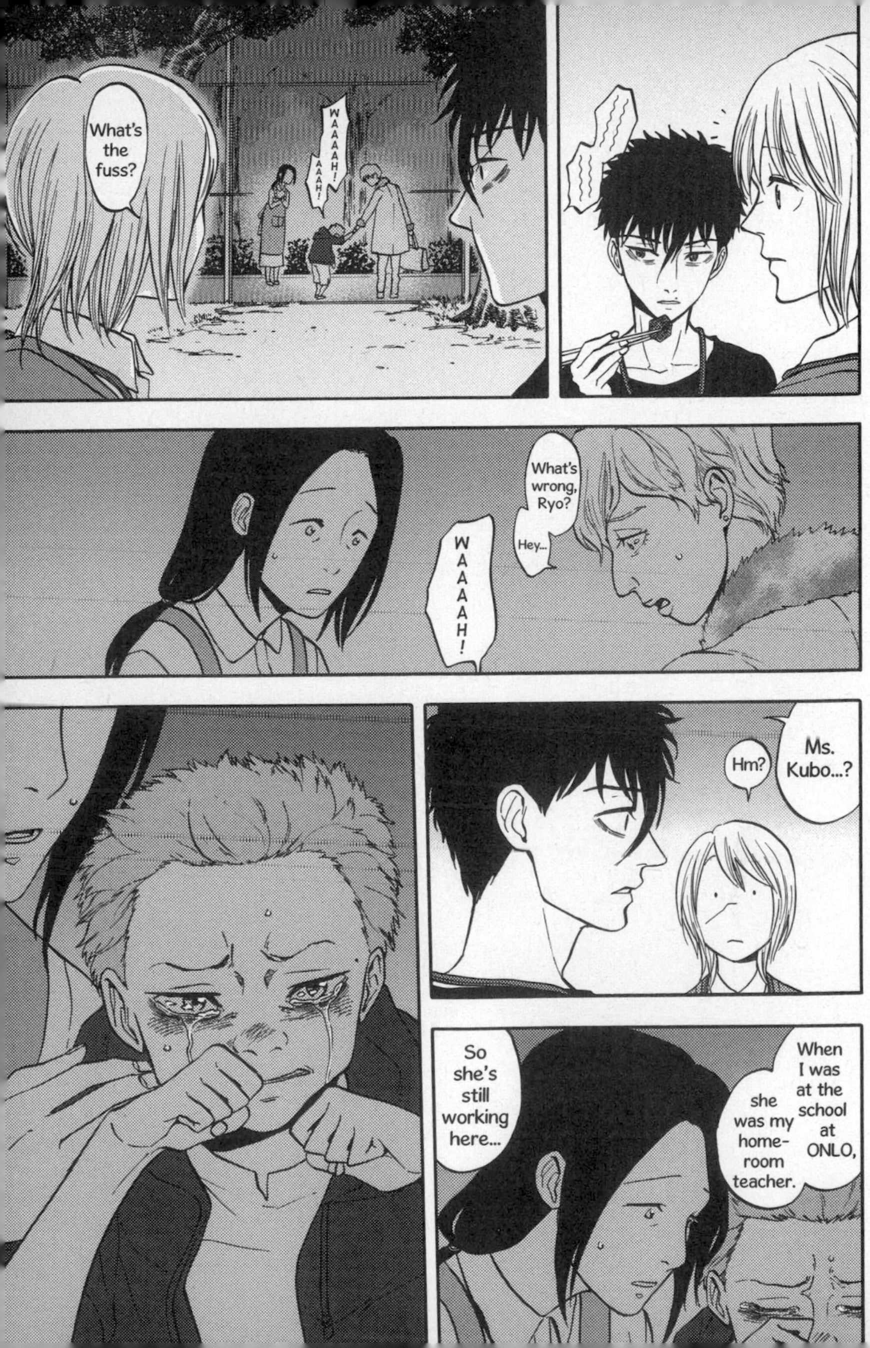
WAAAAH!
AAAH!
What's the fuss?
What's wrong, Ryo?
Hey...
WAAAAH!
Ms. Kubo...?
Hm?
When I was at the school at ONLO,
she was my home-room teacher.
So she's still working here...

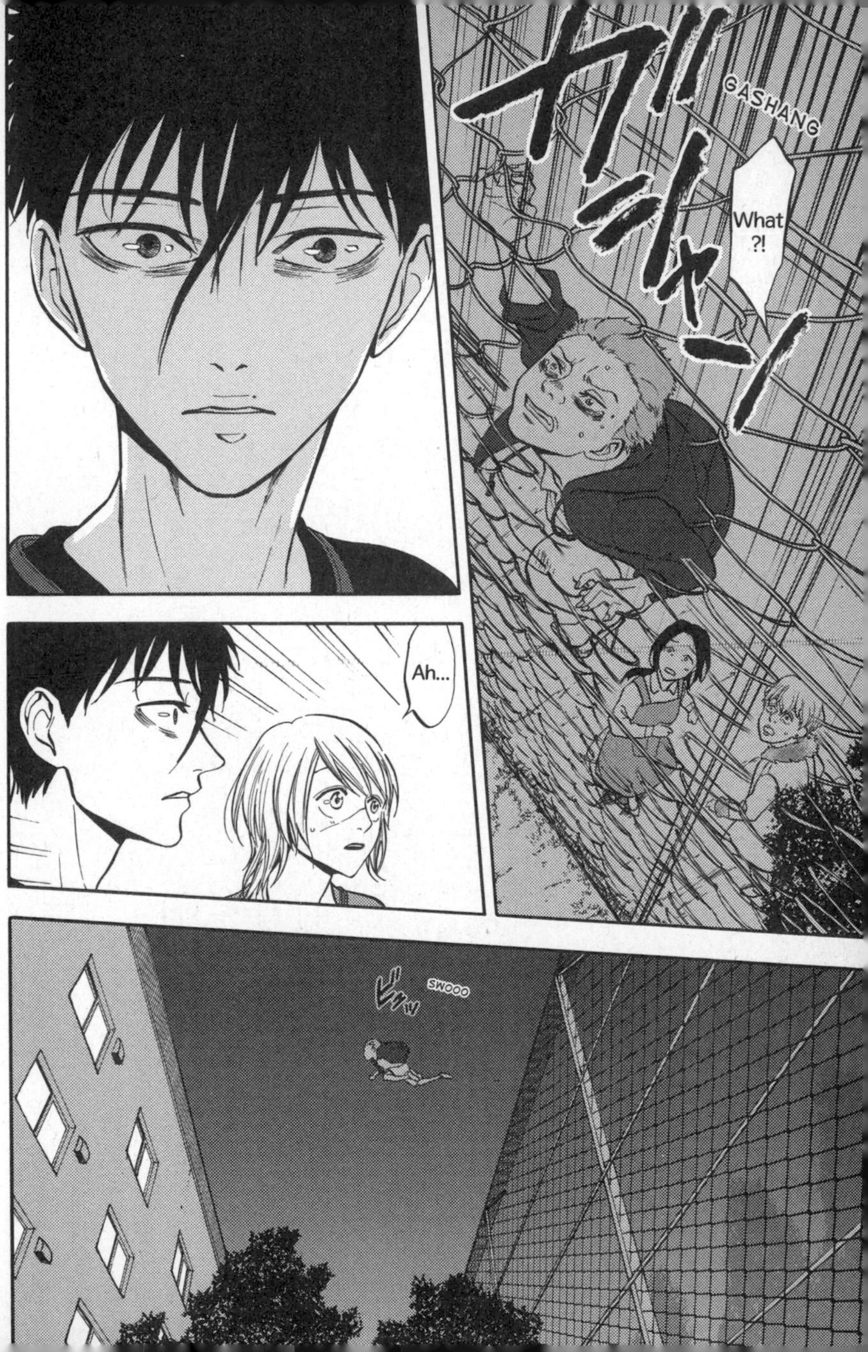

GASHANG
What ?!
Ah...
SWOOO

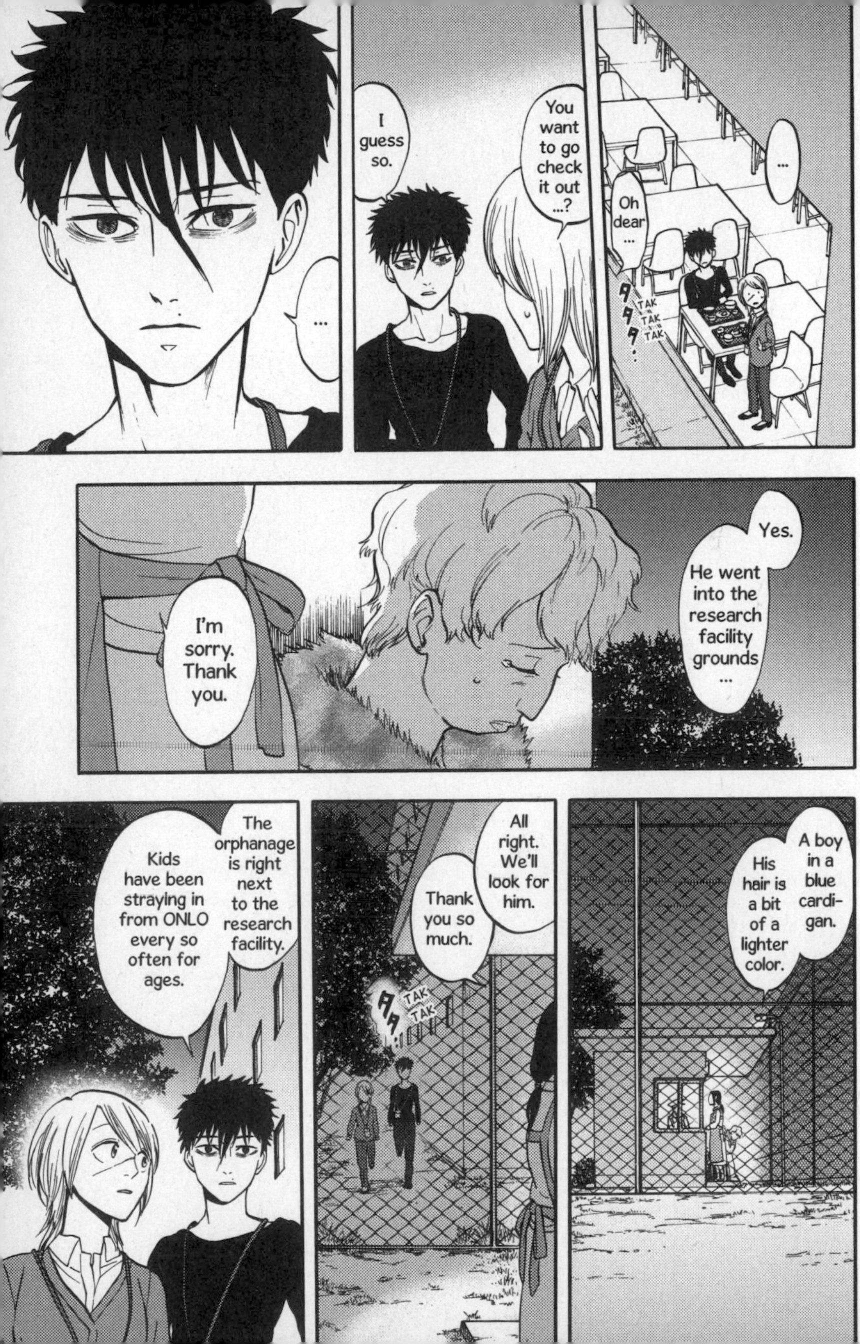
...
Oh dear ...
TAK TAK TAK
You want to go check it out ...?
I guess so.
...
Yes.
He went into the research facility grounds ...
I'm sorry. Thank you.
A boy in a blue cardi-gan.
His hair is a bit of a lighter color.
All right. We'll look for him.
Thank you so much.
TAK TAK
The orphanage is right next to the research facility.
Kids have been straying in from ONLO every so often for ages.

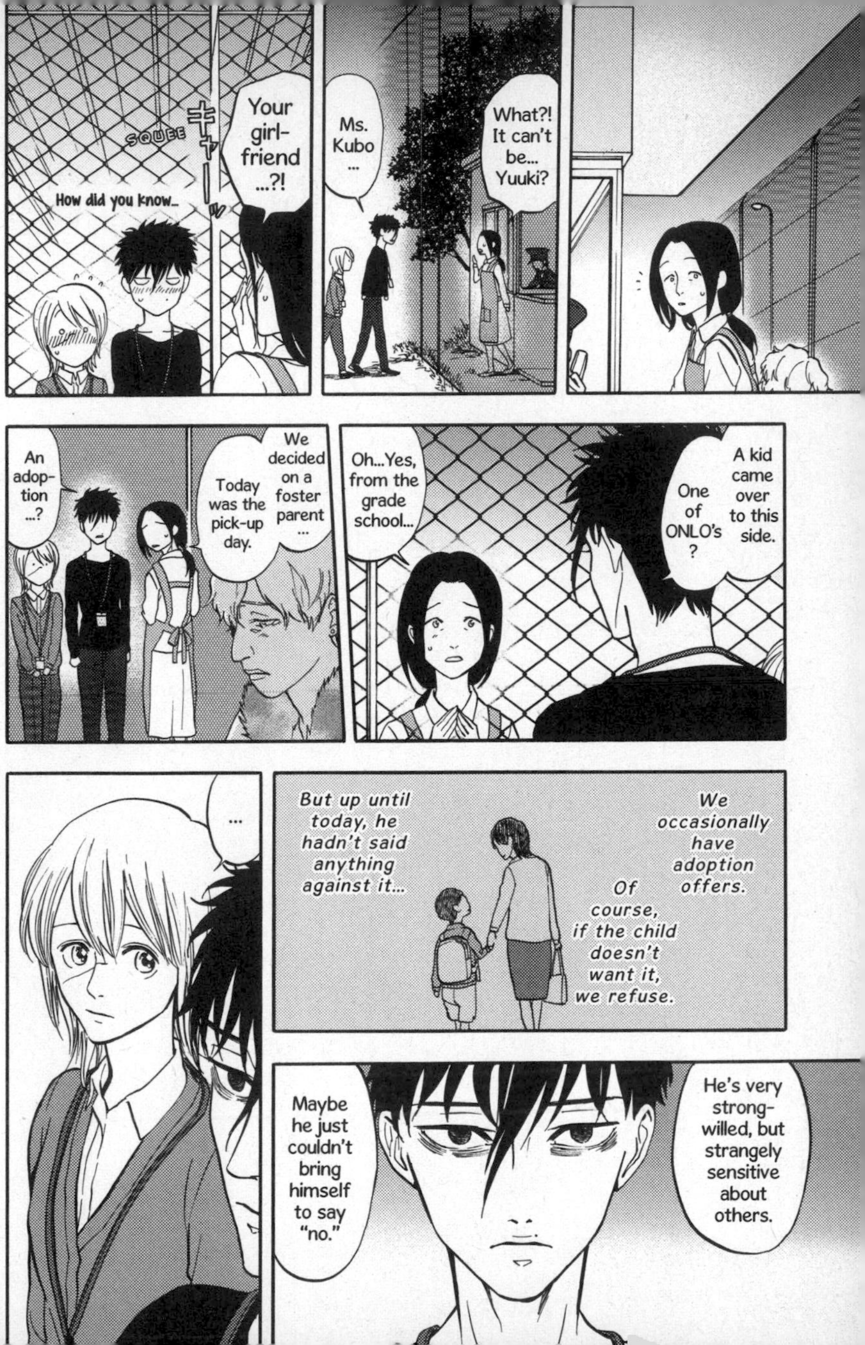
What?! It can't be... Yuuki?
Ms. Kubo ...
Your girl-friend ...?!
SQUEE
How did you know...
A kid came over to this side.
One of ONLO's ?
Oh...Yes, from the grade school...
We decided on a foster parent ...
Today was the pick-up day.
An adop-tion ...?
We occasionally have adoption offers.
Of course, if the child doesn't want it, we refuse.
But up until today, he hadn't said anything against it...
He's very strong-willed, but strangely sensitive about others.
Maybe he just couldn't bring himself to say "no."
...

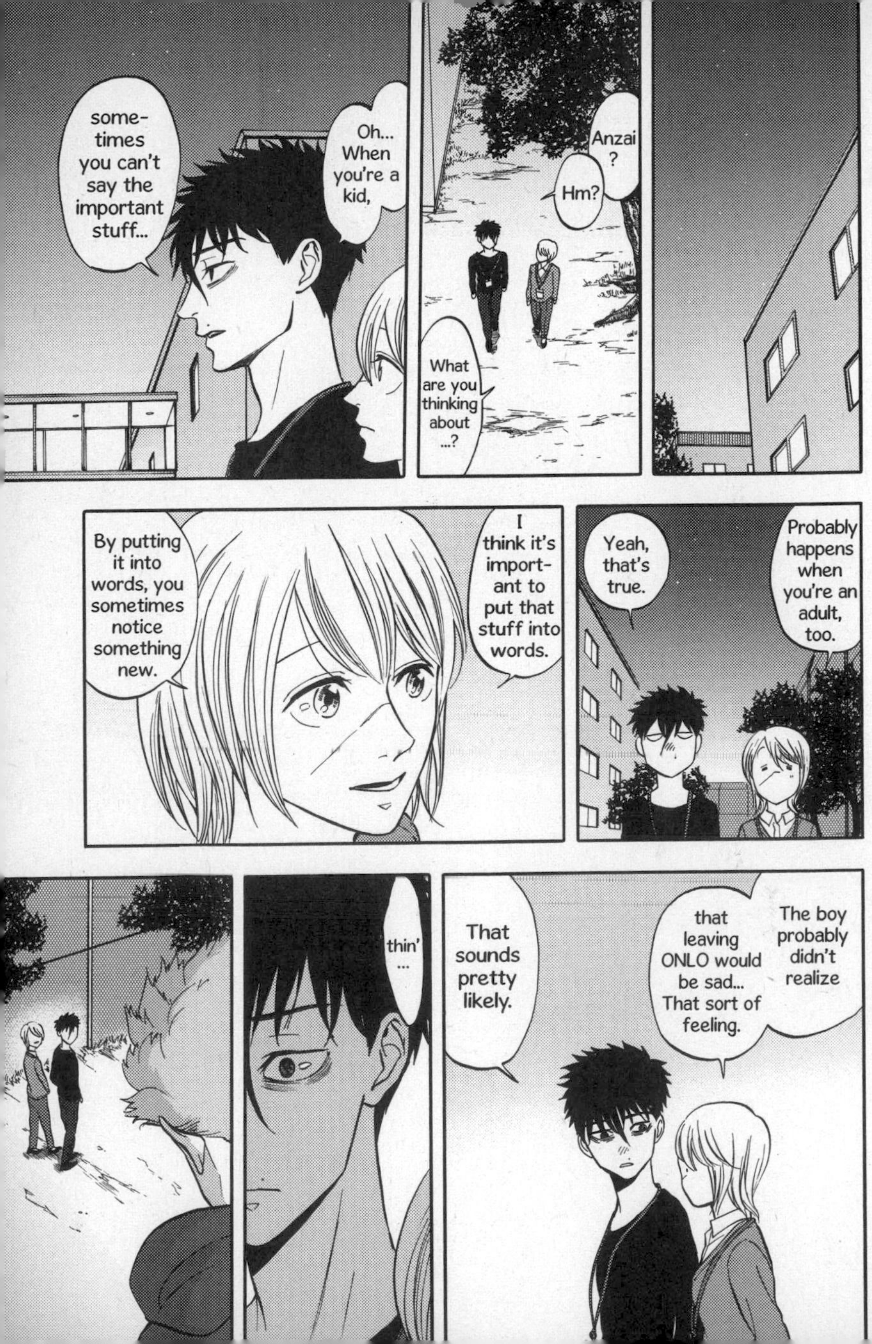
Anzai?
Hm?
What are you thinking about...?
Oh... When you're a kid,
sometimes you can't say the important stuff...
Probably happens when you're an adult, too.
Yeah, that's true.
I think it's important to put that stuff into words.
By putting it into words, you sometimes notice something new.
The boy probably didn't realize
that leaving ONLO would be sad... That sort of feeling.
That sounds pretty likely.
thin' ...

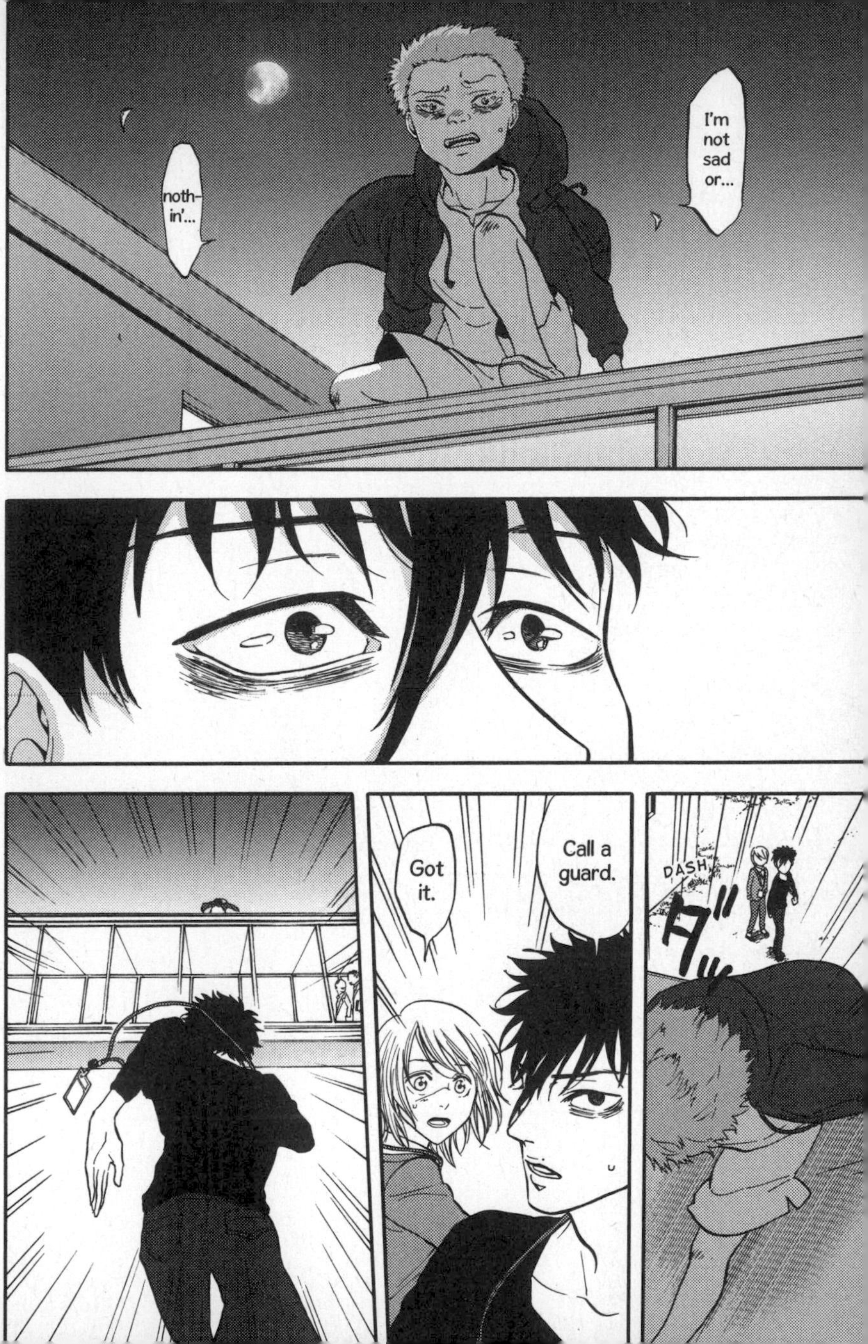
I'm not sad or...
noth-in'...
DASH
ダッ
Call a guard.
Got it.

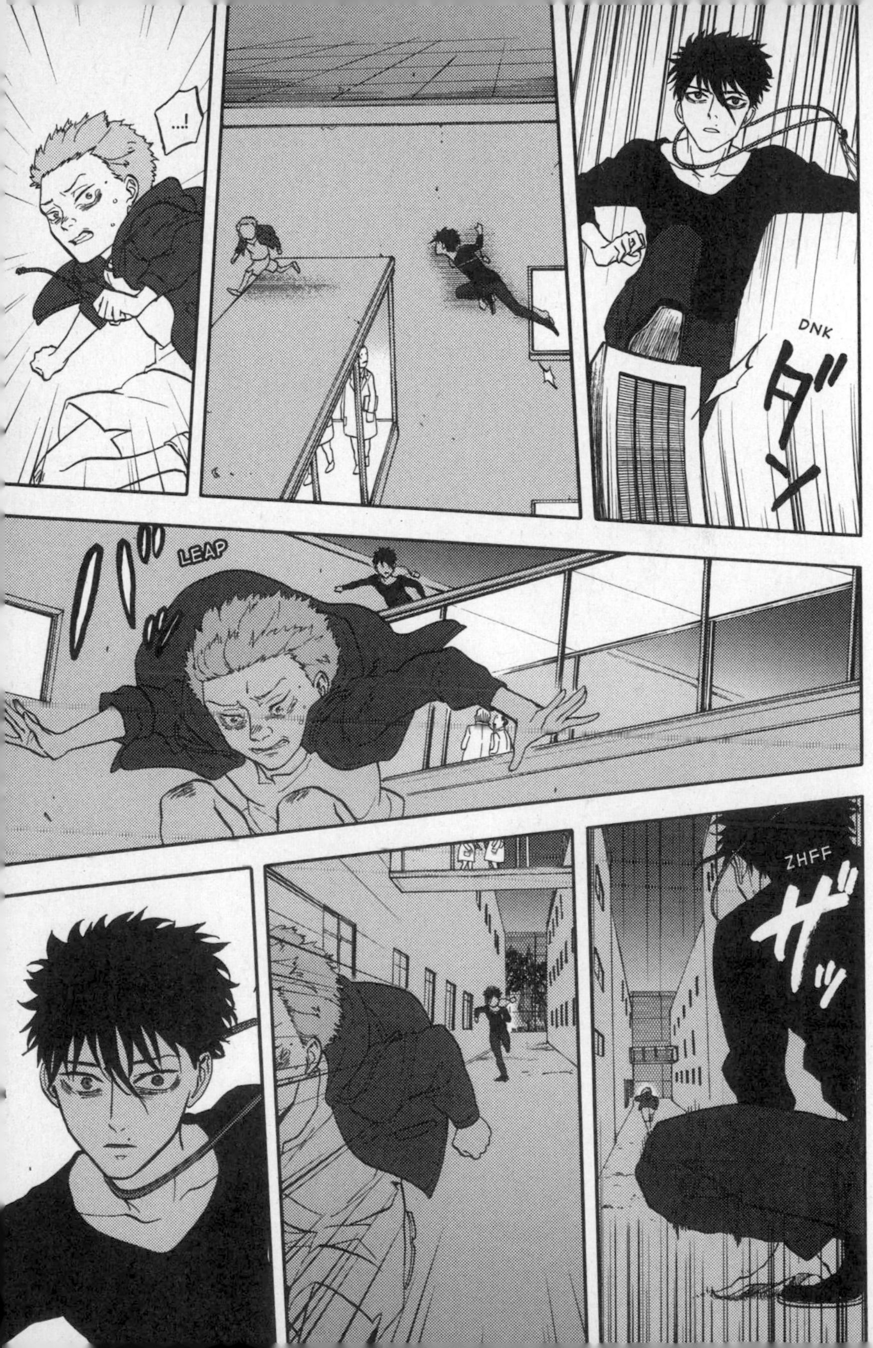
DNK
ダン
...!
LEAP
ZHFF
ザッ

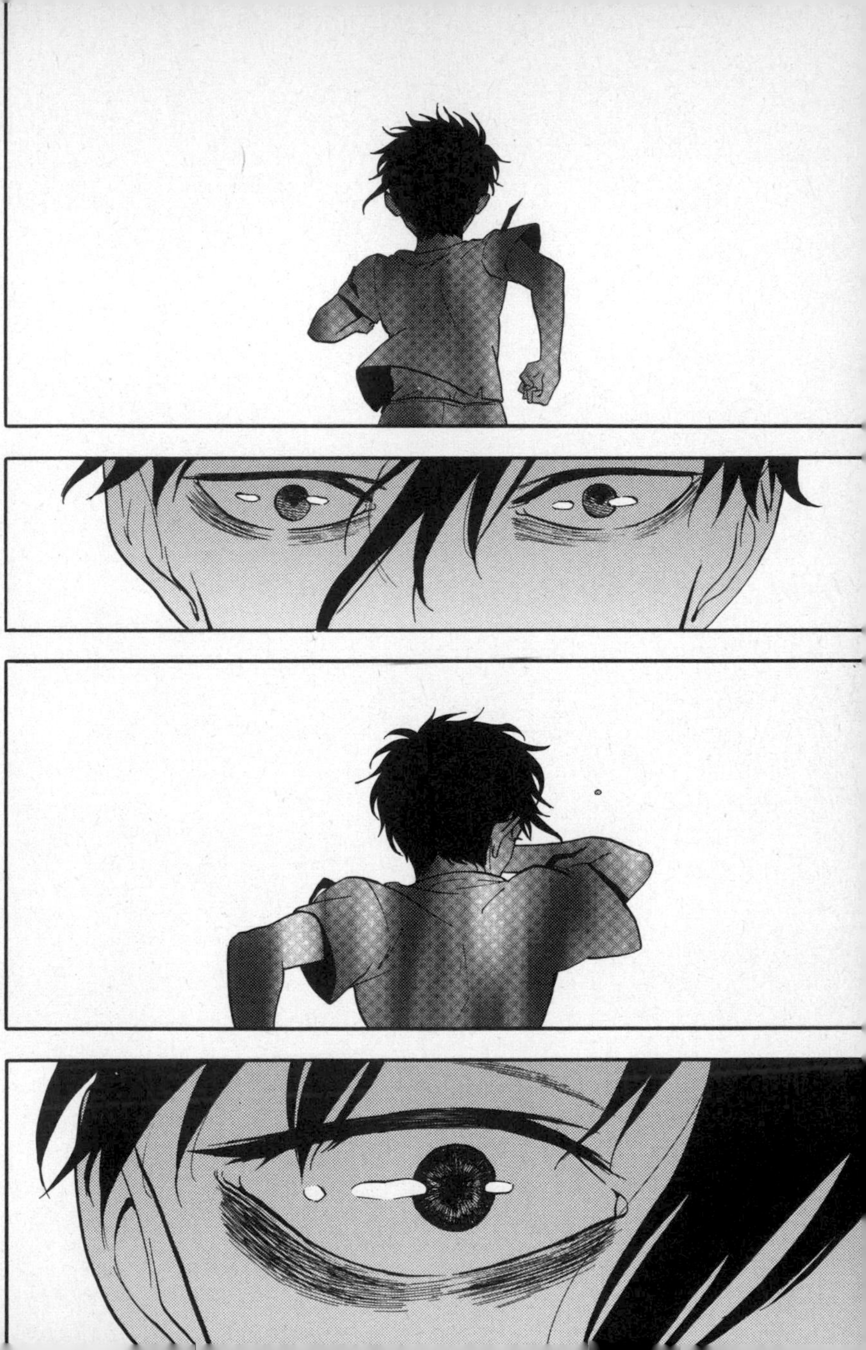

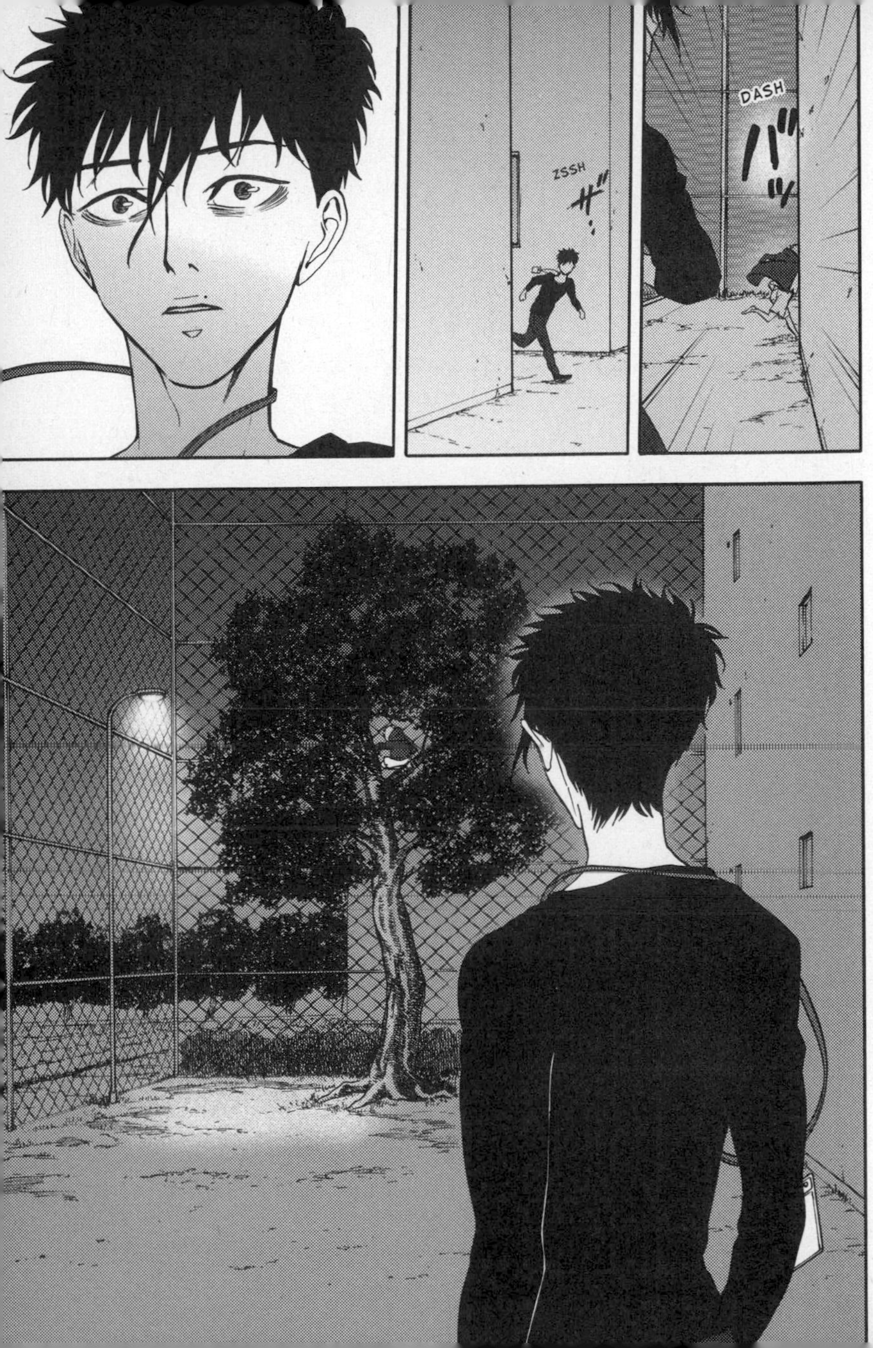
DASH
バッ
ZSSH
ザ

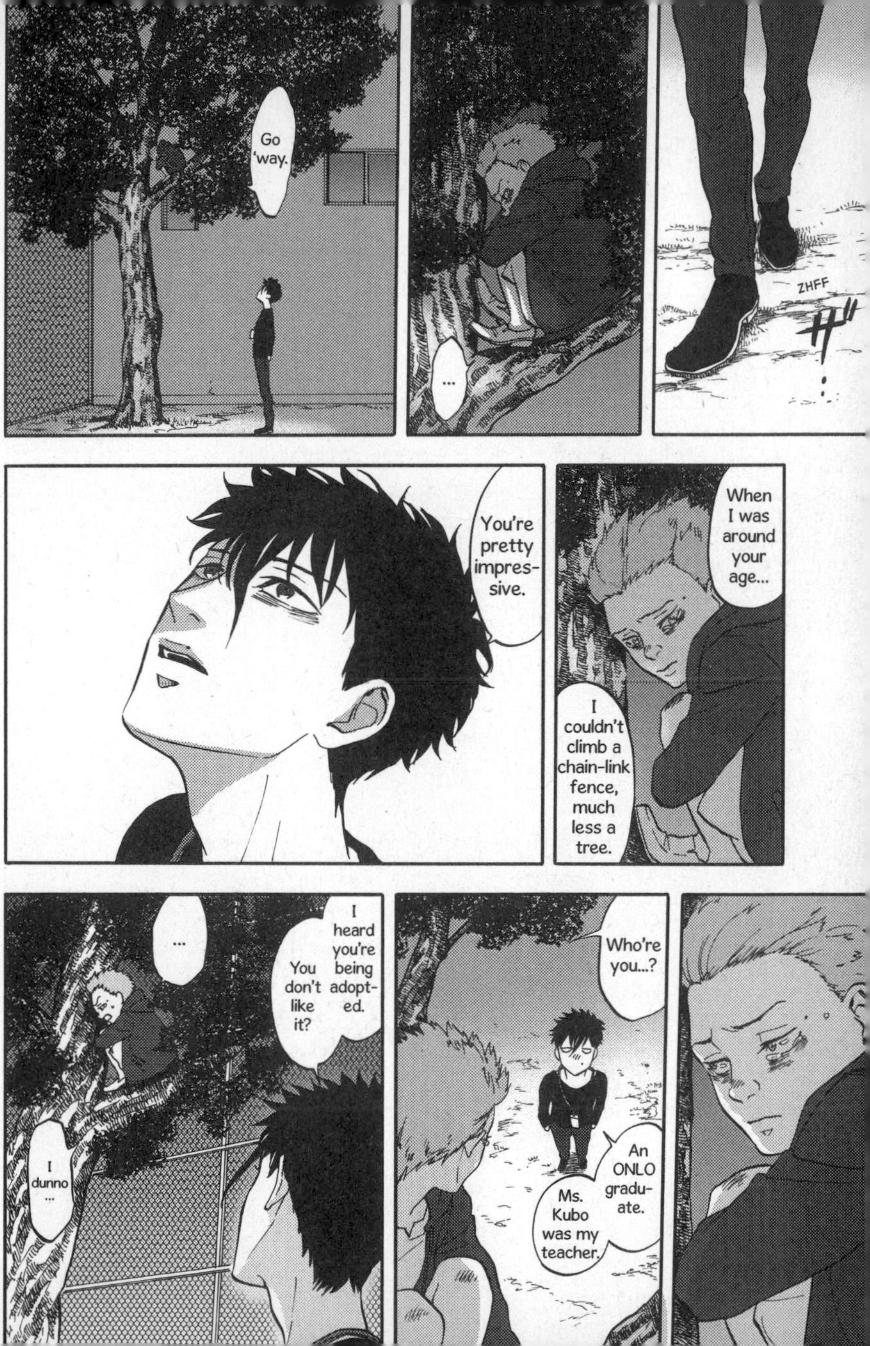
ZHFF
...
Go 'way.
When I was around your age...
I couldn't climb a chain-link fence, much less a tree.
You're pretty impressive.
Who're you...?
An ONLO graduate.
Ms. Kubo was my teacher.
I heard you're being adopted.
You don't like it?
...
I dunno...

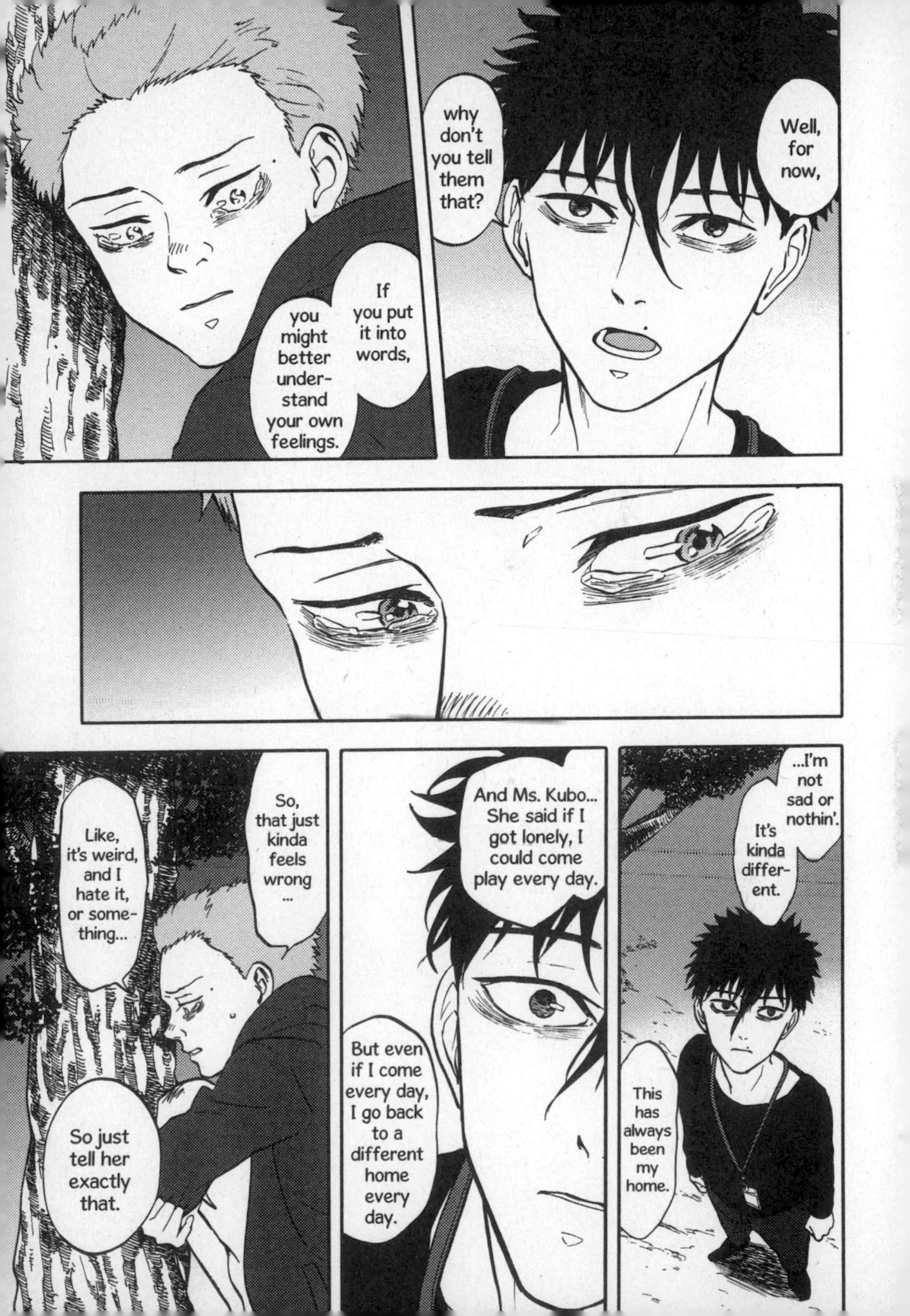
Well, for now,
why don't you tell them that?
If you put it into words,
you might better under-stand your own feelings.
...I'm not sad or nothin'.
It's kinda differ-ent.
This has always been my home.
And Ms. Kubo... She said if I got lonely, I could come play every day.
But even if I come every day, I go back to a different home every day.
So, that just kinda feels wrong ...
Like, it's weird, and I hate it, or some-thing...
So just tell her exactly that.

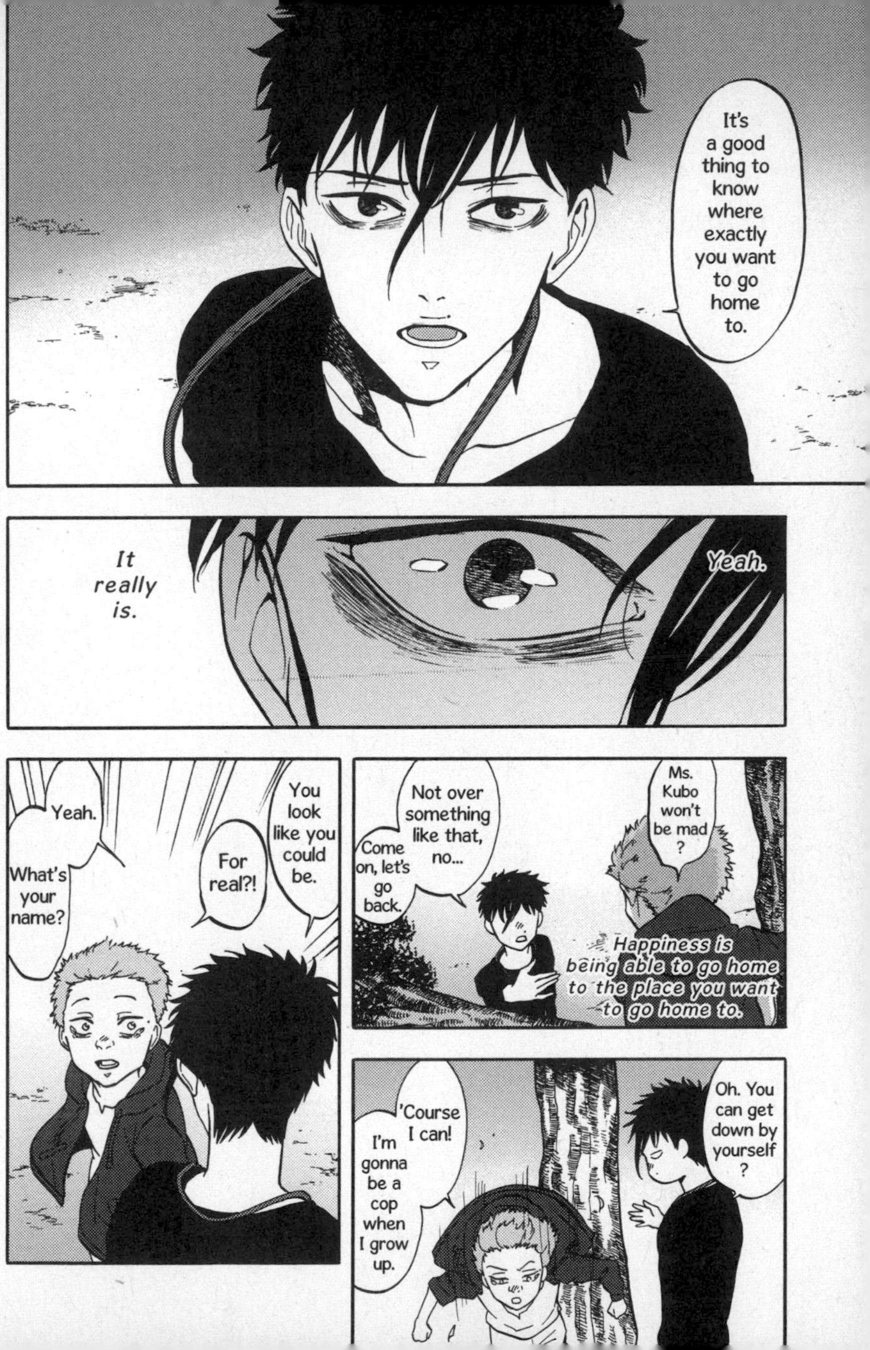
It's a good thing to know where exactly you want to go home to.
Yeah.
It really is.
Ms. Kubo won't be mad?
Not over something like that, no...
Come on, let's go back.
Happiness is being able to go home to the place you want to go home to.
Oh. You can get down by yourself?
'Course I can!
I'm gonna be a cop when I grow up.
You look like you could be.
For real?!
Yeah.
What's your name?

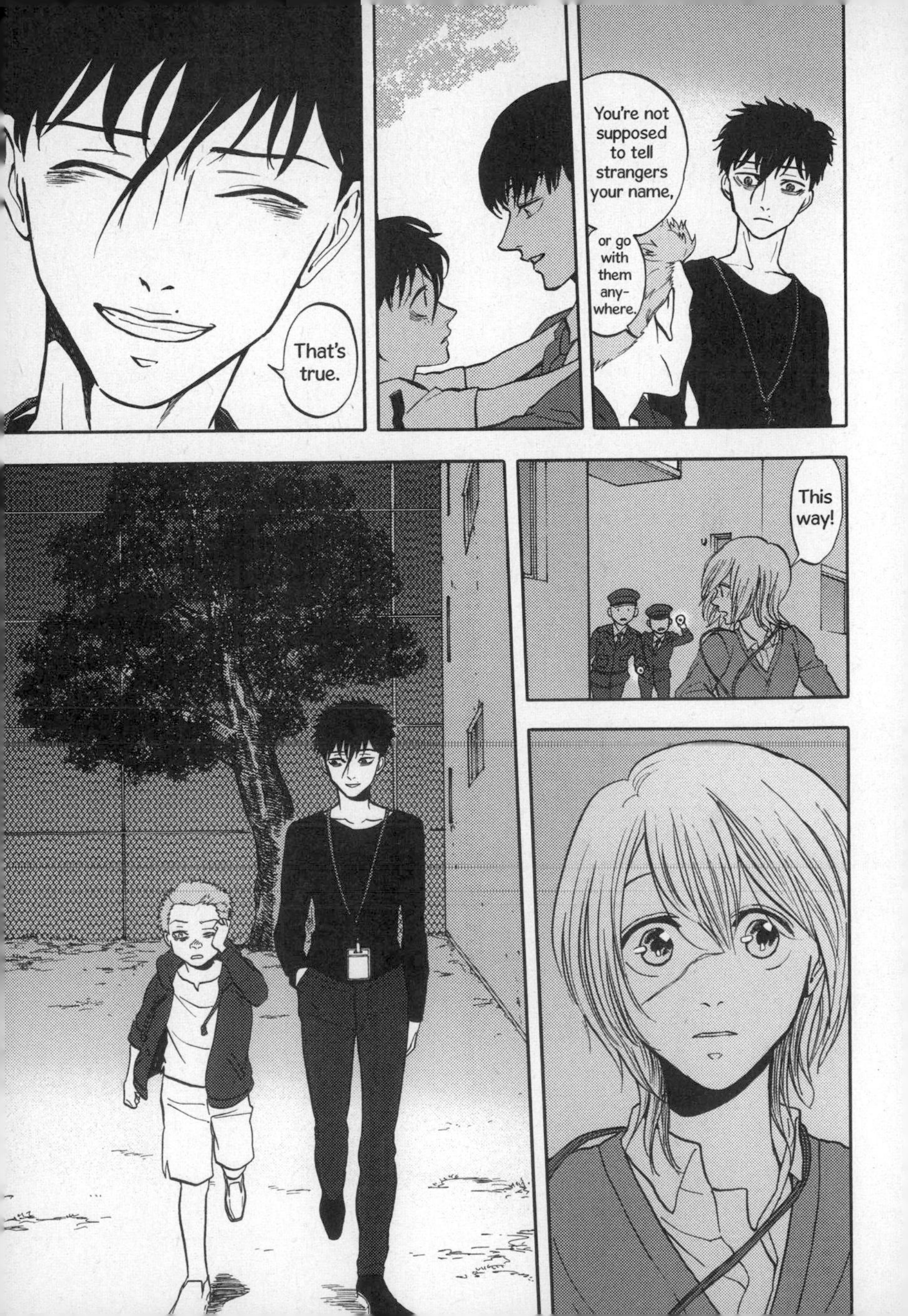
You're not supposed to tell strangers your name,
or go with them any-where.
That's true.
This way!

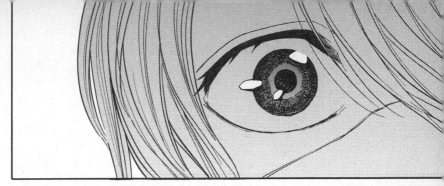

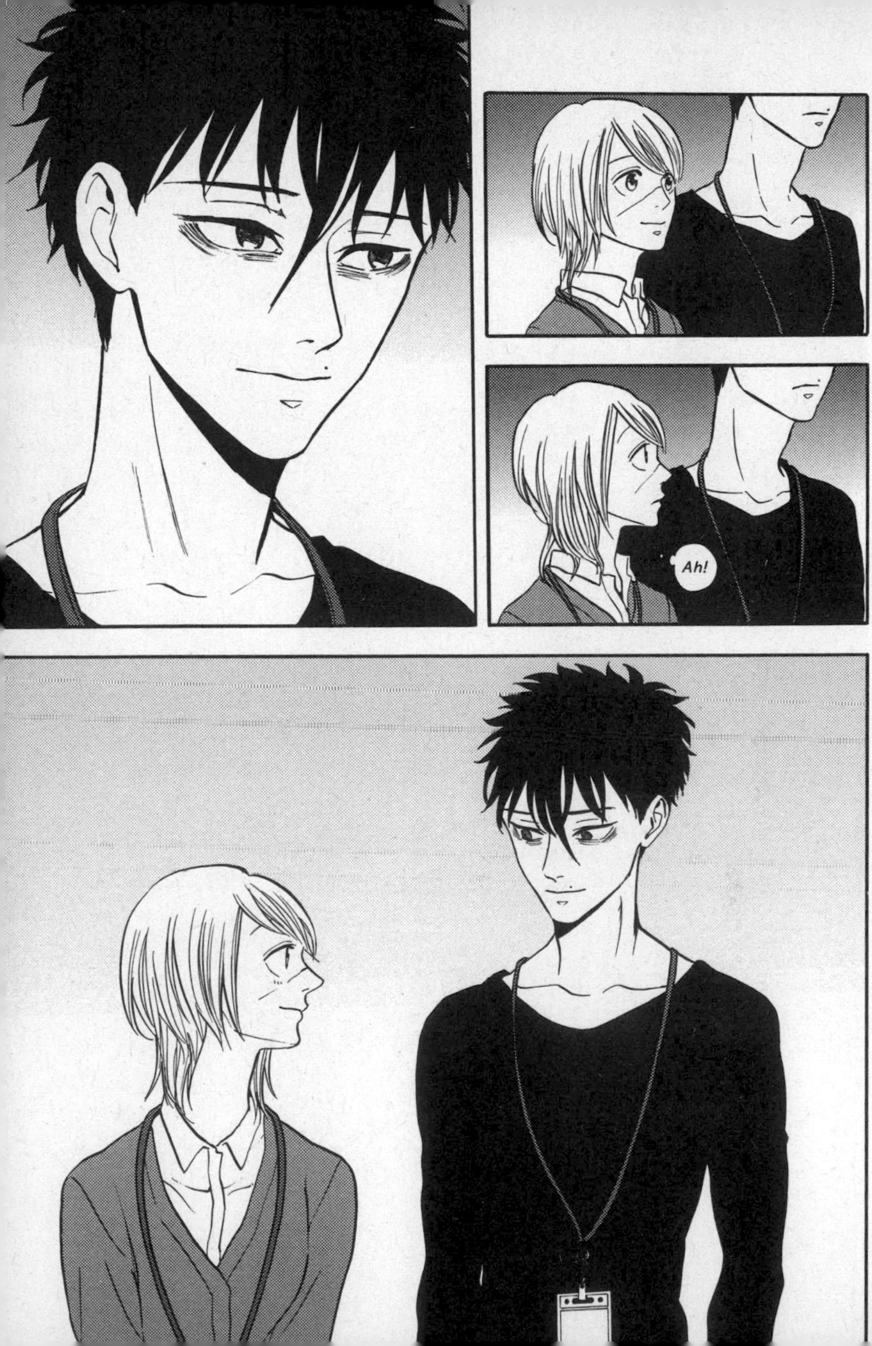
Ah!

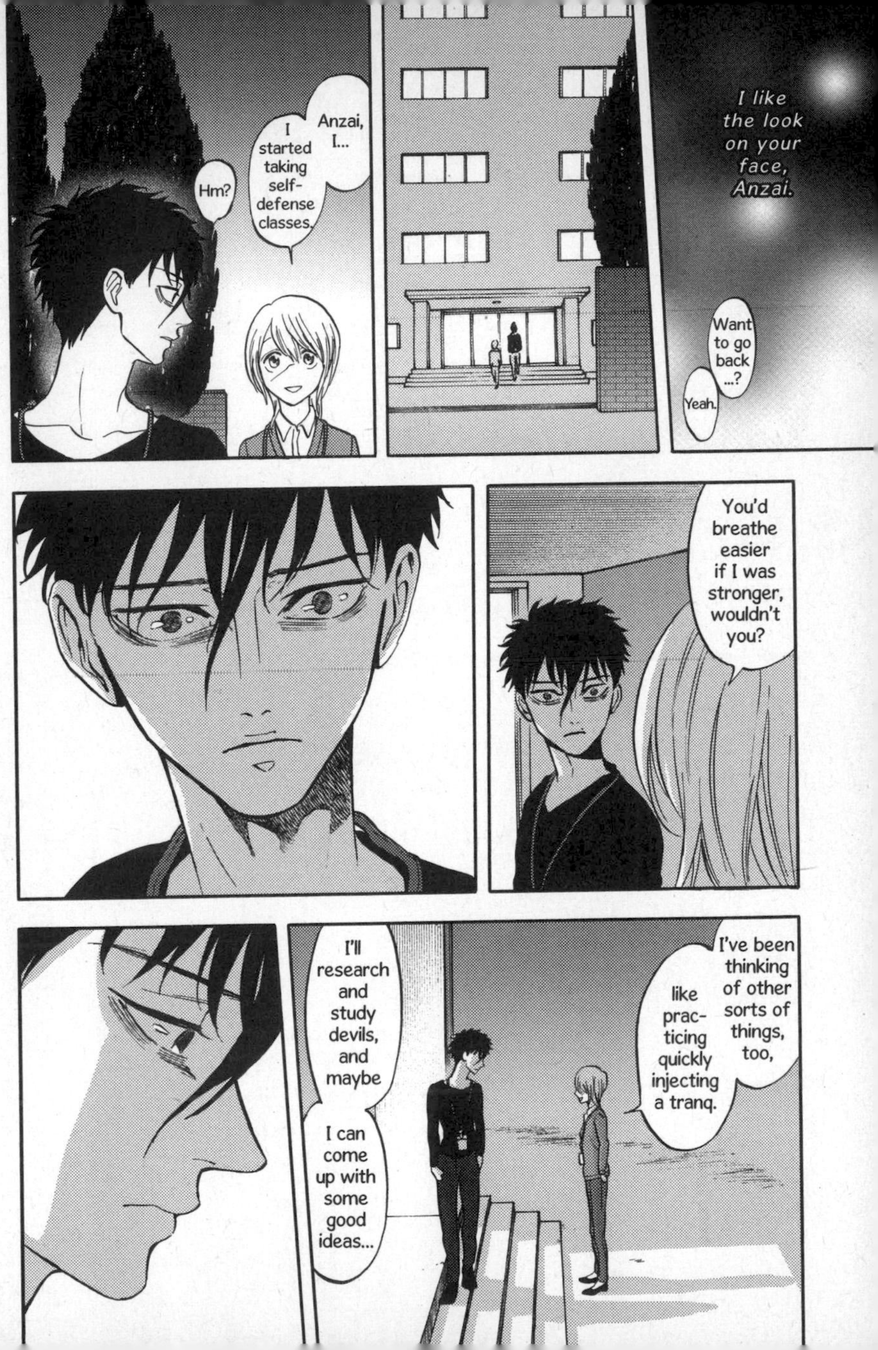
I like the look on your face, Anzai.
Want to go back...?
Yeah.
Anzai, I...
I started taking self-defense classes.
Hm?
You'd breathe easier if I was stronger, wouldn't you?
I've been thinking of other sorts of things, too,
like practicing quickly injecting a tranq.
I'll research and study devils, and maybe
I can come up with some good ideas...

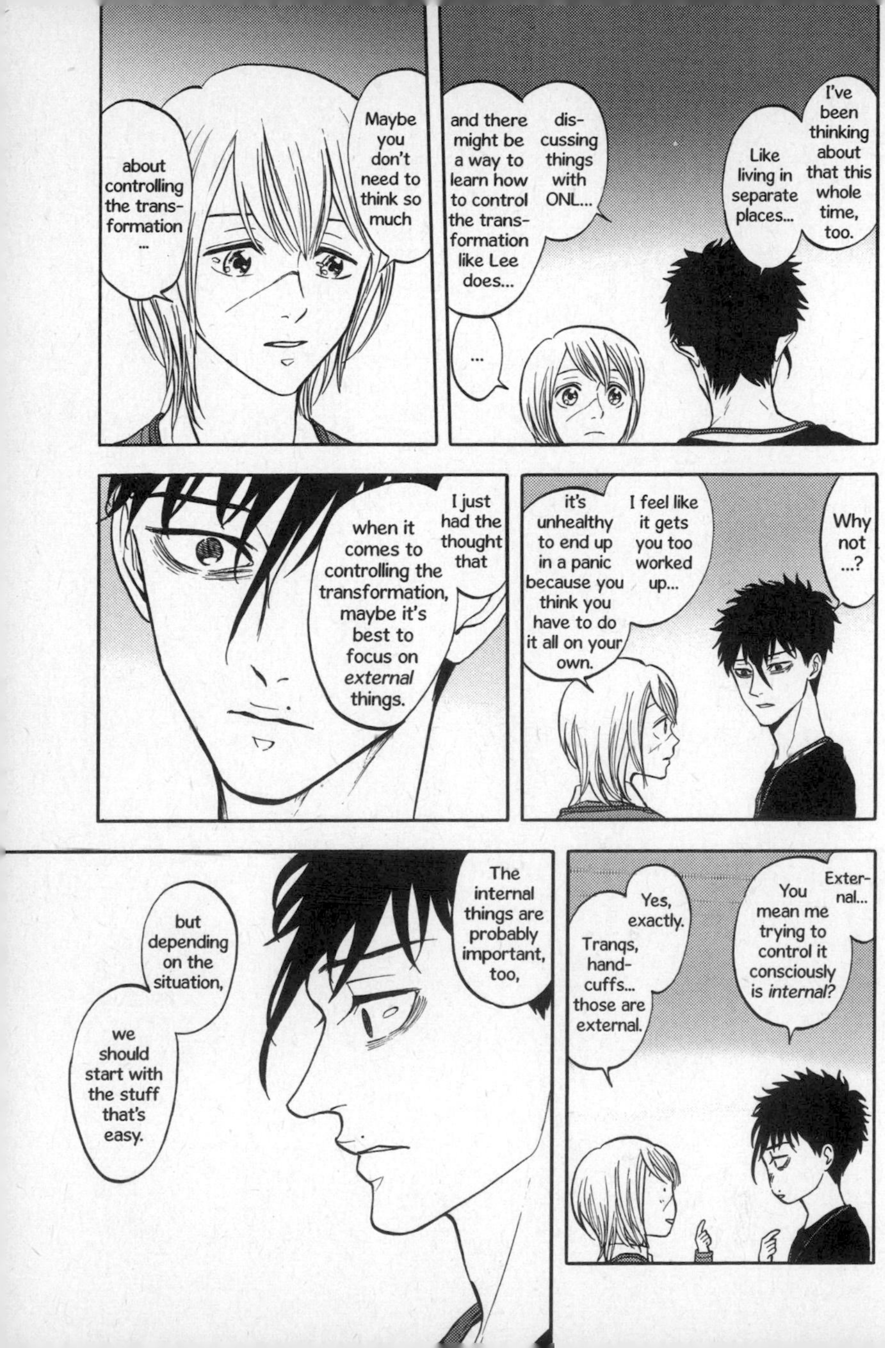
I've been thinking about that this whole time, too.
Like living in separate places...
dis-cussing things with ONL...
and there might be a way to learn how to control the trans-formation like Lee does...
...
Maybe you don't need to think so much
about controlling the trans-formation ...
Why not ...?
I feel like it gets you too worked up...
it's unhealthy to end up in a panic because you think you have to do it all on your own.
I just had the thought that
when it comes to controlling the transformation, maybe it's best to focus on *external* things.
Exter-nal...
You mean me trying to control it consciously is *internal?*
Yes, exactly.
Tranqs, hand-cuffs... those are external.
The internal things are probably important, too,
but depending on the situation,
we should start with the stuff that's easy.

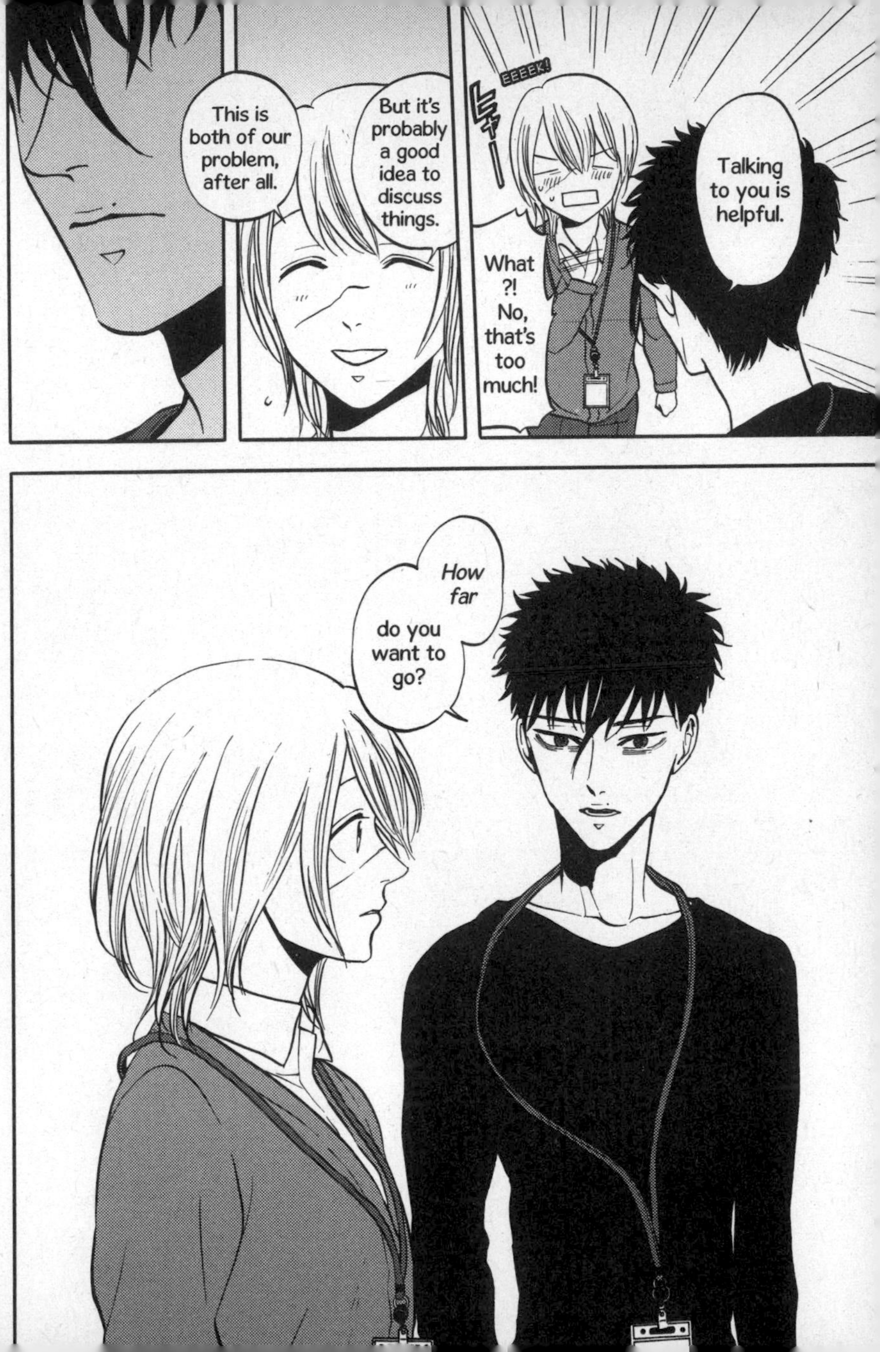
Talking to you is helpful.
EEEEK!
What?! No, that's too much!
But it's probably a good idea to discuss things.
This is both of our problem, after all.
How far do you want to go?

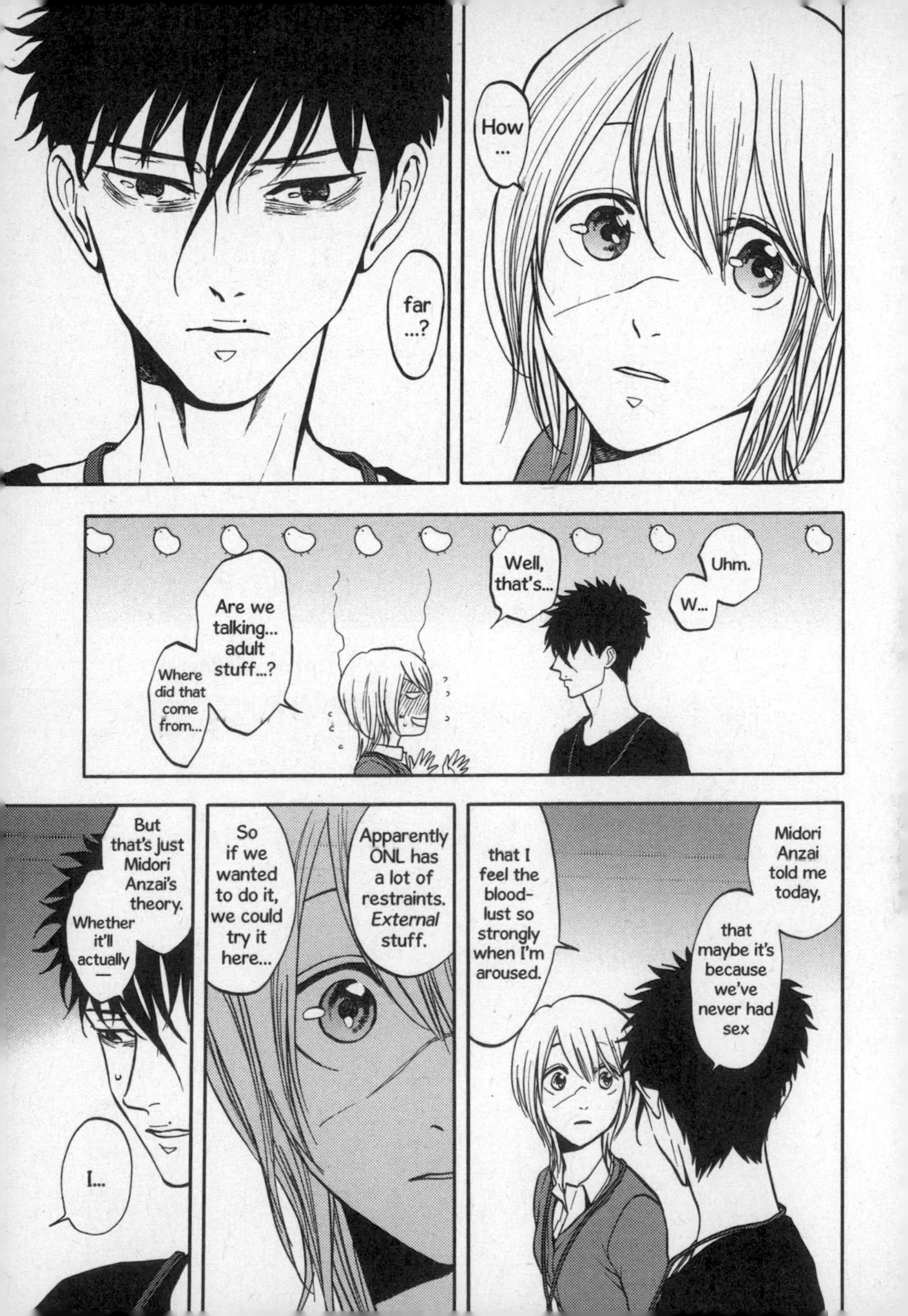
How ...
far ...?
Uhm.
W...
Well, that's...
Are we talking... adult stuff...?
Where did that come from...
Midori Anzai told me today,
that maybe it's because we've never had sex
that I feel the blood-lust so strongly when I'm aroused.
Apparently ONL has a lot of restraints. *External* stuff.
So if we wanted to do it, we could try it here...
But that's just Midori Anzai's theory.
Whether it'll actually —
I...

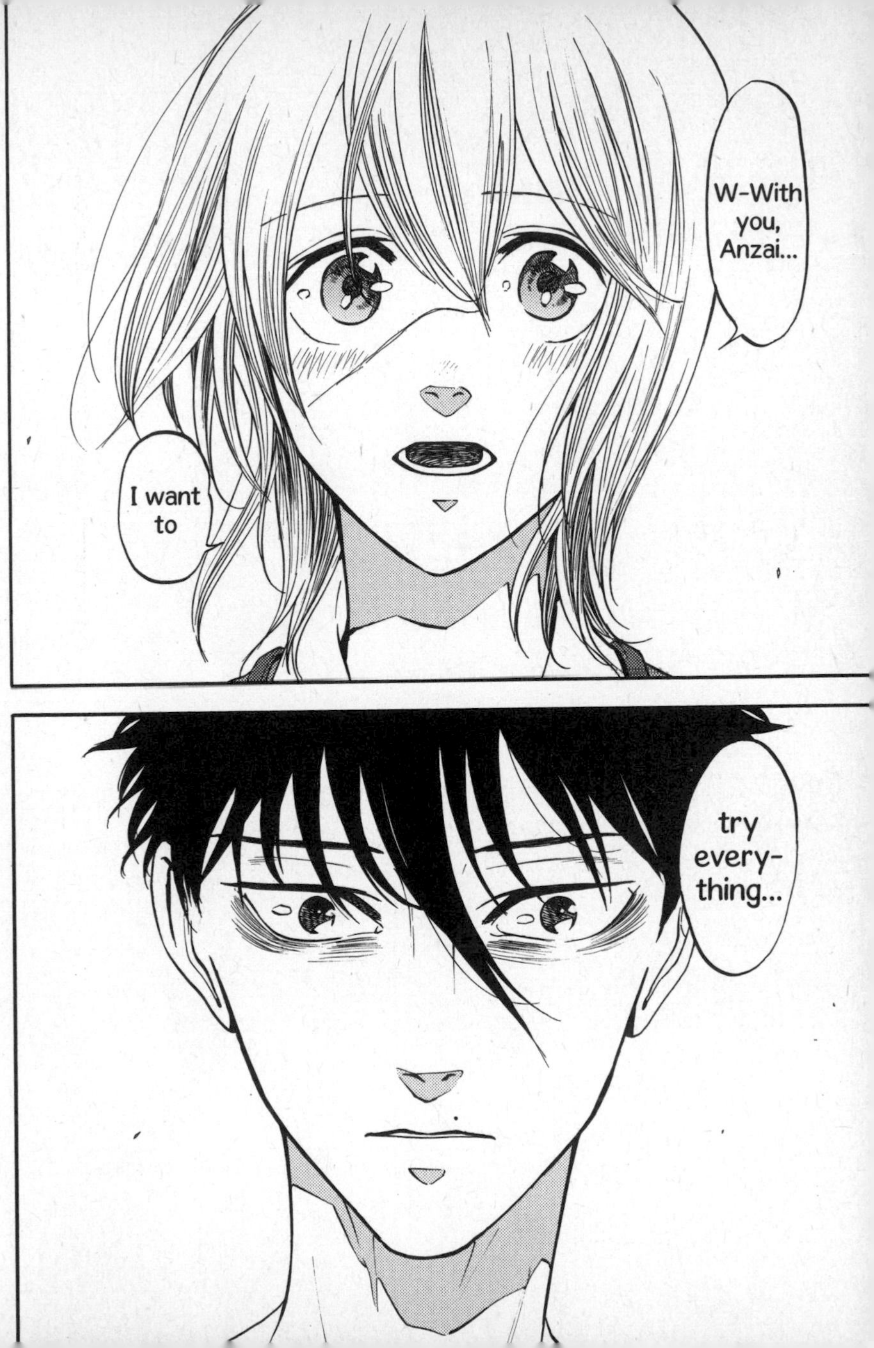
W-With you, Anzai...
I want to
try every-thing...

How far do *you* want to go?!

WHPP

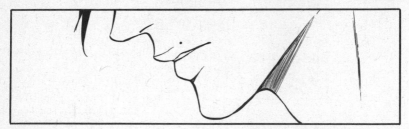

I want to do all the things

that we can...

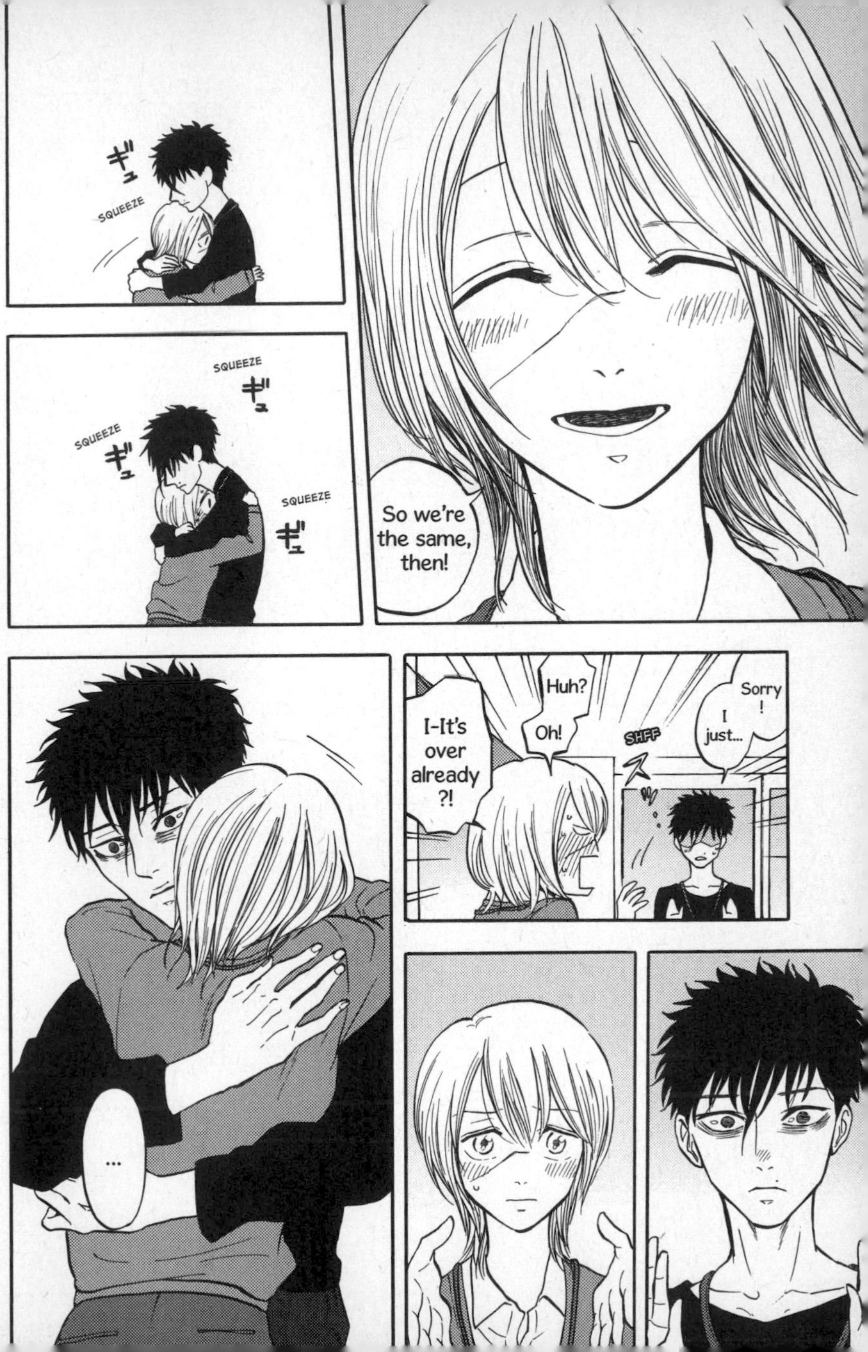
So we're the same, then!
ギュ
SQUEEZE
SQUEEZE
ギュ
SQUEEZE
ギュ
SQUEEZE
ギュ
Sorry! I just...
SHFF
ス
Huh?
Oh!
I-It's over already?!
...

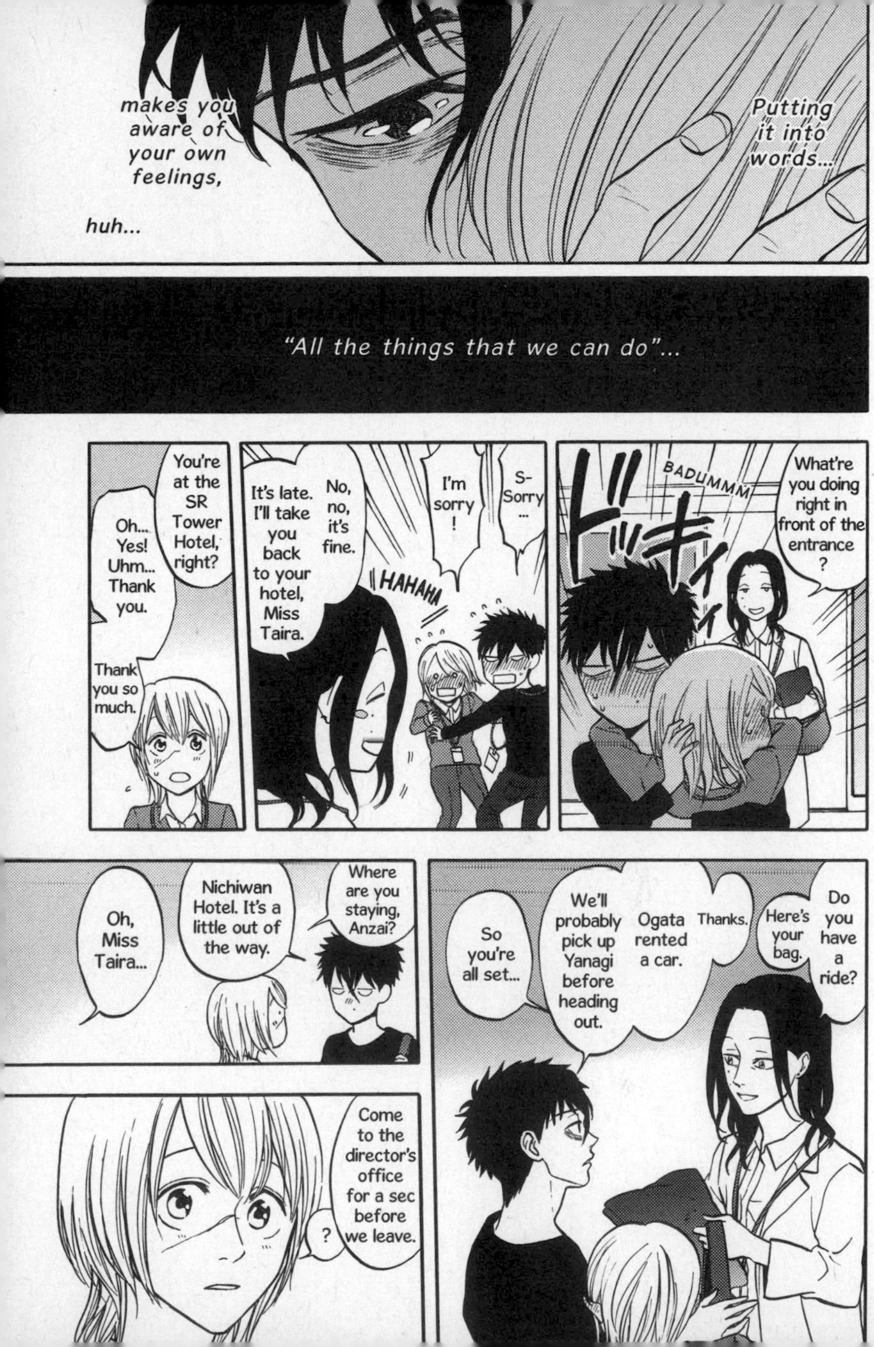
Putting it into words...
makes you aware of your own feelings,
huh...
"All the things that we can do"...
What're you doing right in front of the entrance?
BADUMMM
ドッキイ
S-Sorry...
I'm sorry!
No, no, it's fine.
It's late. I'll take you back to your hotel, Miss Taira.
HAHAHA
You're at the SR Tower Hotel, right?
Oh... Yes! Uhm... Thank you.
Thank you so much.
Do you have a ride?
Here's your bag.
Thanks.
Ogata rented a car.
We'll probably pick up Yanagi before heading out.
So you're all set...
Where are you staying, Anzai?
Nichiwan Hotel. It's a little out of the way.
Oh, Miss Taira...
Come to the director's office for a sec before we leave.
?

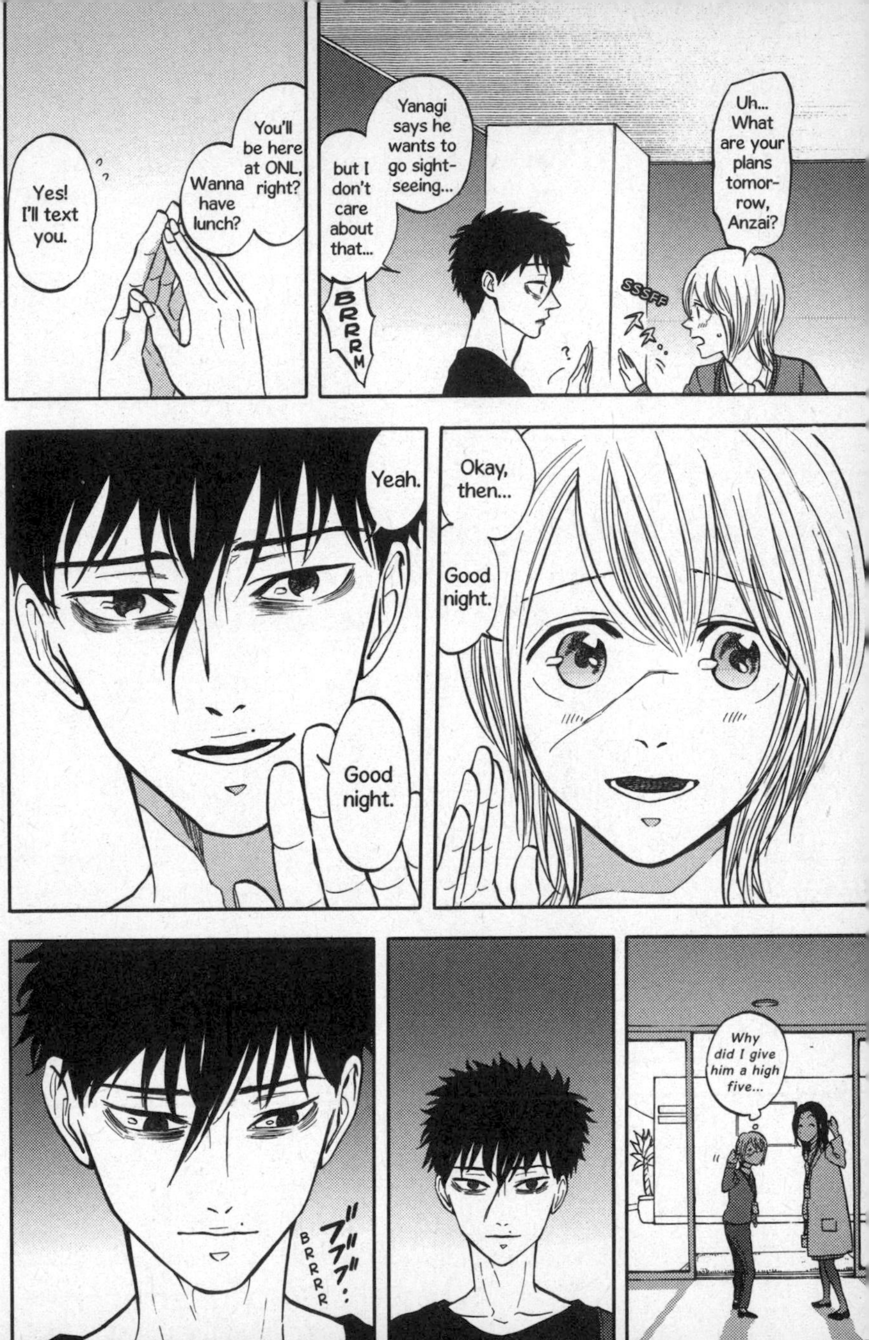
Uh... What are your plans tomorrow, Anzai?
SSSFF
Yanagi says he wants to go sight-seeing...
but I don't care about that...
BRRRM
You'll be here at ONL, right?
Wanna have lunch?
Yes! I'll text you.
Okay, then...
Good night.
Yeah.
Good night.
Why did I give him a high five...
BRRRR

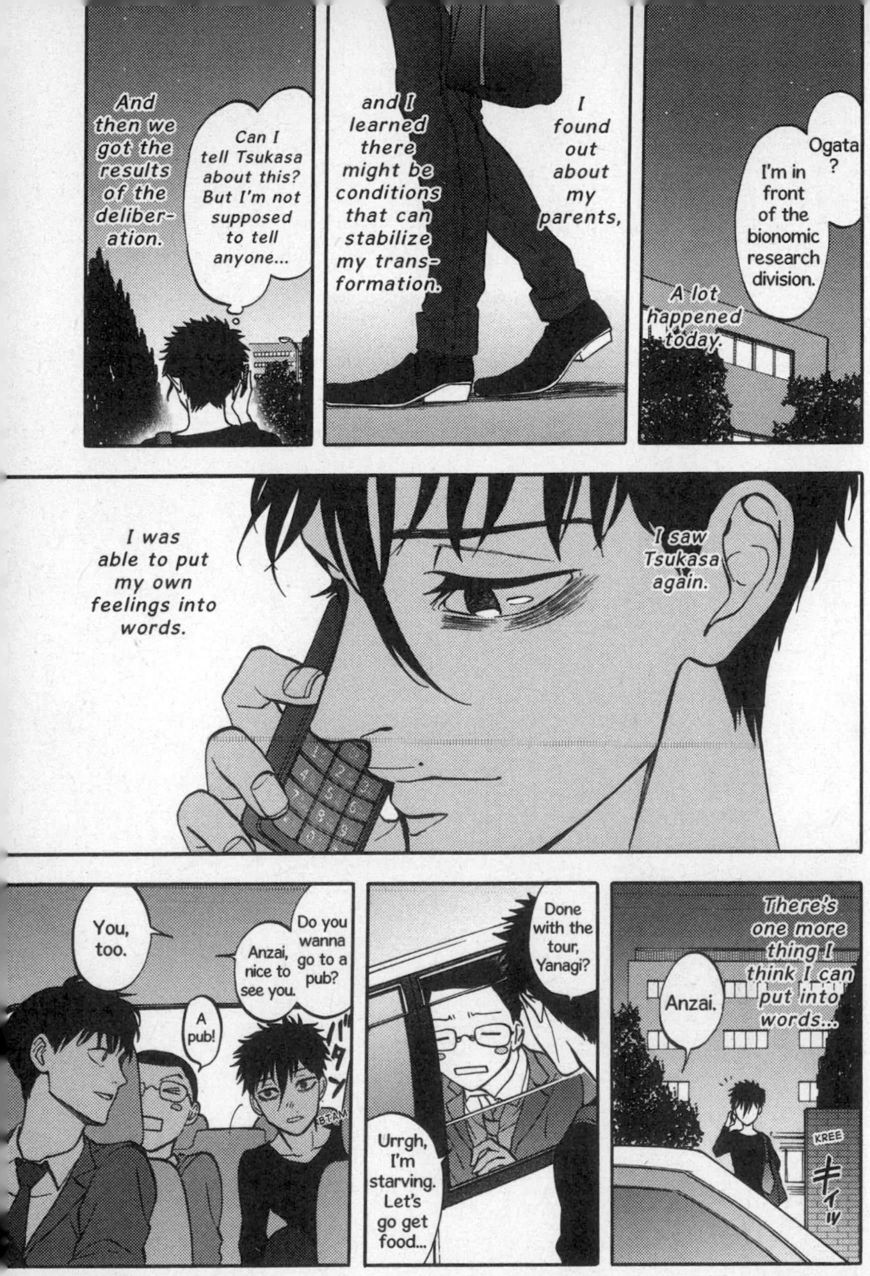
Ogata?
I'm in front of the bionomic research division.
A lot happened today.
I found out about my parents,
and I learned there might be conditions that can stabilize my transformation.
And then we got the results of the deliberation.
Can I tell Tsukasa about this? But I'm not supposed to tell anyone...
I saw Tsukasa again.
I was able to put my own feelings into words.
There's one more thing I think I can put into words...
Anzai.
KREE
キィ
Done with the tour, Yanagi?
Urrgh, I'm starving. Let's go get food...
Do you wanna go to a pub?
Anzai, nice to see you.
You, too.
A pub!
バタン
BTAM

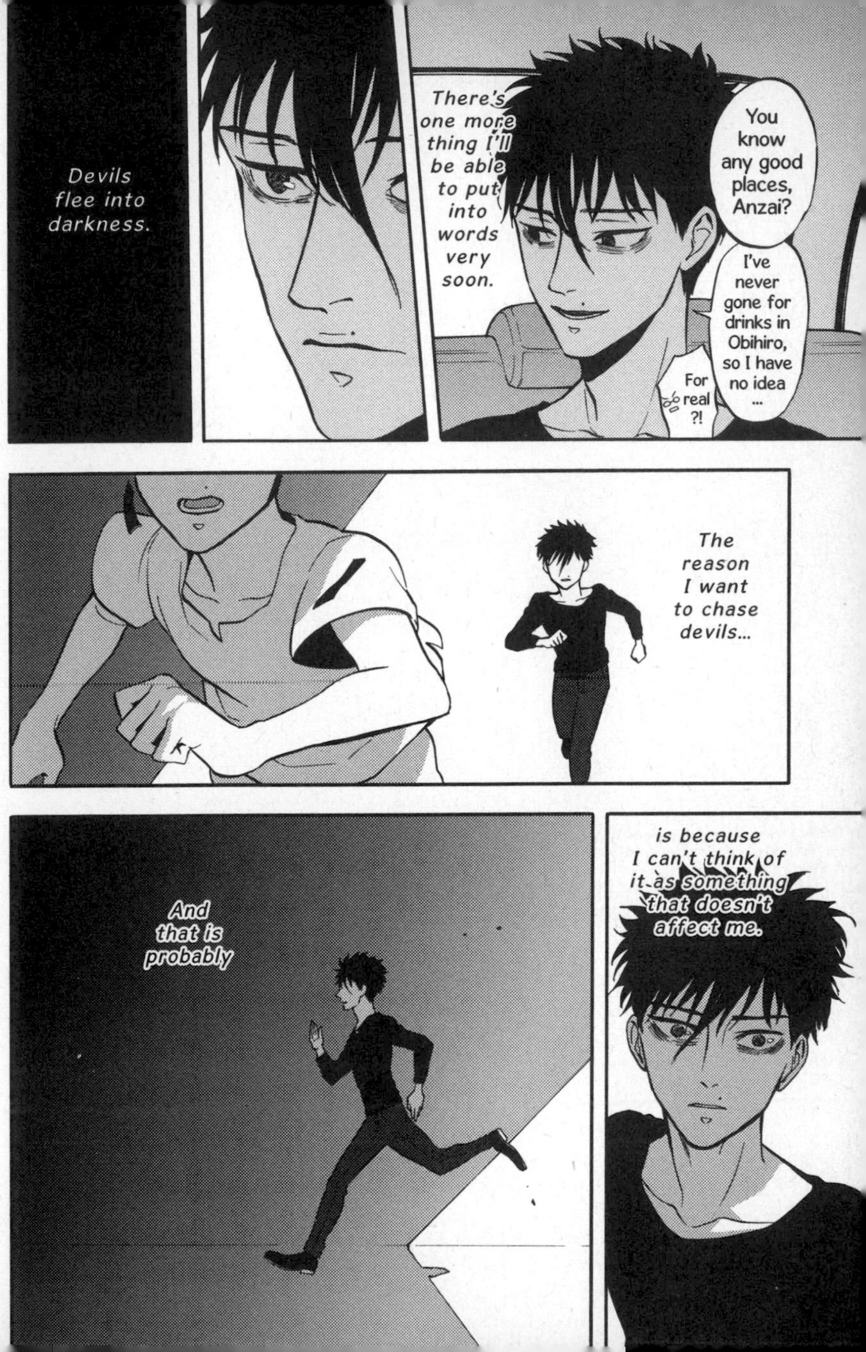
You know any good places, Anzai?
I've never gone for drinks in Obihiro, so I have no idea ...
For real ?!
There's one more thing I'll be able to put into words very soon.
Devils flee into darkness.
The reason I want to chase devils...
is because I can't think of it as something that doesn't affect me.
And that is probably

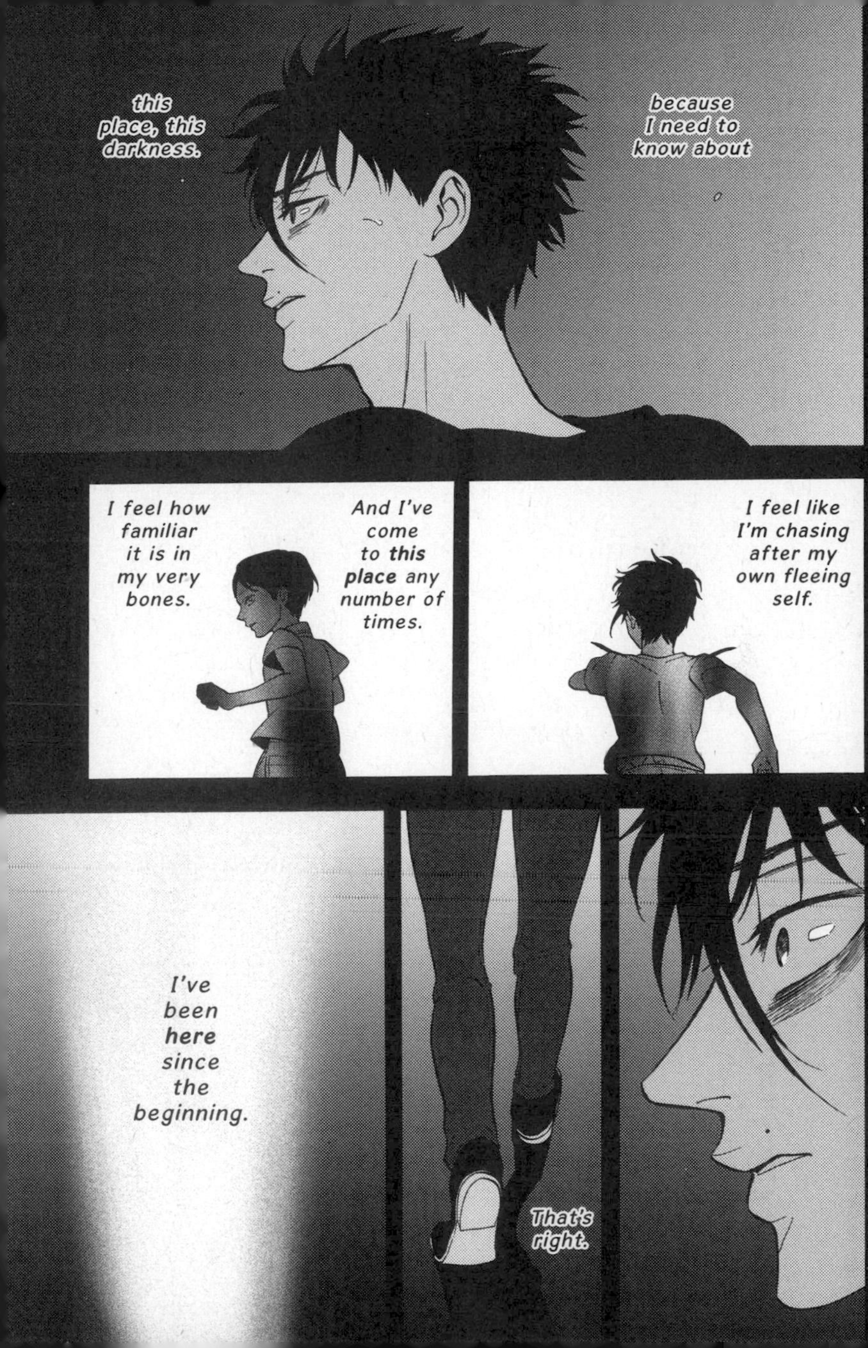
because I need to know about
this place, this darkness.
I feel like I'm chasing after my own fleeing self.
And I've come to **this place** any number of times.
I feel how familiar it is in my very bones.
That's right.
I've been **here** since the beginning.

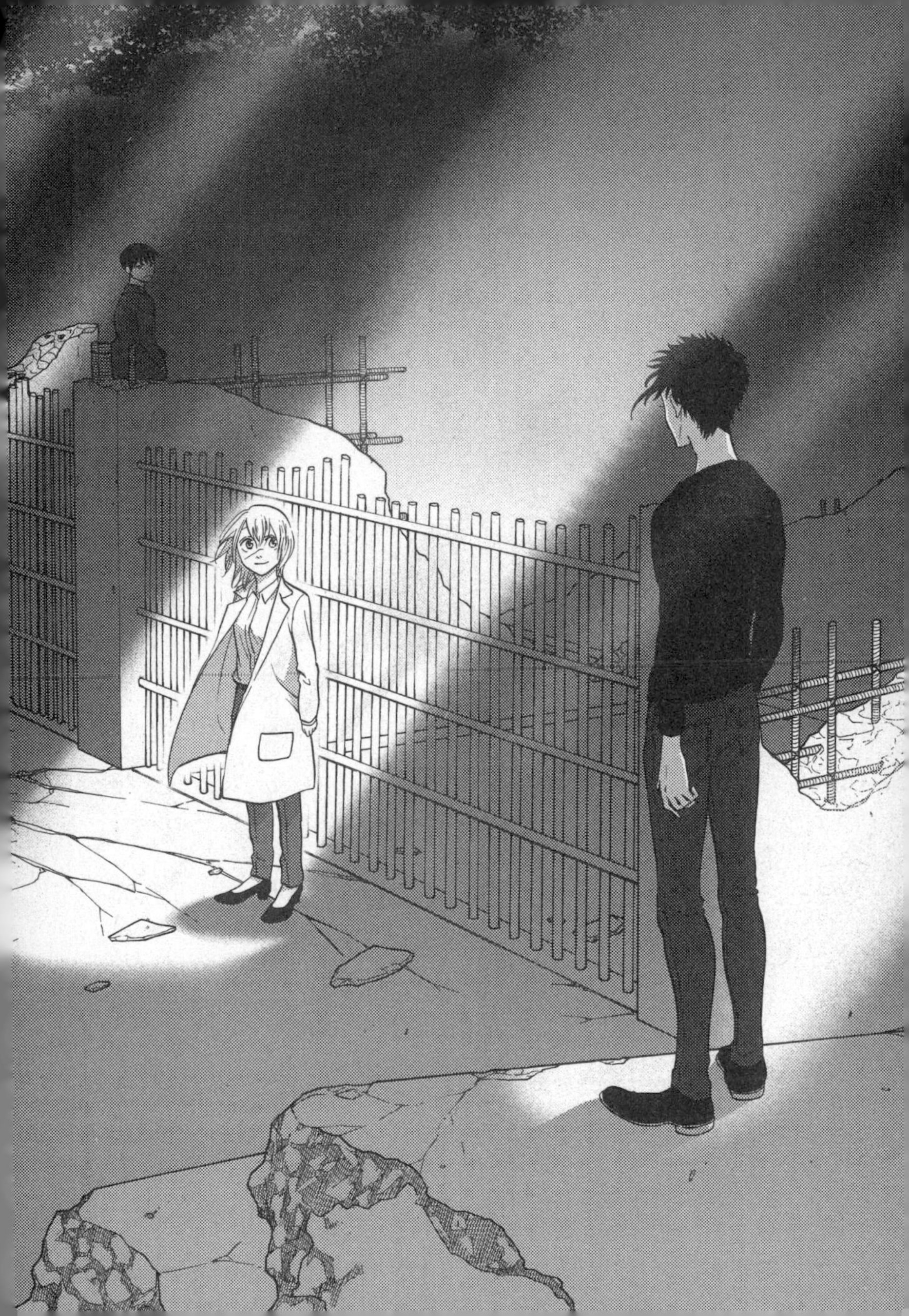

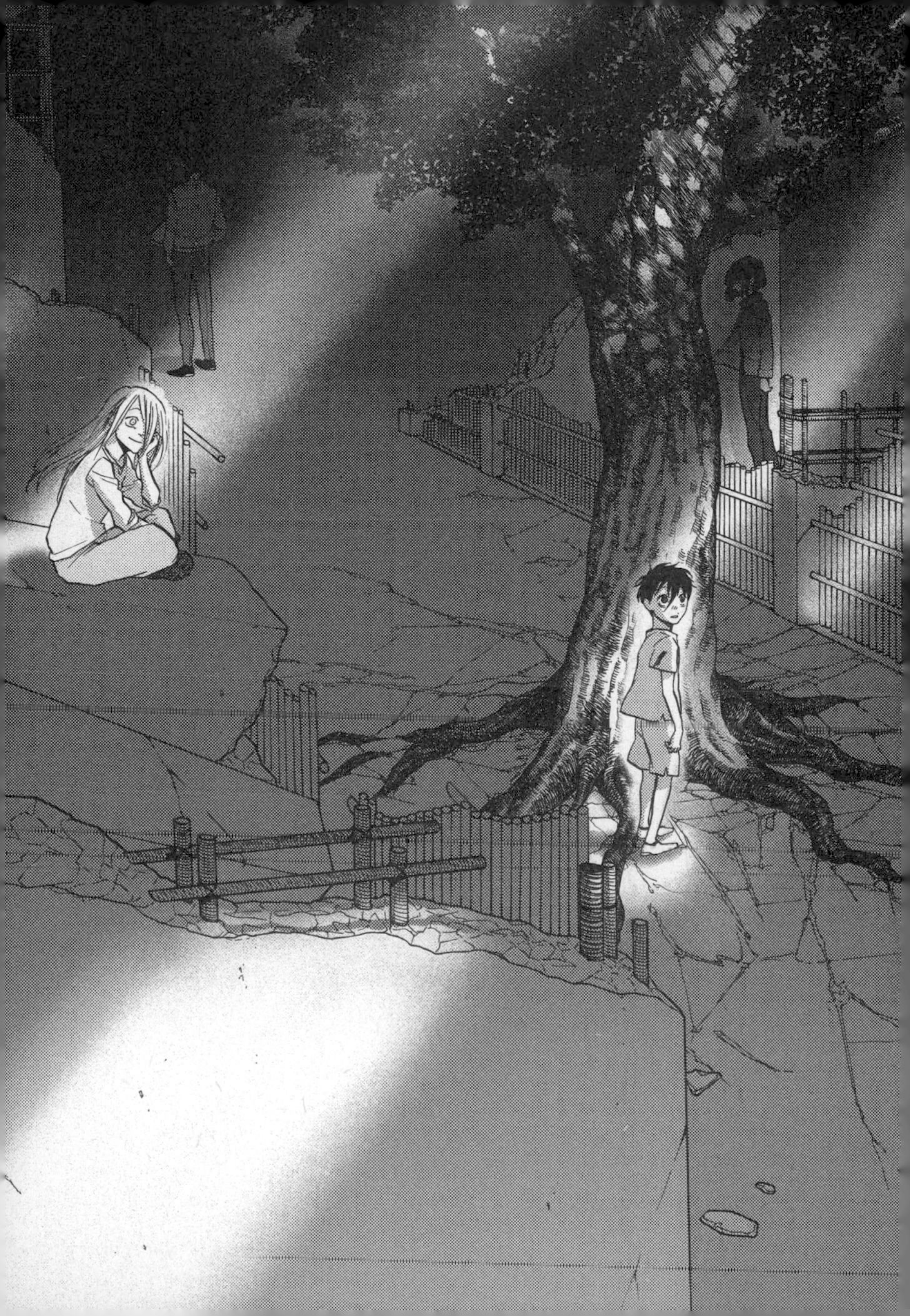

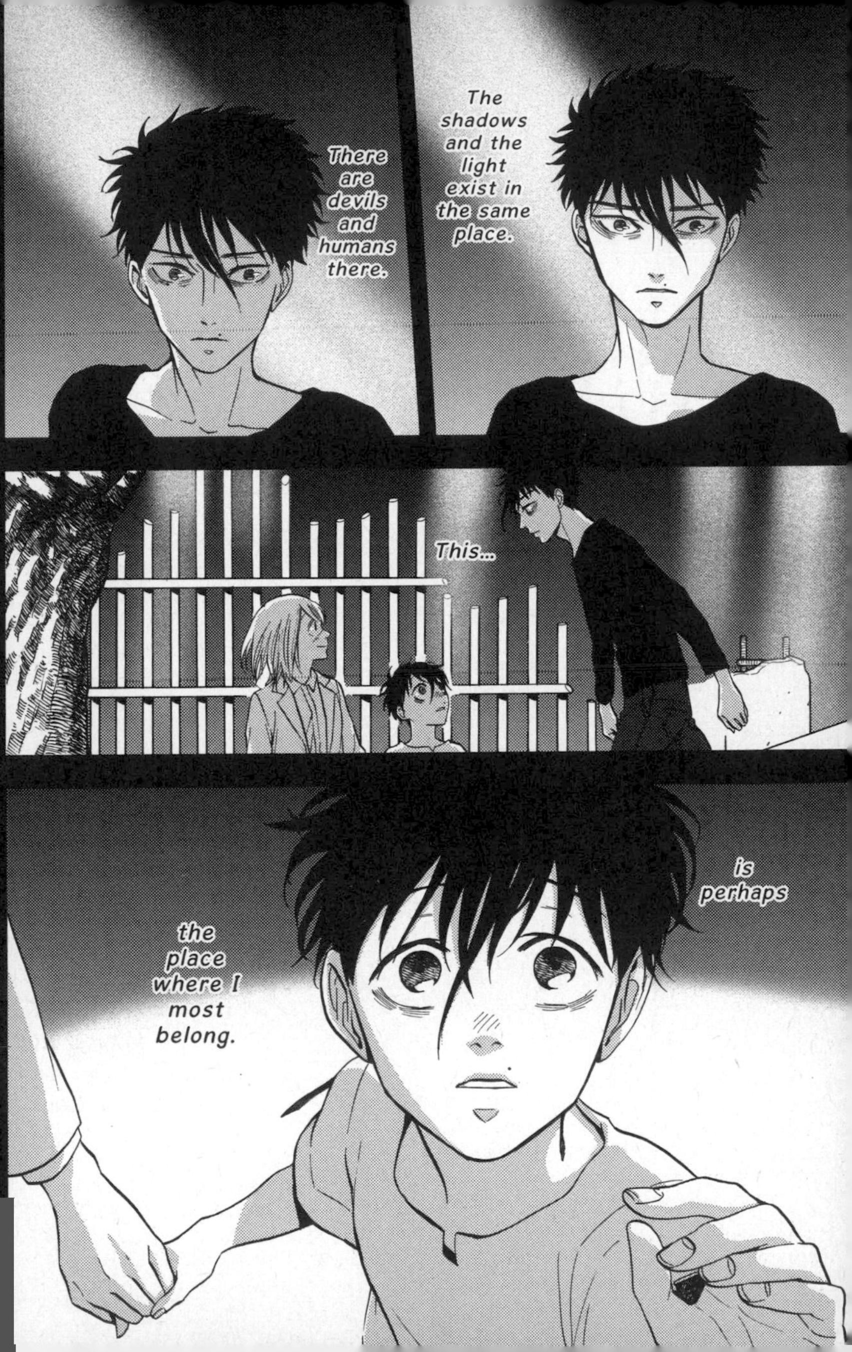
The shadows and the light exist in the same place.
There are devils and humans there.
This...
is perhaps
the place where I most belong.

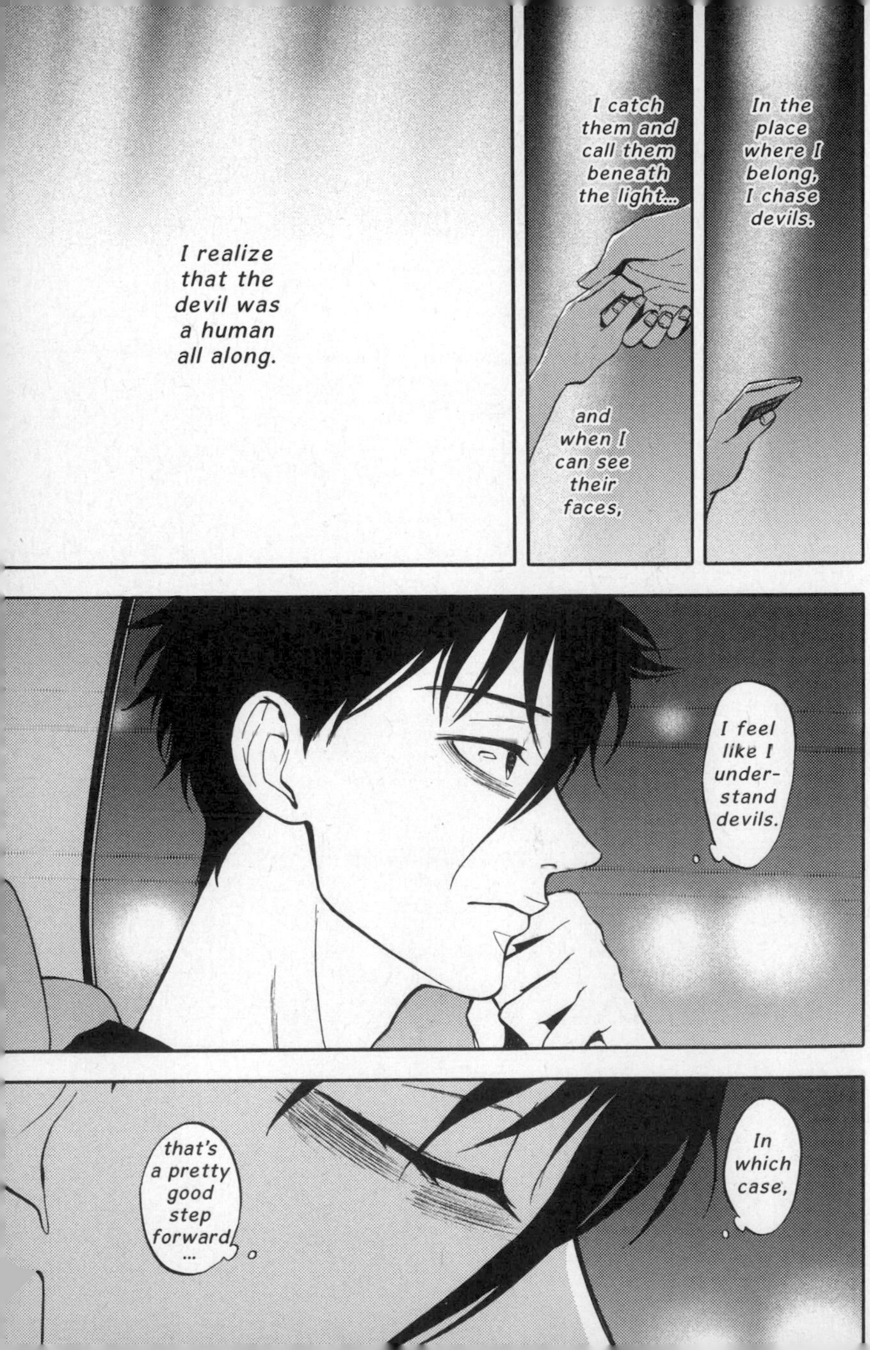
In the place where I belong, I chase devils.
I catch them and call them beneath the light...
and when I can see their faces,
I realize that the devil was a human all along.
I feel like I understand devils.
In which case,
that's a pretty good step forward...

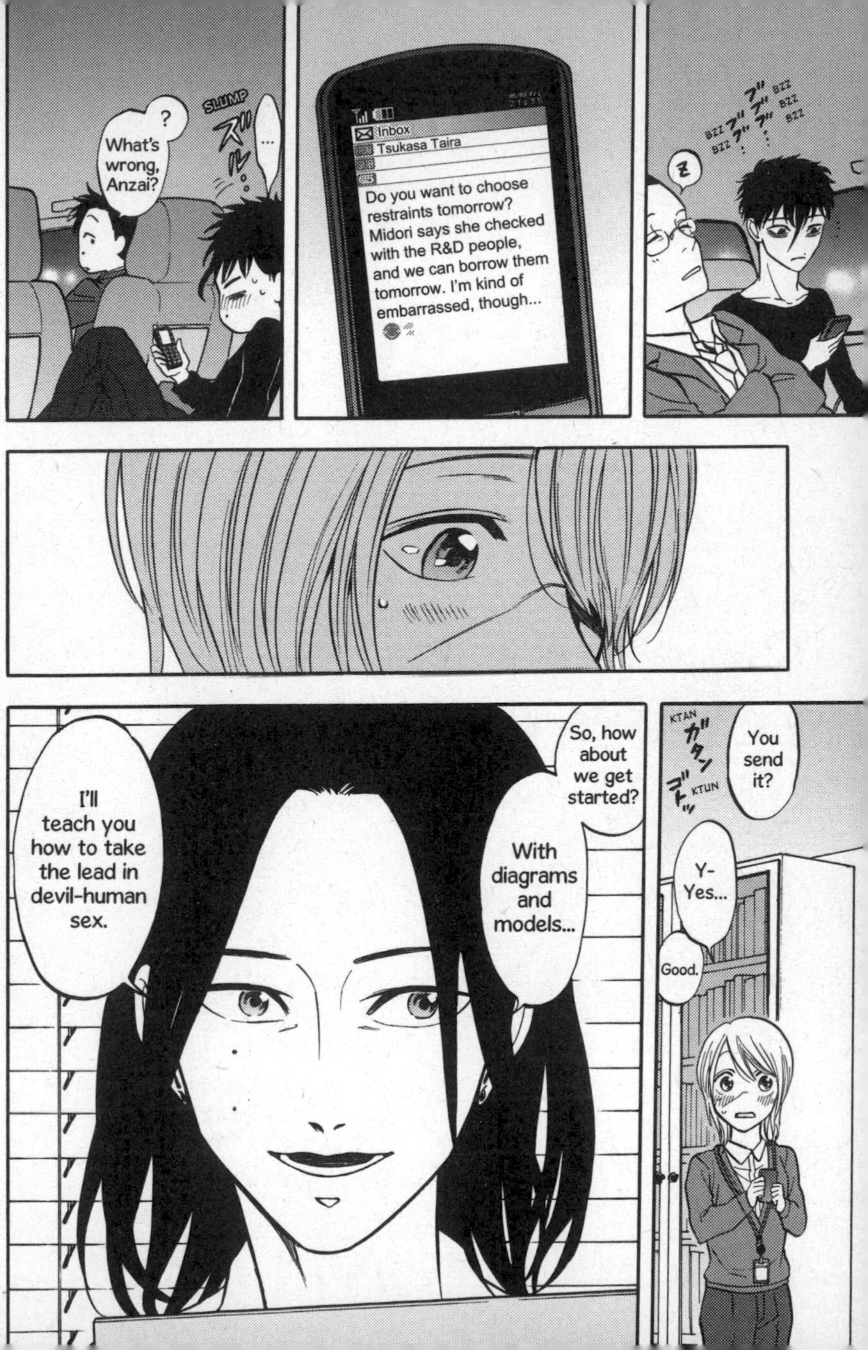
BZZ BZZ BZZ BZZ BZZ BZZ
Z
Inbox
Tsukasa Taira
Do you want to choose restraints tomorrow? Midori says she checked with the R&D people, and we can borrow them tomorrow. I'm kind of embarrassed, though...
...
SLUMP
?
What's wrong, Anzai?
KTAN KTUN
You send it?
Y- Yes...
Good.
So, how about we get started?
With diagrams and models...
I'll teach you how to take the lead in devil-human sex.

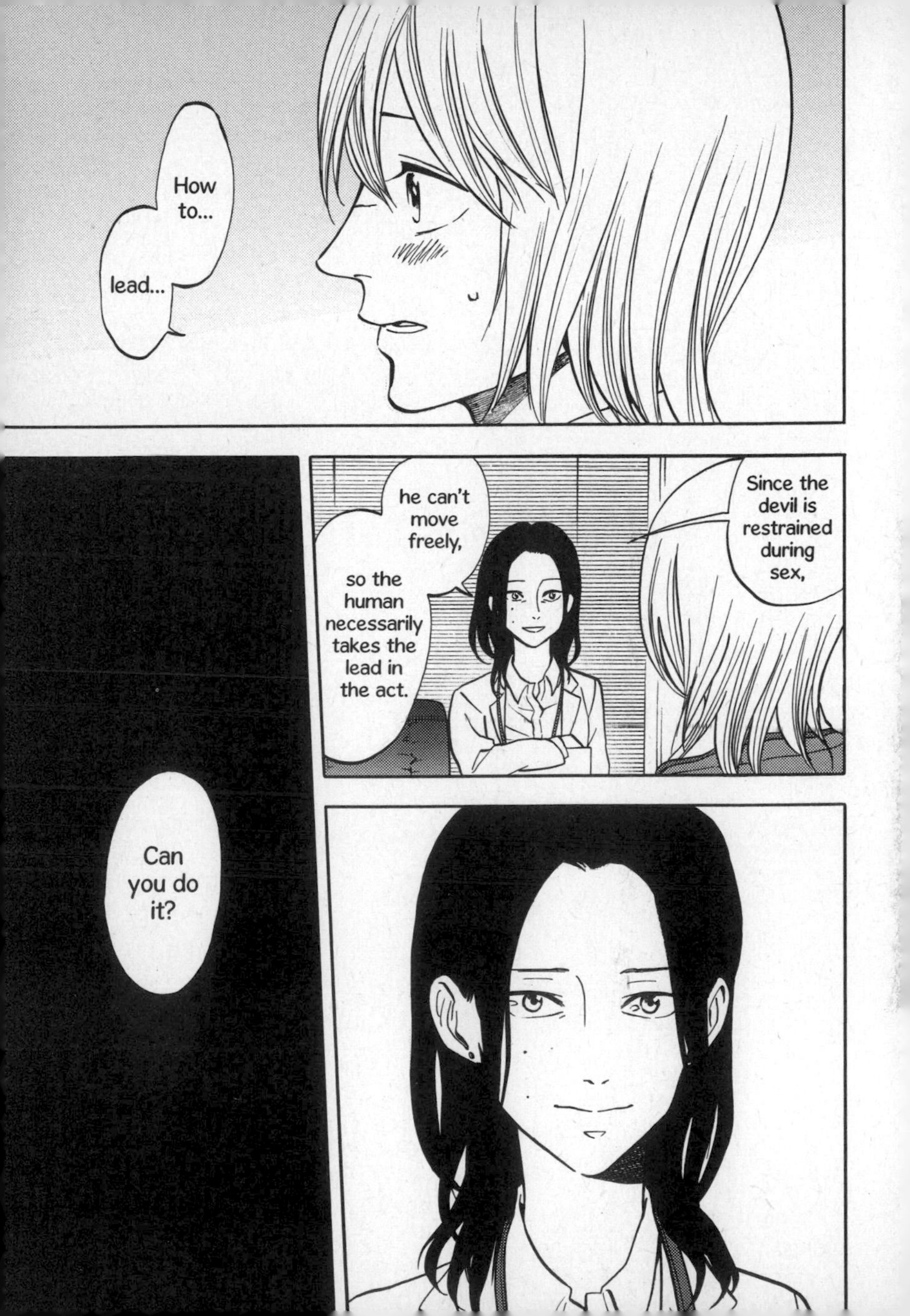
How to... lead...
Since the devil is restrained during sex,
he can't move freely,
so the human necessarily takes the lead in the act.
Can you do it?

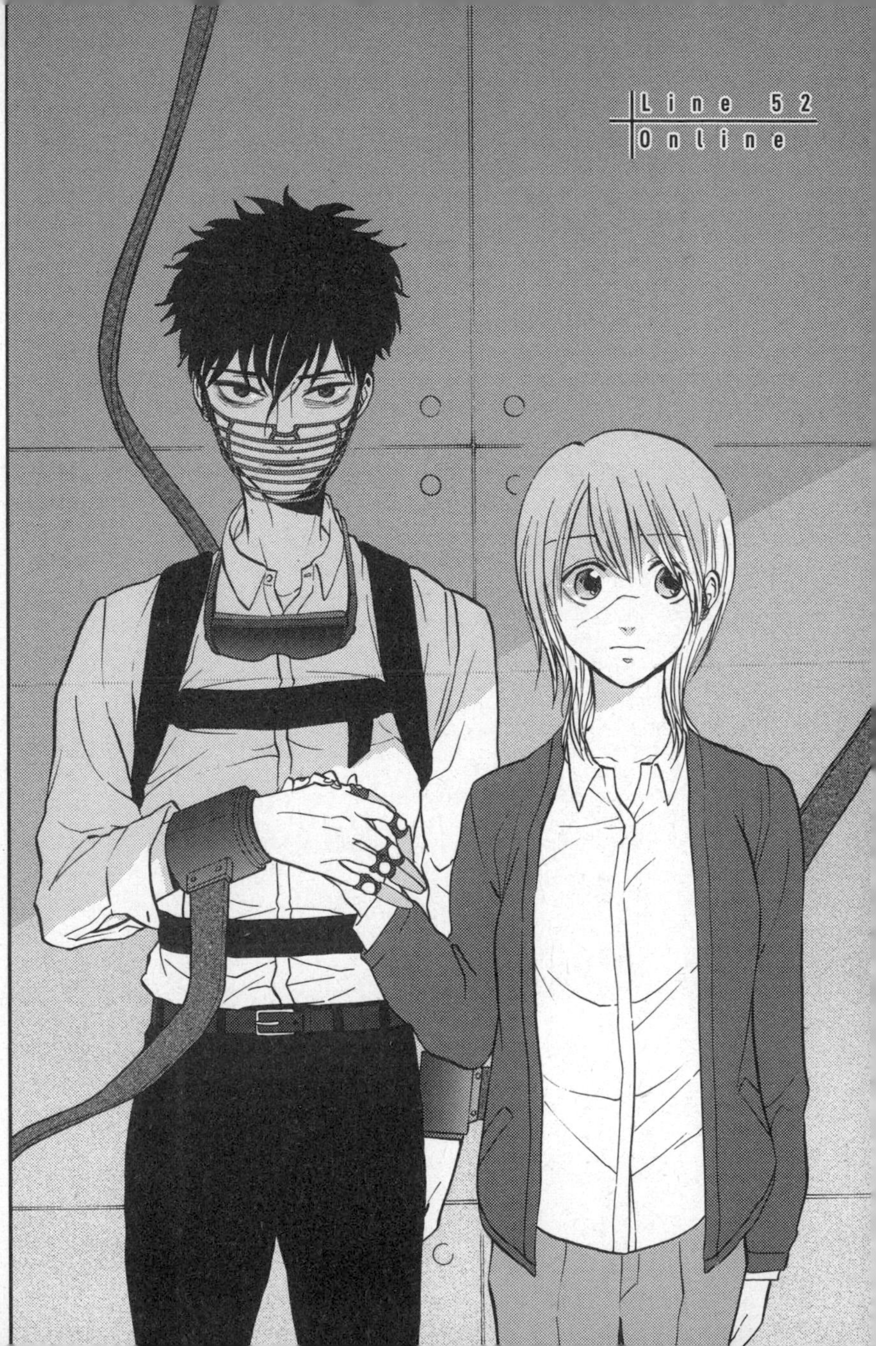

Line 52
Online

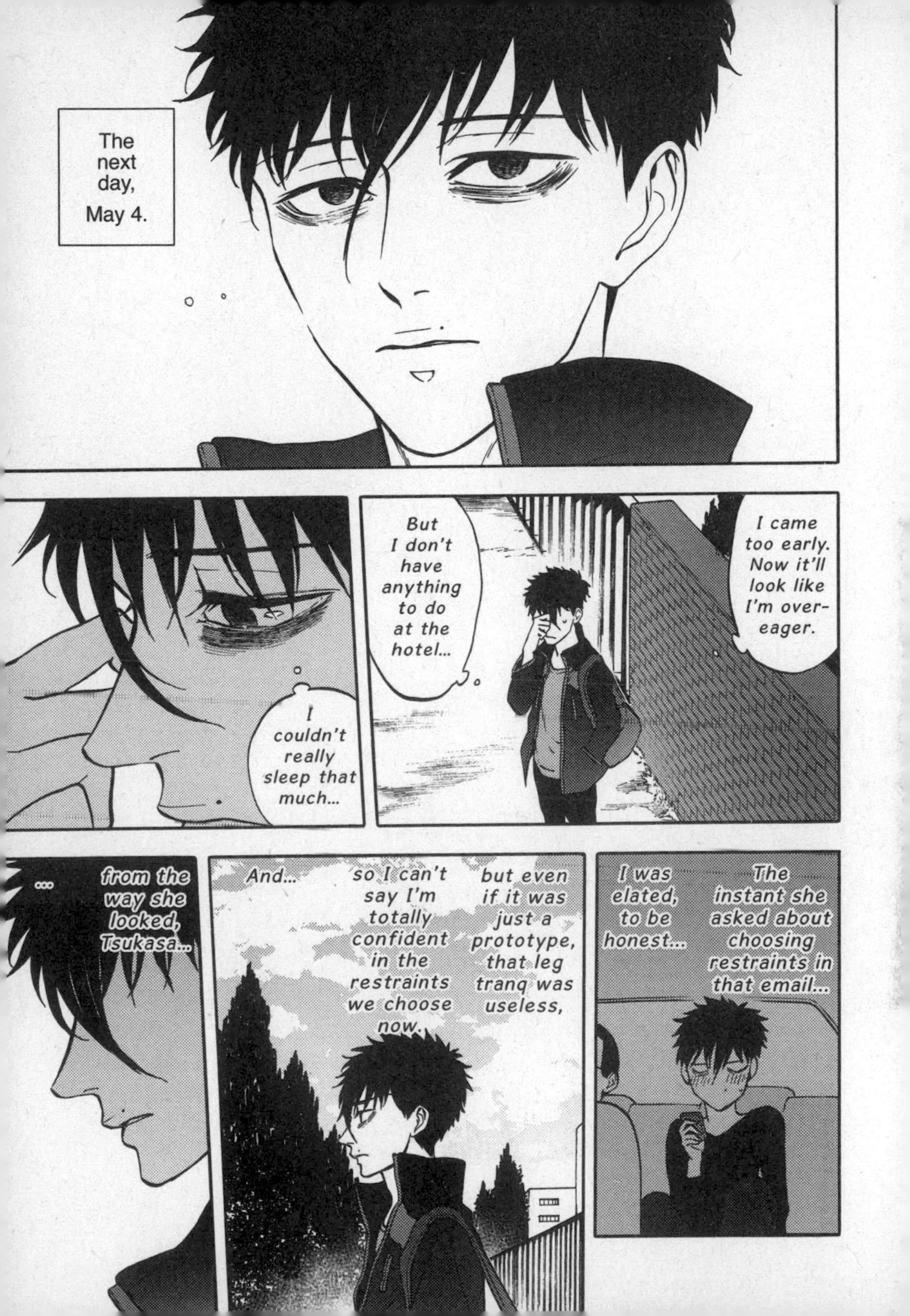
The next day, May 4.
I came too early. Now it'll look like I'm over-eager.
But I don't have anything to do at the hotel...
I couldn't really sleep that much...
The instant she asked about choosing restraints in that email...
I was elated, to be honest...
but even if it was just a prototype, that leg tranq was useless,
so I can't say I'm totally confident in the restraints we choose now.
And...
from the way she looked, Tsukasa...
...

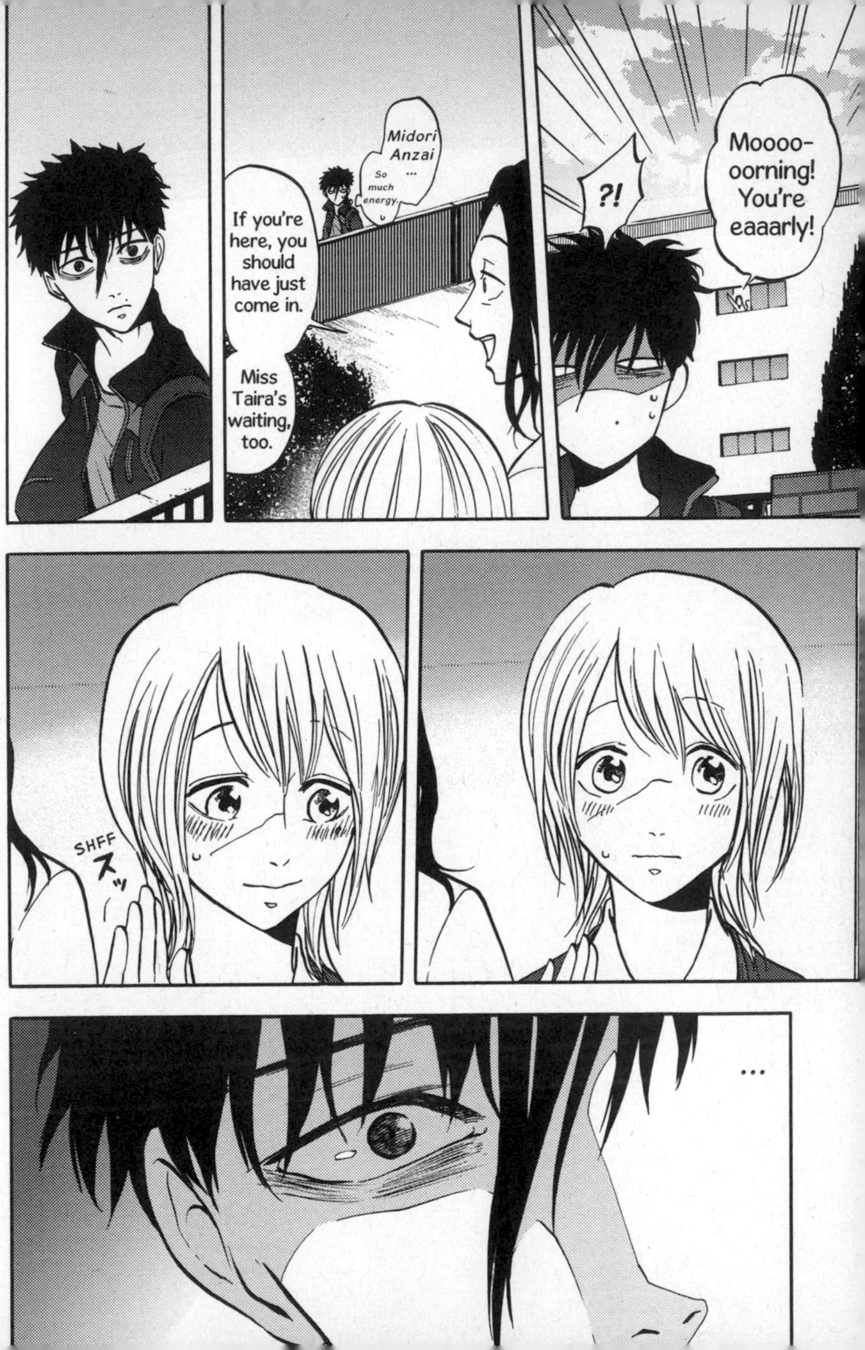
Moooo-oorning! You're eaaarly!
?!
Midori Anzai ...
So much energy.
If you're here, you should have just come in.
Miss Taira's waiting, too.
SHFF
スッ
...

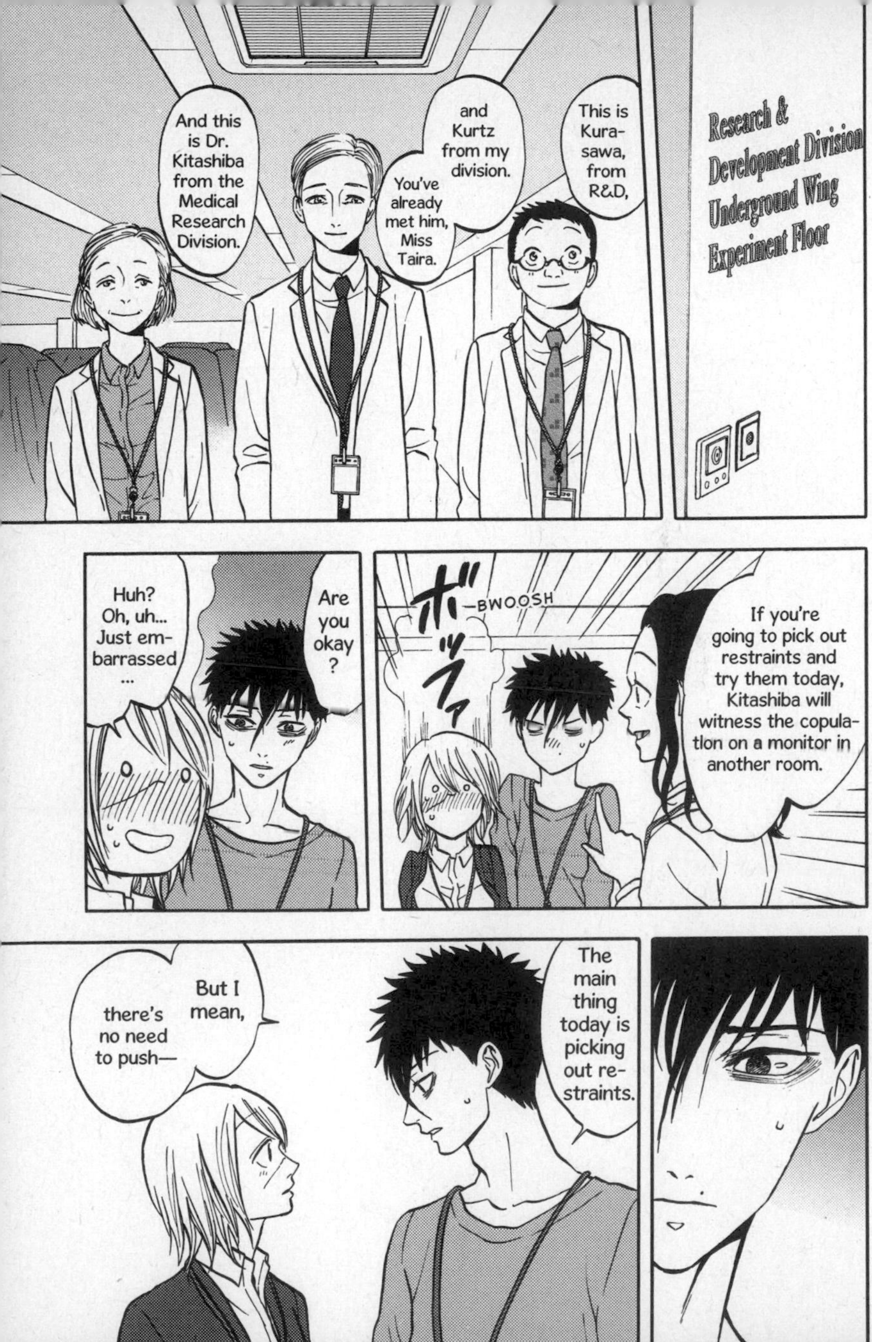
Research & Development Division Underground Wing Experiment Floor
This is Kura-sawa, from R&D,
and Kurtz from my division.
You've already met him, Miss Taira.
And this is Dr. Kitashiba from the Medical Research Division.
ボッ —BWOOSH
If you're going to pick out restraints and try them today, Kitashiba will witness the copula-tion on a monitor in another room.
Are you okay?
Huh? Oh, uh... Just em-barrassed...
The main thing today is picking out re-straints.
But I mean,
there's no need to push—

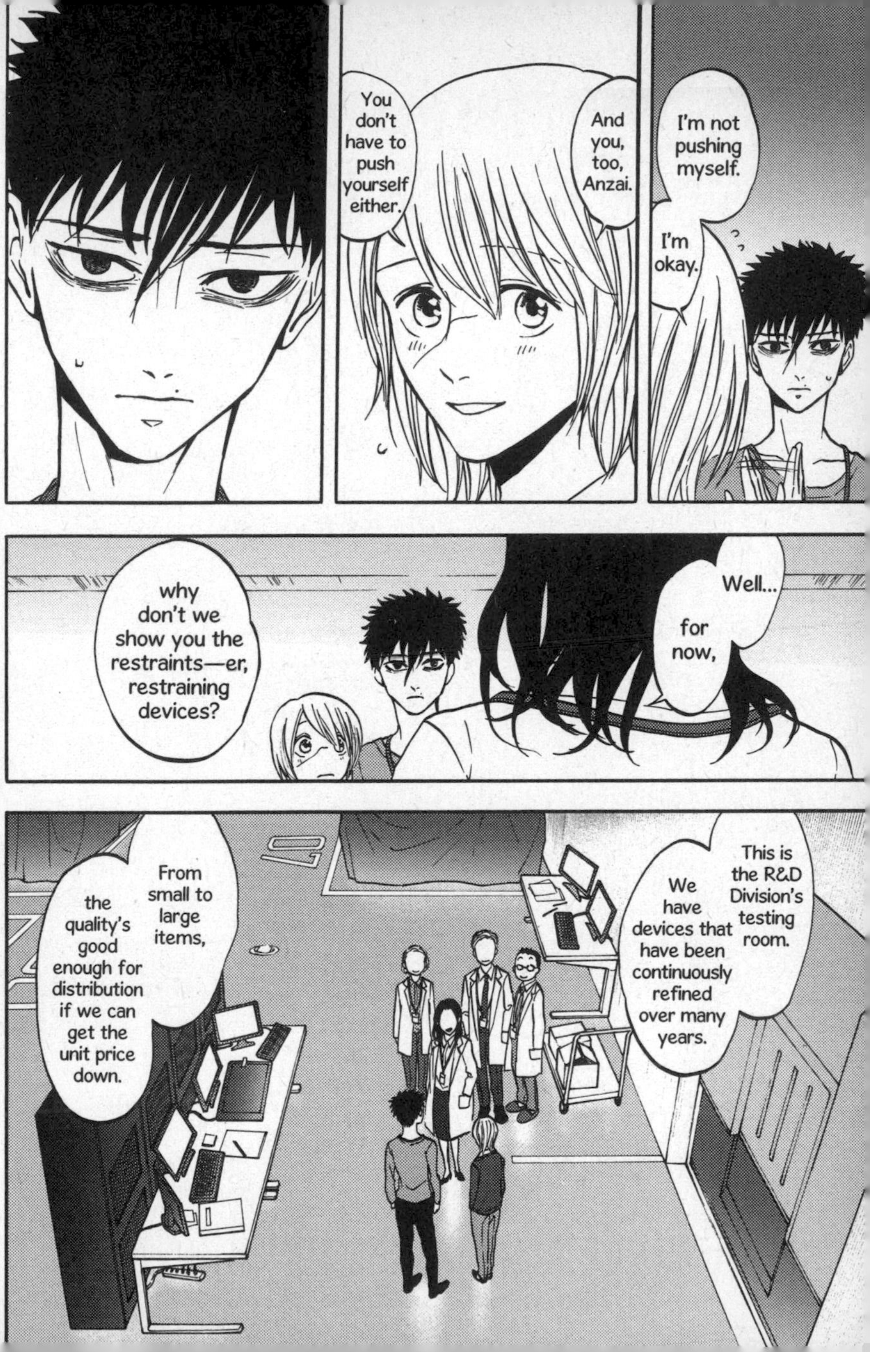
I'm not pushing myself.
I'm okay.
And you, too, Anzai.
You don't have to push yourself either.
Well...
for now,
why don't we show you the restraints—er, restraining devices?
This is the R&D Division's testing room.
We have devices that have been continuously refined over many years.
From small to large items,
the quality's good enough for distribution if we can get the unit price down.

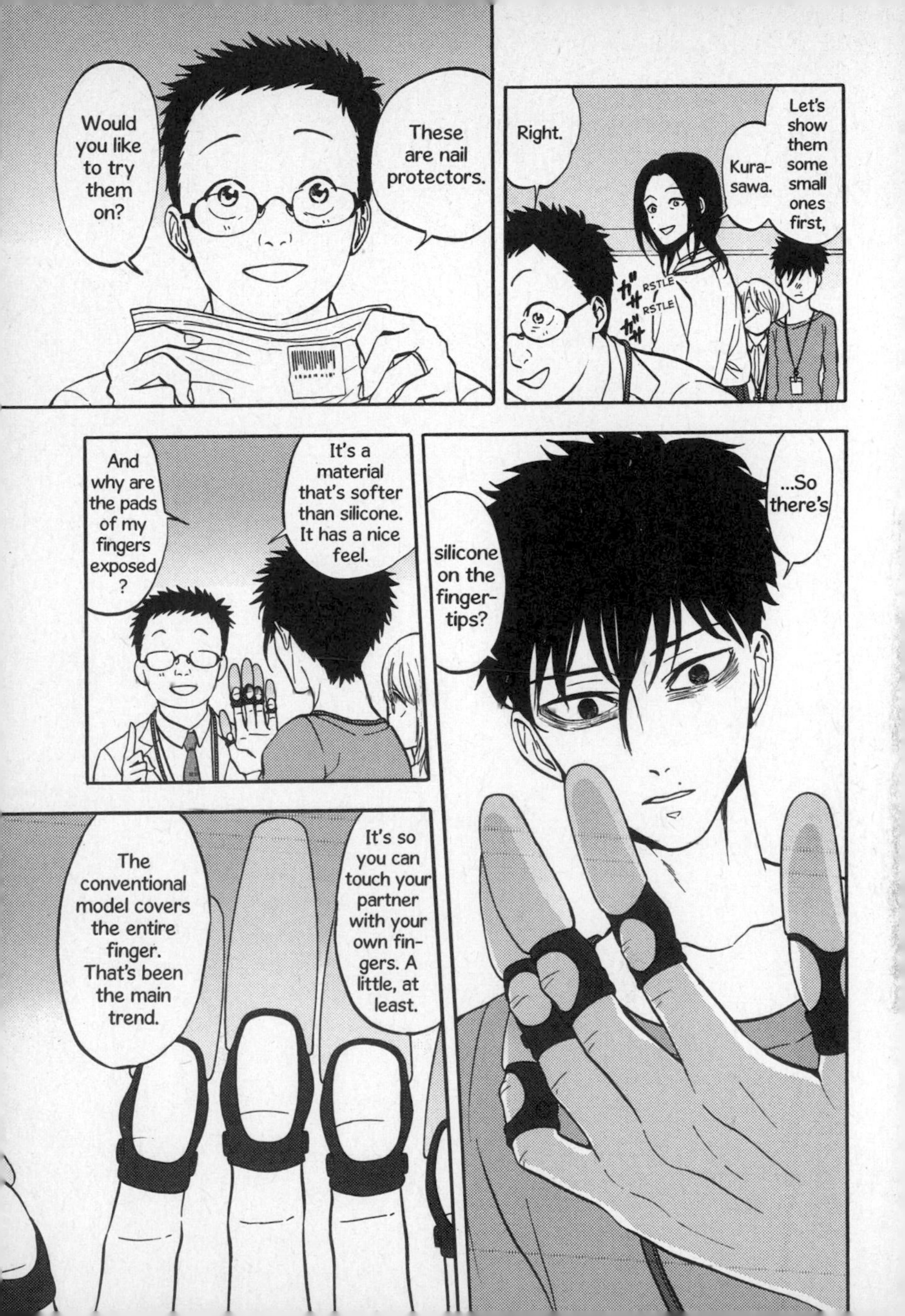
Let's show them some small ones first,
Kurasawa.
Right.
RSTLE RSTLE
These are nail protectors.
Would you like to try them on?
...So there's
silicone on the finger-tips?
It's a material that's softer than silicone. It has a nice feel.
And why are the pads of my fingers exposed?
It's so you can touch your partner with your own fingers. A little, at least.
The conventional model covers the entire finger. That's been the main trend.

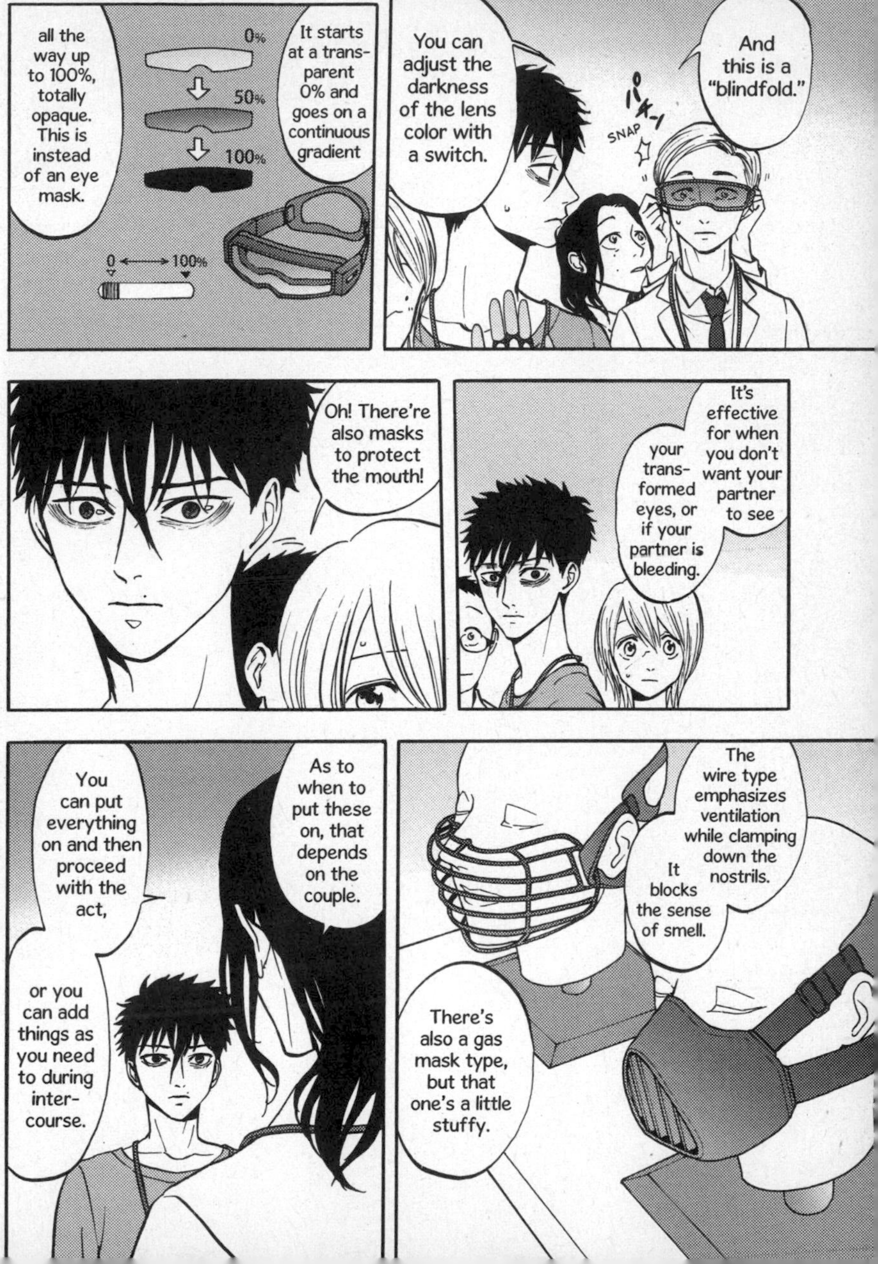
And this is a "blindfold."
SNAP
You can adjust the darkness of the lens color with a switch.
It starts at a transparent 0% and goes on a continuous gradient
0%
50%
100%
0 ⟷ 100%
all the way up to 100%, totally opaque. This is instead of an eye mask.
It's effective for when you don't want your partner to see
your transformed eyes, or if your partner is bleeding.
Oh! There're also masks to protect the mouth!
The wire type emphasizes ventilation while clamping down the nostrils.
It blocks the sense of smell.
There's also a gas mask type, but that one's a little stuffy.
As to when to put these on, that depends on the couple.
You can put everything on and then proceed with the act,
or you can add things as you need to during intercourse.

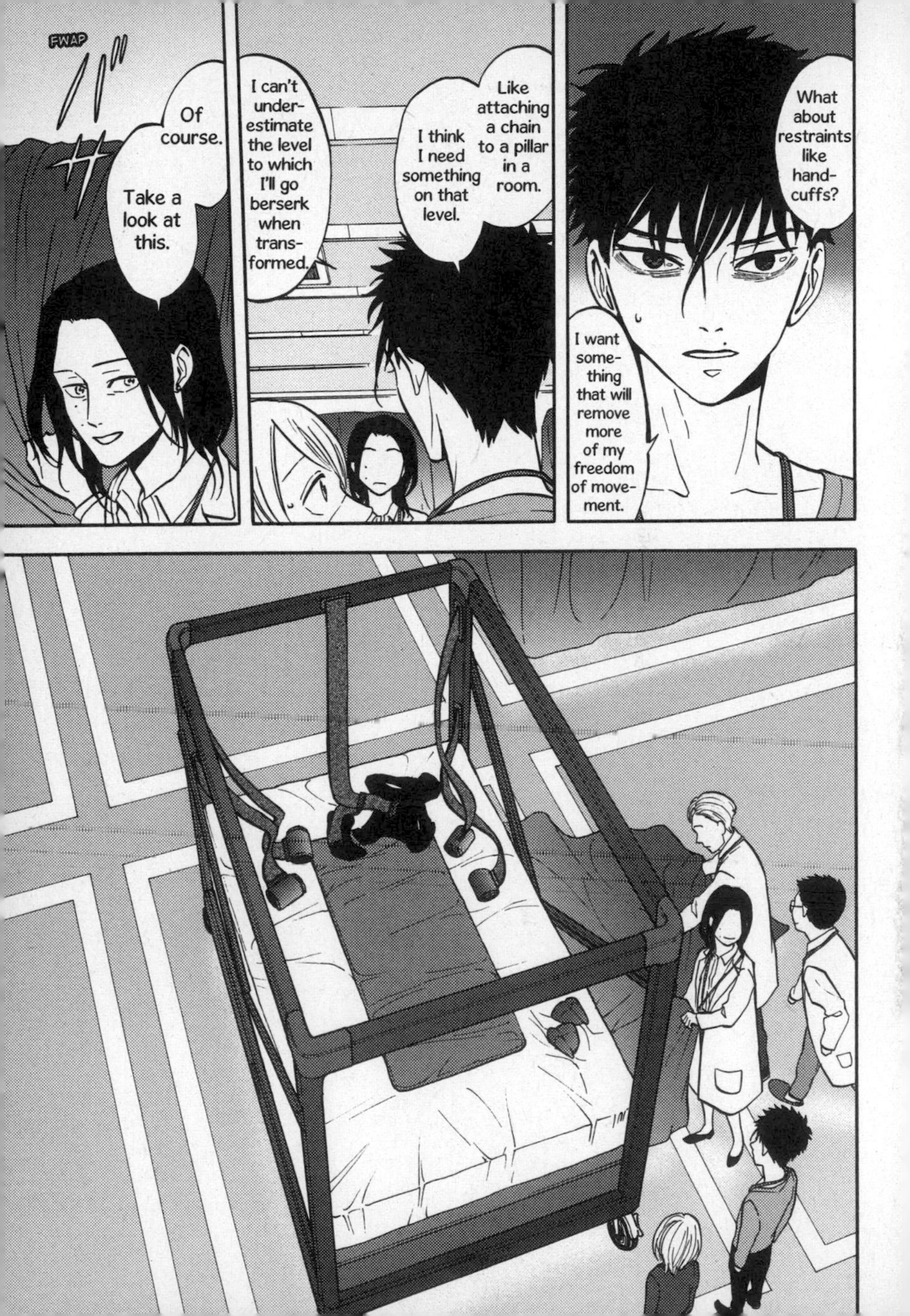
What about restraints like handcuffs?
I want something that will remove more of my freedom of movement.
Like attaching a chain to a pillar in a room.
I think I need something on that level.
I can't underestimate the level to which I'll go berserk when transformed.
FWAP
Of course.
Take a look at this.

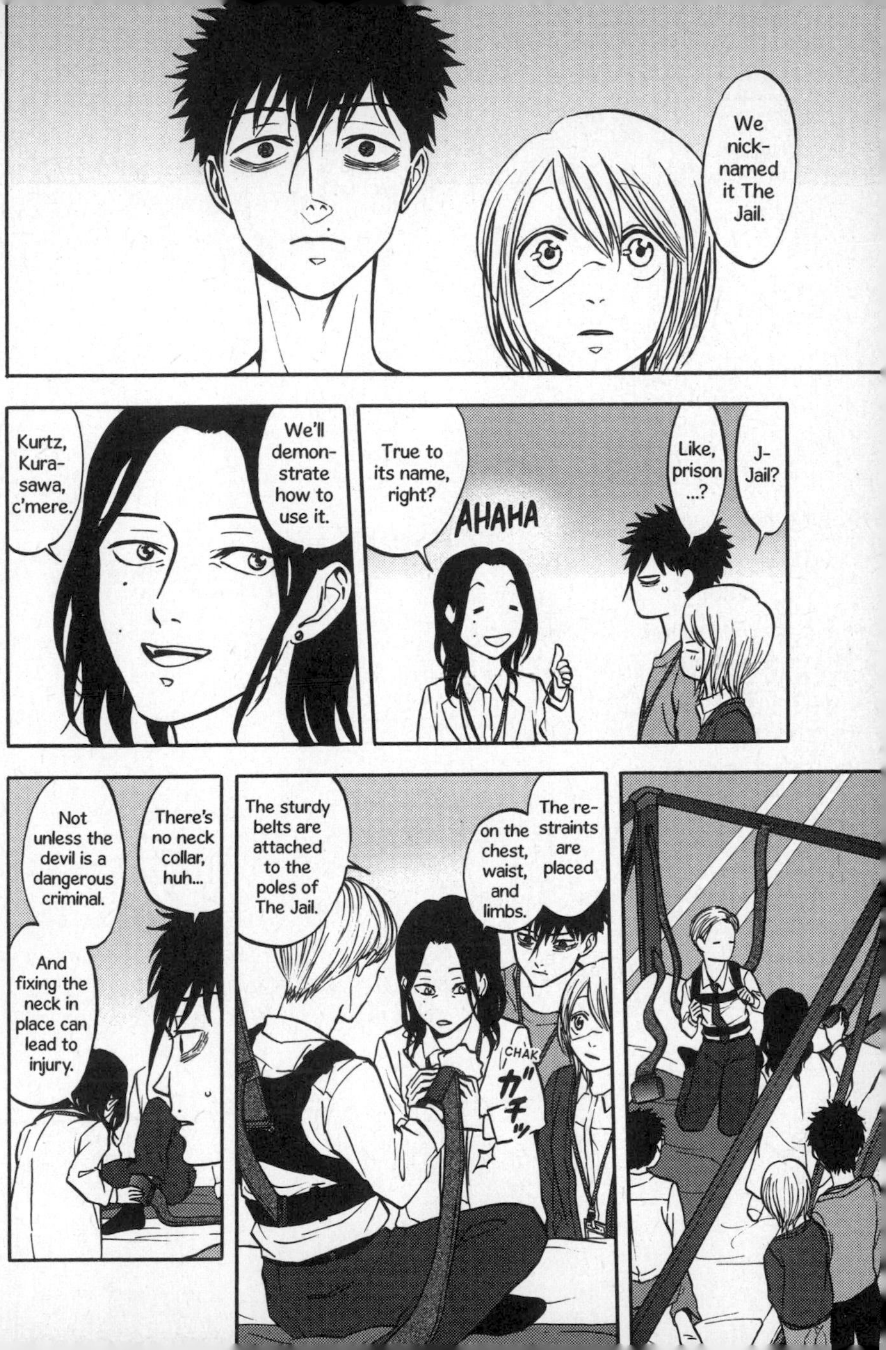
We nick-named it The Jail.
J-Jail?
Like, prison ...?
AHAHA
True to its name, right?
We'll demon-strate how to use it.
Kurtz, Kura-sawa, c'mere.
The re-straints are placed
on the chest, waist, and limbs.
CHAK
ガチッ
The sturdy belts are attached to the poles of The Jail.
There's no neck collar, huh...
Not unless the devil is a dangerous criminal.
And fixing the neck in place can lead to injury.

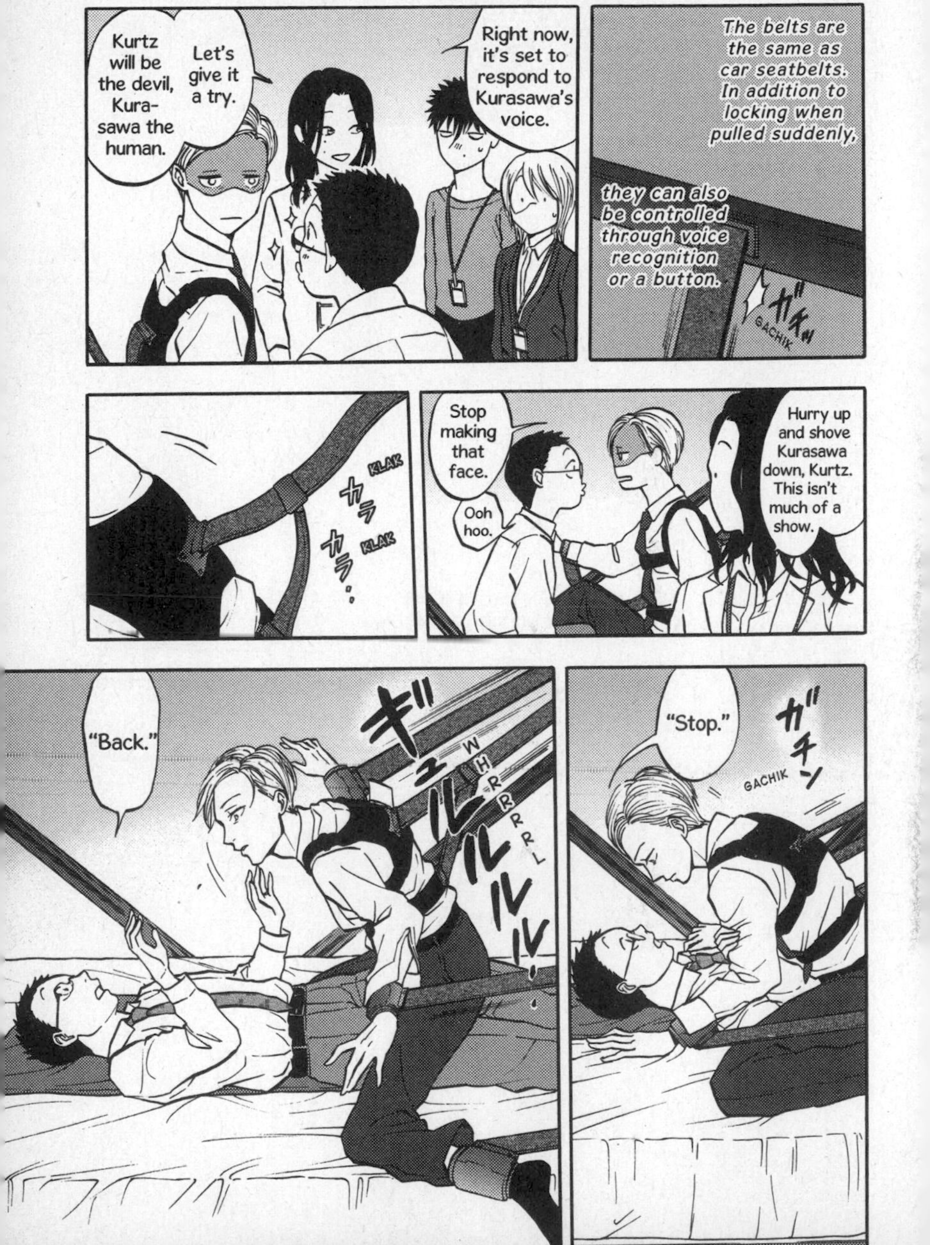
The belts are the same as car seatbelts. In addition to locking when pulled suddenly,
they can also be controlled through voice recognition or a button.
GACHIK
Right now, it's set to respond to Kurasawa's voice.
Let's give it a try.
Kurtz will be the devil, Kurasawa the human.
Hurry up and shove Kurasawa down, Kurtz. This isn't much of a show.
Stop making that face.
Ooh hoo.
KLAK
KLAK
"Stop."
GACHIK
"Back."
WHRRRRL

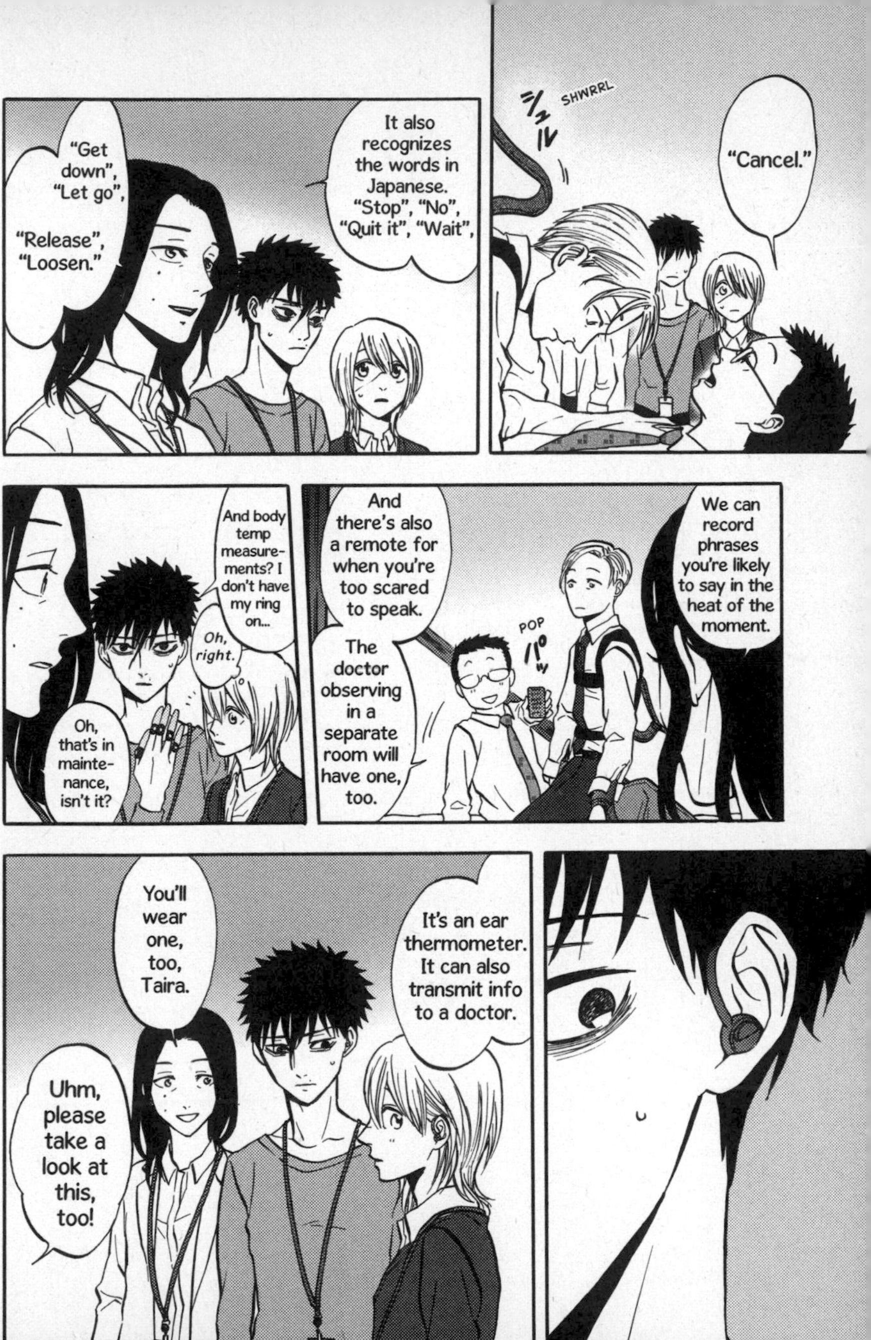
SHWRRL
"Cancel."
It also recognizes the words in Japanese. "Stop", "No", "Quit it", "Wait",
"Get down", "Let go",
"Release", "Loosen."
We can record phrases you're likely to say in the heat of the moment.
And there's also a remote for when you're too scared to speak.
POP
The doctor observing in a separate room will have one, too.
And body temp measurements? I don't have my ring on...
Oh, right.
Oh, that's in maintenance, isn't it?
It's an ear thermometer. It can also transmit info to a doctor.
You'll wear one, too, Taira.
Uhm, please take a look at this, too!

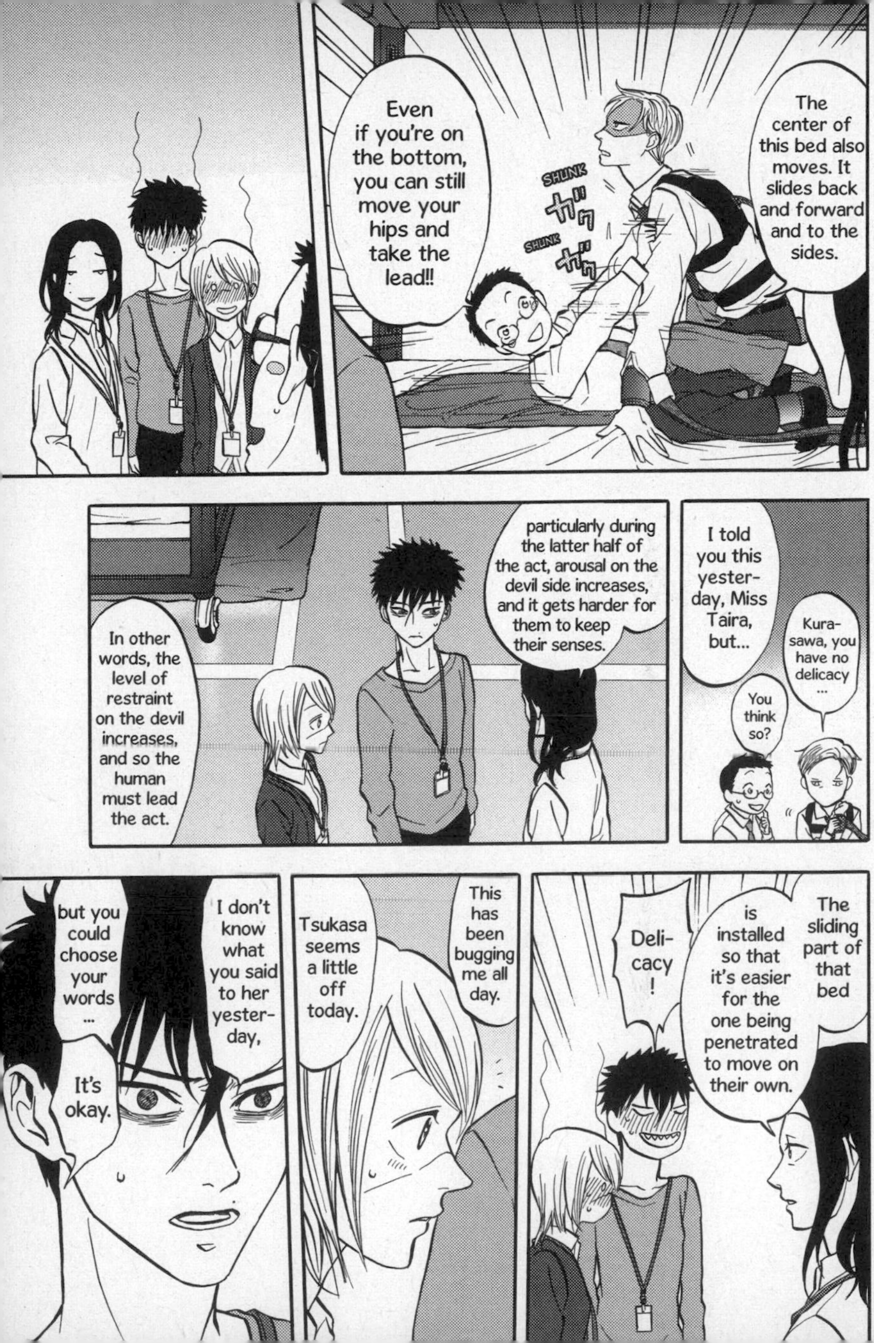
The center of this bed also moves. It slides back and forward and to the sides.
Even if you're on the bottom, you can still move your hips and take the lead!!
SHUNK
ガク
SHUNK
ガク
I told you this yesterday, Miss Taira, but...
Kura-sawa, you have no delicacy ...
You think so?
particularly during the latter half of the act, arousal on the devil side increases, and it gets harder for them to keep their senses.
In other words, the level of restraint on the devil increases, and so the human must lead the act.
The sliding part of that bed
is installed so that it's easier for the one being penetrated to move on their own.
Deli-cacy!
This has been bugging me all day.
Tsukasa seems a little off today.
I don't know what you said to her yester-day,
but you could choose your words ...
It's okay.

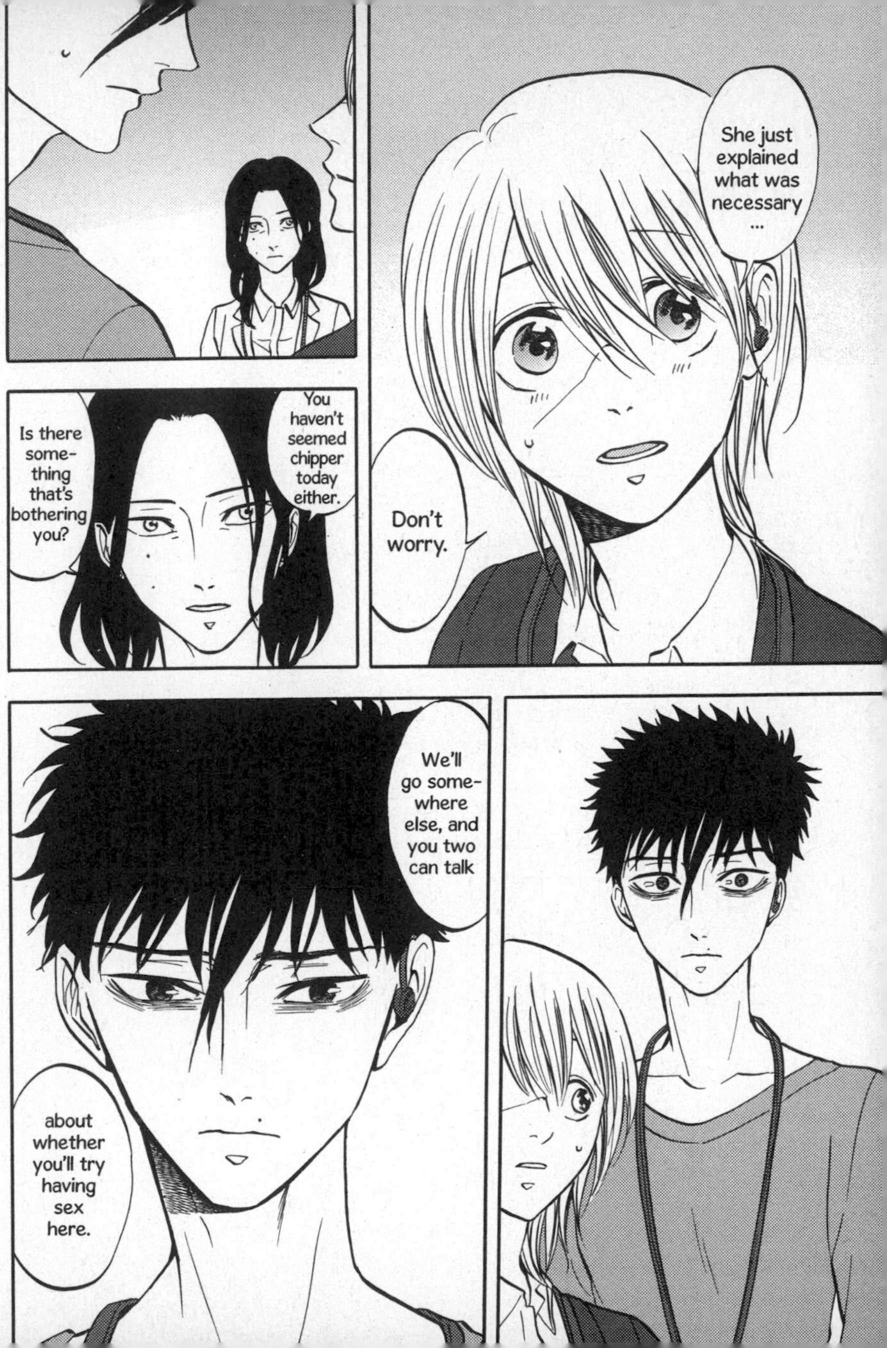
She just explained what was necessary ...
Don't worry.
You haven't seemed chipper today either.
Is there some-thing that's bothering you?
We'll go some-where else, and you two can talk
about whether you'll try having sex here.

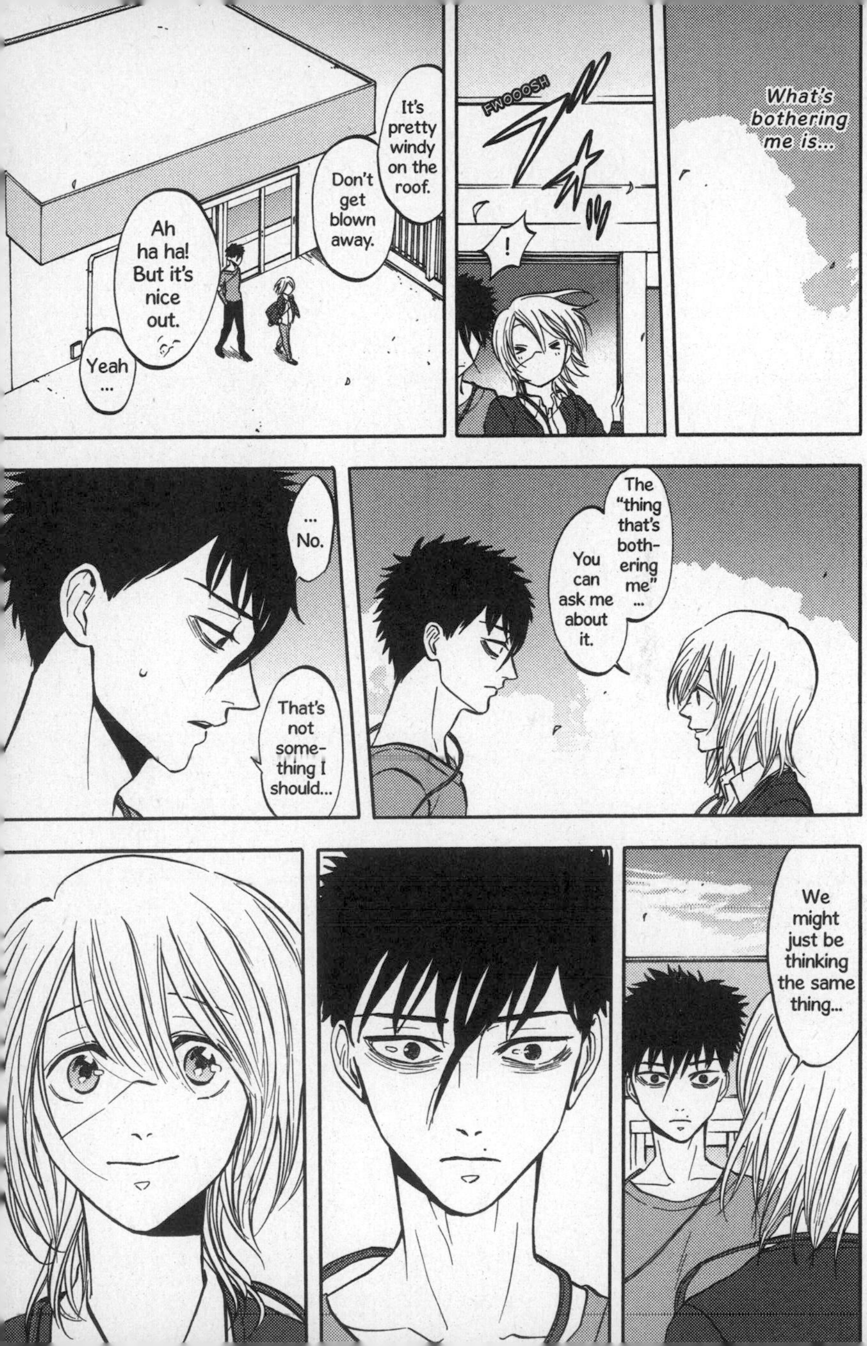
What's bothering me is...
FWOOOSH
!
It's pretty windy on the roof.
Don't get blown away.
Ah ha ha! But it's nice out.
Yeah ...
The "thing that's bothering me" ...
You can ask me about it.
... No.
That's not something I should...
We might just be thinking the same thing...

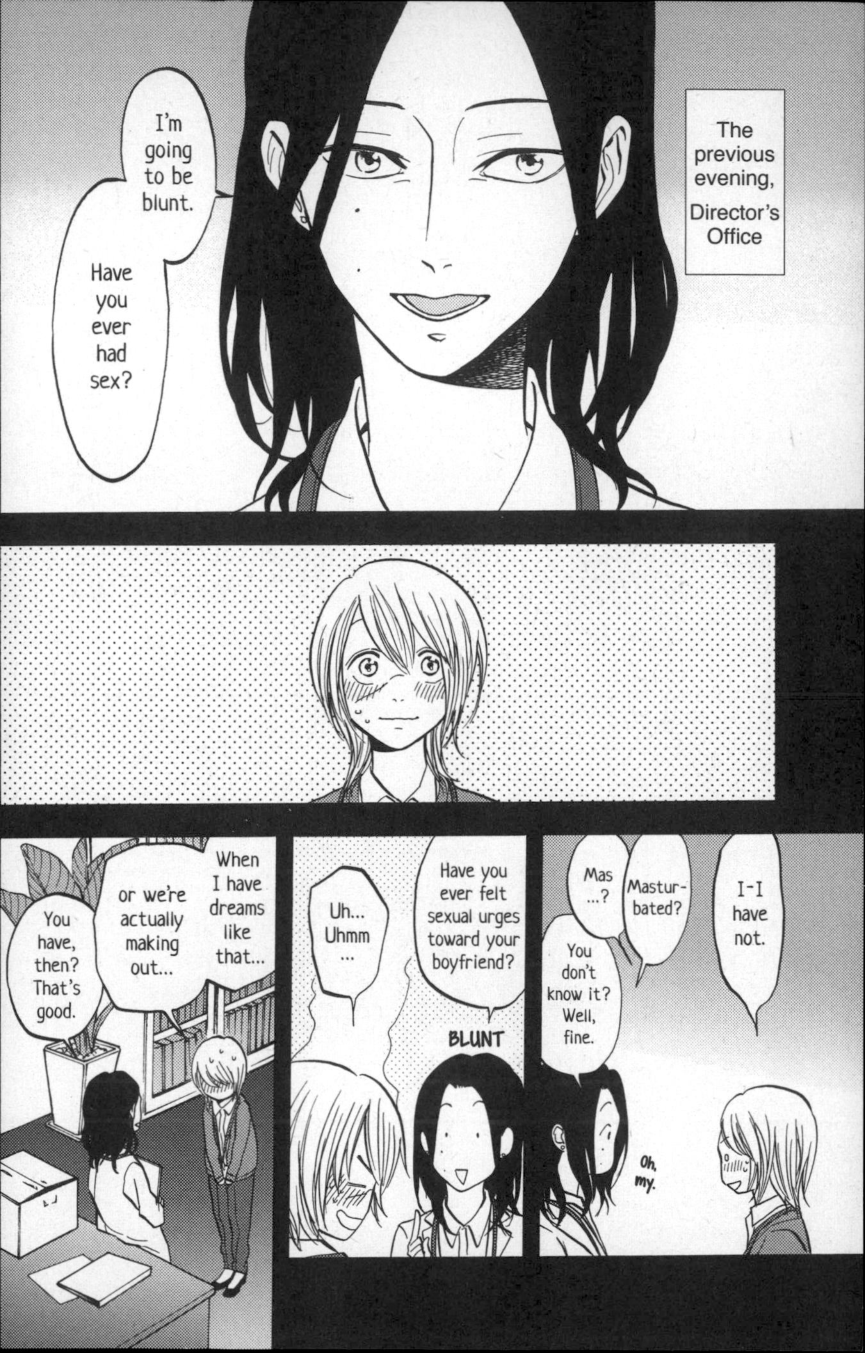
The previous evening, Director's Office
I'm going to be blunt.
Have you ever had sex?
I-I have not.
Mastur-bated?
Mas ...?
You don't know it? Well, fine.
Oh, my.
Have you ever felt sexual urges toward your boyfriend?
BLUNT
Uh... Uhmm ...
When I have dreams like that...
or we're actually making out...
You have, then? That's good.

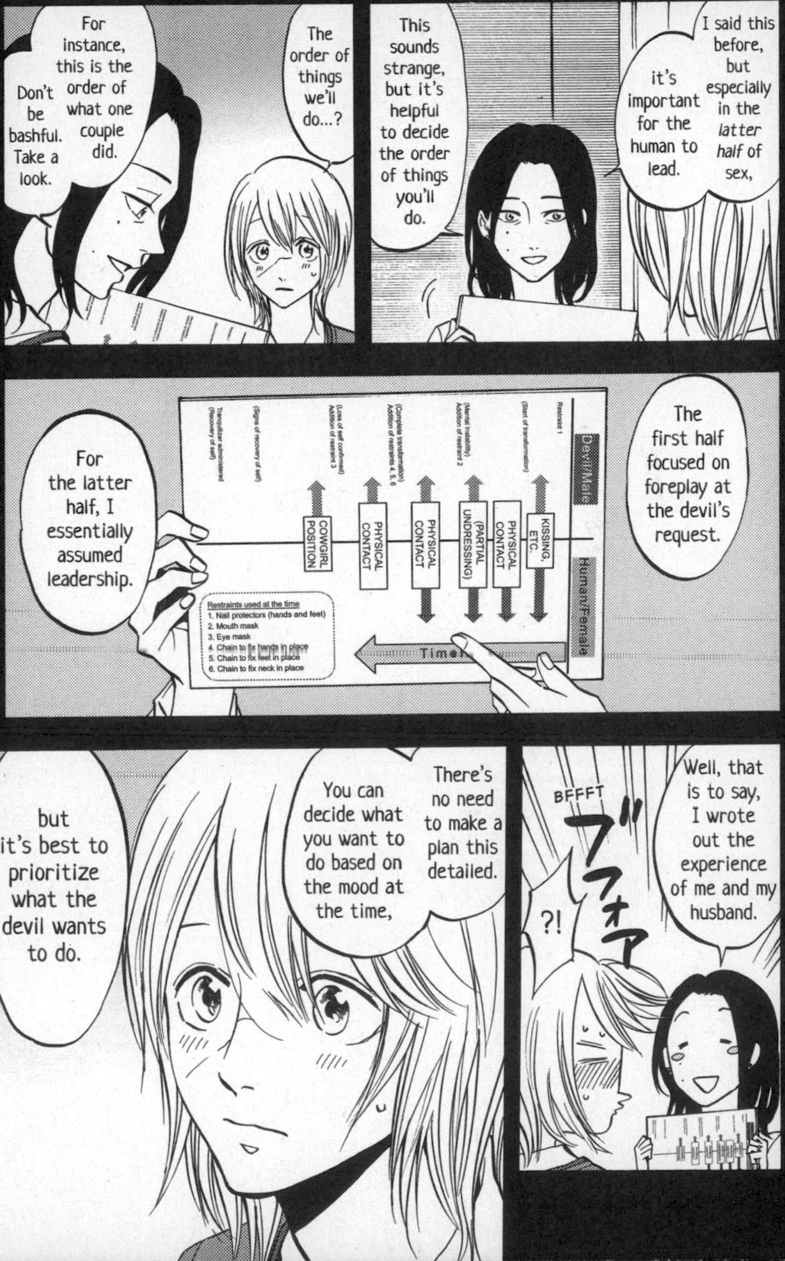
I said this before, but especially in the *latter half* of sex,
it's important for the human to lead.
This sounds strange, but it's helpful to decide the order of things you'll do.
The order of things we'll do...?
For instance, this is the order of what one couple did.
Don't be bashful. Take a look.
The first half focused on foreplay at the devil's request.
Devil/Male
Human/Female
Restraint 1
(Start of transformation)
(Mental instability)
Addition of restraint 2
(Complete transformation)
Addition of restraints 4, 5, 6
(Loss of self confirmed)
Addition of restraint 3
(Signs of recovery of self)
Tranquilizer administered
(Recovery of self)
KISSING, ETC.
PHYSICAL CONTACT
(PARTIAL UNDRESSING)
PHYSICAL CONTACT
PHYSICAL CONTACT
COWGIRL POSITION
Restraints used at the time
1. Nail protectors (hands and feet)
2. Mouth mask
3. Eye mask
4. Chain to fix hands in place
5. Chain to fix feet in place
6. Chain to fix neck in place
Time
For the latter half, I essentially assumed leadership.
Well, that is to say, I wrote out the experience of me and my husband.
BFFFT
ブフォア
?!
There's no need to make a plan this detailed.
You can decide what you want to do based on the mood at the time,
but it's best to prioritize what the devil wants to do.

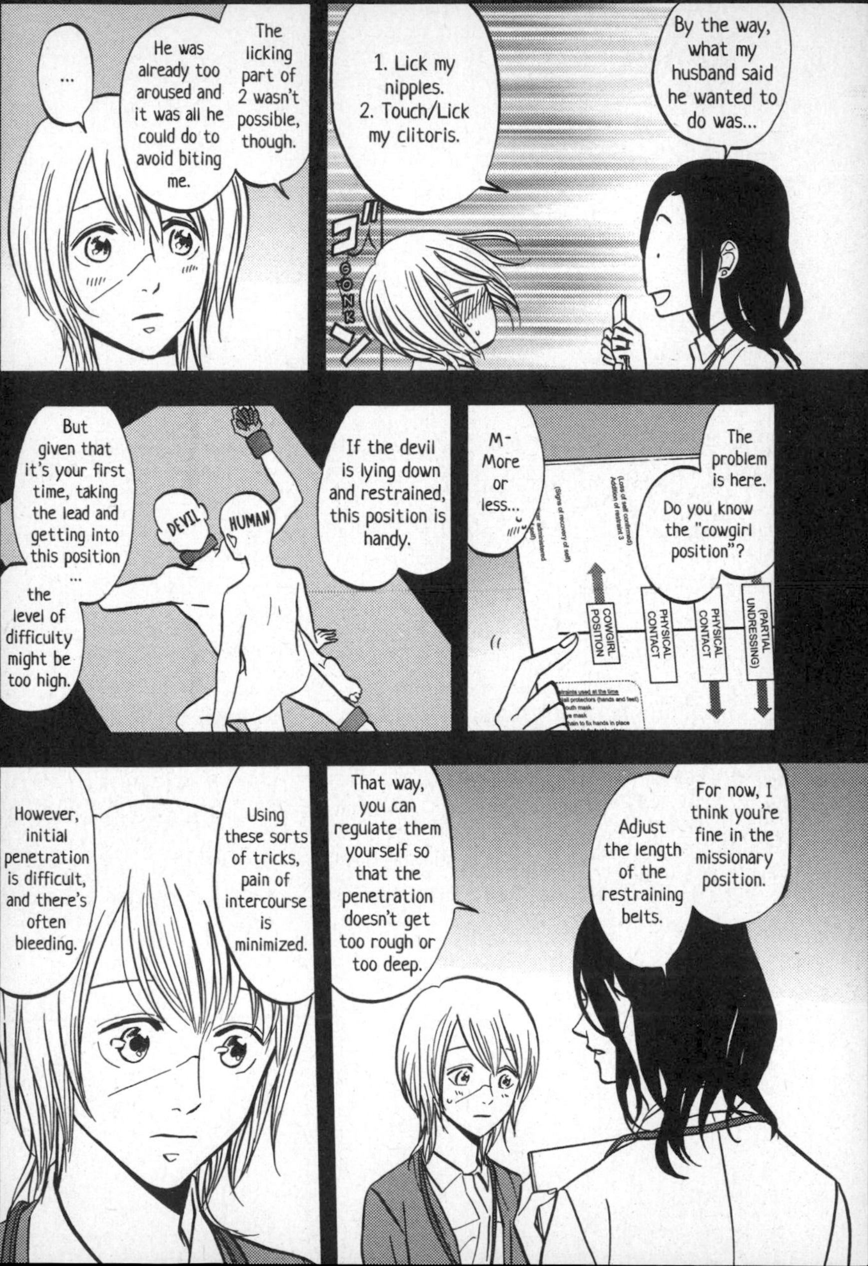
By the way, what my husband said he wanted to do was...
1. Lick my nipples.
2. Touch/Lick my clitoris.
GONK
The licking part of 2 wasn't possible, though.
He was already too aroused and it was all he could do to avoid biting me.
...
The problem is here.
Do you know the "cowgirl position"?
(PARTIAL UNDRESSING)
PHYSICAL CONTACT
PHYSICAL CONTACT
COWGIRL POSITION
(Loss of self confirmed)
Addition of restraint 3
M- More or less...
If the devil is lying down and restrained, this position is handy.
DEVIL
HUMAN
But given that it's your first time, taking the lead and getting into this position ...
the level of difficulty might be too high.
For now, I think you're fine in the missionary position.
Adjust the length of the restraining belts.
That way, you can regulate them yourself so that the penetration doesn't get too rough or too deep.
Using these sorts of tricks, pain of intercourse is minimized.
However, initial penetration is difficult, and there's often bleeding.

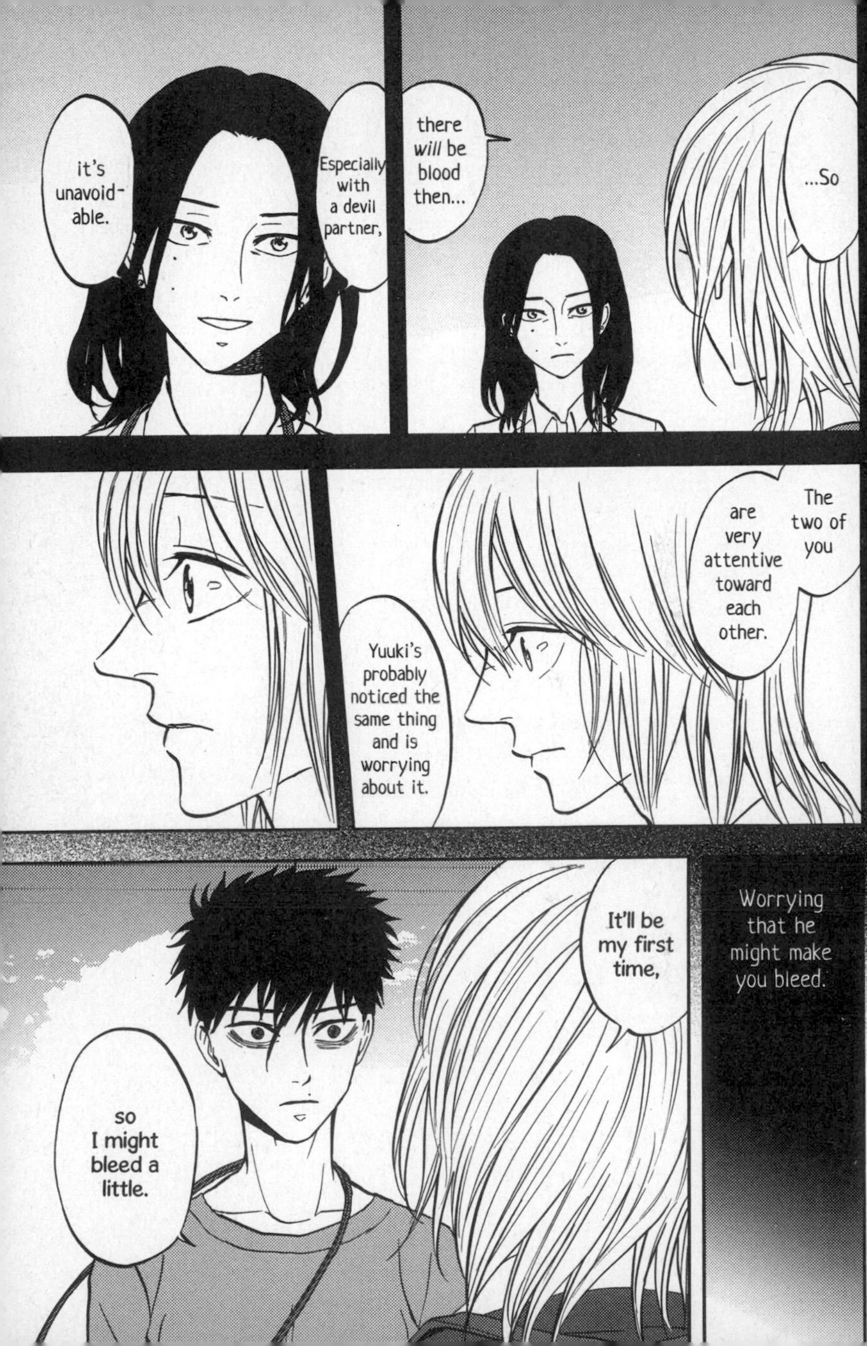
...So
there *will* be blood then...
Especially with a devil partner,
it's unavoidable.
The two of you are very attentive toward each other.
Yuuki's probably noticed the same thing and is worrying about it.
Worrying that he might make you bleed.
It'll be my first time,
so I might bleed a little.

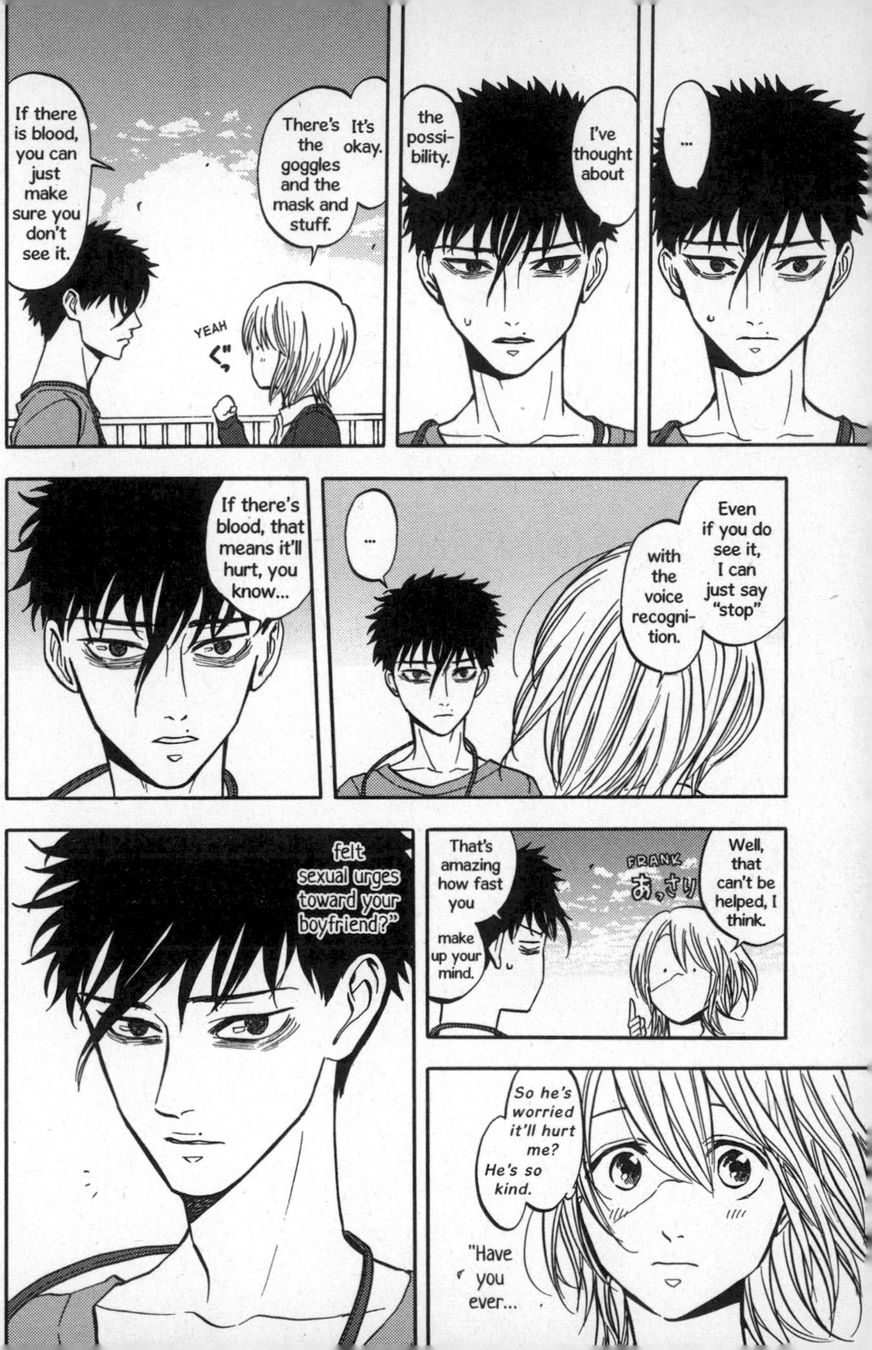
...
I've thought about
the possibility.
It's okay.
There's the goggles and the mask and stuff.
If there is blood, you can just make sure you don't see it.
YEAH
ぐっ
Even if you do see it, I can just say "stop"
with the voice recognition.
...
If there's blood, that means it'll hurt, you know...
Well, that can't be helped, I think.
FRANK
あっさり
That's amazing how fast you
make up your mind.
So he's worried it'll hurt me? He's so kind.
"Have you ever...
felt sexual urges toward your boyfriend?"

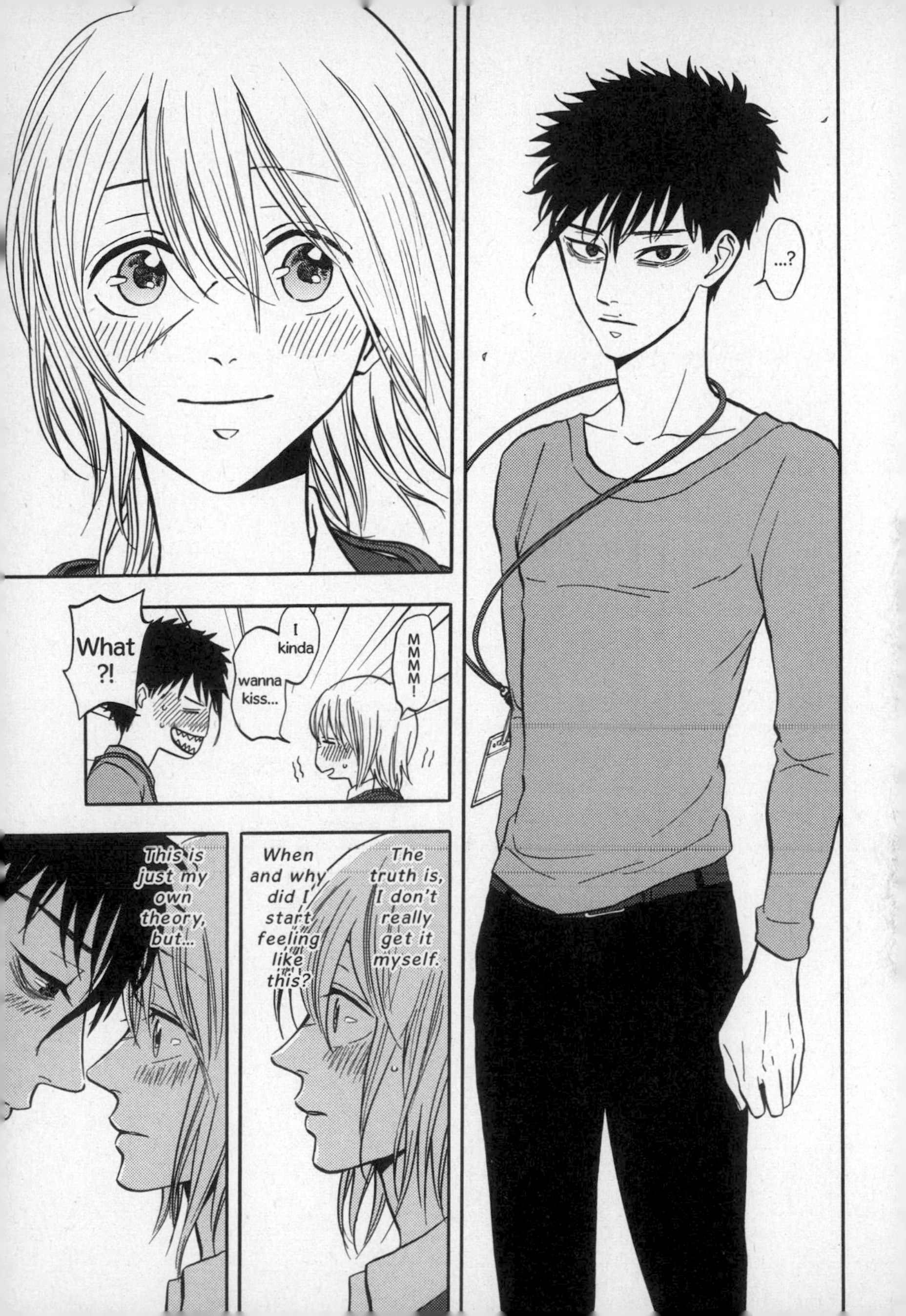
...?
MMMM!
I kinda wanna kiss...
What?!
The truth is, I don't really get it myself.
When and why did I start feeling like this?
This is just my own theory, but...

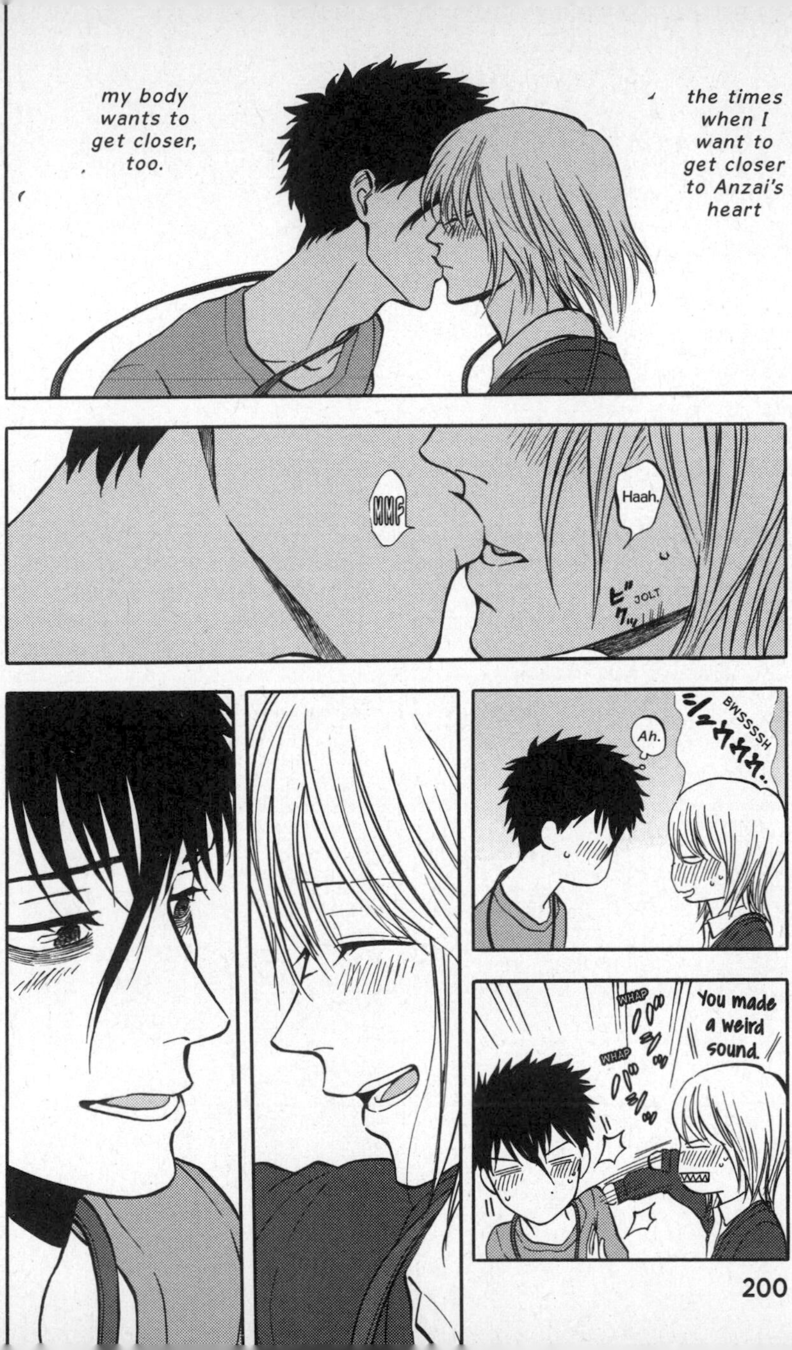
the times when I want to get closer to Anzai's heart
my body wants to get closer, too.
Haah.
ビクッ
JOLT
MMF
Ah.
シュウウウ..
BWSSSSH
You made a weird sound.
WHAP
WHAP

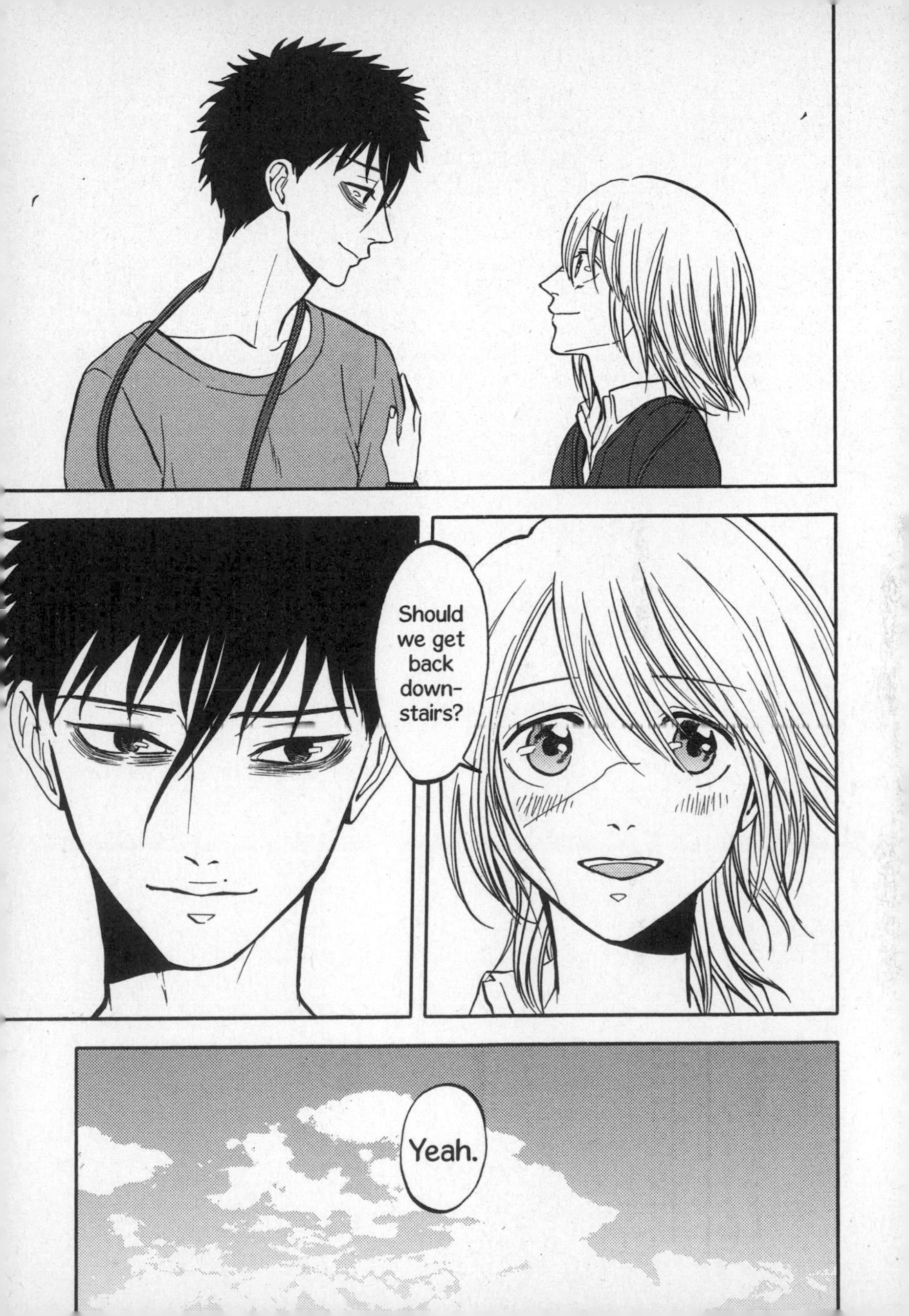
Should we get back down-stairs?
Yeah.

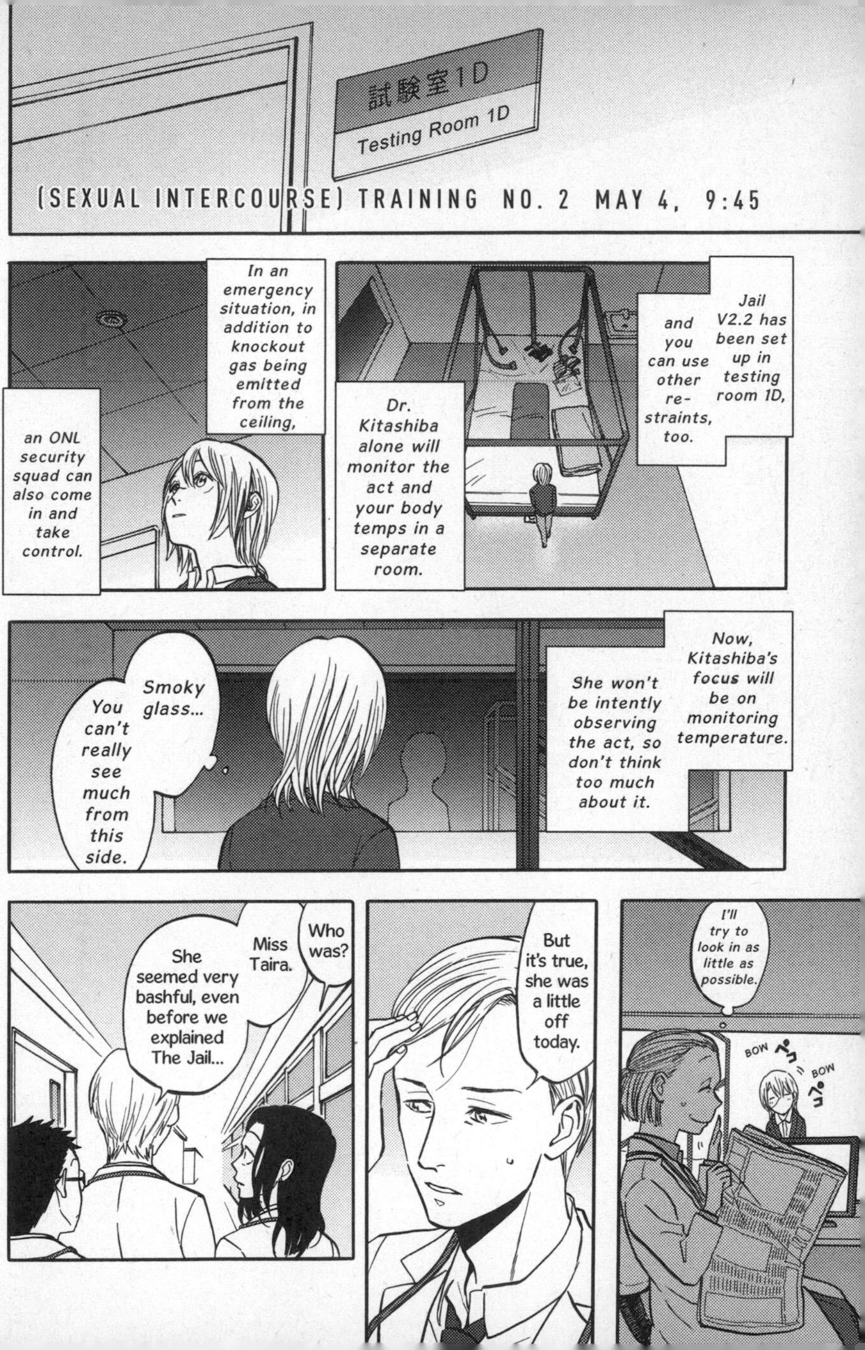

試験室1D
Testing Room 1D
(SEXUAL INTERCOURSE) TRAINING NO. 2 MAY 4, 9:45
Jail V2.2 has been set up in testing room 1D,
and you can use other re-straints, too.
Dr. Kitashiba alone will monitor the act and your body temps in a separate room.
In an emergency situation, in addition to knockout gas being emitted from the ceiling,
an ONL security squad can also come in and take control.
Now, Kitashiba's focus will be on monitoring temperature.
She won't be intently observing the act, so don't think too much about it.
Smoky glass...
You can't really see much from this side.
I'll try to look in as little as possible.
BOW
ペコ
BOW
ペコ
But it's true, she was a little off today.
Who was?
Miss Taira.
She seemed very bashful, even before we explained The Jail...

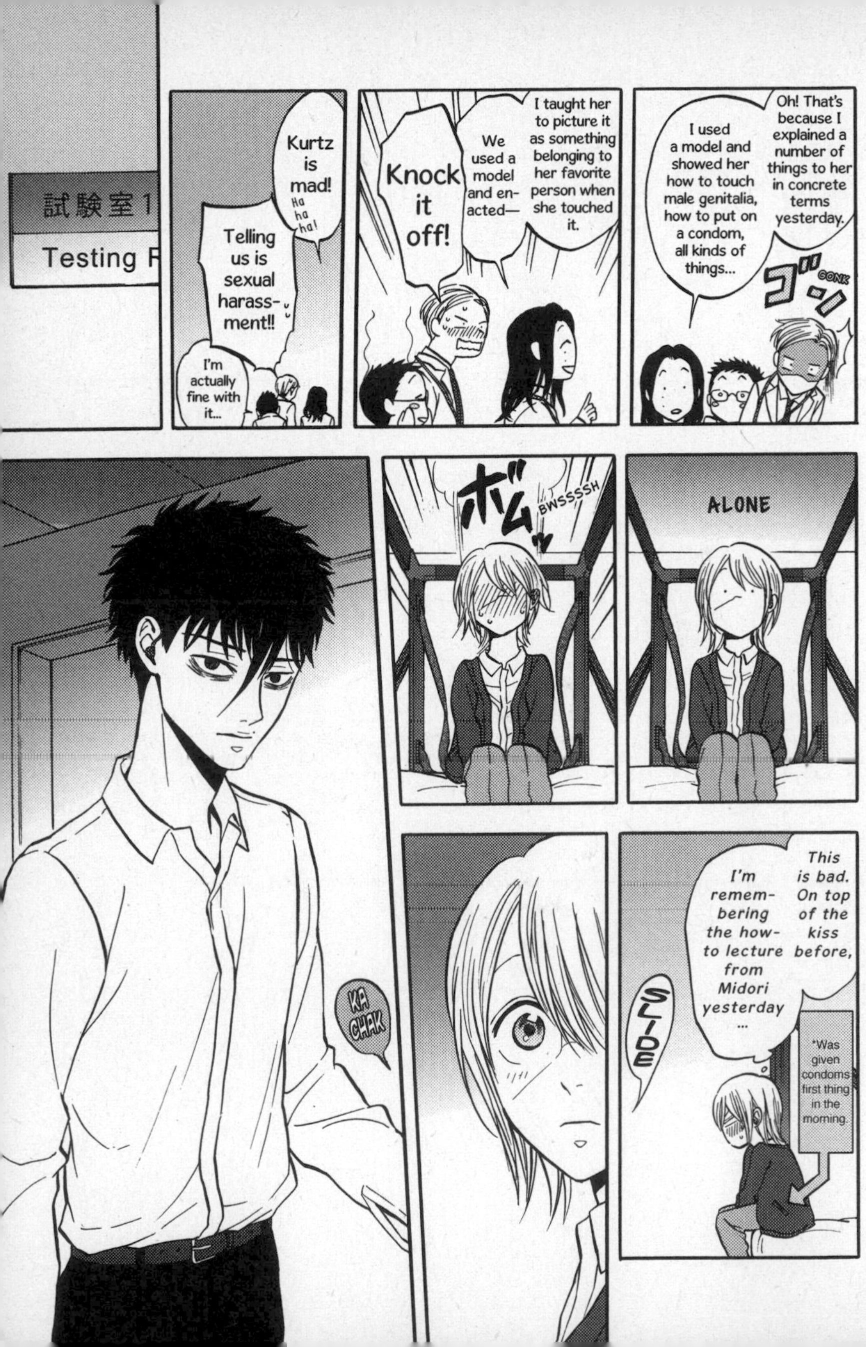
Oh! That's because I explained a number of things to her in concrete terms yesterday.
I used a model and showed her how to touch male genitalia, how to put on a condom, all kinds of things...
GONK
I taught her to picture it as something belonging to her favorite person when she touched it.
We used a model and en-acted—
Knock it off!
Kurtz is mad!
Ha ha ha!
Telling us is sexual harass-ment!!
I'm actually fine with it...
試験室1
Testing R
ALONE
BWSSSSH
This is bad. On top of the kiss before,
I'm remem-bering the how-to lecture from Midori yesterday ...
*Was given condoms first thing in the morning.
SLIDE
KA CHAK

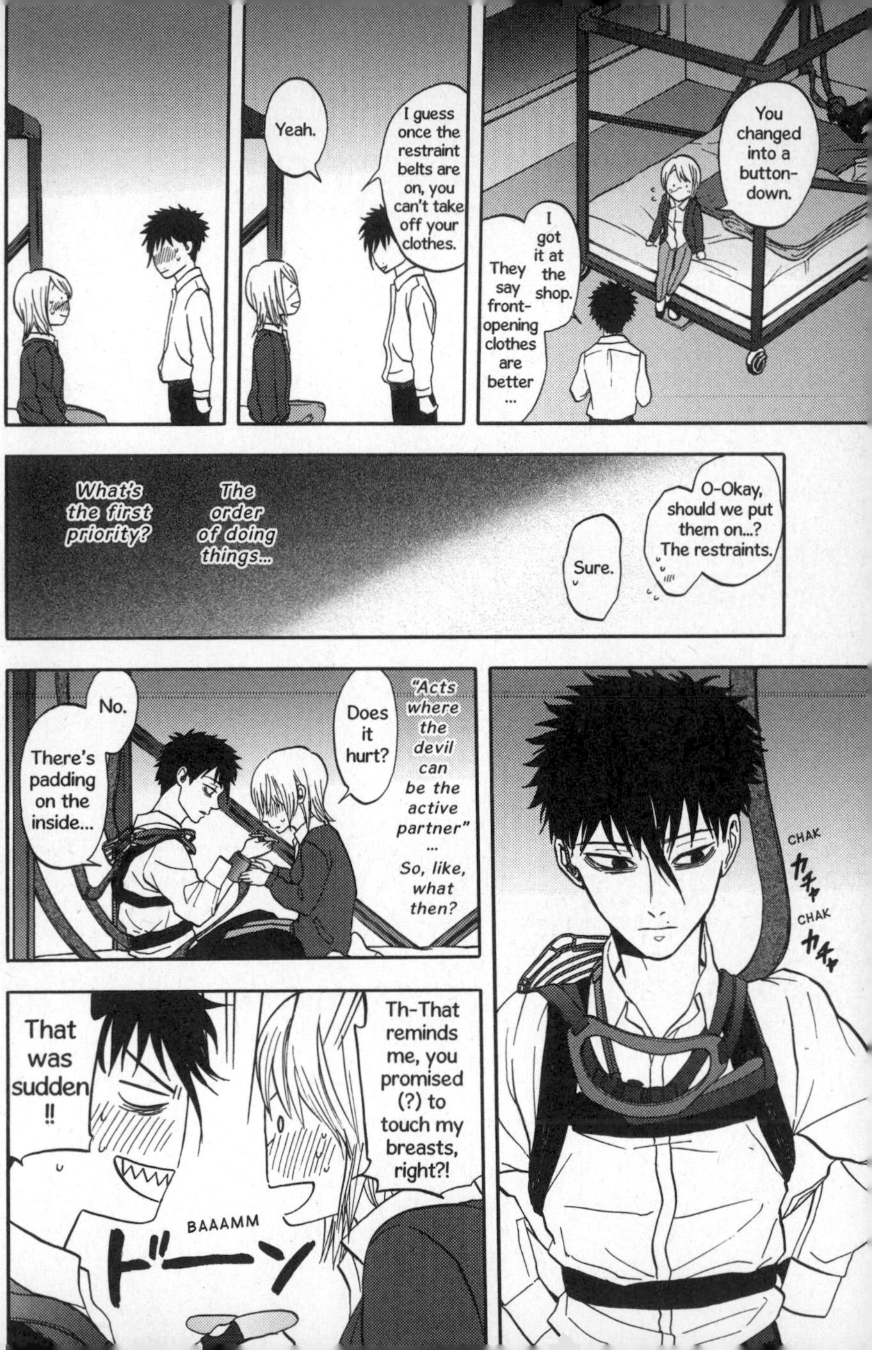
You changed into a button-down.
I got it at the shop.
They say front-opening clothes are better ...
I guess once the restraint belts are on, you can't take off your clothes.
Yeah.
O-Okay, should we put them on...? The restraints.
Sure.
The order of doing things...
What's the first priority?
CHAK
CHAK
"Acts where the devil can be the active partner" ... So, like, what then?
Does it hurt?
No.
There's padding on the inside...
Th-That reminds me, you promised (?) to touch my breasts, right?!
That was sudden!!
BAAAMM
ドーン

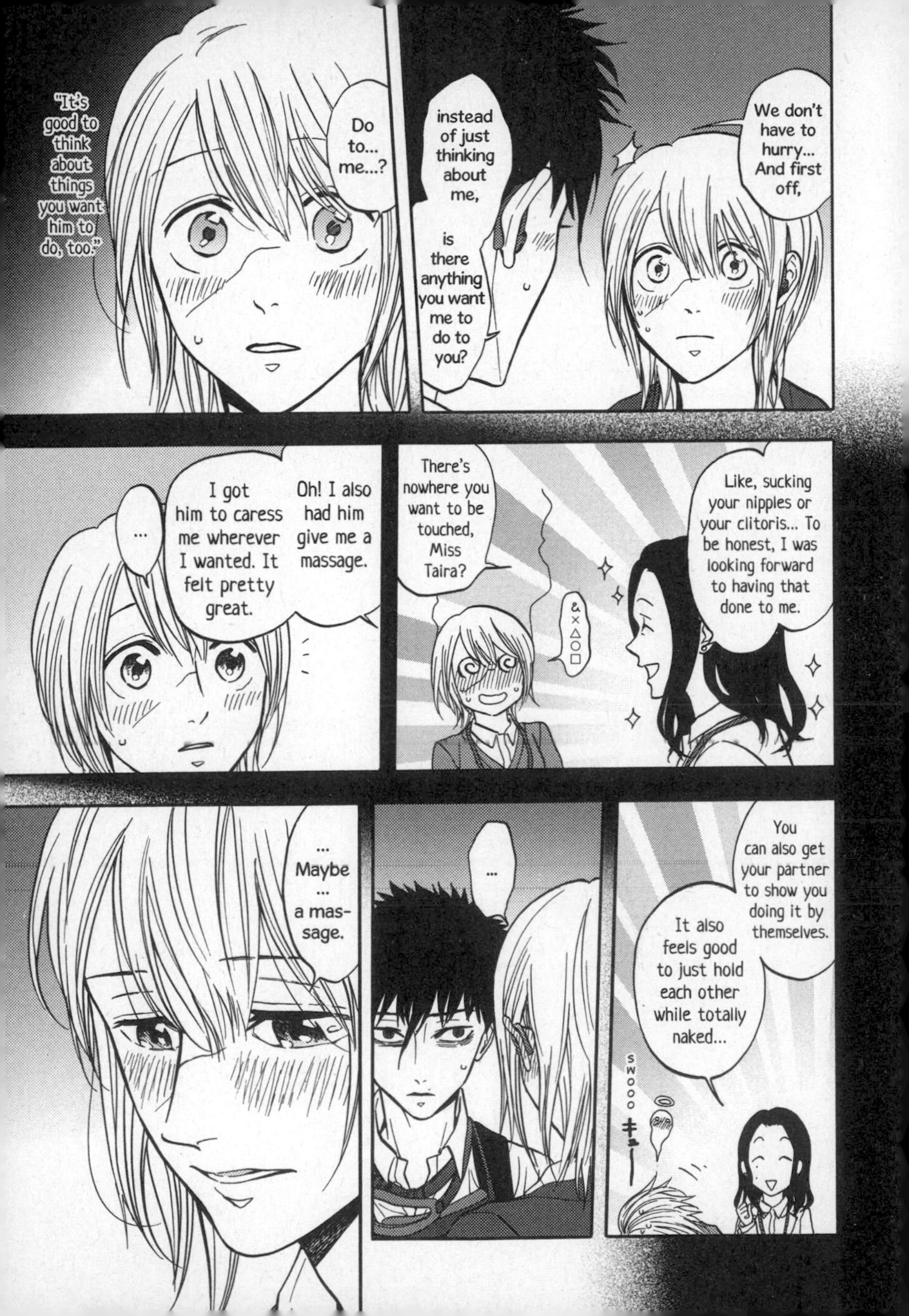
We don't have to hurry... And first off,
instead of just thinking about me,
is there anything you want me to do to you?
Do to... me...?
"It's good to think about things you want him to do, too."
Like, sucking your nipples or your clitoris... To be honest, I was looking forward to having that done to me.
There's nowhere you want to be touched, Miss Taira?
&×△○□
Oh! I also had him give me a massage.
I got him to caress me wherever I wanted. It felt pretty great.
...
You can also get your partner to show you doing it by themselves.
It also feels good to just hold each other while totally naked...
SWOOO
...
... Maybe ... a massage.

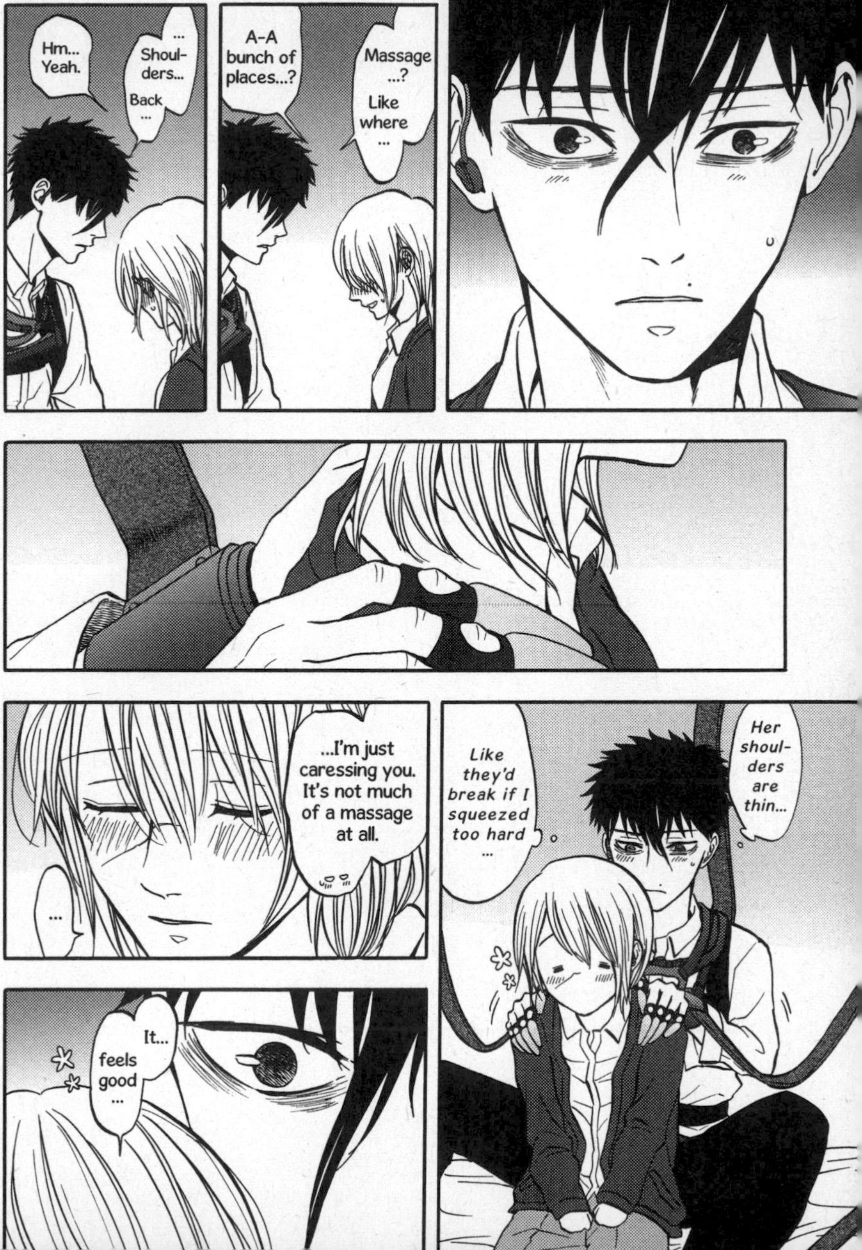
Massage ...? Like where ...
A-A bunch of places...?
... Shoulders... Back ...
Hm... Yeah.
Her shoulders are thin...
Like they'd break if I squeezed too hard ...
...I'm just caressing you. It's not much of a massage at all.
...
It... feels good ...

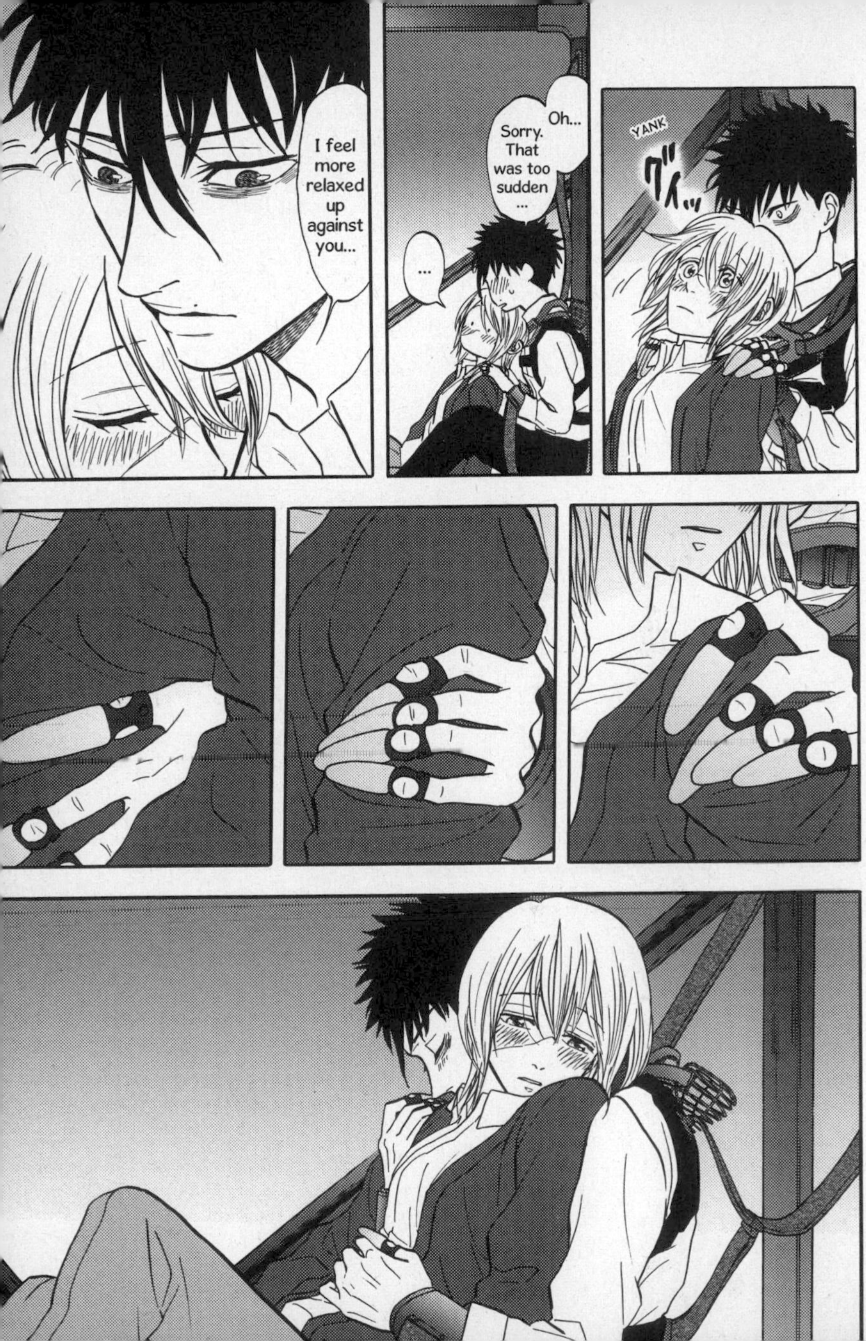
YANK
グイッ
Oh... Sorry. That was too sudden ...
...
I feel more relaxed up against you...

He's so gentle...

TWITCH

ピク。

SHFF

This feels good.

His touch, his body heat.

Yeah.

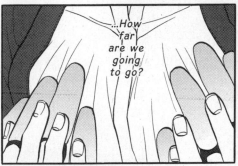

...How far are we going to go?

...

How far...

...sk.

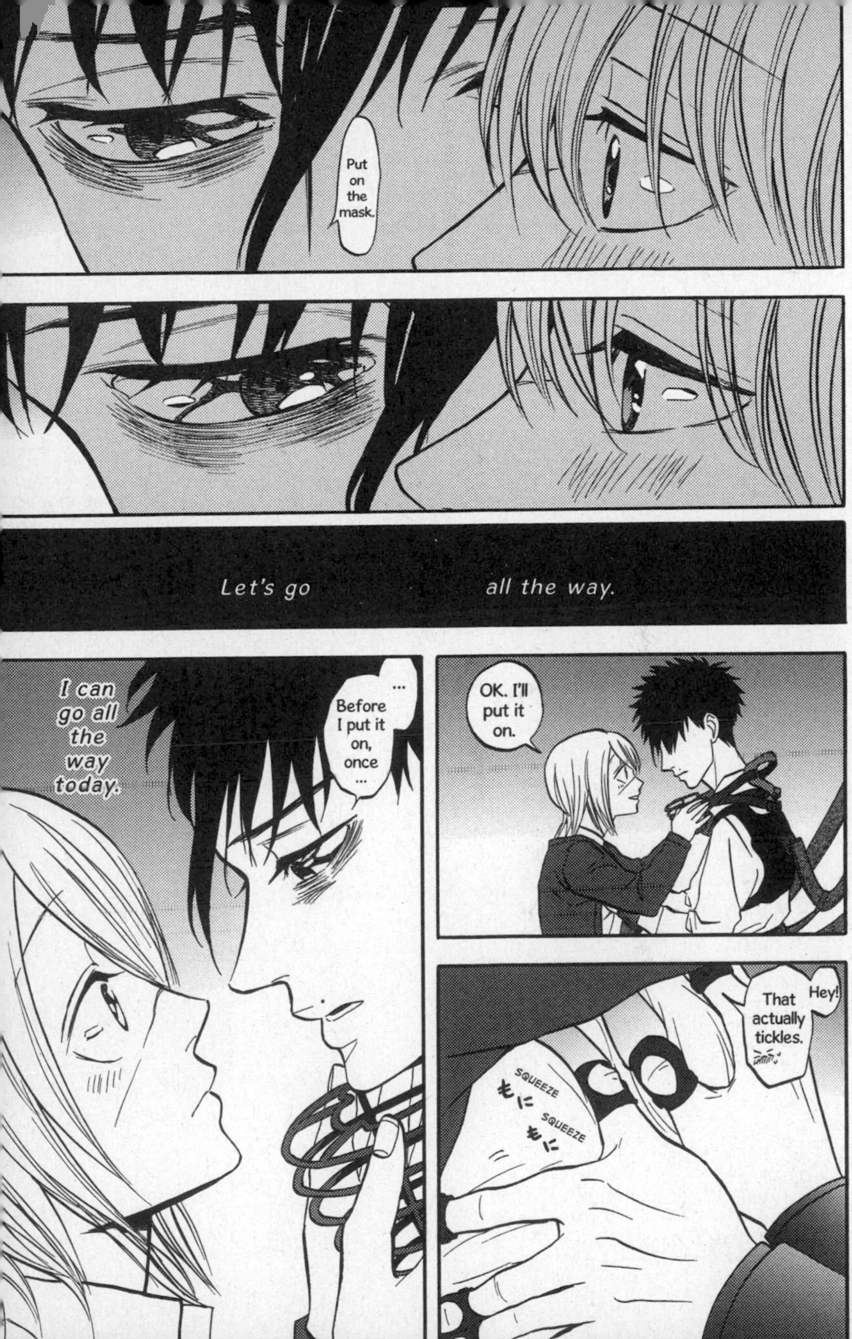
Put on the mask.
Let's go all the way.
OK. I'll put it on.
Hey!
That actually tickles.
SQUEEZE
もに
SQUEEZE
もに
... Before I put it on, once ...
I can go all the way today.

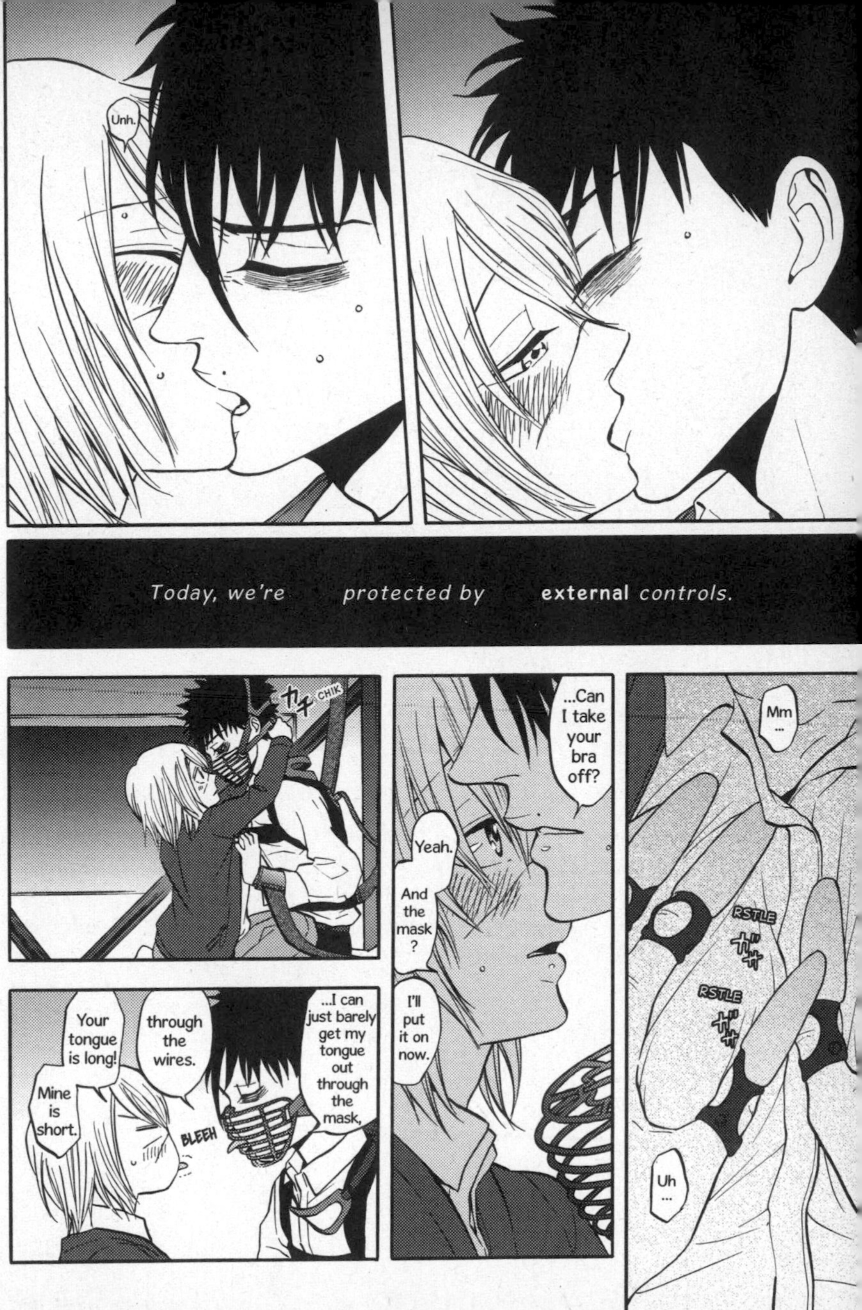
Unh.
Today, we're protected by external controls.
Mm ...
RSTLE
RSTLE
Uh ...
...Can I take your bra off?
Yeah.
And the mask?
I'll put it on now.
CHIK
...I can just barely get my tongue out through the mask,
through the wires.
Your tongue is long!
Mine is short.
BLEEH

Eeep!

LICK

That's the first time I've ever had a kiss that was just a lick.

PLP

W-Wait.

Um.

I'll take my shirt off...

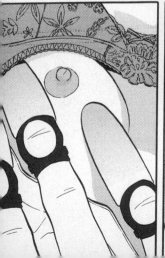

Take... my bra...

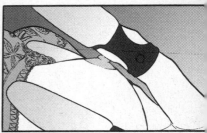

...

It tickles ...

He's touching me with the pads of his fingers.

Ah ...

Mm.

... licking them...

I want you to... try...

Uhm ...

Aaah...

FWMP

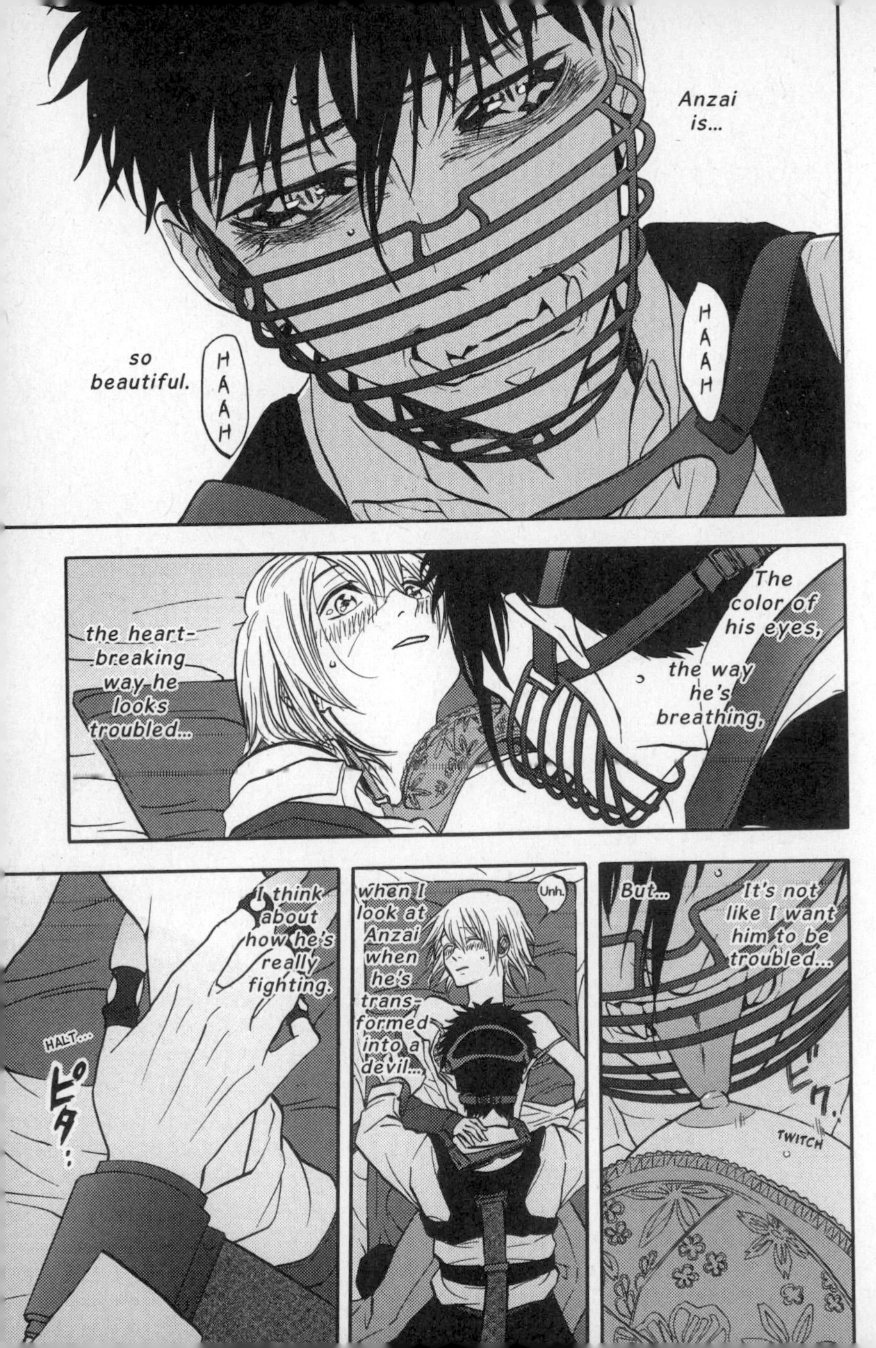
Anzai is...
HAAAH
HAAAH
so beautiful.
The color of his eyes,
the way he's breathing,
the heart-breaking way he looks troubled...
It's not like I want him to be troubled...
But...
TWITCH
Unh.
when I look at Anzai when he's transformed into a devil...
I think about how he's really fighting.
HALT...
ピタ…

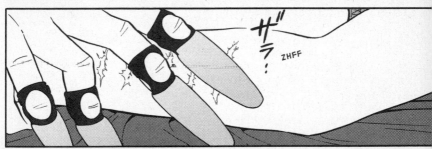

ザッ!
ZHFF

214

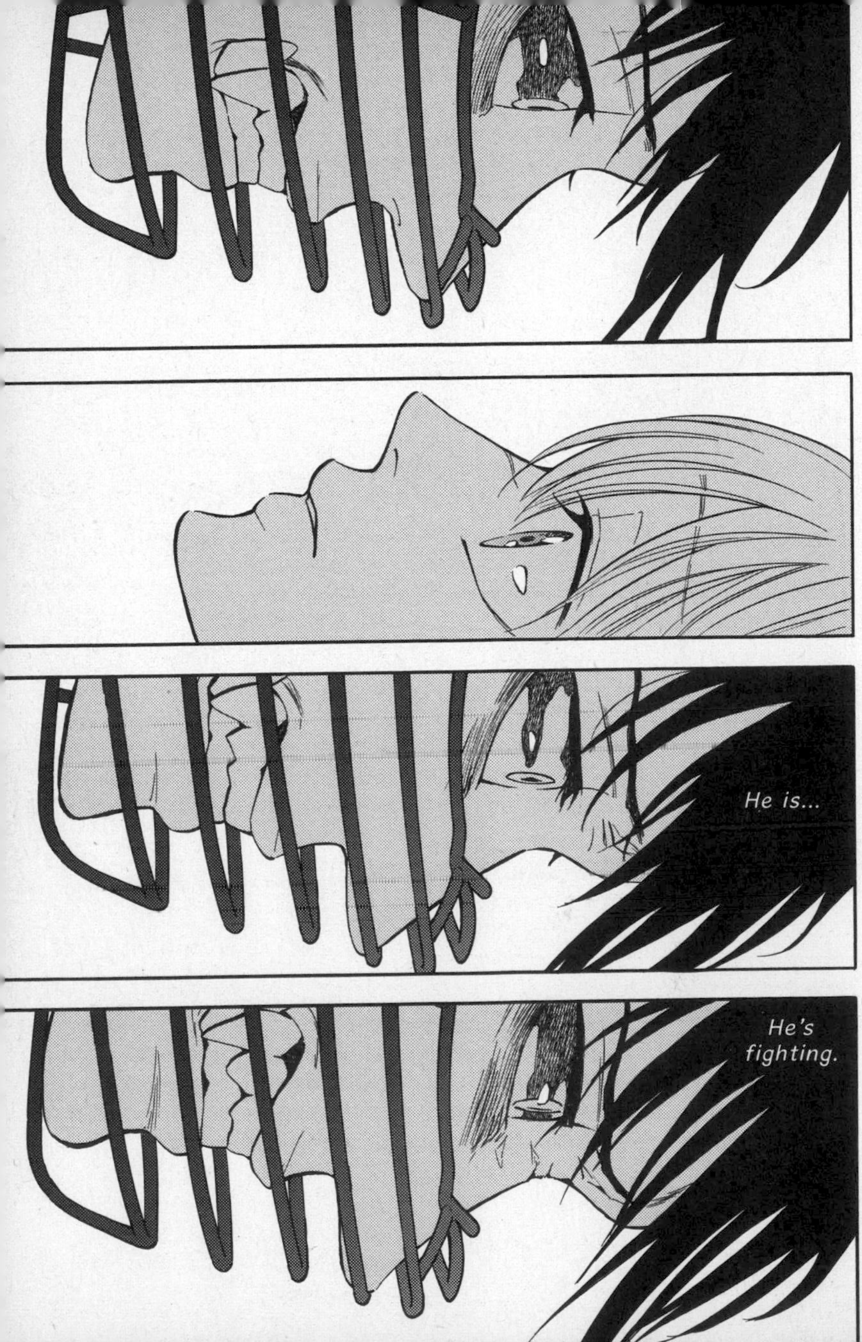
He is...
He's fighting.

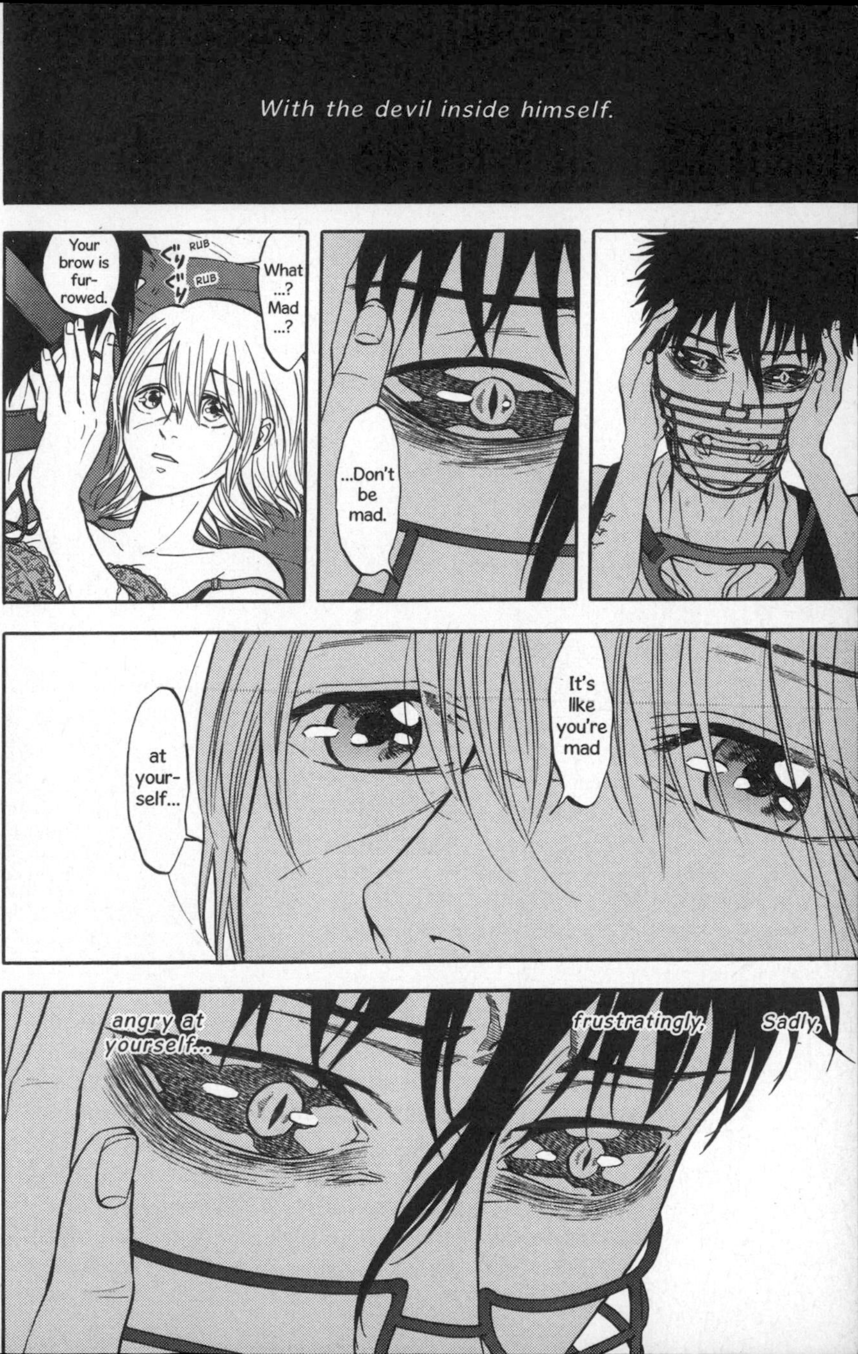

With the devil inside himself.
...Don't be mad.
What ...? Mad ...?
RUB
RUB
Your brow is fur-rowed.
It's like you're mad
at your-self...
Sadly,
frustratingly,
angry at yourself...

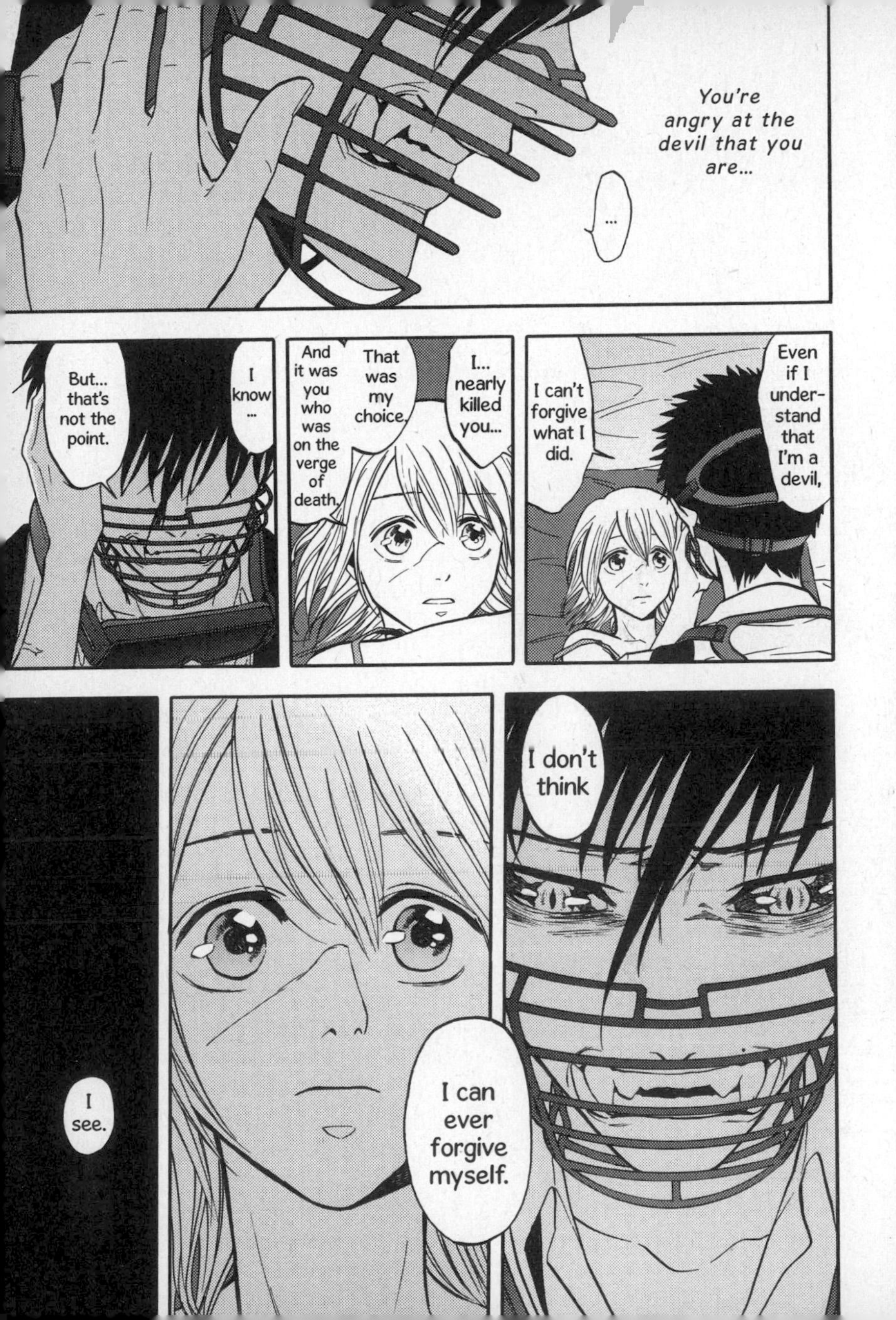
You're angry at the devil that you are...
...
Even if I understand that I'm a devil,
I can't forgive what I did.
I... nearly killed you...
That was my choice.
And it was you who was on the verge of death.
I know...
But... that's not the point.
I don't think
I can ever forgive myself.
I see.

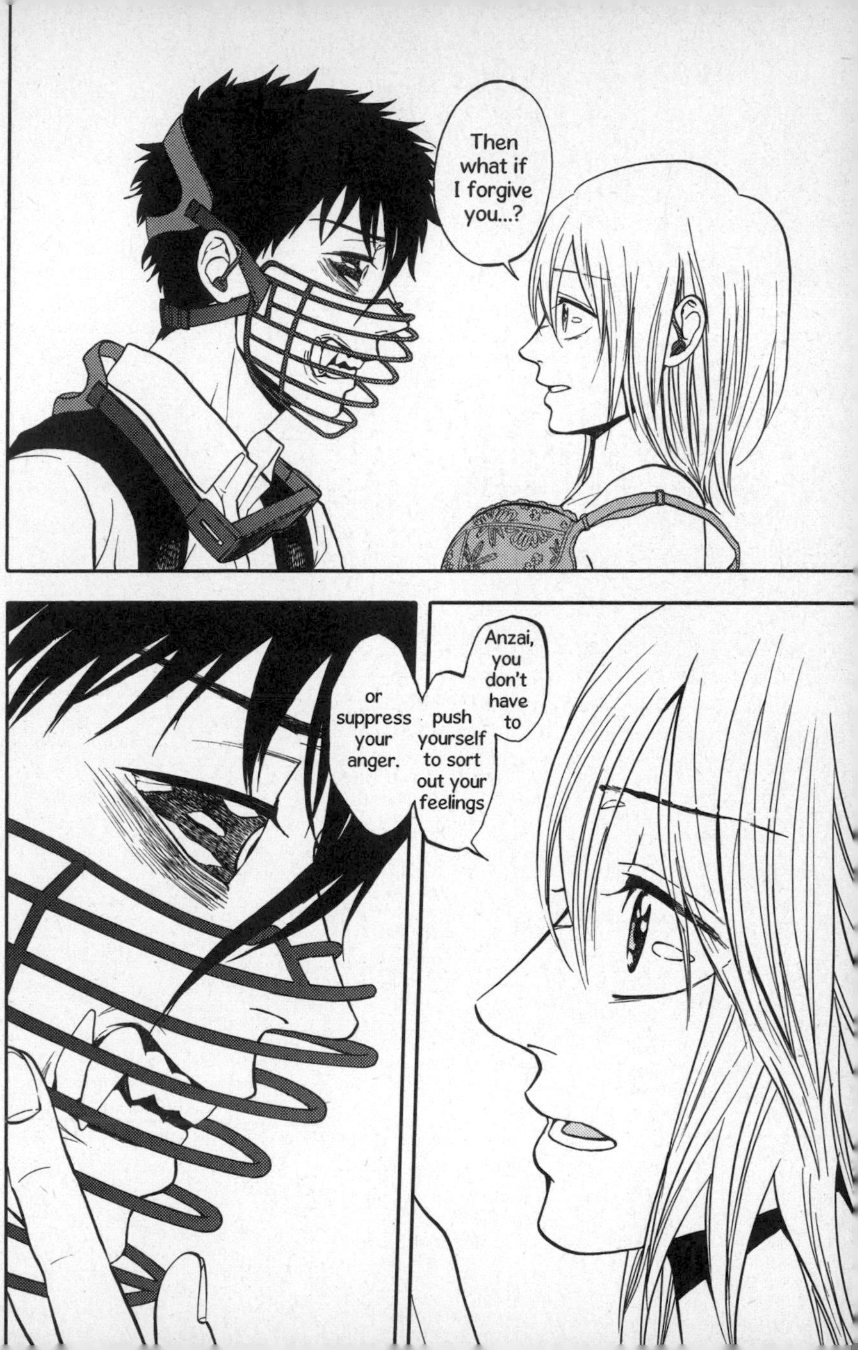
Then what if I forgive you...?
Anzai, you don't have to push yourself to sort out your feelings or suppress your anger.

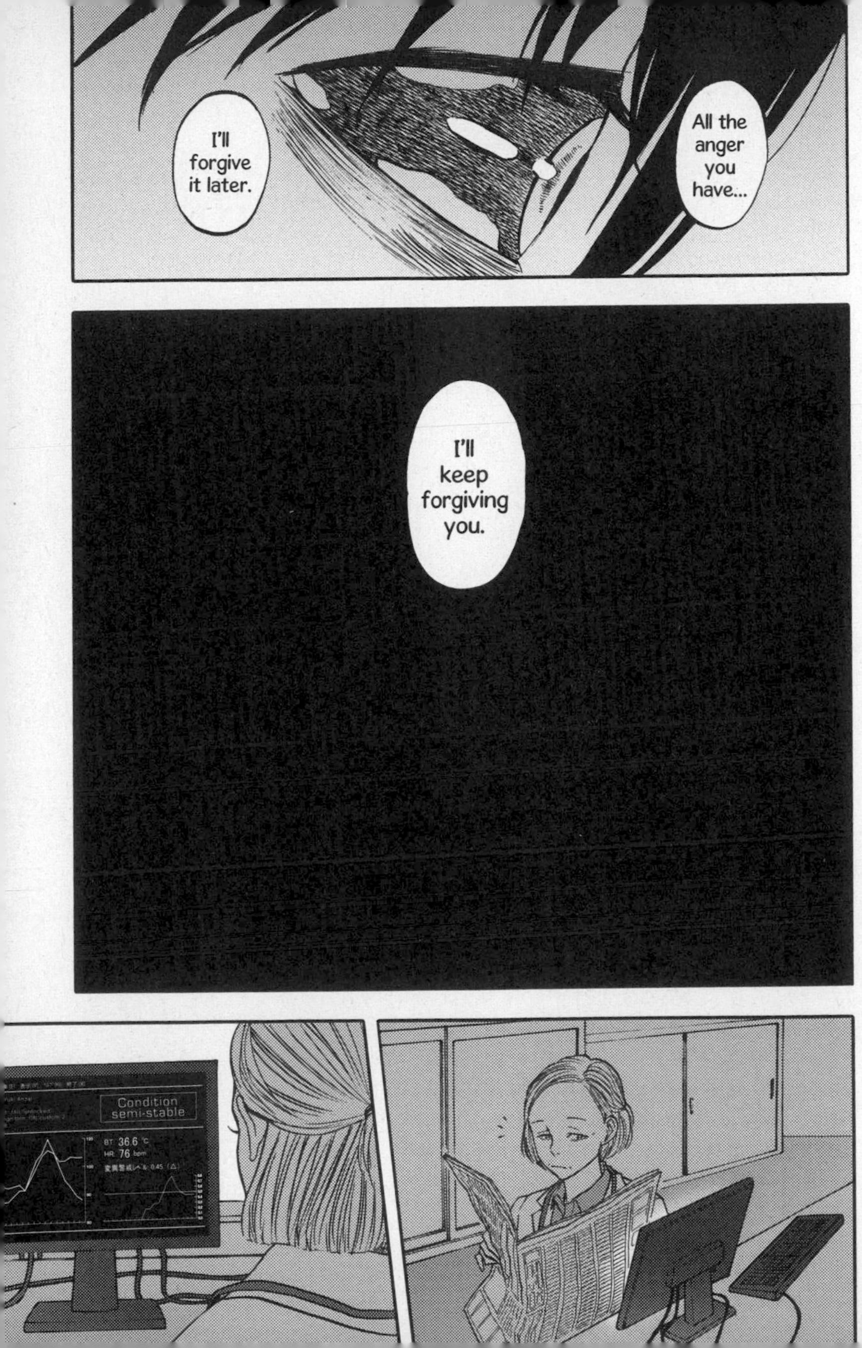
All the anger you have...
I'll forgive it later.
I'll keep forgiving you.
Condition semi-stable
BT 36.6 °C
HR 76 bpm

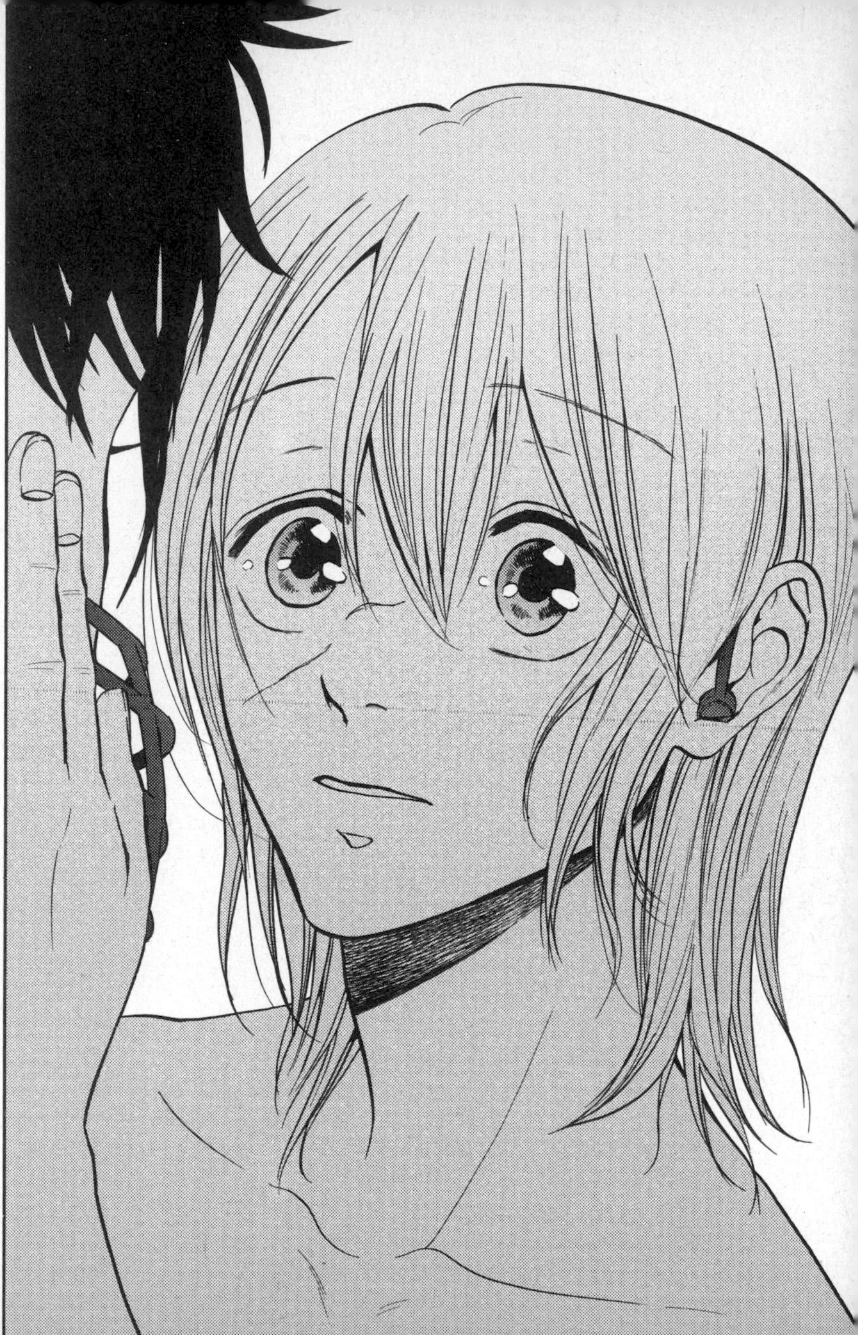

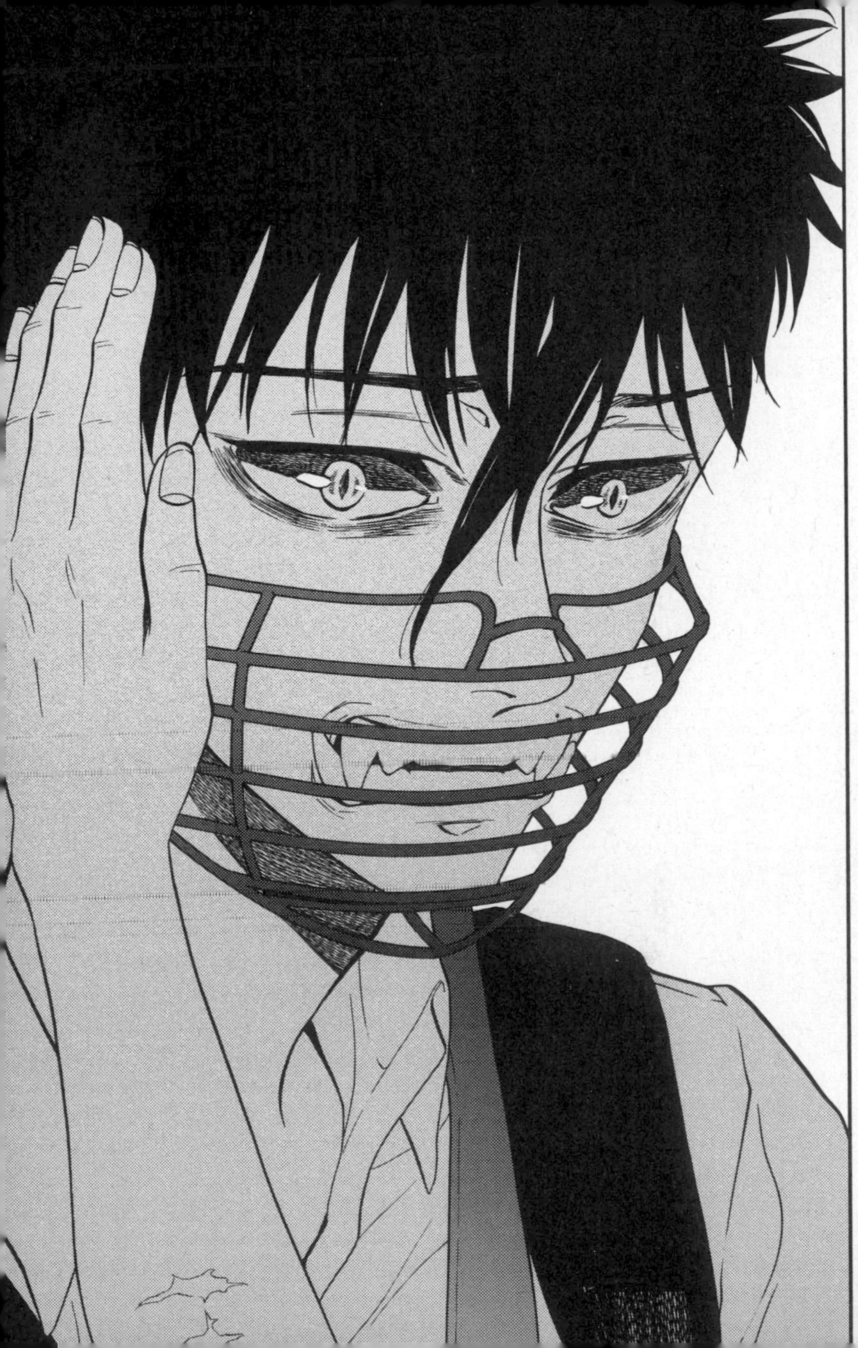

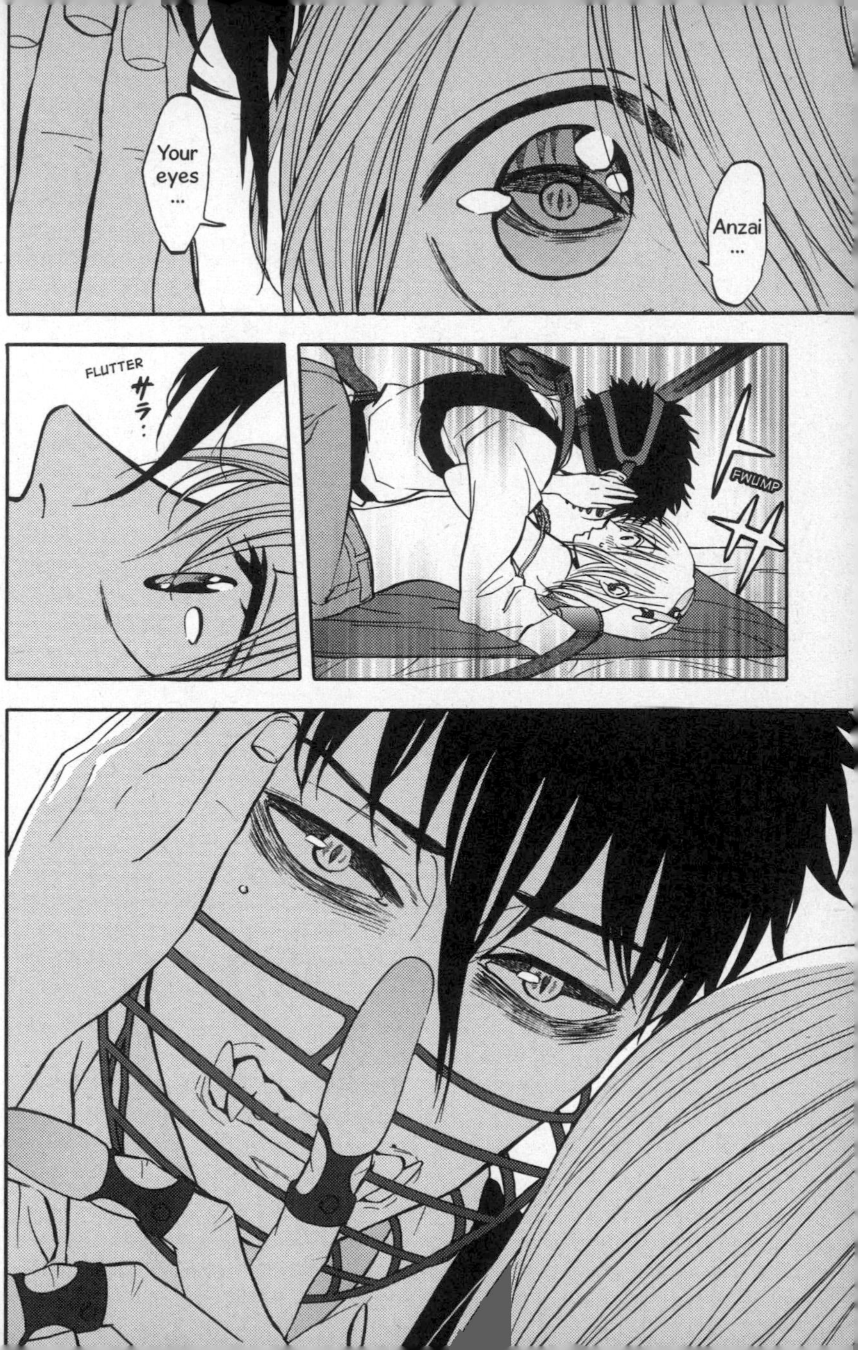
Anzai ...
Your eyes ...
FWUMP
FLUTTER
サラ…

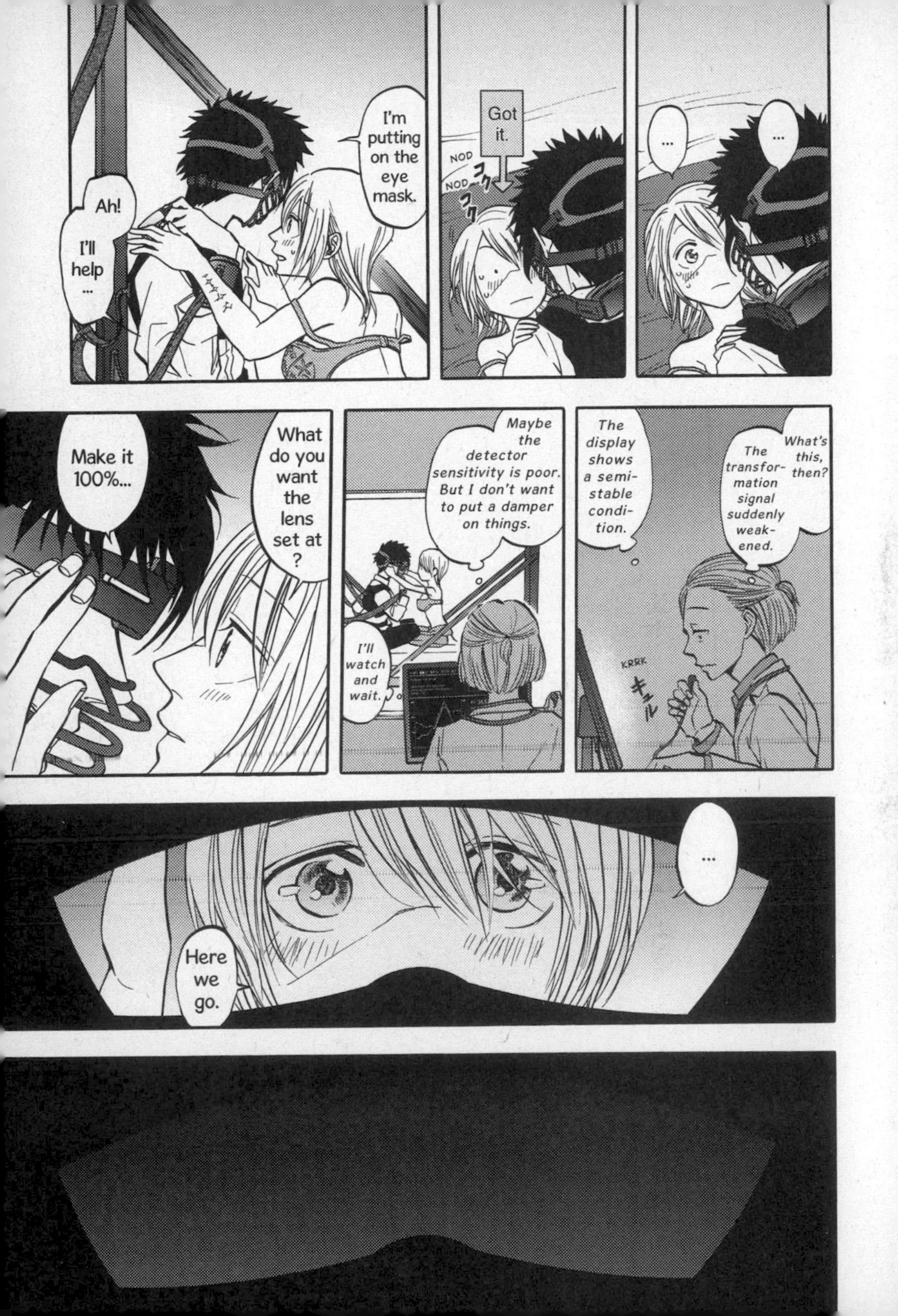
...
...
Got it.
NOD
NOD
I'm putting on the eye mask.
Ah! I'll help ...
What's this, then?
The transformation signal suddenly weakened.
The display shows a semi-stable condition.
KRRK
Maybe the detector sensitivity is poor. But I don't want to put a damper on things.
I'll watch and wait.
What do you want the lens set at?
Make it 100%...
...
Here we go.

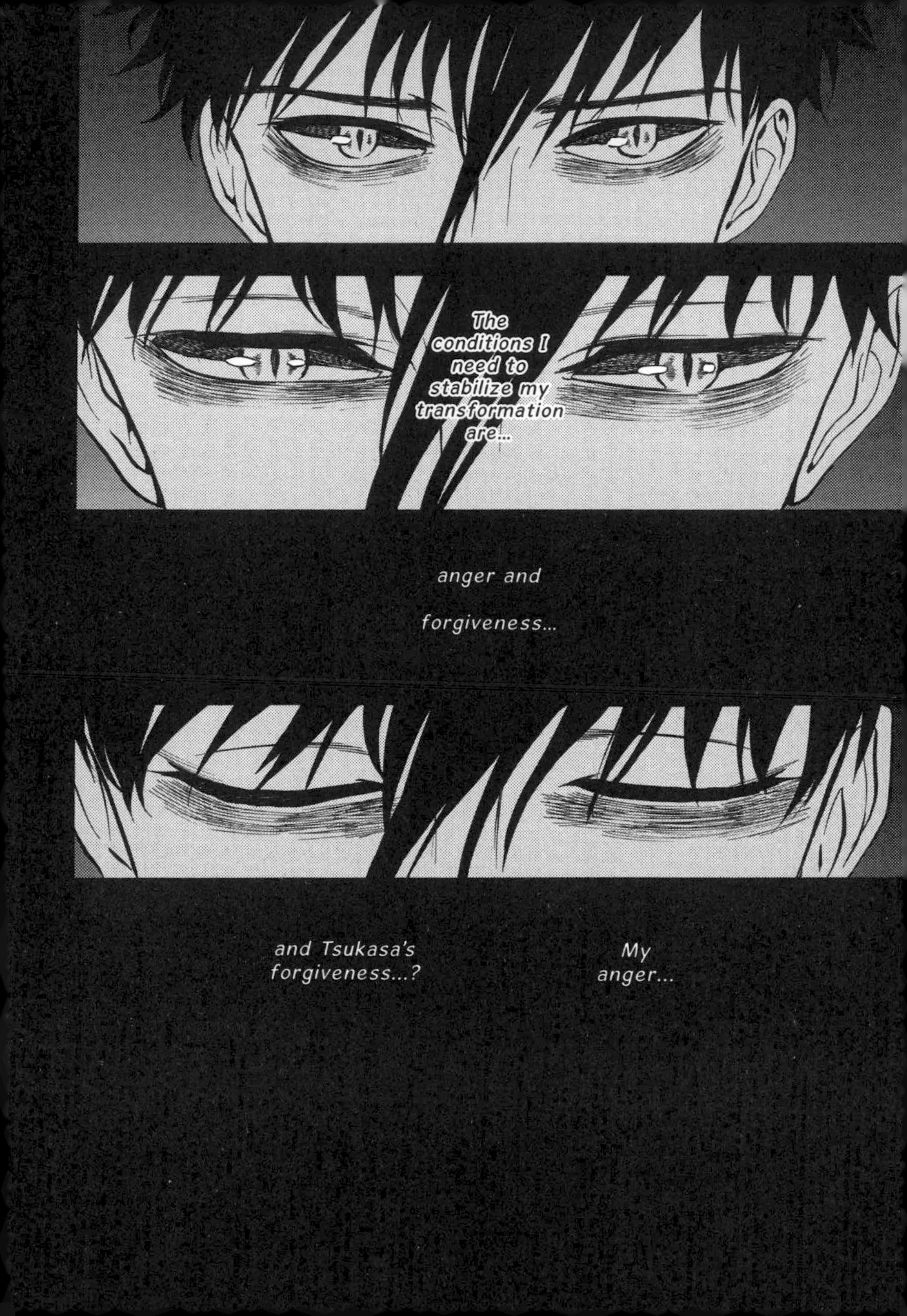
The conditions I need to stabilize my transformation are...
anger and forgiveness...
My anger...
and Tsukasa's forgiveness...?

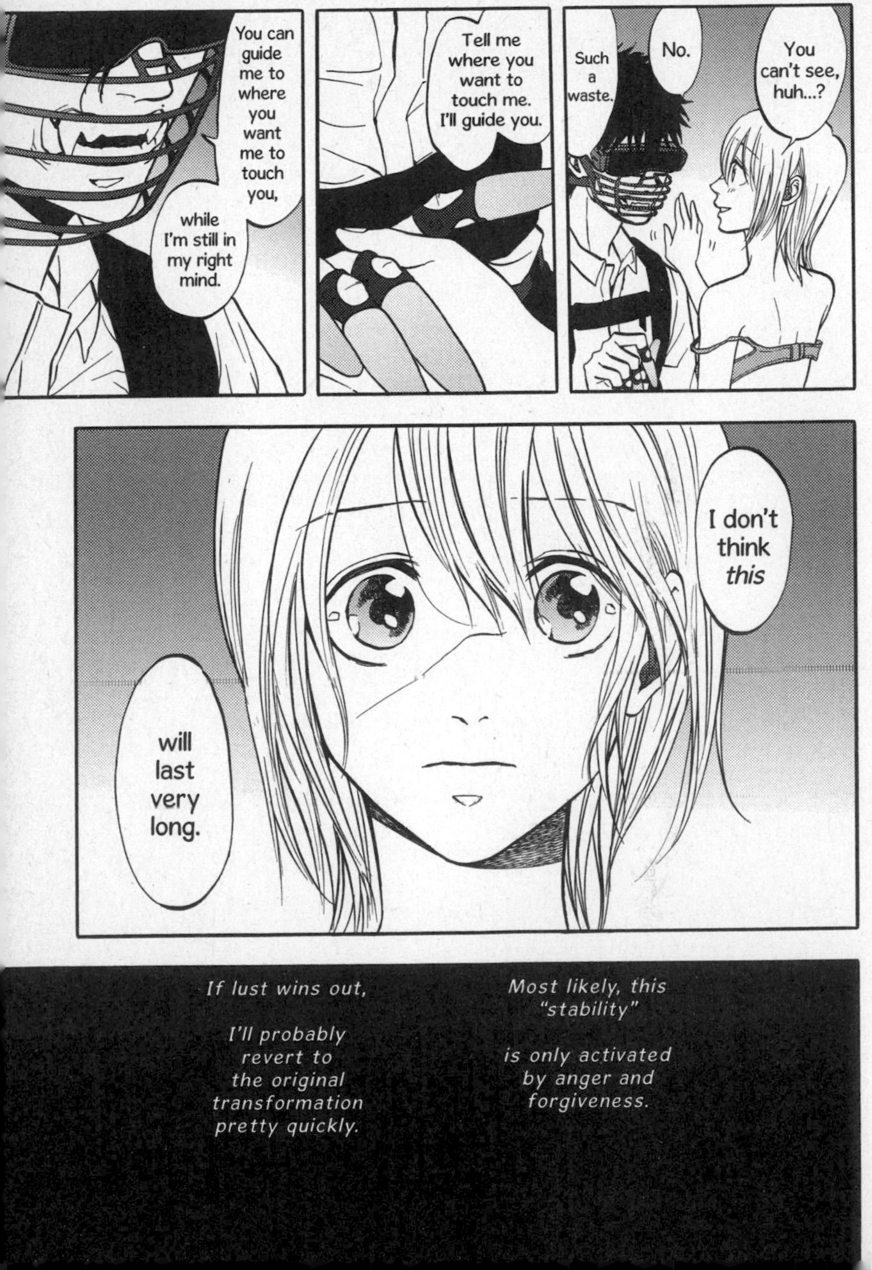
You can't see, huh...?
No.
Such a waste.
Tell me where you want to touch me. I'll guide you.
You can guide me to where you want me to touch you,
while I'm still in my right mind.
I don't think *this*
will last very long.
Most likely, this "stability"
is only activated by anger and forgiveness.
If lust wins out,
I'll probably revert to the original transformation pretty quickly.

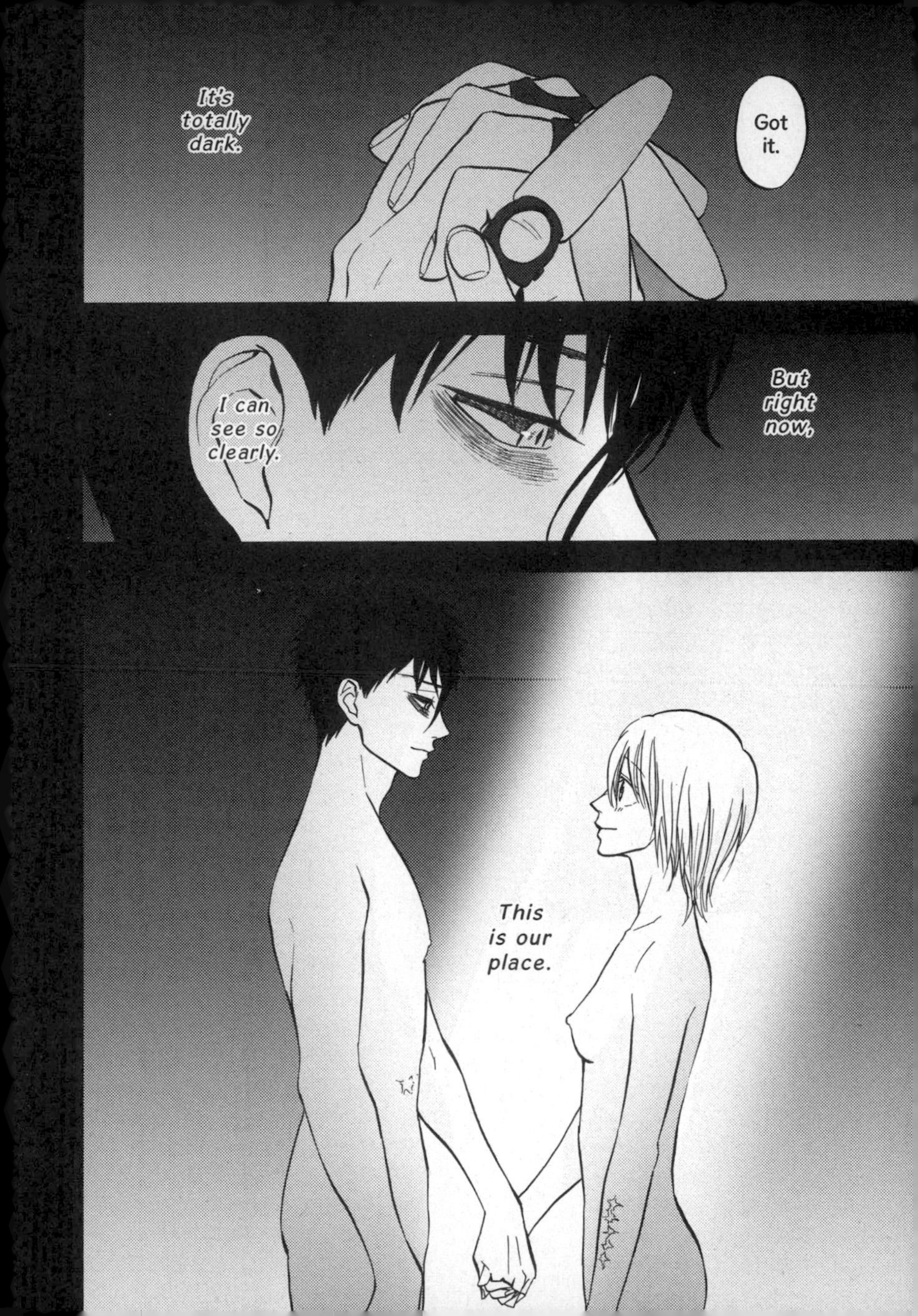
Got it.
It's totally dark.
But right now,
I can see so clearly.
This is our place.

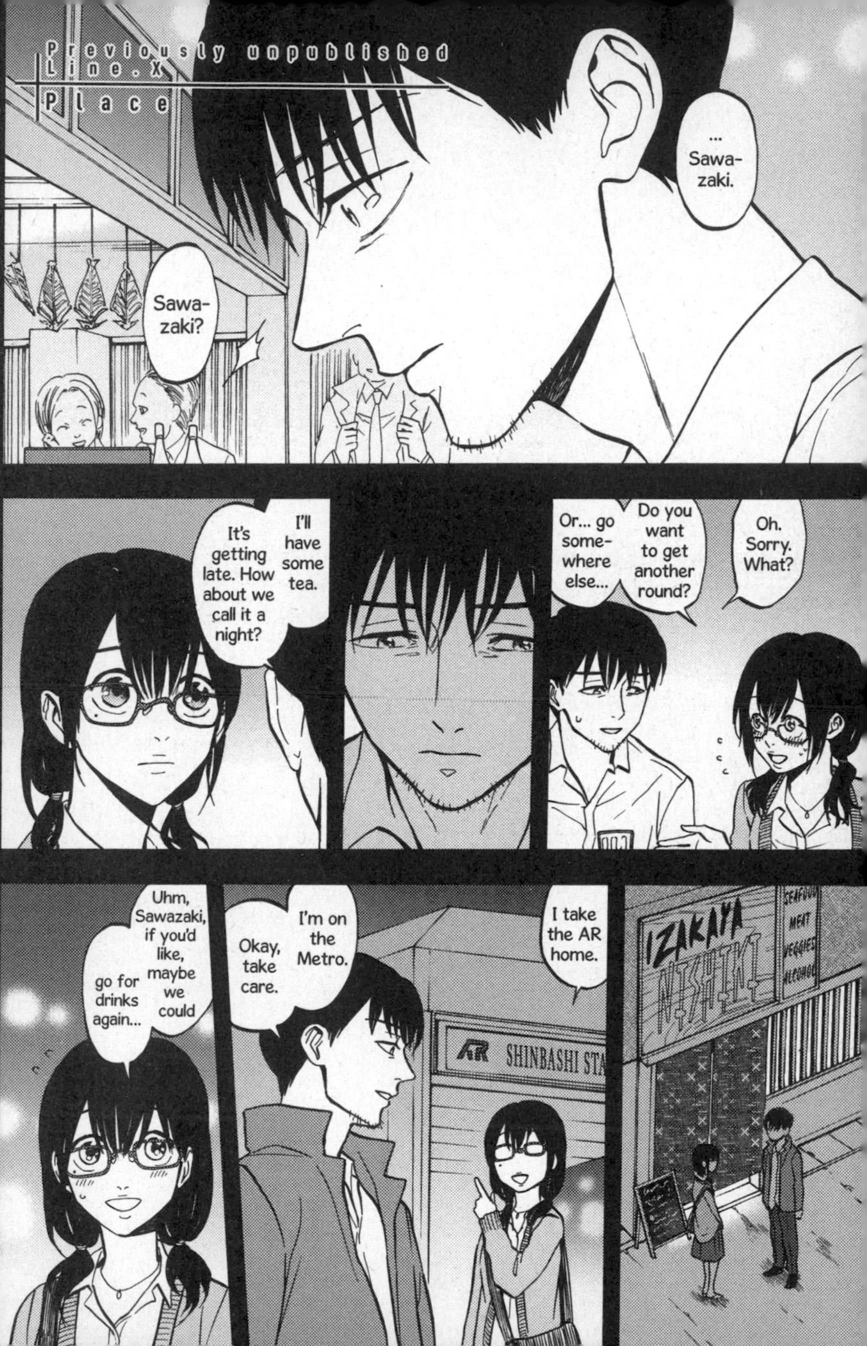
Previously unpublished Line.X Place
... Sawazaki.
Sawazaki?
Oh. Sorry. What?
Do you want to get another round?
Or... go somewhere else...
I'll have some tea.
It's getting late. How about we call it a night?
IZAKAYA NISHIKI
MEAT VEGGIES ALCOHOL
I take the AR home.
I'm on the Metro.
Okay, take care.
AR SHINBASHI STA
Uhm, Sawazaki, if you'd like, maybe we could go for drinks again...

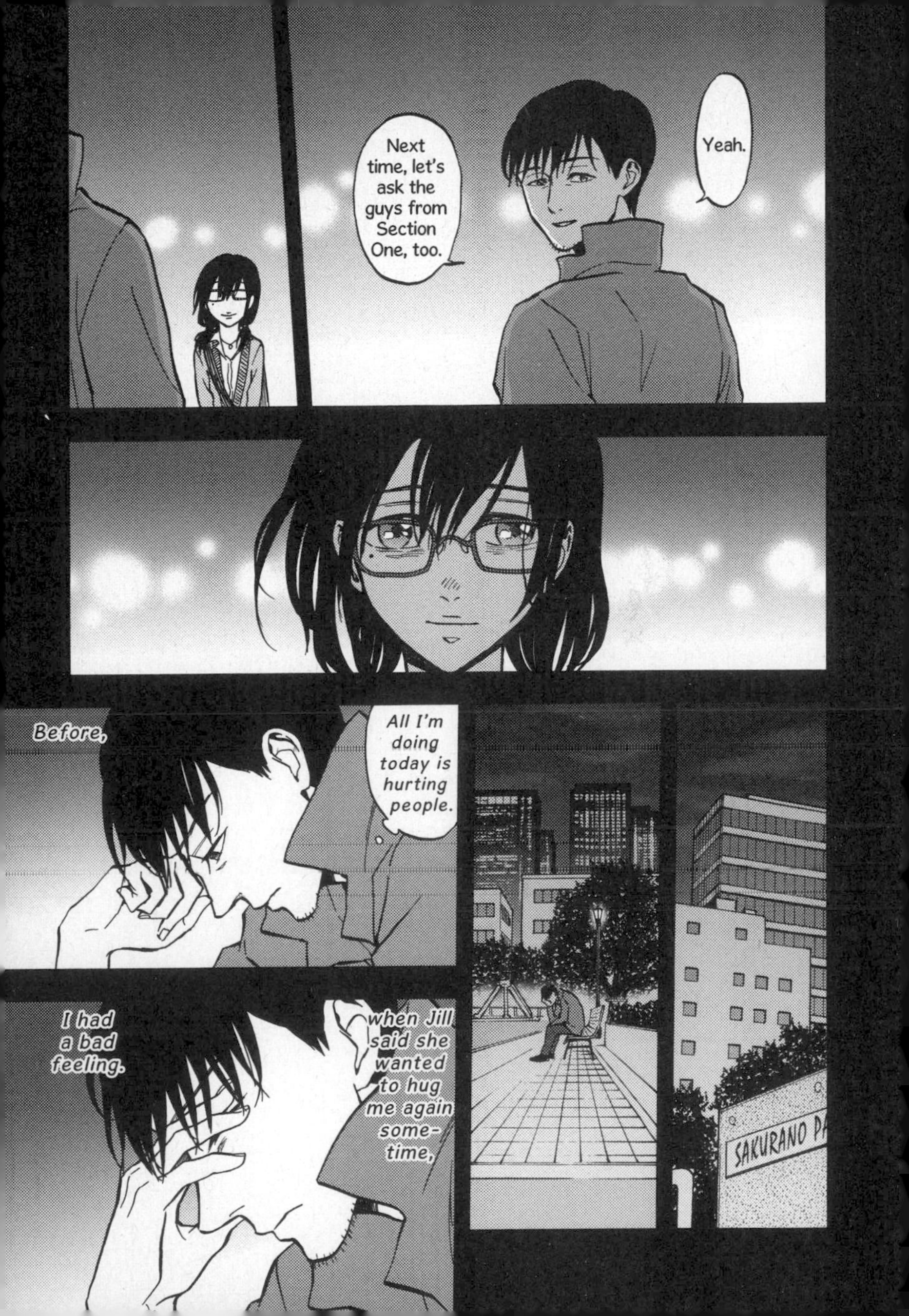
Yeah.
Next time, let's ask the guys from Section One, too.
SAKURANO PA
All I'm doing today is hurting people.
Before,
when Jill said she wanted to hug me again some-time,
I had a bad feeling.

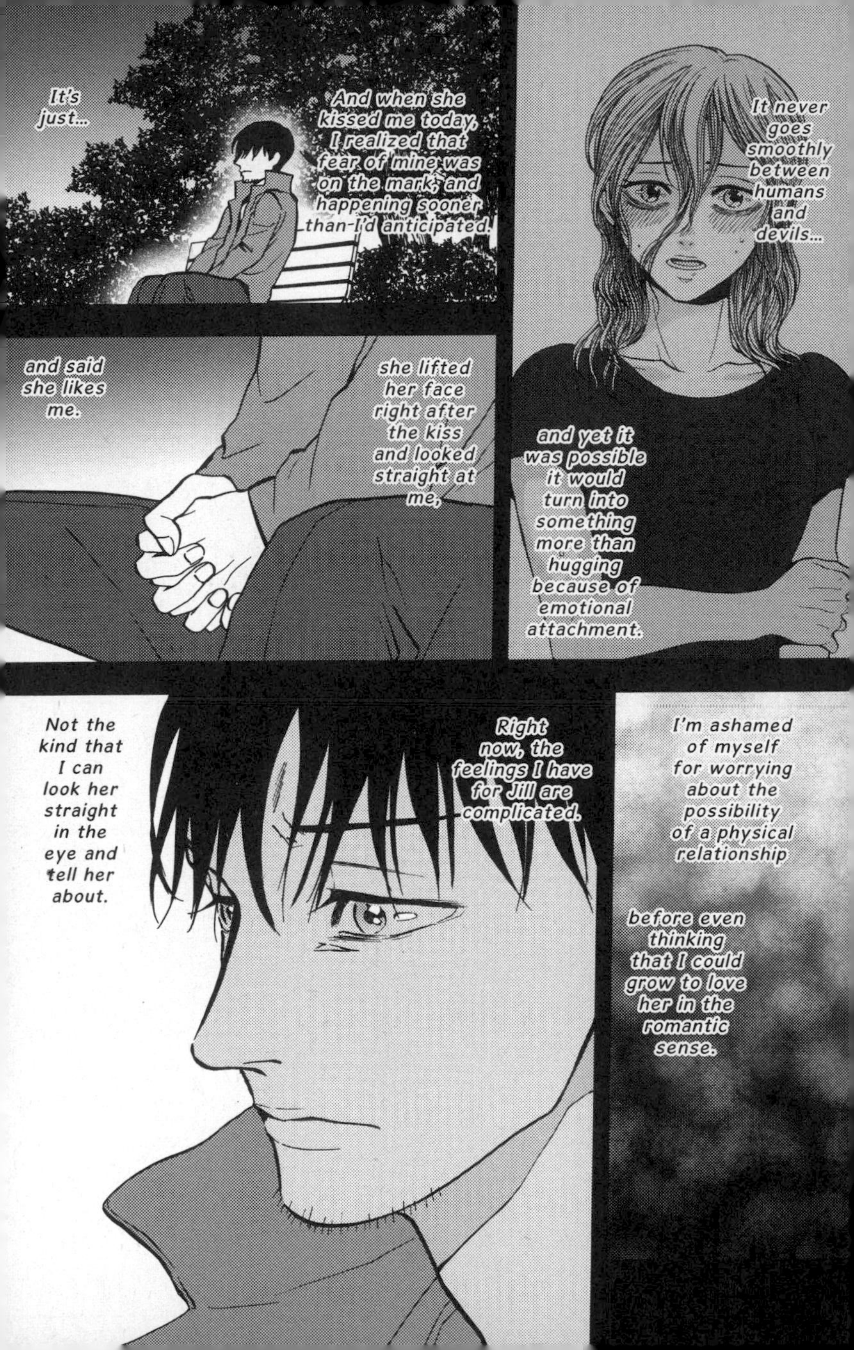
It never goes smoothly between humans and devils...
and yet it was possible it would turn into something more than hugging because of emotional attachment.
And when she kissed me today, I realized that fear of mine was on the mark, and happening sooner than I'd anticipated.
It's just...
she lifted her face right after the kiss and looked straight at me,
and said she likes me.
I'm ashamed of myself for worrying about the possibility of a physical relationship
before even thinking that I could grow to love her in the romantic sense.
Right now, the feelings I have for Jill are complicated.
Not the kind that I can look her straight in the eye and tell her about.

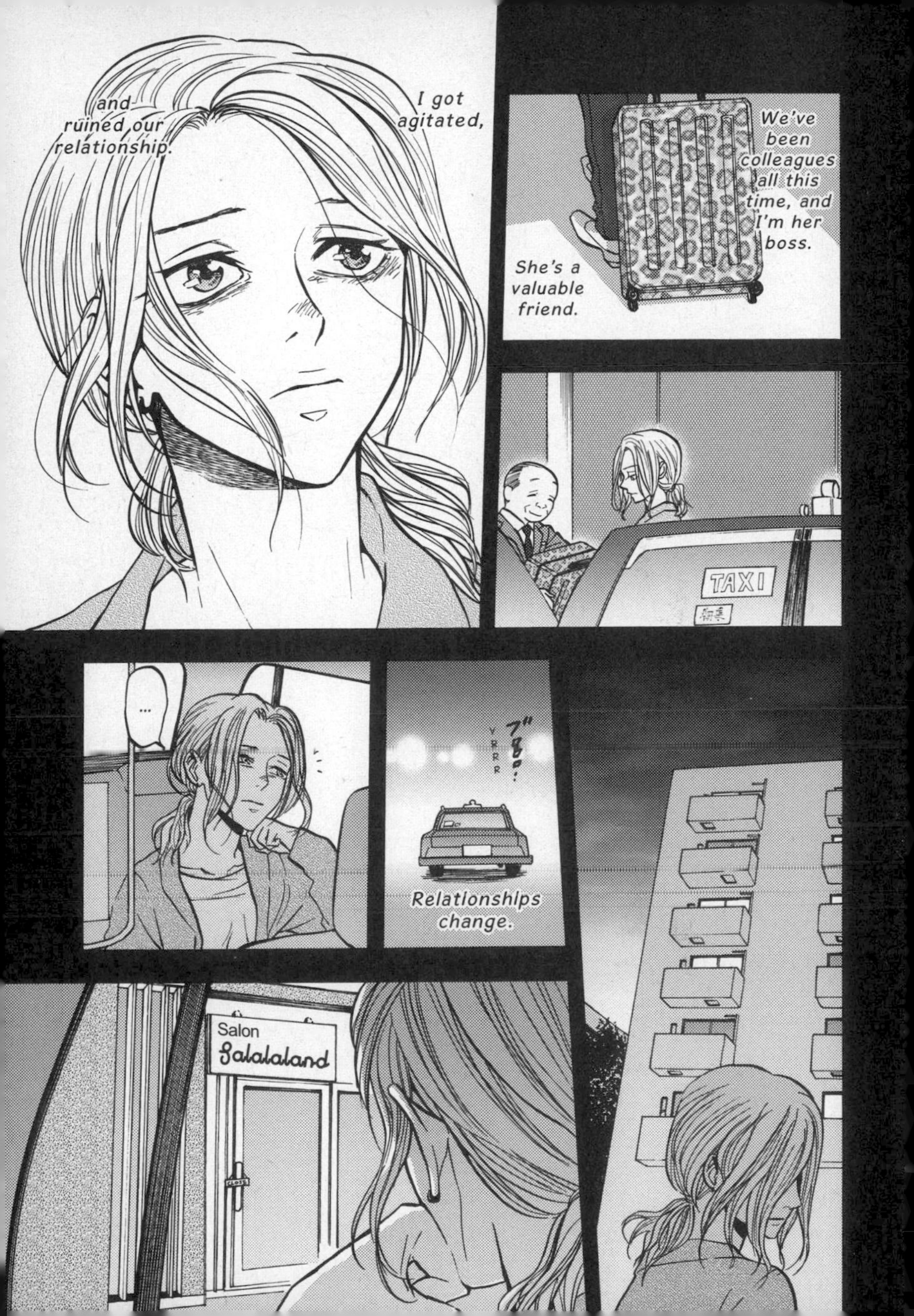
We've been colleagues all this time, and I'm her boss.
She's a valuable friend.
TAXI
I got agitated,
and ruined our relationship.
VRRR
Relationships change.
...
Salon
Salalaland

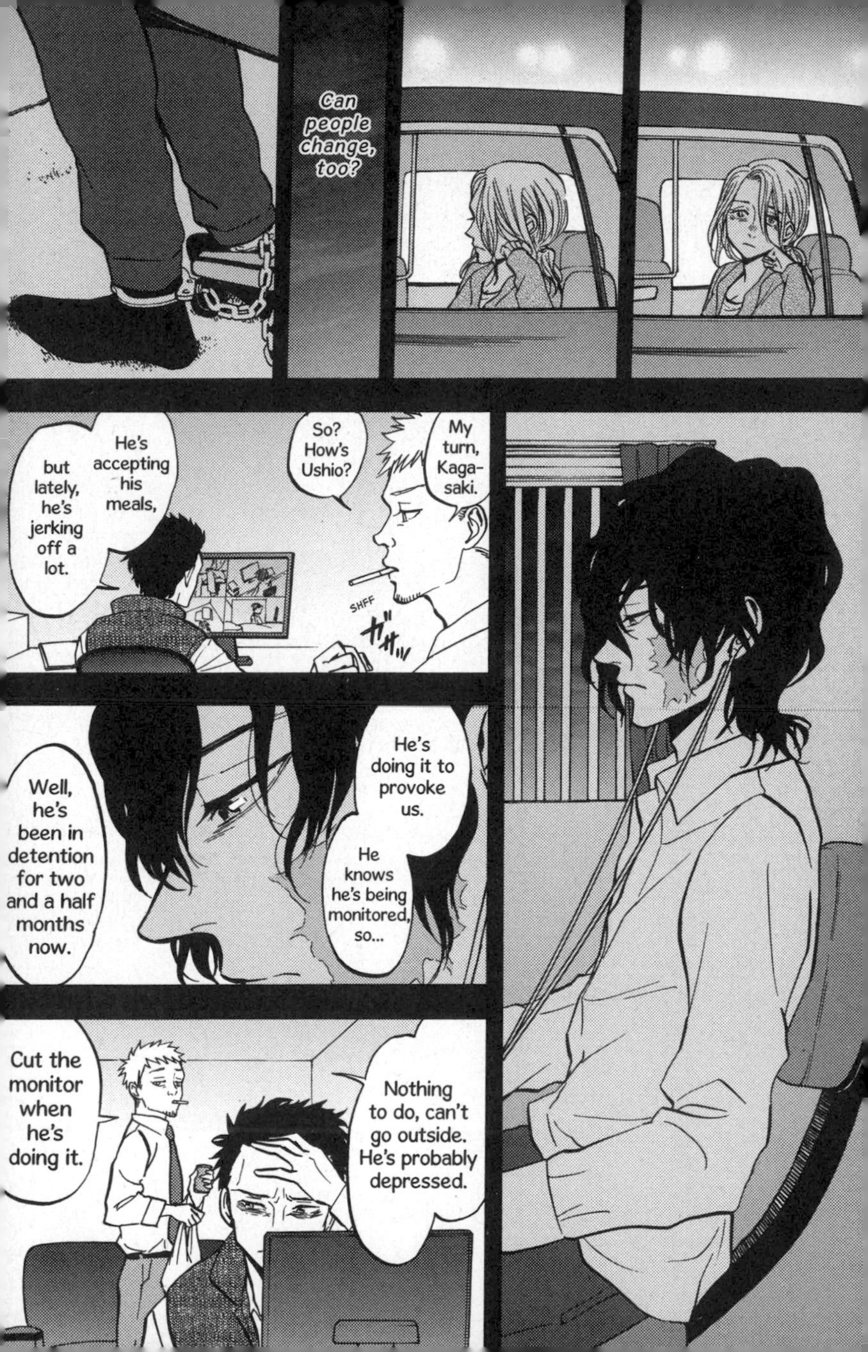
Can people change, too?
My turn, Kagasaki.
So? How's Ushio?
He's accepting his meals,
but lately, he's jerking off a lot.
SHFF
ガサッ
He's doing it to provoke us.
He knows he's being monitored, so...
Well, he's been in detention for two and a half months now.
Nothing to do, can't go outside. He's probably depressed.
Cut the monitor when he's doing it.

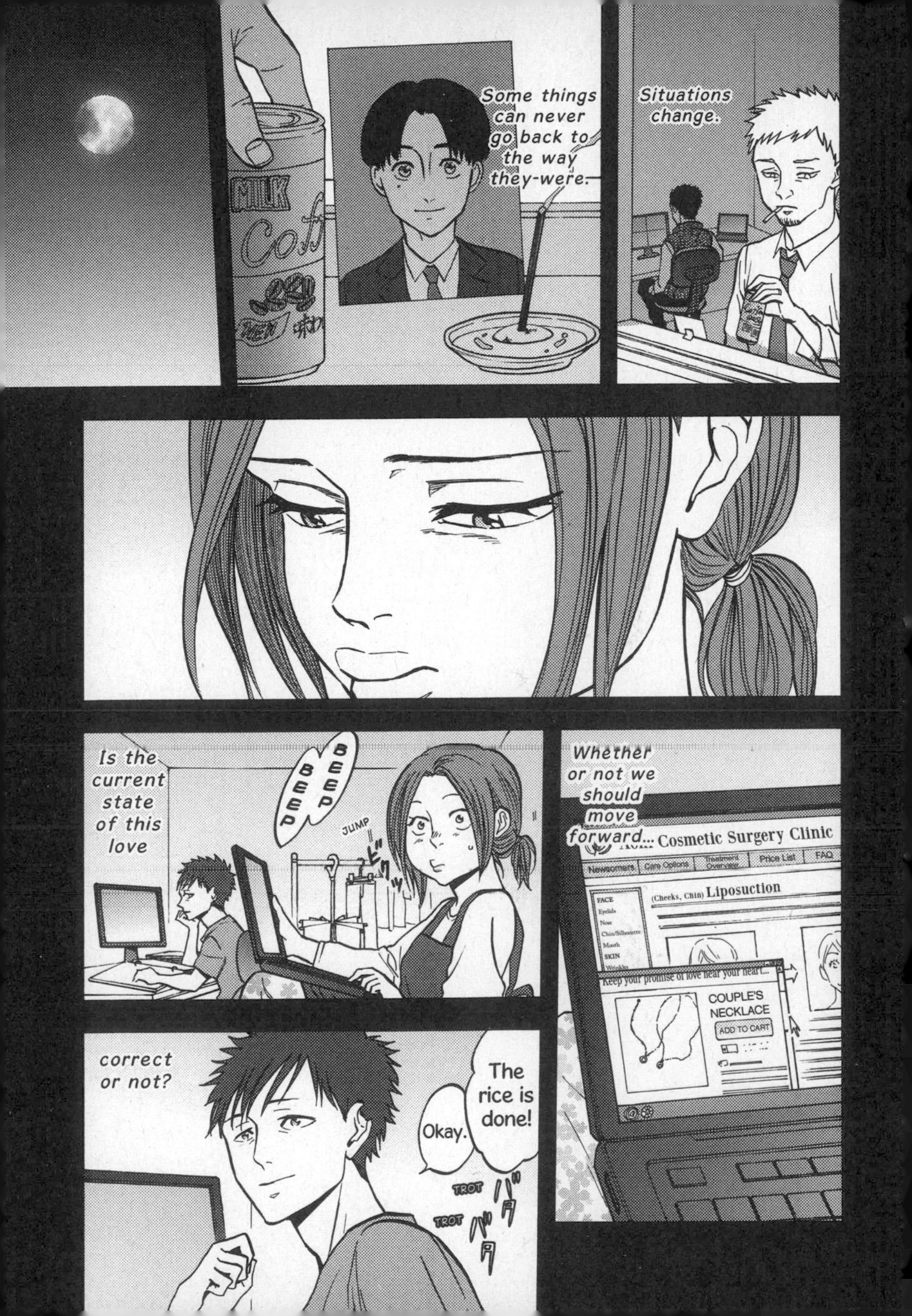
Situations change.
Some things can never go back to the way they-were.
Whether or not we should move forward...
Cosmetic Surgery Clinic
Newsomers
Care Options
Treatment Overview
Price List
FAQ
(Cheeks, Chin) Liposuction
FACE
Eyelids
Nose
Chin/Silhouette
Mouth
SKIN
Keep your promise of love near your heart...
COUPLE'S NECKLACE
ADD TO CART
Is the current state of this love
BEEP BEEP BEEP
JUMP
correct or not?
The rice is done!
Okay.
TROT
TROT

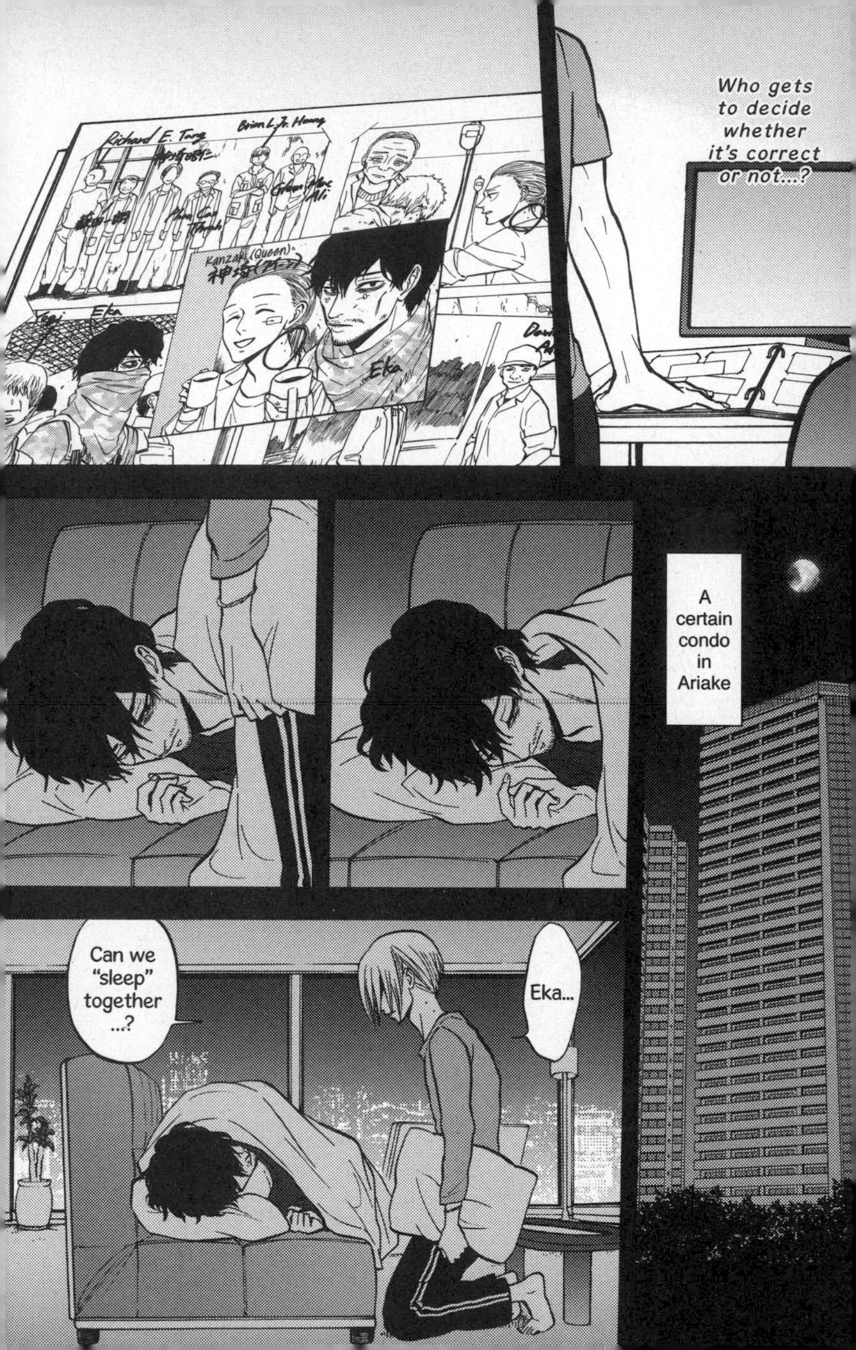
Who gets to decide whether it's correct or not...?
Richard E. Tang
Kanzaki (Queen)
Eka
Eka
A certain condo in Ariake
Eka...
Can we "sleep" together ...?

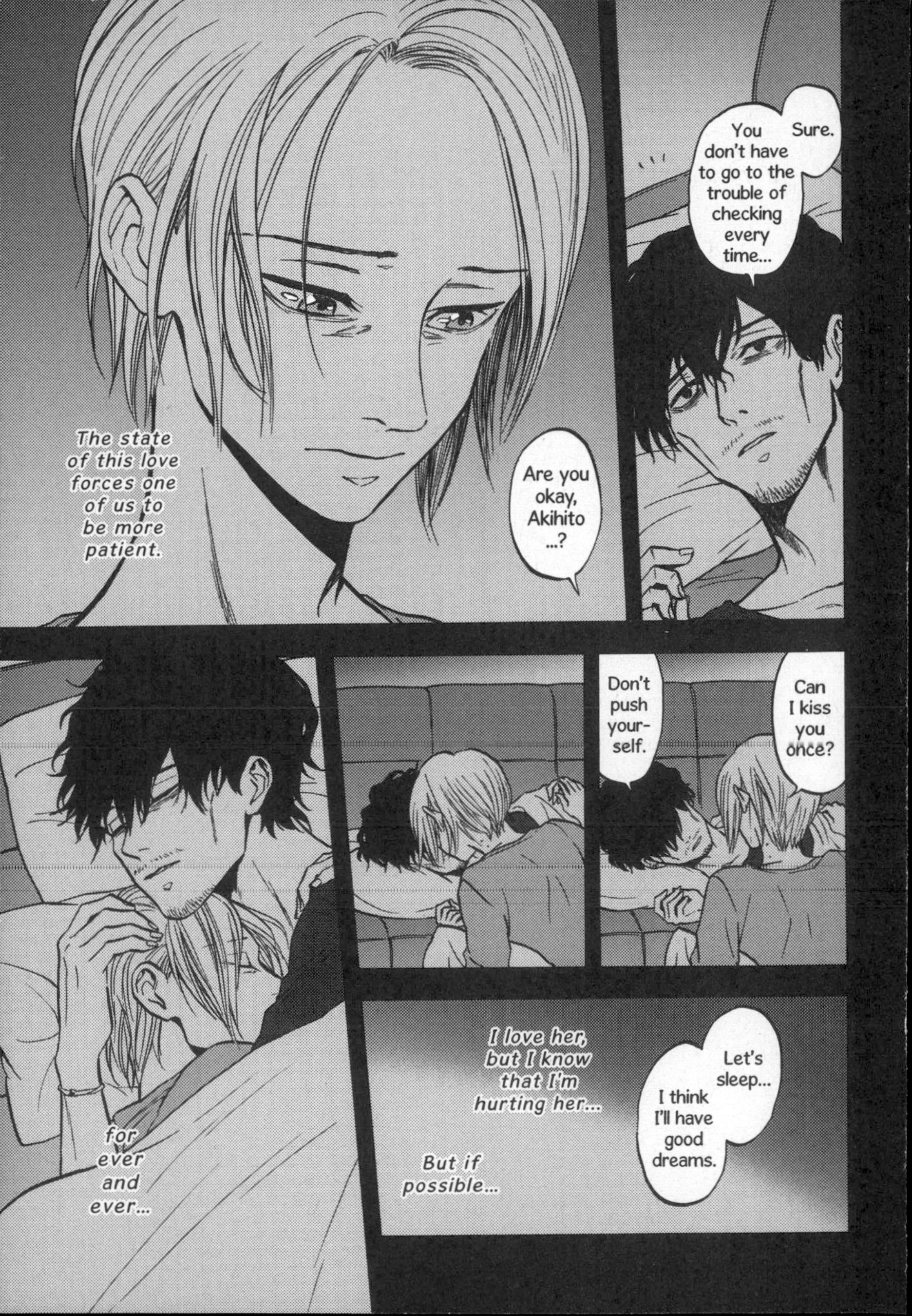
Sure.
You don't have to go to the trouble of checking every time...
Are you okay, Akihito ...?
The state of this love forces one of us to be more patient.
Can I kiss you once?
Don't push yourself.
Let's sleep...
I think I'll have good dreams.
I love her, but I know that I'm hurting her...
But if possible...
for ever and ever...

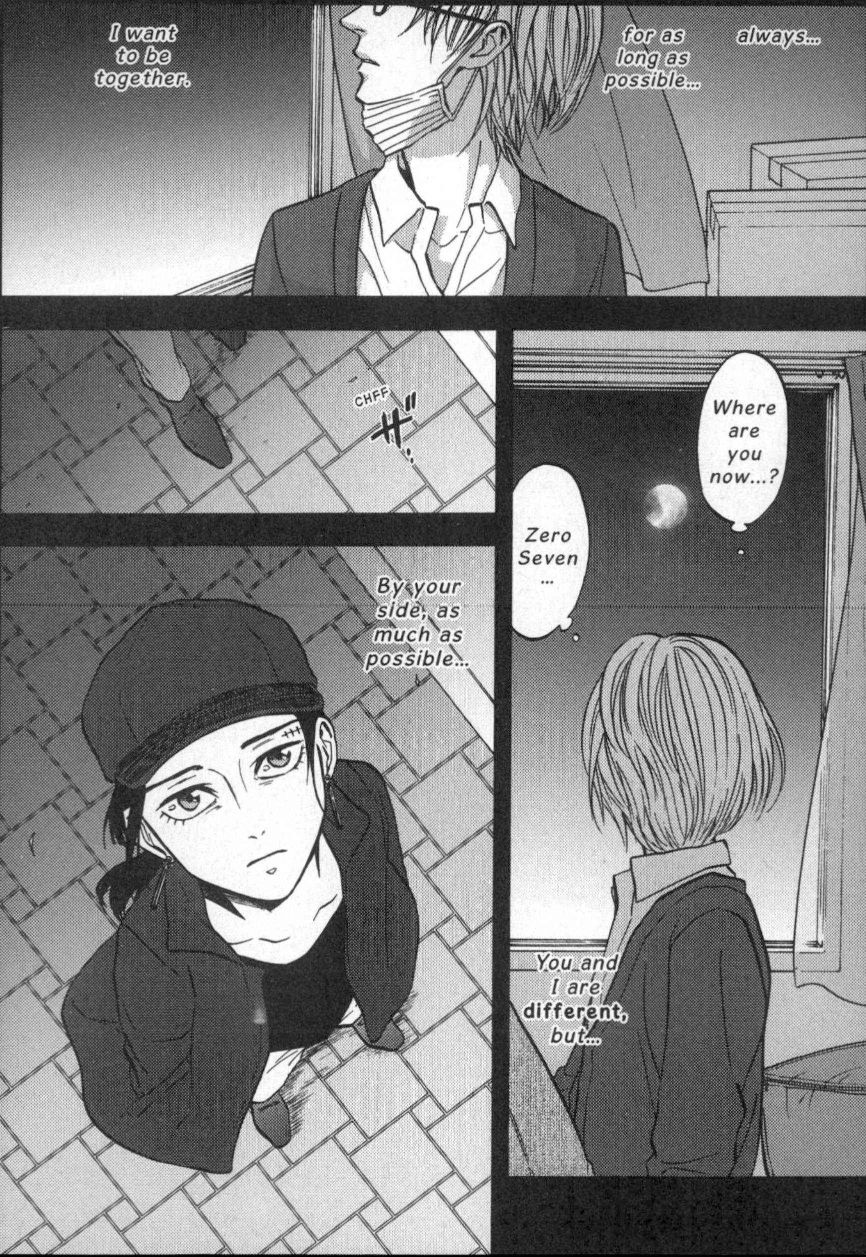
always...
for as long as possible...
I want to be together.
Where are you now...?
Zero Seven ...
You and I are different, but...
CHFF
By your side, as much as possible...

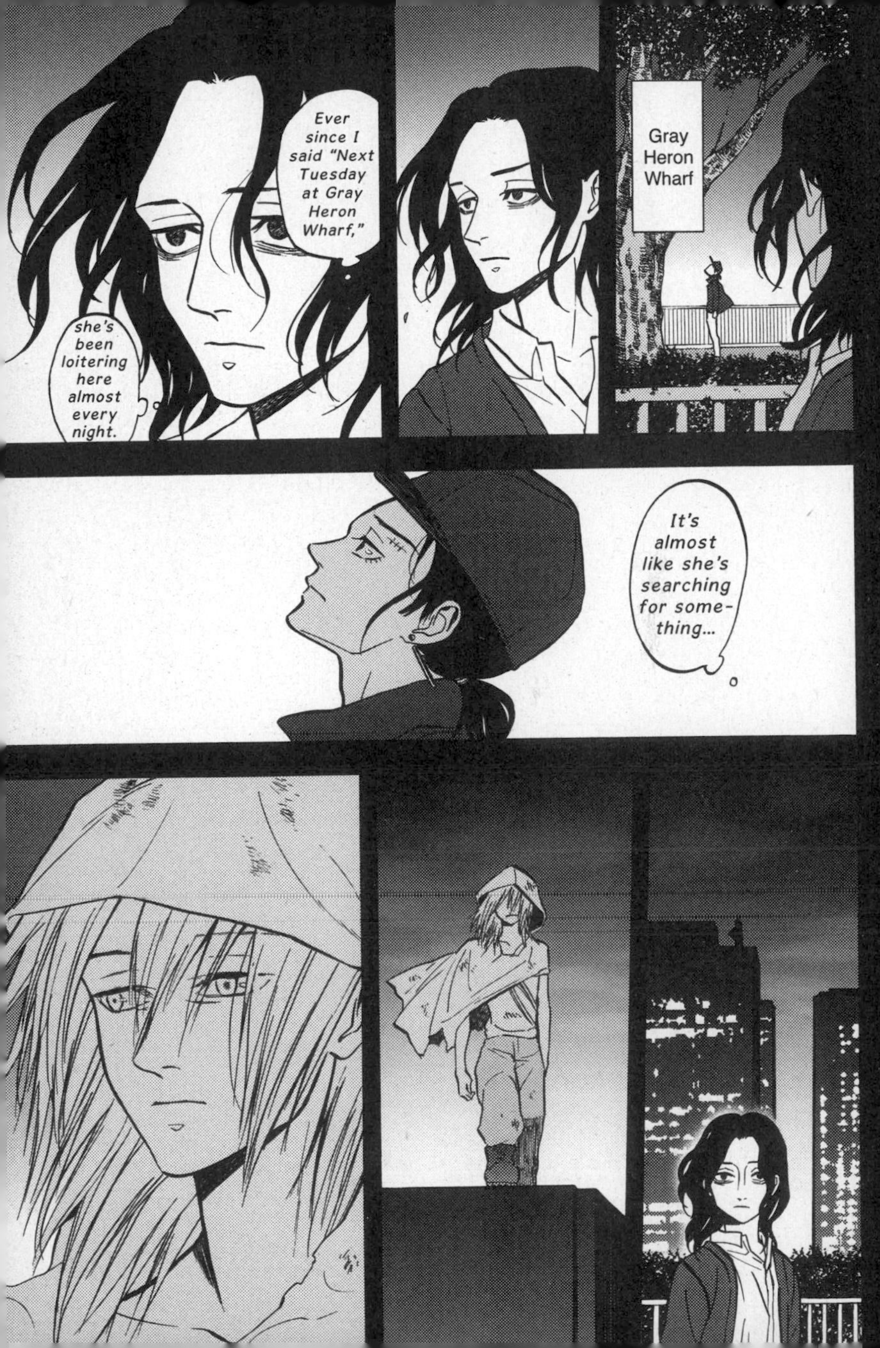
Gray Heron Wharf
Ever since I said "Next Tuesday at Gray Heron Wharf,"
she's been loitering here almost every night.
It's almost like she's searching for some-thing...

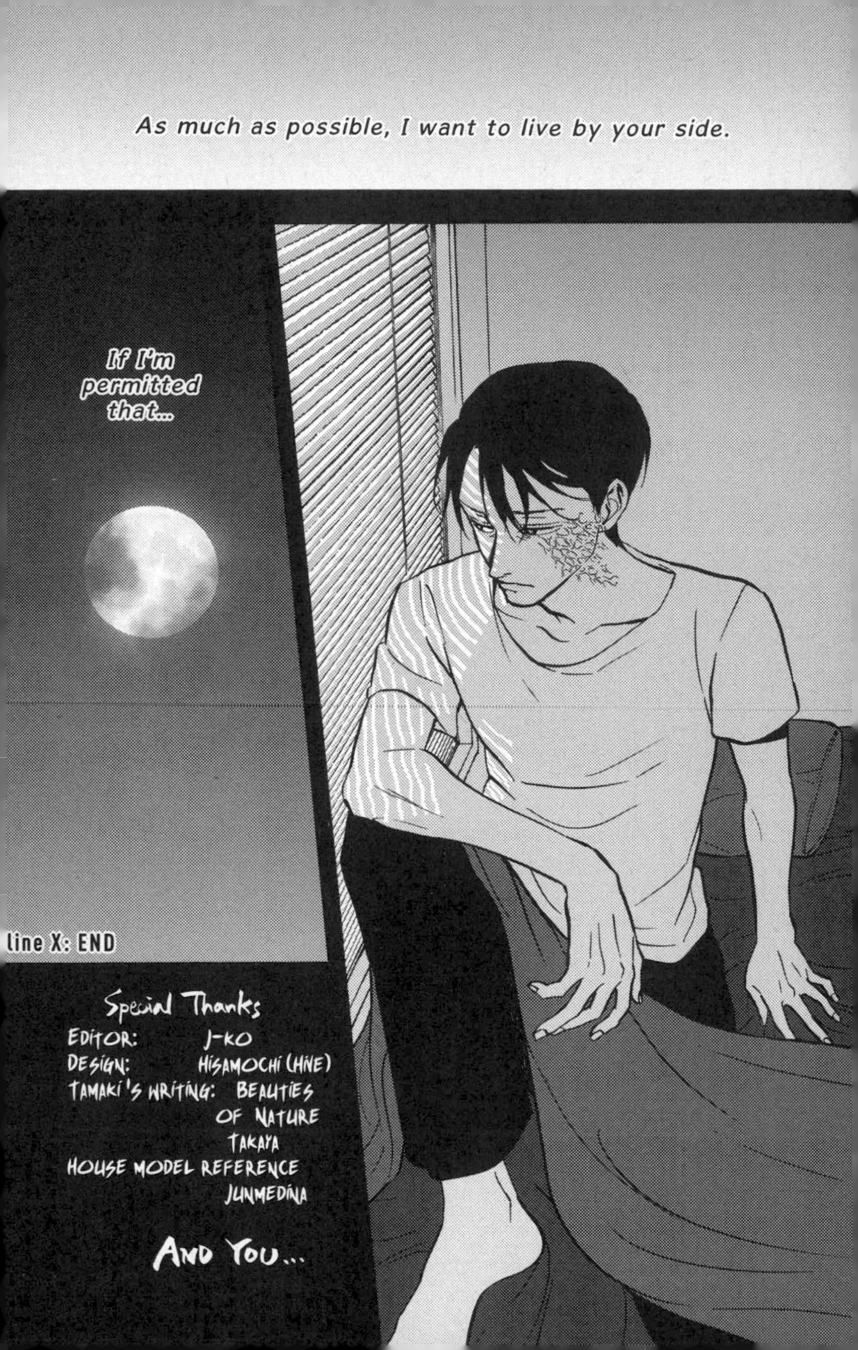
As much as possible, I want to live by your side.
If I'm permitted that...
line X: END
Special Thanks
EDITOR: J-KO
DESIGN: HISAMOCHI (HIVE)
TAMAKI'S WRITING: BEAUTIES OF NATURE TAKAYA
HOUSE MODEL REFERENCE JUNMEDINA
AND YOU...

Kurtz and Tamaki Talk

*I think this story's more understandable after you read the book.

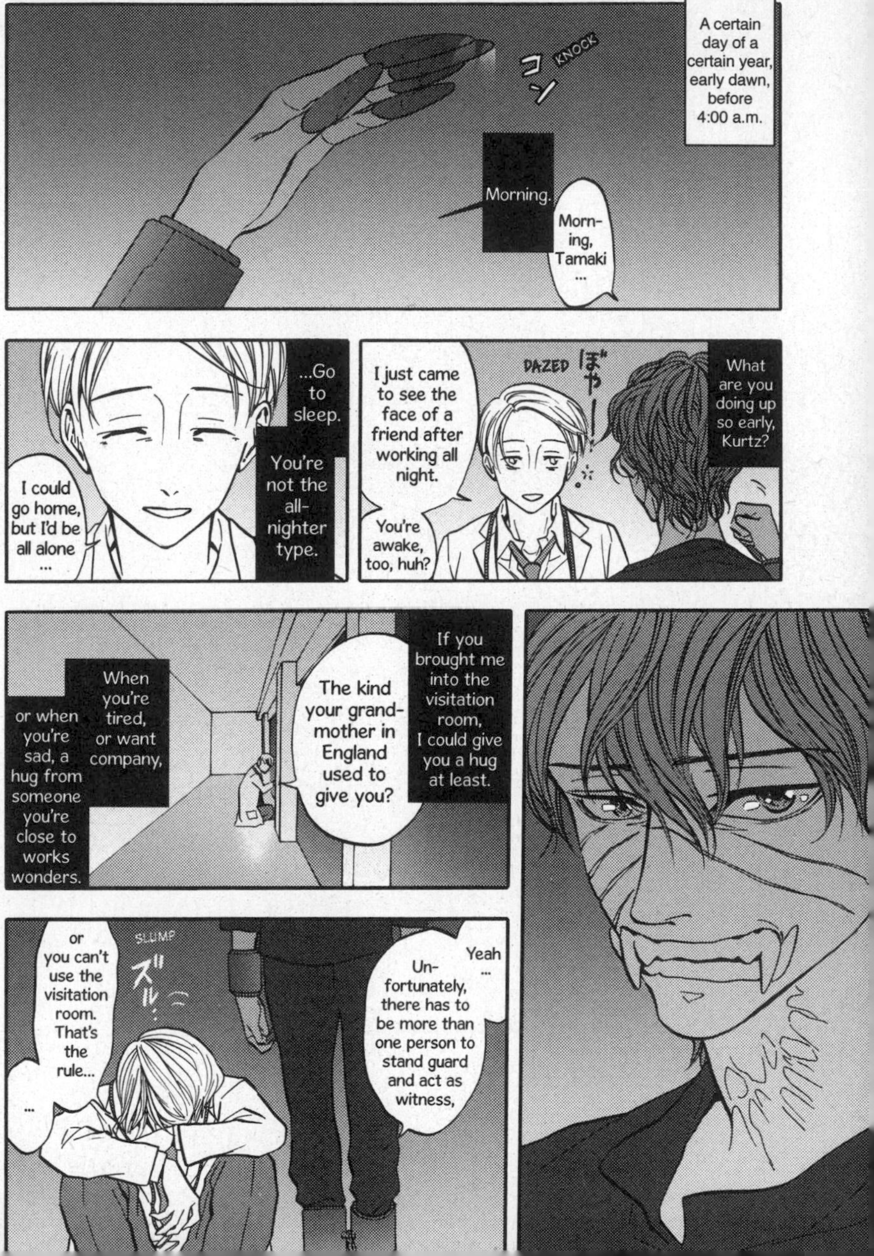
A certain day of a certain year, early dawn, before 4:00 a.m.
KNOCK
Morn-ing, Tamaki ...
Morning.
What are you doing up so early, Kurtz?
DAZED
I just came to see the face of a friend after working all night.
You're awake, too, huh?
...Go to sleep.
You're not the all-nighter type.
I could go home, but I'd be all alone ...
If you brought me into the visitation room, I could give you a hug at least.
The kind your grand-mother in England used to give you?
When you're tired, or want company,
or when you're sad, a hug from someone you're close to works wonders.
Yeah ...
Un-fortunately, there has to be more than one person to stand guard and act as witness,
SLUMP
or you can't use the visitation room. That's the rule...
...

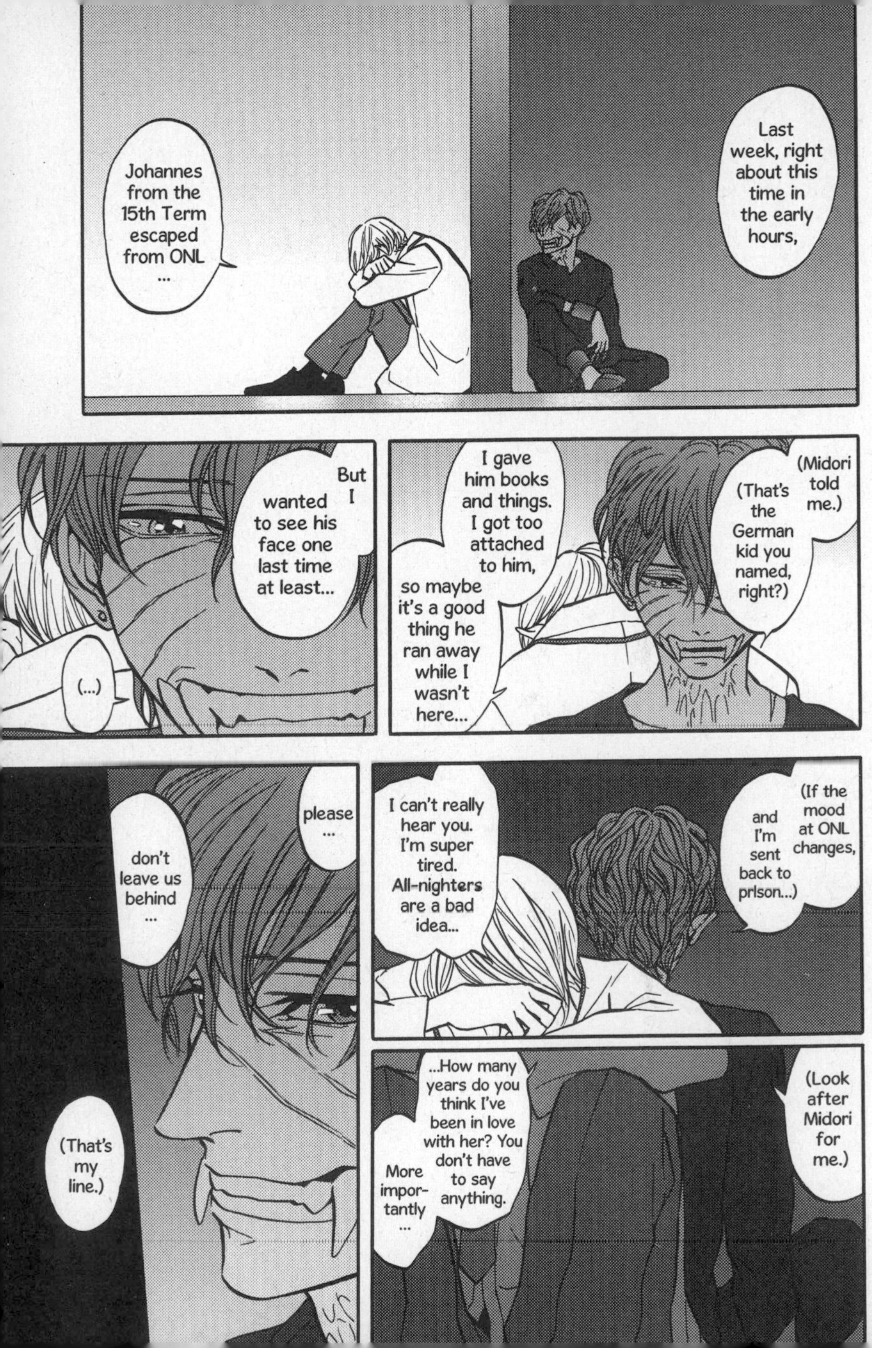

Last week, right about this time in the early hours,
Johannes from the 15th Term escaped from ONL ...
(Midori told me.)
(That's the German kid you named, right?)
I gave him books and things. I got too attached to him,
so maybe it's a good thing he ran away while I wasn't here...
But I wanted to see his face one last time at least...
(...)
(If the mood at ONL changes,
and I'm sent back to prison...)
I can't really hear you. I'm super tired. All-nighters are a bad idea...
(Look after Midori for me.)
...How many years do you think I've been in love with her? You don't have to say anything.
More impor-tantly ...
please ...
don't leave us behind ...
(That's my line.)

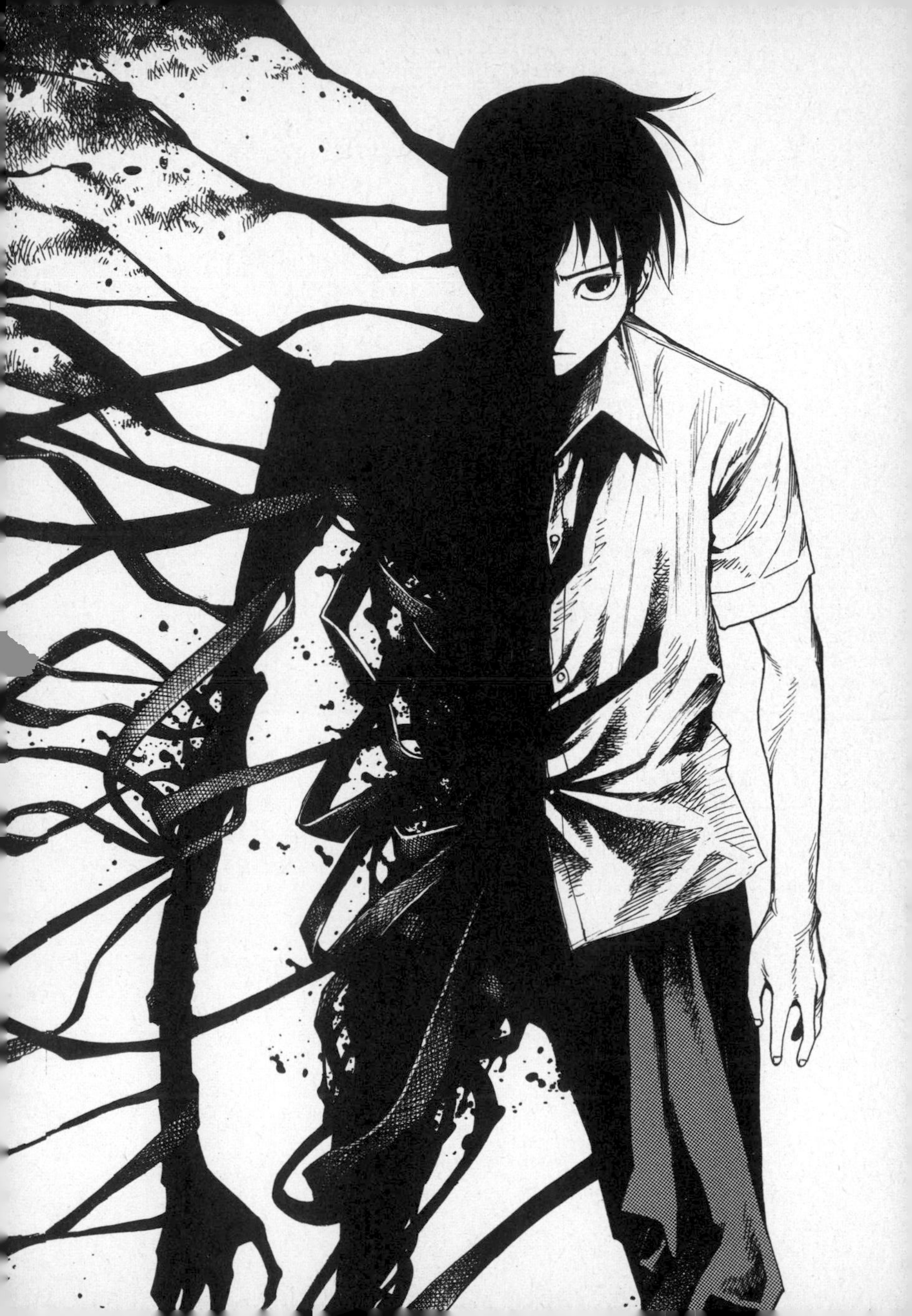

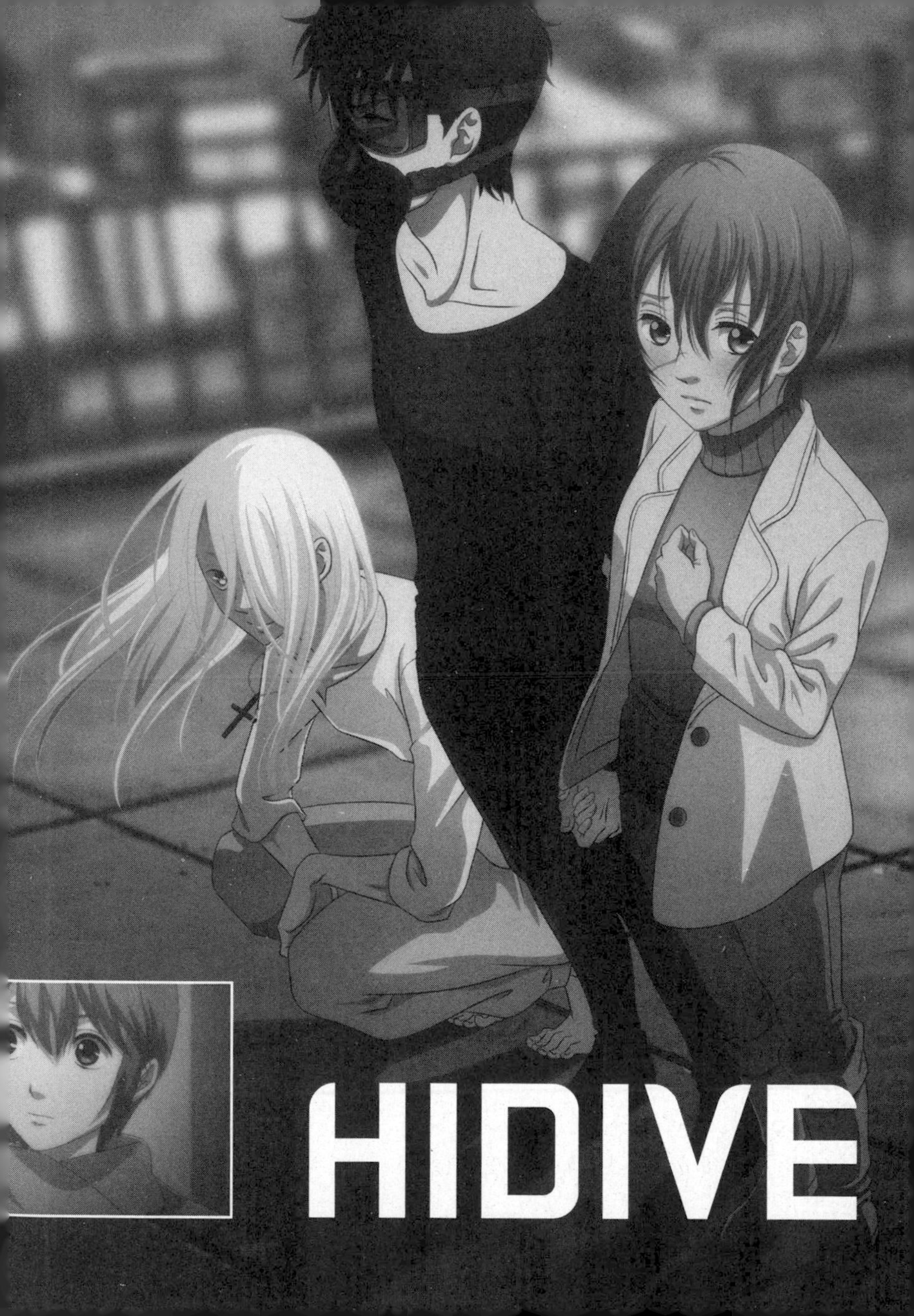
HIDIVE